Aquinas and the Early Chinese Masters

THOMISTIC RESSOURCEMENT SERIES

Volume 30

SERIES EDITORS

Matthew Levering, Mundelein Seminary

Thomas Joseph White, OP, Pontifical University of St. Thomas Aquinas

EDITORIAL BOARD

Serge-Thomas Bonino, OP, Pontifical University of St. Thomas Aquinas

Gilles Emery, OP, University of Fribourg

Reinhard Hütter, Duke University

Bruce Marshall, Southern Methodist University

Emmanuel Perrier, OP, Dominican Studium, Toulouse

Richard Schenk, OP, University of Freiburg (Germany)

Kevin White, The Catholic University of America

Aquinas and the Early Chinese Masters

Chinese Philosophy and Catholic Theology

JOSHUA R. BROWN

The Catholic University of America Press
Washington, D.C.

Copyright © 2024
The Catholic University of America Press
All rights reserved
The paper used in this publication meets the minimum
requirements of American National Standards for Information
Science—Permanence of Paper for Printed Library Materials,
ANSI Z39.48-1992.
∞

Cataloging-in-Publication Data is available
from the Library of Congress
ISBN: 978-0-8132-3894-4
eISBN: 978-0-8132-3895-1

For Matthew Levering, in gratitude and friendship

Contents

Acknowledgments	ix
Preface	xi
Introduction	1
1. A Thomistic Assessment of the *Mengzi* on *Tian*	38
2. A Thomistic Reading of the *Mozi* on Divine Will	89
3. A Thomistic Assessment of the Confucian Debate on *Renxing*	128
4. A Thomistic Reading of Mohist *Jian ai*	173
5. Thomistic Christology and Xunzi's *Shengren*	210
6. Thomas's Reading of Matthew 8:21–22 and Confucian Filiality	247
A Brief Conclusion	284
Appendix: Introduction to Early Confucianism and Mohism	289
Bibliography	297
Index	319

Acknowledgments

Writing this book has been a difficult process, and far more challenging than I originally imagined. At many junctures, I have feared the task I set myself was beyond me, and that I would fail to adequately express the riches I discovered for myself while writing this book. Thus, I have incurred many debts of gratitude. First, I must acknowledge the support of my wife Jamie and four children (Elliott, Emmett, Sophia, and Selah, born to us in heaven) whose gifts of presence, laughter, and prayers made it possible to push through the hard times of writing a difficult book. I must also thank my good friends and colleagues at Mount St. Mary's University for their support and encouragement of the project, especially Pete Dorsey, Paige Hochschild, Barrett Turner, and Luis Vera. In addition to my colleagues at the Mount, I am especially grateful for the conversations and feedback on parts of my research from Trent Pomplun and Xueying Wang. I owe a profoundly deep thank you to friends who read chapters of the book and provided helpful responses, including Jason Heron and Josh Hochschild. I must single out the generosity of Michael Hahn, who read the entire book in its earliest form and gave immeasurably valuable critique and encouragement.

I am honored that the book is part of the prestigious Thomistic Ressourcement series and thank Fr. Thomas Joseph White for that honor. John Martino has been a tremendous help not only as an acquisitions editor, but in helping to make key decisions on the book—I thank him for his immense help. I would also like to thank the editorial board at the Catholic University of America Press and the blind reviewers of the book for helpful comments and critiques that have massively improved the book.

The most thanks are owed to Matthew Levering, my friend and mentor, to whom this book is dedicated. Matthew was first and foremost supremely gracious with his time, having read the book at least twice and parts of the book several times over and offering extensive and trenchant comments. Here I must also thank Joy Levering, Matthew's gracious wife, for letting me steal so much of Matthew's time. But more importantly, Matthew has been a true friend as I have written this book. He has believed in the value of my work and my abilities as a scholar more than I have myself many times. I cannot express how great a blessing his friendship has been to me.

Finally, I would like to thank all those men and women who long before me have attempted to understand and articulate the beauty of the Christian faith in light of Chinese culture and thought. I offer this book as a form of filial service (*xiao shi* 孝事), and I hope I do honor to my intellectual forebears. All praise and thanksgiving are owed to the Triune God, who has loved and embraced me despite my severe shortcomings, and who has placed in my heart the desire to learn to see his face in light of Chinese wisdom. May this book be an offering pleasing to the Lord, to whom it is offered in humility and love.

Thank you to the editors of *Nova et Vetera* (English edition) for permission to republish parts of "Christ our Ritual Sage? A Chinese Articulation of Christ's Priesthood," *Nova et Vetera* 17, no. 1 (2019): 15–38.

Preface

In this book, I seek to provide foundations for the continued development of Chinese Catholic theology. I use "Chinese" Catholic theology not to refer to a specific geographical location in which Catholic theology is done, but to refer to any Catholic theology that would take the engagement with Chinese intellectual traditions (which I call "philosophies" for sake of convention)[1] as a primary resource for theological articulation and analysis, with an eye toward the theological formation of culturally Chinese Christians. Admittedly, calling this kind of project "Chinese Catholic theology" seems inadequate, and I am happy to entertain suggestions for better labels. But "Chinese Catholic theology" helps avoid jargonistic and clunky descriptors and so I embrace it for now.

For many, however, the appeal to "Chinese" Catholic theology signals work written from the Chinese experience and meant to serve the Chinese experience. I hope my work is of service to those of Chinese cultural background, but I can make no claim to write from the Chinese experience as such. Rather, I am a theologian residing in the modern West who does not come from Chinese lineage, and—perhaps worst of all in the eyes of some potential critics—a white man. In our interesting times, my claim to be writing Chinese

---

1. Scholars debate how classical Chinese texts and traditions can be labeled as "philosophies" or "religions" among other options. The labels are, of course, the provenance of Western liberal modernity and anachronistic to Chinese traditions themselves—even the Chinese analogs for "philosophy" and "religion" are modern distinctions. Since my appeal to these traditions is roughly equivalent to traditional theological appeals to thinkers like Plato, Aristotle, and Plotinus, labeling them "philosophies" conveniently signals their function in the book.

xi

Catholic theology is therefore vulnerable to construal as cultural appropriation, intellectual colonialism, or something of that nefarious sort.

Consequently, it is helpful to preface this book by clarifying why I seek to contribute to Chinese Catholic theology. As I partly explained in my previous book, *Balthasar in Light of Early Confucianism*, my theological vocation has been profoundly shaped by two major events in my life, when in the space of a few years I married a wonderful woman of Chinese-Malaysian heritage and converted to Catholicism.[2] Through my marriage, I began to be introduced to Chinese cultural practices and language, and during my doctoral studies in theology I became consumed with the question of what it would mean for my children to grow up as Catholics of Chinese (and American) descent, and for me to be their father in a home formed by both Catholicism and a Chinese heritage. How could our family respectfully combine our now shared identities as Catholics who participate in Chinese culture and heritage in various ways?

And so, in my doctoral work I sought out additional language training in classical Chinese and the study of classical Chinese texts, leading to an intensive research agenda engaging Chinese philosophical traditions. Over time, it has become clear to me that my heart as a scholar lies in attending to the reconciliation of Chinese philosophy and Catholic theology and offering my humble gifts to the broader work of building "Chinese Catholic theology"—that is, an approach to Catholic theology that deeply resonates with Chinese culture and thought.

For a considerable time, however, I hesitated to write in explicit service of this larger project. After all, I am not Chinese, and I have a deep respect for the vitality and breadth of Chinese intellectual culture as well as a profound awareness of the often difficult history of those of Chinese descent in the United States.[3] However, through

---

2. Joshua Brown, *Balthasar in Light of Early Confucianism* (Notre Dame, IN: University of Notre Dame Press, 2020), x.

3. My reference here is to the way the first wave of Chinese immigrants to the United States, in particular, were typically met with scorn and contempt from Americans culminating in the Chinese Exclusion Act of 1882. Along with other famous anti-Asian movements such as the internment of Japanese Americans during World War II, these events testify to the difficulty many East Asian peoples have had in forging homes and identities in the modern

the ministrations of my gracious wife, children, and wise friends, I realized that other Catholic theologians work in domains within the Church to which they lay claim through conversion and personal interest, for example the large number of American theologians who work constructively within German theological and philosophical traditions. In the Church as in marriage, cultures can be shared, and not merely appropriated or stolen. More to the point, as a father I have some responsibility for helping my own children to see the possible unity of the Catholic faith we practice and the Chinese heritage that shapes their lives and our home in diverse and often subtle ways. And additionally, as I have sought to learn more about Chinese Catholicism from its rich history of devotion and thought, I have grown to love this tradition and cannot help but seek to contribute to its flourishing. Therefore, my commitment to my children—and to all Catholics of Chinese descent who yearn for a genuine and faithful Chinese Catholic theology—inspires me along this path.

West. Hence, the experience of Asian Americans as caught "betwixt and between" (in the words of Peter Phan) or the "liminal" experience of Asian Americans (to borrow from Sang H. Lee) is impossible to ignore. For a compelling historical account of the struggles of Chinese immigrants to the US, see, *inter alia*, Erika Lee, *At America's Gates: Chinese Immigration during the Exclusion Era, 1882–1943* (Chapel Hill: University of North Carolina Press, 2003). For theological treatments of the complexity of Asian American identity, see Peter C. Phan, "Betwixt and Between: Doing Theology with Memory and Imagination," in *Journeys at the Margin: Towards and Auto-Biographical Theology in Asian-American Perspective*, ed. Peter C. Phan and Jung Young Lee (Collegeville, MN: The Liturgical Press, 1999), 113–34; and Sang H. Lee, *From a Liminal Place: An Asian American Theology* (Minneapolis, MN: Fortress Press, 2010).

Aquinas and the Early Chinese Masters

Introduction

After several years of arduous study of the Chinese language, the Jesuit missionary Michelle Ruggieri (1543–1607) published the first Chinese catechism in 1584.[1] Although it was a modest literary accomplishment, Ruggieri's catechism was the first flower of Chinese Catholic theology, the work of understanding and articulating Catholic theology out of an engagement with Chinese intellectual culture, written to help those of Chinese cultural background discover and live out the gospel of Jesus Christ. Since Ruggieri's publication to the present, a number of skilled and faithful thinkers have probed the relationship between Catholic theology and Chinese philosophical traditions. Writers such as Matteo Ricci, SJ, Giulio Aleni, SJ, Yang Tingyun, Yan Mo, Wu Li, and John C. H. Wu have all left impressive legacies. Yet despite the riches and successes of these authors, there is still one principal task of Chinese Catholic theology that—perhaps somewhat surprisingly—has not yet been accomplished: that of finding a rapprochement between Catholic theological science and Chinese philosophy.

---

1. This text was originally entitled the *Tianzhu Shilu* 天主實錄, but was reprinted in 1640 as *Tianzhu shengjiao shilu* 天主圣教实录. For the text of the *Tianzhu Shilu*, see Nicholas Standaert and Adrian Dudink, eds., *Chinese Christian Texts from the Roman Archives of the Society of Jesus*, vol. 1 (Taipei: Taipei Ricci Institute, 2002), 1–86. For the text of the *Tianzhu shengjiao shilu*, see Michele Ruggieri (as Luo Mingxian 罗明坚), *Tianzhu shengjiao shilu* 天主圣教实录, printed as volume 1 of Zheng Ande 郑安德 (Andrew Chung), ed. *Mingmo Qingchu Yesuhui sixiang wenxian hui bian* 明末清初耶稣会思想文献汇编 (Beijing: Beijing University Press, 2000). For a comparison of both editions, see Wang Huiyu, "Adjustments to the 'Accommodation Strategy' of the Early Jesuit Mission to China: The Case of Michele Ruggieri's *Tianzhu shilu* (1584) and its Revised Edition (ca. 1640)," *Journal of Religious History* 46, no. 1 (March 2022): 82–96.

By "Catholic theological science," I mean to signify that the Catholic theological tradition is, notwithstanding its rich and welcome diversity, a body of knowledge in its own right with its own first principles (i.e., divine revelation as handed on in sacred scripture and sacred tradition) and discursive norms (e.g., its historical problems and dominant conceptual frameworks). Put in the language of Alasdair MacIntyre, my use of the phrase "Catholic theological science" intends to affirm that Catholic theology is "an historically extended, socially embodied argument."[2] As I discuss in the next section of the introduction, however, many theologians who appeal to Chinese philosophy today (in Western scholarship, at least) do so in order to establish theology's "cultural relevance" in Chinese thought-forms, and largely ignore (or actively undermine) the relationship between Chinese philosophical ideas and the principles and norms of Catholic theological science. Thus, the claim that Chinese philosophy can and does have a place within the tradition of Catholic theological science can appear paradoxical since it has been employed as a "cultural disruptor" that, we are told, breaks the shackles of Western hegemony that have long plagued Christian thought. Yet this perspective fails to adequately address how the theological tradition claims to be a body of knowledge whose principles and discursive norms are not simply cultural expressions of power, but communications of truth, indeed saving truth.

In this way, the rapprochement between Chinese philosophy and Catholic theological science is both largely ignored (at least in Western literature) and sorely needed. Although many writers such as those listed above have illustrated deep resonances between Catholic theology and Confucianism in particular, there is still lacking a full integration of Chinese philosophy into Catholic theological science. Consequently, the appeal to Chinese philosophy threatens to make Chinese Catholic theology a purely nationalized form of theological discourse, rather than a communication of the Church's proclamation of truth in a manner suitably expressing the gifts and patrimony of Chinese culture. What is needed, therefore, is an approach

---

2. Alasdair MacIntyre, *After Virtue: A Study in Moral Theory*, 3rd ed. (Notre Dame, IN: University of Notre Dame Press, 2007), 222.

Introduction 3

allowing Chinese Catholic theology to speak from a perspective rooted both in Chinese intellectual traditions and in the fullness of the Catholic Church's faith.[3] My purpose in this book is to model and promote a concrete way of addressing this task.

In my view, one major obstacle to the full integration of Chinese philosophy into Catholic theological science is the lack of a rigorous and systematic framework for adjudicating how Chinese philosophical concepts—on their own terms and without adaptation—can and cannot be used within Catholic theological science. As I describe in more detail below, there is often a simple and uncritical deployment of Chinese philosophical concepts within an articulation of Catholic theology (for example, as found in the Jesuit missionary texts). When Catholic theologians such as Zhao Binshi have gone on to test the relationship between Catholic theological science and Chinese philosophy, the testing framework itself typically fails to be sophisticated enough to appreciate how concepts such as *renxing* 人性, for example, possess multiple layers of meaning that must each be assessed for possible integration into the multivalent tradition of Catholic theological science.

Consequently, Chinese Catholic theologians have not yet been able to undertake in a sustained fashion the long yet fruitful labor of submitting the Chinese philosophical heritage to the clarifying light of Christ's gospel. Recall the ways in which thinkers such as Justin Martyr, Gregory of Nazianzus, Augustine of Hippo, and Thomas Aquinas held Greek philosophical thought in tremendous esteem, while recognizing that Greek philosophy had to undergo a "conversion" in order to serve the Church. Concretely, this led to the rejection of many Greek theses. For example, Justin Martyr turned away from Plato's theory of the transmigration of the soul, and Aquinas disagreed with Aristotle's position on the eternal existence of matter. Yet these thinkers also recognized that Greek philosophy had valuable insights that could help the Church to understand what happened in and through Jesus Christ, as God's covenant with Israel

---

3. As an example, in 1961, the Catholic Conference of San Francisco noted there was a need "to reconcile the tenets of Chinese philosophy with the doctrines of the Catholic Church." Cited from Jeffrey M. Burns, Ellen Skerret, and Joseph M. White, eds., *Keeping Faith: European and Asian Catholic Immigrants* (Maryknoll, NY: Orbis Books, 2000), 242–43.

4   Introduction

was opened to the nations. These thinkers brought Greek philosophy with them into the Church and therein found this philosophy alive yet changed (perhaps even transfigured) by the light of Christ.[4]

Today the same must be done for Chinese philosophy by those seeking to articulate a fully Chinese Catholic theology. However, because the ministrations of the Holy Spirit have a history, we cannot solely appeal to scripture but must also appeal to the conciliar and doctrinal tradition of the Catholic Church (as the bedrock of the proper interpretation of scripture) in order to develop a Chinese Catholic theology that conforms to the truth of divine revelation.

Any Catholic theologian who has read the classical texts of Chinese philosophy in even a cursory manner can attest that they contain true wisdom, beauty, and goodness. Though the Chinese tradition bears different philosophical gifts than Greek and Latin philosophy, it nonetheless has gifts in abundance, which can and should be used by Catholic theologians to understand, proclaim, and adore the Triune God. Yet in order to use such gifts well, we must first do what our forefathers and mothers in the Church were able to accomplish, and submit the gifts of Chinese philosophy to a charitable scrutiny. We must test the capacity of these offerings to serve or hinder Catholic theological science in service to the proclamation of the Gospel of Jesus Christ.

And so, in this book my central purpose is to propose and exhibit an analytical approach that I contend best serves the development of Chinese Catholic theology in the direction I have outlined above. The chapters work together to offer a concrete model for bringing together Chinese philosophy and Catholic theology. I offer a model not as a strict path for others to follow, but rather as an example of the synthesis of sinological, philosophical, and theological analysis that I believe is necessary in order to continue the development of Chinese Catholic theology. As such, the chapters are intended to illustrate an approach to identifying the challenges and fruitfulness of integrating Chinese philosophy into Catholic theology. The

---

4. See Joseph Ratzinger, *Truth and Tolerance: Christian Belief and World Religions*, trans. Henry Taylor (San Francisco, CA: Ignatius Press, 2004), 87–89. Here Ratzinger argues that the notion of Catholic dogma as a form of Hellenistic thinking ignores the fact that Christianity always involves a cultural "exodus" and does not simply valorize or affirm any culture as such. It is always an agent of cultural change.

Introduction 5

book is united by the theological and philosophical work of Aquinas, which I use as a means to assess the theological fittingness of Chinese philosophical concepts in their classical context. Just as Aquinas received and expanded upon a tradition of incorporating Greek philosophy into Catholic theology, I seek to build foundations for allowing Chinese philosophy to serve as an *ancilla* or "handmaiden" of Catholic theology.[5] My basic approach is to use the following question as a heuristic device: What if Aquinas had read the Chinese masters as he did Aristotle and the other Greek sources, in order to draw them into his masterful synthesis of faith and reason?[6]

I should clarify that while Aquinas is the theological exemplar I use in this book, I do not mean to argue Aquinas is the only thinker who can serve my approach. I have myself advocated for the value of other theological voices in dialogue with Chinese philosophy, such as that of Hans Urs von Balthasar.[7] My use of Aquinas, then, is aimed

5. See *ST* Ia, q. 1, art. 5, s.c. For excellent studies of Aquinas's use of non-Christian philosophers and its impact on his theology, see Leo J. Elders, *Thomas Aquinas and His Predecessors: The Philosophers and the Church Fathers in His Work* (Washington, DC: The Catholic University of America Press, 2018), 1–100; and Gilles Emery, OP, and Matthew Levering, eds., *Aristotle in Aquinas's Theology* (New York: Oxford University Press, 2015).

6. Interest in Aquinas in dialogue with Chinese traditions is a small but growing field. The most important classic study still heavily cited today remains Lee H. Yearley, *Mencius and Aquinas: Theories of Virtue and Conceptions of Courage* (Albany, NY: SUNY Press, 1990). Other more recent work includes Vincent Shen, "From Gift to Law: Thomas's Natural Law and Laozi's Heavenly *Dao*," *International Philosophical Quarterly* 53, no. 3 (September 2013): 251–70; Anselm Kyongsuk Min, "The Trinity of Aquinas and the Triad of Zhu Xi: Some Comparative Reflections," in *Word and Spirit: Renewing Christology and Pneumatology in a Globalizing World* (Berlin: Water De Gruyter, 2014), 151–70; Catherine Hudak Klancer, *Embracing Our Complexity: Thomas Aquinas and Zhu Xi on Power and the Common Good* (Albany, NY: SUNY Press, 2016); Jude Chua Soo Meng, "Nameless Dao: A Rapprochement Between the *Tao-Te Ching* and St. Thomas Aquinas' Metaphysics of Unlimited Being," *Journal of Chinese Philosophy* 30, no. 1 (March 2003): 99–113. I should also note that Alasdair MacIntyre has often commented on the importance of the future Thomistic engagement with Confucianism in particular. See MacIntyre, "Incommensurability, Truth and the Conversation between Confucians and Aristotelians about the Virtues," in *Culture and Modernity: East-West Philosophic Perspectives*, ed. Eliot Deutsch (Honolulu, HI: University of Hawaii Press, 1991), 104–23; and Alasdair MacIntyre, "Once More on Confucian and Aristotelian Conceptions of the Virtues: A Response to Professor Wang," in *Chinese Philosophy in an Era of Globalization*, ed. Robin R. Wang (Albany, NY: SUNY Press, 2004), 151–62; Alasdair MacIntyre, "Questions for Confucianism: Reflections on Essays in *Comparative Study of Self, Autonomy, and Community*," in *Confucian Ethics: A Comparative Study of Self, Autonomy, and Community*, ed. Kwong-loi Shun and David B. Wong (Cambridge: Cambridge University Press, 2004), 195–210.

7. Most of my previous publications concern integrating Confucian philosophy into the *Nouvelle théologie* style theology of Hans Urs von Balthasar, though I have also drawn upon the

at demonstrating the "intellectual virtues" I think are needed in Chinese Catholic theology, regardless of whether Aquinas's thought is given the role I allow it here. Not only was Aquinas himself a very charitable reader of pre-Christian pagan philosophy, he was also an exemplar of one who sought to think fully from within the Catholic tradition. Aquinas's thought is not *sui generis*—throughout his writings, there is a constant appeal to the sacred scriptures as the soul of his theology, and a perpetual respect for the tradition preceding him, both the Greek and Latin Fathers as well as the conciliar tradition. Given these qualities of his thought, and the important impact he has had on magisterial teaching at Trent and beyond, we can find in him a rich form of Catholic theological science that puts us into touch with many of the most foundational texts and resources of Catholic theological tradition.

Consequently, placing St. Thomas in conversation with the masters of early China allows for a robust, theologically deep engagement with their philosophical principles and concepts that more or less expresses the principles and norms of Catholic theological science. Aquinas helps to ground my project in an efficient and illuminating access to the "historically embodied and socially extended" tradition of Catholic theological science. He helps us to gain greater clarity about how Chinese philosophical concepts might and might not resonate with the principles and norms of Catholic theological science. There will be need occasionally to make a distinction between his personal perspective and the broader bounds of Catholic orthodoxy. For example, his view on the transmission of original sin is distinctive; Catholic theological science admits of other ways of considering this doctrine. However, in general, he provides an efficient means for expressing that which is needful for Catholic theological science, and therefore for understanding how Chinese philosophy does and does not supply these needful things. Put differently, Aquinas provides a fruitful way to "test everything, hold on to what is good" (1 Thes 5:21), regarding early Chinese philosophy.

The approach I offer here is not, then, an attempt to finagle

---

theology of Pseudo-Dionysius for a reading of the *Daodejing*. See, e.g., Brown, *Balthasar in Light of Early Confucianism*; Joshua R. Brown and Alexus McLeod, *Transcendence and Non-naturalism in Early Chinese Thought* (London: Bloomsbury, 2020).

Introduction 7

Chinese philosophy into a Thomistic system. Rather, my proposal is that Catholic theologians ought to read and assess Chinese philosophical texts in the way someone like Aquinas would have done, with intellectual rigor, charity, and a stubborn commitment to the truth found in scripture, tradition, and the historically normative articulations of Catholic theological science. My heuristic question of asking what would have been the result if Aquinas had read early Chinese texts is simply the means I use to gain access to a truly integrative path for Chinese Catholic theology, given my own intellectual gifts and limitations.

To this point, I have referred broadly to "Chinese philosophy" because I believe that the analytical approach that I demonstrate here is fruitful for reflecting upon the theological application of any Chinese tradition. However, the actual chapters of the book are far more specific and limited in scope, since obviously one short book cannot provide a rigorous testing of all of the philosophical concepts that were significant in early China. I have elected to focus on providing rigorous, concrete analyses of just a few important philosophical concepts as they appear in texts of early Chinese thought, focusing on the textual traditions of early Confucianism and Mohism.[8]

The reason for this focused approach is that it allows for a more substantial engagement with Chinese philosophical concepts on their own terms. In this way, my approach borrows heavily from the methodology of what has been called the new comparative theology.[9] Francis X. Clooney, SJ, in particular, has encouraged comparative theologians to focus on rereading and engaging concrete textual traditions—and thus eschewing scholarly abstractions as much as possible—in order to discern the theological value of non-Christian texts.[10] Although my goal is formally distinct from the kind

8. Although early Confucians and Mohists were true rival schools, they were also very similar in many of their basic assumptions, terminology, and approaches. Historically, it has even been suggested that the founder of Mohism, Mo Di, was originally a Confucian student. At the least, it is undeniable that many of the central concepts in each tradition, such as the focus on *Tian*, *ren* 仁, and *yi* 義 evince broad similarities between the two schools making them excellent companions for this book. For more on the differences between the schools, see the appendix below.

9. See Francis X. Clooney, SJ, ed., *The New Comparative Theology: Thinking Interreligiously in the 21st Century* (London: T & T Clark, 2010).

10. See Francis X. Clooney, *Theology after Vedanta: An Experiment in Comparative Theology* (Albany, NY: SUNY Press, 1993), 4–9.

of interreligious dialogue modeled by many comparative scholars, I agree with most contemporary comparativists that the concrete textual approach is preferable to one based on generic abstractions. Though the concrete textual approach requires nuanced and challenging historical and linguistic analysis, it arguably yields a more fruitful and more interesting theological engagement with Chinese ideas.

One of the most important advantages of following the concrete textual approach is that it allows access to the deeper levels of a concept's meaning in a given author, which in turn allows theological engagement with diverse aspects of the philosophical concept. This is important because in Chinese philosophy, there are often features that, if stated in a simple propositional form, may contradict Christian thought, but, if analyzed more deeply, are in genuine harmony with it. For example, in chapter 3, I examine the Confucian view of *renxing* 人性 (human moral nature) found in Mengzi and Xunzi. On the face of it, it would seem a Catholic would agree with Mengzi, who holds that *renxing* is good (*shan* 善) and disagree with Xunzi who hold *renxing* is bad or evil (*e* 惡)—indeed, Zhao Binshi assumes this to be the case. While there are ways Catholic theological science would indeed disagree with Xunzi's position, in other ways his insights about *renxing* deeply resonate with Catholic commitments. The trick is that accessing the resonances requires a deeper, more comprehensive reading of Xunzi in order to see how his intellectual concerns and specific take on the concept of *renxing* inform his thought. Without a concrete textual analysis of *renxing* it would be difficult to see the theological utility of Xunzi's thought on the matter.

Since neither the chapters nor the book as a whole can be comprehensive or exhaustive, I should explain why I have chosen to analyze these particular topics and texts. I focus on Confucianism and Mohism because I hope to demonstrate the ability of my approach to expose both the weaker spots of Chinese philosophy for Catholic theology and, more importantly, to show the theological promise of Chinese thought. I have also elected to focus on those traditions and arguments for which I think Aquinas would have most

Introduction 9

sympathy and interest. Put simply, I suspect Aquinas would have been drawn to more engagement with Confucianism and Mohism than other Chinese traditions such as Daoism or Legalism. This is because Confucianism and Mohism had a more robust way of dealing with the concept of the divine (this holds especially for Mozi), and because Confucianism and Mohism focused on issues of morality and human flourishing that strike very close to issues Aquinas makes central in his own writings.

A helpful contrast to the Confucians and Mohists is early Daoism, which was also influential for significant thinkers like the Legalist Han Feizi, and which tended to be very critical of the concept of virtue for naming and inculcating proper moral behavior, preferring instead an appeal to the ethical naturalism and apophatic epistemology that, according to its proponents, effects genuine flourishing. For example, the *Daodejing* teaches that it was only when the great *dao* was lost that the conceptions of virtue of *ren* 仁 and *yi* 義 appeared.[11] *Ren* and *yi* were cardinal virtues that Confucians like Mengzi argued needed to be cultivated, and so the *Daodejing* means that the attention to which virtues are needed and how to acquire them is a sign of a loss of the *dao*, and not a way to gain it. For the *Daodejing*, we should abandon artificial "wisdom"—such as virtue ethics—in order to return to the state of "spontaneity" (*ziran* 自然) that harmonizes with the *dao*.[12] Although it is feasible to understand the Daoist viewpoint and come to defend the theological applicability of its approach to ethics, it would be much more difficult to articulate the theological value of Daoist ethics within a Thomistic guiding framework, since the latter takes a positive conception of moral virtue as fundamental.[13] Thus, for the present book, focusing on Confucianism and Mohism is preferable.

The topics I examine in my six chapters have been chosen on the grounds of their significance for both the Chinese texts and Catholic theological science. In some chapters, admittedly, the significance

---

11. *Daodejing*, 18

12. See *Daodejing*, 19

13. I provide one such recovery of the Daoist approach in Joshua R. Brown, "A Catholic Spirituality of Non-action: Rereading Hans Urs von Balthasar with the *Daodejing*," *Communio* (forthcoming). Another option would be to seize upon St. Augustine's soft critique of virtue in *City of God*, XIX.4, in which he discusses virtue as at best a continual war against the vices.

for Catholic theological science will be more immediately evident. For example, in chapter 1, I explore Mengzi's account of *Tian* (Heaven) in light of a Catholic (and Thomistic) doctrine of God. I do not think this approach does violence to how Mengzi understands *Tian*, but it does focus on *Tian* more than Mengzi typically did, and with a greater emphasis on the theistic features of *Tian* than Mengzi scholars typically provide. On the other side of the equation, chapter 3 examines the Confucian debate on *renxing*, thus focusing on a debate that is more significant in early China than for Catholic theological science. Overall, the chapters aim to foster a genuine theological assessment of Chinese philosophical concepts, but in a way that strives to honor the contexts and concerns of the Chinese texts themselves.

As a final clarification about the rationale of the book, I should add that I have intentionally risked the possibility that the chapters will feel episodic rather than be clearly a linear argument. First, this is because, again, the approach *is* the argument, and so it must be exhibited in case studies rather than simply proposed or explained. Second, the episodic feel has its foundation in my wish to retain a modicum of comprehensiveness by demonstrating the theological fruitfulness of Chinese thought for several areas of Catholic theology. The chapters that follow are thus intended to engage the fields of natural theology, moral theology, Christology, soteriology, sacramental theology, the theology of creation, and other areas as well. Put differently, the chapters of the book are meant to enable readers to recognize and analyze something of the breadth of possibilities for Catholic theological utilization of Chinese philosophy, beyond the limits of a particular subdiscipline of theological science.

The chapters are arranged on the basis of the heuristic question governing the work, and so they are arranged in keeping with the organization of topics found in Aquinas's *Summa theologiae*. Chapters 1–2 correspond to questions arising in conversation between the *Prima pars* and the understanding of *Tian* as divine in the Confucian (chapter 1) and Mohist (chapter 2) traditions. The next two chapters touch on ethical concerns and are connected with the *Secunda pars*—namely, the moral goodness of human nature (chapter 3) and a discussion of the virtue of charity and the Mohist doctrine of

Introduction 11

"universal love" or *jian ai* 兼愛 (chapter 4). The final two chapters are inspired by the *Tertia pars*, and test how the Chinese conception of the sage (*shengren* 聖人) may be fitting for Christological use. In particular, I look at two aspects of the sage: ritual sagehood (chapter 5) and the sage as moral teacher (chapter 6).

It is worth underscoring that many of the ideas I examine in this book have a much greater sinological and theological body of literature about them than I deal with here. Consequently, there are some assumptions I take on board as an interpreter of Chinese philosophers, or as interpreter of Aquinas, that I do not explain as fully as a sinological specialist or Thomistic specialist might wish. I have attempted as best I can to signal my awareness of the controversies surrounding the concepts I am analyzing here, but often I cannot explain in detail the rationale for my specific position within intra-sinological or intra-Thomistic controversies. This is because doing so would often require longer excursions into the debates within prodigious bodies of secondary literature. Since the scholarship on each Chinese philosopher I study and on Aquinas is voluminous, engaging every point of controversial interpretation would weigh down the book and distract from my larger purpose. Ultimately, then, I have erred on the side of saying something imperfectly rather than fearing to say anything at all. Naturally, I beg the indulgence of specialist readers whenever I have failed to explain how I would respond to other interpretative options or deal with debates about the texts I touch upon in the chapters that follow.

The remainder of the introduction provides further context. First, I describe why this book is needed within my own theological context by showing how the theological engagement with Chinese philosophical concepts in Western literature currently lacks a sufficient theological assessment of the philosophical concepts. Second, I show how this book contributes to other historical and contemporary projects of Chinese Catholic theology. As noted above, I argue that until now, there have been two main problems with the theological application of Chinese philosophy: a tendency either to uncritically employ Chinese philosophical concepts within the theological endeavor, and a tendency to fail to develop an assessment

12   Introduction

framework of sufficient sophistication for measuring the true theological limits and possibilities of Chinese philosophical concepts. Showing that these problems are present even in otherwise admirable works of Chinese Catholic theology will help me to clarify the value of this book.

THE NEED FOR A BETTER APPROACH: THE WESTERN THEOLOGICAL CONTEXT

The development of Chinese Catholic theology is inherently contextual. Although there are commonalities and cross-contextual aspects of Chinese Catholic theology that can be seen as forming a common project, the theologians who have contributed to Chinese Catholic theology have done so in specific academic, cultural, and political contexts. For example, in mainland China, the modern Christian experience has been shaped by the political context after the Communist rise to power in 1949.[14] Indeed, it is fair to say that the work of building a Chinese Catholic theology in mainland China since 1949 has in many ways been justifiably pushed aside given the serious practical difficulties for Catholics under the Communist regime.[15] In the decades following 1949, the key tension for all Christians in China was to articulate how they were genuinely Chinese and not simply tools of imperialism as popular rhetoric claimed. Very soon, the terms of Christian participation in new China fell within the boundaries demarcated by the Three-Self Movement begun in 1951, one that led to schisms of a sort within both the Catholic and Protestant churches in China. Many Protestant theologians in mainland China have embraced the Three-Self Framework, particularly as the keystone in the process of the "Sinicization" (*zhongguohua* 中國化)

---

14. See, e.g., John H. Tong, "The Church from 1949 to 1990," in *The Catholic Church in Modern China: Perspectives*, ed. Edmond Tang and Jean-Paul Wiest (Maryknoll, NY: Orbis Books, 1993), 7–27; Cindy Yik-yi Chu, ed., *Catholicism in China, 1900–Present* (New York: Palgrave-Macmillan, 2014), 87–218; R. G. Tiedemann, ed. *Handbook of Christianity in China*, vol. 2, *1800–Present* (Leiden: Brill, 2010), 848–66.

15. For works discussing some of the problems faced by the Church in China since 1949, see Geralomo Fazzini, ed., *The Red Book of the Chinese Martyrs* (San Francisco, CA: Ignatius, 2009); Joseph Cardinal Zen, *For the Love of My People, I Will Not Remain Silent* (San Francisco, CA: Ignatius, 2019).

Introduction

of Christianity.[16] For theologians in mainland China, the development of Chinese Christian theology stresses negotiating the civic context of modern China more than the interpretation of Christianity through traditional Chinese cultural resources.

Similarly, in modern Taiwan, the preferred term for the development of Chinese Catholic theology is "indigenization" (*benweihua* 本位化), which is location specific. In a classic essay on the indigenization of Catholic theology in Chinese Taiwan, Aloysius Zhang Chunshen, SJ, defined indigenization as involving "the adoption of contemporary Chinese (*zhongguoren* 中國人) thought, developing and enhancing what has been revealed by God, while at the same time using the logic of revelation to create a new Chinese culture (*zhongguo wenhua* 中國文化)."[17] Zhang also emphasized that indigenization "is not solely the responsibility of professors of academic theology, but is something that must be created by the entire community of a particular place."[18] As these elucidations show, the development of Chinese Catholic theology is therefore deeply contextual, and contains many aspects that cannot be reduced to intellectual, academic activity, even though theologians have an important role to play in these processes.

This book, then, is primarily aimed to aid the development of Chinese Catholic theology in my own intellectual milieu of the modern West and Western language theology. I do not mean that the proposals I make in this book are insignificant to the various projects of Chinese Catholic theologians in other contexts. In fact, I believe the engagement with Chinese philosophy I lay out in this book would be a boon to the development of Chinese Catholic theology in places such as mainland China, Taiwan, Singapore, and so forth. But the concerns that animate this book stem from an engagement

---

16. See, e.g., Alexander Chow, *Theosis, Sino-Christian Theology and the Second Chinese Enlightenment: Heaven and Humanity in Unity* (New York: Palgrave MacMillan, 2013); Alexander Chow, *Chinese Public Theology: Generational Shifts and Confucian Imagination in Chinese Christianity* (New York: Oxford, 2018); Peter Tze Ming Ng, *Chinese Christianity: An Interplay Between Local and Global Perspectives* (Leiden: Brill, 2012); Zhuo Xinping, ed., *Christianity* (Leiden: Brill, 2013); Zhang Yangwen, ed. *Sinicizing Christianity* (Leiden: Brill, 2017).

17. Zhang Chunshen 張春申, "Zhongguo jiaohui de benweihua shenxue 中國教會的本位化神學," *Fujen daxue shenxue lunji* 42 (1979): 407.

18. Zhang Chunshen 張春申, 407.

14 Introduction

with theology written within the Western context, and it is here I must begin.

In the modern West, the project of building Chinese Catholic theology is today still only beginning, and few (if any) scholars would identify their work in these terms. Here, I use "Chinese Catholic theology" to describe the use of Chinese intellectual traditions or resources in producing Catholic theology. While it is a fitting label for some intellectual work, the scholars producing this work I describe as Chinese Catholic theology would not describe their projects as such. Unfortunately, there are exceedingly few Catholic theologians who have offered an intellectual project engaging Chinese traditions at all, and fewer still have been developing a systematic or constructive theology out of this engagement.[19] If one broadens the scope to Chinese Christian theology, there is a modest expansion of literature upon which to draw from Protestant traditions. With the exceptions of evangelical scholars such as K. K. Yeo and Paulos Huang, most such theologians are firmly within the tradition of Protestant liberalism.[20]

19. The most prominent works in this area are historical projects, such as those of Nicholas Standaert, SJ, and Anthony E. Clark. Other scholars have provided Catholic theological engagement with Chinese traditions in order develop Catholic theology, notably the comparative work of Bede Benjamin Bidlack, Xueying Wang, and Stephanie Wong, though Wang's latest work takes a more historical approach. See the following representative works from these authors: Nicholas Standaert, *Yang Tingyun, Confucian and Christian in Late Ming China: His Life and Thought* (Leiden: Brill, 1988); Anthony E. Clark, *China's Saints: Catholic Martyrdom during the Qing (1644–1911)* (Bethlehem, PA: Lehigh University Press, 2011); Bede Benjamin Bidlack, *In Good Company: The Body and Divinization in Pierre Teilhard de Chardin, SJ and Daoist Xiao Yingsou* (Leiden: Brill, 2015); Xueying Wang, "Mengzi, Xunzi, Augustine, and John Chrysostom on Childhood Moral Cultivation," in *Confucianism and Catholicism: Reinvigorating the Dialogue* (Notre Dame, IN: University of Notre Dame Press, 2020), 109–35; Stephanie Wong, "The Mind's Dynamism in Chinese Catholic Theology: A Comparative Study of Metaphysics and Knowledge in the Thought of Wang Yangming and Joseph Maréchal," *Journal of World Christianity* 8, no. 2 (December 2018): 109–33.

20. See e.g., K. K. Yeo, *What does Jerusalem Have to do with Beijing? Biblical Interpretation from a Chinese Perspective* (Harrisburg, PA: Trinity Press International, 1998); K. K. Yeo, "Messianic Predestination in Romans 8 and Classical Confucianism," in *Navigating Romans through Cultures: Challenging Readings by Charting a New Course*, ed. K. K. Yeo (Edinburgh: T&T Clark, 2004), 259–89; and K. K. Yeo, *Musing with Confucius and Paul: Toward a Chinese Christian Theology* (Cambridge: James Clarke & Co., 2008). Huang may be the best current scholar in terms of understanding the complexity of the way that Christianity and Confucianism have been related in Chinese intellectual circles. See esp. Paulos Huang, *Confronting Confucian Understandings of the Christian Doctrine of Salvation: A Systematic Analysis of the Basic Problems in the Confucian-Christian Dialogue* (Leiden: Brill, 2009); and Paulos Huang, "A Response

Introduction 15

The vast majority of Western language scholars who seek to build a Chinese Catholic or Chinese Christian theology do so from the methodological vantage point of liberation theology. For a variety of reasons, these scholars have failed to develop a framework for assessing the standing of Chinese philosophical concepts vis-à-vis the principles of Catholic theological science. Here I will cite two prominent examples in order to first of all demonstrate that this lacuna exists, and second to show that the lacuna is a product of questionable assumptions that I challenge.

Within Catholic theology, Peter C. Phan is the most well-known theologian who has attempted to develop Catholic theology in light of Chinese intellectual traditions. Phan is admittedly not a comparative scholar by training and is not an expert in Chinese philosophy. Yet Phan has, more than any other Western theologian since Vatican II, drawn attention to the theological fruitfulness of engaging Chinese religious and philosophical thought. At the same time, Phan has actively avoided developing a theological framework for assessing the relationship between Chinese philosophy and Catholic theological science, stemming from the nature of his appeal to Chinese thought.

In an earlier essay touching most explicitly upon the relationship between Catholic theology and Chinese philosophy, Phan challenges the position of John Paul II in *Fides et Ratio*, wherein the pontiff argues that philosophy and especially metaphysics are essential to the inculturation of the faith.[21] Phan argues this is not really possible in Confucian cultures of Asia, which do not conform to the metaphysical and philosophical presuppositions John Paul II himself holds when he makes this argument. Rather, Phan holds that in these contexts, inculturation requires that Christian faith be willing to enter into the language and framework of more native

---

to Professor He Guanghu: Different Reactions to the Similarities between Christianity and Traditional Chinese Religions," in *Christianity and Chinese Culture*, ed. Miikka Ruokanen and Paulos Huang (Grand Rapids, MI: Eerdmans, 2010), 70–84.

21. Peter C. Phan, "Inculturation of the Christian Faith in Asia through Philosophy: A Dialogue with John Paul II's *Fides et Ratio*," in *Christianity with An Asian Face* (Maryknoll, NY: Orbis Books, 2003), 47–71. Chinese philosophy is not Phan's sole subject in this study, but I focus on his reading of it here.

16   Introduction

traditions—"almost always at the cost of abandoning its own categories"—in order that "a new *tertium quid* will emerge."[22]

For Phan, the commitment to Chinese thinking and the commitment to traditional Christian categories are exclusive and possibly even diametric commitments, such that holding closer to one requires the diminishment of the other. Phan explicitly argues the Catholic tradition should be willing to "abandon its own categories" in order to become "relevant" and truly "enter into" the intellectual context of Chinese thought. Particularly illuminating is Phan's desire to see a new "*tertium quid*" emerge from this intercultural theology. Consequently, Phan suggests that the best one can do in creating a culturally relevant form of Chinese Catholic theology is to produce some hybrid entity (Confucian-Catholic, specifically) that does not have the quiddity or nature of Catholic theology, inasmuch as this means being able to embrace and work within the conceptual and doctrinal norms of the Christian tradition.

The upshot of this observation is that according to Phan's approach, taking Chinese philosophy seriously as a theological resource inherently requires a willingness to see the very substance and not simply the form of Catholic theology be transformed by the process. Consequently, there is no need to develop an approach to help one understand the relationship between Chinese philosophy and Catholic theological science. According to Phan, in the exchange between Chinese philosophy and Catholic theology, Catholic theology must be willing to divest itself of the principles of its theological science in order to accommodate genuine dialogue with Chinese commitments. Underlying this position, we should note, is a rather stringent commitment to understanding Chinese philosophy and (Western) Catholic theology as fundamentally opposed worldviews.

Notably, Phan's commitment to an opposition between Chinese thought and Catholic theology seems deeply dependent upon his sources. As I mentioned above, Phan does not possess first-hand specialist knowledge of Chinese philosophical traditions (though his later work has improved in this regard).[23] Rather, he is especially

22. Phan, 64.

23. See, e.g., Peter C. Phan, "Catholicism and Confucianism," in *Catholicism and Interreligious Dialogue*, ed. James L. Heft, SM (New York: Oxford University Press, 2011), 170–87.

Introduction

dependent on secondary literature, namely the work of David L. Hall and Roger T. Ames.[24] This is important not least because Hall and Ames are perhaps the most significant Anglophone version of a tradition in Western sinology (particularly among French sinologists such as Marcel Granet, Jacques Gernet, and François Jullien) that casts China as the cultural counterpoint to Western culture. Hall and Ames particularly consider Chinese thought to be fundamentally opposed to the principles animating Christian thought in the West.[25] Yet this is far from a consensus view. In fact, as Edward Slingerland has recently argued, one sees in Hall and Ames's oppositional treatment of China and the West a more amicable form of Orientalism, trading in a cultural essentialism that overlooks the richness of diverse philosophical commitments and arguments found in the Chinese context, many of which are in fact very resonant with Western thought in several respects.[26]

Though this reading of Chinese philosophy is clearest in some of Phan's earlier work, his more recent publications touching on Confucianism show a largely unchanged perspective, though as I mentioned Phan's understanding of the Confucian tradition has admirably expanded. However, the dialectical contrast between Christian categories and Chinese thought presented by Hall and Ames remains a primary foundation in Phan's development of Asian Catholic theology. The irony here is, then, that Phan's theological interpretation of the meeting of Chinese philosophy and Catholic theology reads very much like an offshoot of the cultural essentialism found in Orientalism that liberation theologians often inveigh against.

But more importantly, the seepage of this cultural essentialism into Phan's understanding helps us understand why his theological

---

24. See Phan, "Inculturation," 63n28. Notably, Hall and Ames are the only authors Phan cites for his understanding of Chinese philosophy in this earlier essay.

25. The central pillars of Hall and Ames's project (apart from translations of key texts) are David L. Hall and Roger T. Ames, *Thinking through Confucius* (Albany, NY: SUNY Press, 1987); David L. Hall and Roger T. Ames, *Anticipating China: Thinking Through the Narratives of Chinese and Western Culture* (Albany, NY: SUNY Press, 1995); and David L. Hall and Roger T. Ames, *Thinking from the Han: Self, Truth, and Transcendence in Chinese and Western Culture* (Albany, NY: SUNY Press, 1998). N.B.: Hall died in 2001, while Ames continues to be an active and influential scholar.

26. Edward Slingerland, *Mind and Body in Early China: Beyond Orientalism and the Myth of Holism* (New York: Oxford University Press, 2019). For a shorter yet illuminating version of this account, see Slingerland, 1–7. A more substantial treatment is Slingerland, 22–61.

18   Introduction

reading of Chinese philosophy never turns to develop an adequate framework for testing the standing of Chinese concepts vis-à-vis Catholic theological science. The presuppositions of his approach mean that is impossible for Catholic theological science to incorporate Chinese philosophical concepts without ceasing to be Catholic theological science. Instead of testing Chinese philosophical concepts, Catholic theological science can only give ground, and indeed lose itself to become something new. We see this at work, for example, in Phan's idea of "multiple religious belonging" which is essentially a kind of conceptual and spiritual bilocation within two traditions that are mutually exclusive on the levels of belief, practice, and intellectual disposition.

What I would like to emphasize here is that Phan's reticence to develop a framework for testing the relationship between Chinese philosophical concepts and Catholic theological science ultimately rests upon a presupposition that Chinese and Catholic thought are mutually opposed conceptual worldviews. As I hope this volume helps to illustrate, there are a host of very good reasons for rejecting this presupposition. Though it is clear the Chinese philosophical tradition(s) uses different categories than and entertains distinct problems from Catholic theological science, there is no clear reason to assume the two are fundamentally opposed.[27] Certainly, such a conclusion would have come as a great shock to Christian writers such as Wang Zheng (1571–1644), who believed Christianity fulfilled the classic Confucian exhortation to "fear Heaven and love others."[28] One need not overlook the interesting and important differences between Confucian and Christian ideas of what "fearing Heaven" or

---

27. In my judgment, the differences and divergences between Chinese philosophy and Catholic theological science are neither as deep nor as clear as secular philosophers often presume. For example, Chengyang Li and Francis Perkins have argued that all Chinese philosophy is inherently naturalistic in that it universally rejects the idea of transcendence. As Alexus McLeod and I have argued elsewhere, however, this is because such thinkers do not genuinely understand what Catholic theology, for example, means by transcendence, and instead interpret transcendence in terms set by Enlightenment Deism. We argue that, in fact, Chinese philosophy does have significant forms of transcendence thinking, once we understand the term in the way defended by Catholic theology. See Chengyang Li and Franklin Perkins, introduction to *Chinese Metaphysics and Its Problems*, ed. Chengyang Li and Franklin Perkins (New York: Cambridge University Press, 2015), 1–15; Brown and McLeod, 33–52.

28. Wang Zheng, *Wei Tian ai ren* 畏天爱人. In Zheng Ande, *Mingmo Qingchu Yesuhui sixiang wenxian cihui*, vol. 34.

Introduction 19

"loving others" would mean to see them as having appreciably similarities. And so, once one rejects the oppositional portrait of cultural essentialism, it becomes clear that developing a means to take stock of how Chinese concerns can be understood in light of the principles and norms of theological science is not only possible, but an urgent task for the development of Chinese Catholic theology.

Of course, it is true that even if one does not think Chinese philosophy and Catholic theological science are as incommensurable as some presume, it is inevitable that there are moments of discord between the commitments found in texts of the Chinese tradition and Catholic theological commitments. Where such disagreement occurs, theological science must undoubtedly advance in faithful service of the latter. But more deeply, I am not convinced that the areas of disagreement between Chinese philosophy and Catholic theological science require the sort of resolution that Phan suggests is needed. Justin Martyr, for example, was a devoted Platonist before his conversion to Christianity. In his conversion, he found there were some principles of Platonic thought he must reject, such as the theory of the transmigration of the soul.[29] However, Justin continued to wear the robe of the philosopher and understood himself still to be a Platonist in deep and important ways, even if now his Platonism was subject to the Logos himself.

Similarly, I see no reason why a deep commitment to Chinese philosophy ought to inherently entail diminishing one's commitment to the tradition of Catholic theological science, or vice versa. Indeed, I hope the chapters in this book go a long way to proving this is not the case at all, and that there are significant ways that Chinese philosophy resonates with Catholic theological science. Where Chinese philosophy does not agree with Catholic theological science, those who love Chinese philosophy can admit that such are the weaknesses of human reason, and then strive to find ways to develop Chinese philosophy in keeping with Catholic theological science. This does not remove any of the beauty, wisdom, or utility of Chinese philosophy for Catholic theology; rather such striving purifies and perfects what Chinese philosophy can offer Catholic theology science.

29. See Justin Martyr, *Dialogue with Trypho*, 1.4.

Introduction

Another significant scholar who has worked on the encounter between Chinese philosophy and Christian theology is Heup Young Kim. Here I will focus on his latest book, *A Theology of Dao*.[30] Although Kim's book does not advance a Chinese Catholic theology (it is rather aimed at an East Asian theology within the liberal Protestant perspective), it nonetheless is helpful for analyzing the lacuna I seek to fill through this book.

Kim's fundamental argument is that the concept of *dao* 道 is a more culturally appropriate "root metaphor" for East Asian Christians, and thus should replace the Western frameworks of *logos* and *praxis*.[31] Note that the project of attempting to develop *dao* as a root concept for Chinese Christian theology is clearly justifiable given the importance of *dao* in Chinese traditions and given the deference for this heritage signaled in Chinese translations of the sacred scriptures. When it comes to negotiating this turn to *dao* as a theological root metaphor, however, Kim makes some rather curious decisions. First, Kim never adequately defines the Chinese concept. The most he offers is a footnote citing Herbert Fingarette's "Confucian" definition of *dao*, but this definition is itself ambiguous vis-à-vis Chinese traditions.[32] Otherwise, Kim offers a few quotations from the *Daodejing* and the *Zhuangzi* to identify aspects of the *dao* and establish a connection with *yin-yang* cosmology, but without developing a rigorous account of *dao* either in the texts he cites or as it might relate to a Christian theological context.[33]

This is a problem because *dao* possesses several different meanings and functions in the Daoist tradition alone, and in other contexts (such as Confucianism) can take more diverse meanings. For example, in texts such as the *Daodejing* or *Huainanzi*, the *dao* is explicitly associated with cosmogony and the production of all things. The *Zhuangzi*, in contrast, tends not to consider *dao* cosmogonically, but rather casts *dao* as an important principle of naturalness, which is deeply juxtaposed to the rational tasks of description and classification of things. And in the Confucian tradition broadly (especially

---

30. Heup Young Kim, *A Theology of Dao* (Maryknoll, NY: Orbis Books, 2017).

31. See Kim, 11–13.

32. Kim, 17n6.

33. See Kim, 41–43.

Introduction   21

in the pre-Han), the *dao* is not primarily a metaphysical idea (though it can be), but is more often meant as *rendao* 人道, the moral standards of virtue for humanity. Significantly, the quotation from Fingarette that Kim cites for his understanding of *dao* collapses these various distinctions into one concept in a way that is not found in the texts themselves.[34] Although *dao* was in common usage among early Chinese traditions, accounts of *dao* were variations on a theme rather than one single understanding of *dao*. Hence, Kim's project draws upon *dao* in a sort of abstract way.

Without a clear definition of how *dao* is concretely used in Chinese tradition, it is difficult to see how a concept such as *dao* can come to have a fruitful function within Christian theology. Does Kim mean to use *dao* to supplant Christian metaphysics with something like that of the *Daodejing*? Does he see *dao* as providing a kind of Zhuangist nominalism for establishing Chinese Christian theology? Does he see *dao* as the sum of Confucian moral precepts? Insofar as Kim leans toward seeing *dao* as a replacement of traditional Christian metaphysics (more on this below), he never develops an account of *dao* to clearly define and build toward such a project. This greatly matters because if one wishes to appeal to *dao* in a metaphysical way as a replacement for Western metaphysical concepts, the theologian must recognize and articulate how the shift to a *dao*-metaphysic entails an emendation or rejection of classical Christian metaphysical principles and commitments, as Jung Young Lee did in his *A Theology of Change*.[35] Granted, as I will discuss shortly, Kim is not overly concerned with understanding the relationship between his *dao*-theology and traditional Christian commitments regarding God and the world.[36] But his project does seem to require

34. Herbert Fingarette, *Confucius: The Secular as Sacred* (New York: Harper & Row, 1972), 19.

35. Jung Young Lee, *A Theology of Change: A Christian Concept of God in an Eastern Perspective* (Maryknoll, NY: Orbis Books, 1979). Lee's book posits that the movements of *yin-yang* can apply to God, arguing for God as a kind of perfect principle of change. Yet in his argument, Lee readily admits his view embraces Process theology, and therefore clearly departs from the standards and approach of classical Christian metaphysics.

36. Kim's book does include two comparative essays engaging John Calvin and Karl Barth, respectively. However, these chapters occur in what Kim's section devoted to "bridge-building" between Christianity and East Asian religions. In the book's section that develops his account of "theodao," Kim gives little to no exposition of the Christian theological tradition.

some specificity about the degree to which his appeal to *dao* involves a resistance to traditional Christian metaphysics (which is of central importance to Christian theology) and how such a *dao*-metaphysic can still be genuinely Christian. Kim does not do any of this work; rather he merely asserts that a Christian theology based on *dao* is possible without any demonstration to that effect.[37]

Ultimately, Kim's avoidance of developing either a clear account of *dao* on its own or vis-à-vis Christian theological concepts seems to follow from his presupposition that taking East Asian thought seriously entails diminishing one's commitment to the norms and principles of Christian theology. Kim consistently identifies concern for fidelity to the Christian theological tradition as a form of submission to Western hegemony. For Kim, the doctrinal tradition of the Church is an unjustified misinterpretation of Jesus as a teacher of infallible truth. He writes of the need to move beyond the "myth of orthodoxy," which is dependent upon his consideration of traditional Christian doctrine as merely a construct of Western culture. In Kim's eyes, models of theology as *logos* and as *praxis* (though he is sympathetic with the latter) embody the "dualism" and "historicism" he thinks is indicative of Western thinking, and a culturally responsible East Asian theology must dispense with such Western handicaps. Therefore, Kim appeals to *dao* as a means of disrupting and replacing the conceptual, linguistic, and doctrinal norms of the historical Christian tradition, which he treats as essentially Western.[38]

37. For example, Kim in several places identifies *dao* with the Christian imagery of "the way" (*ho hodos*), and suggests that because the earliest Christians were known as "people of the Way" this means that *dao* is a better foundation for Christian thought than the Johannine conception of *logos*. Similarly, Kim writes that "Jesus did not identify himself either as truly God (*verus Deus*) or truly human (*verus homo*), but he simply said that he is the Way (dao) toward God. He is Christ in such a way that he was the fully embodied Dao of God" (12). But this is a tremendous case of begging the question since the early Church did not identify themselves as "people of the *dao*" but "people of the *hodos*," nor did Christ proclaim Himself to be the *dao* but the *hodos*. Since the Greek term *hodos* lacks the same metaphysical meaning that *dao* has in Chinese, the two are not at all equivalent in the way Kim implies.

38. It is worth noting that such readings of Christianity as a "Western" tradition are themselves historically myopic and ignore the robust and formative contributions of the Christians of the East and Africa. As Philip Jinkins has shown, the identification of Christianity with Western culture is actually a rather late phenomenon, and largely due to the disappearance of Christianity as an institutional force in the Muslim world, rather than any decisive cultural victory of the West. See Philip Jenkins, *The Lost History of Christianity: The Thousand-Year*

Introduction 23

Consequently, Kim treats the norms and principles of Christian theology as a problem of cultural identity. At one point, Kim remarks that because of their commitment to traditional orthodoxy, conservative Korean Christians prove that "there is Christianity in Korea, but not Korean Christianity! There are Christians in Korea but no Korean Christians!"[39] By this, Kim means that the concern for orthodoxy is simply a means of subordinating East Asian identity to the cultural and intellectual hegemony of the West such that those Korean Christians who submit to the orthodoxy undermine their own cultural identity. Instead of perpetuating this hegemony, East Asian Christianity should undermine and move past these Western forms of Christian thought.[40]

Quite revealing in this vein are Kim's reflections on Christology. Kim attempts to submit Christ to the change-dynamics of the cosmos according to the *Yijing*, based on the successive movements of *yin* and *yang* 陰陽. According to Kim, we are entering a time of the *yin* Christ—the feminine principle of change in classical cosmology—which is taking its position after the waning of the *yang* Christ. For Kim, the *yang* Christ is representative of the tradition of Western discourse about Jesus, and its waning is not simply a matter of time and the natural rhythm of the cosmos (as is the transition between *yin* and *yang* in the *Yijing*). As he puts it:

> The millennial crusade of the patriarchal, hegemonic (kataphatic), phallo-onto-Christology with the Western face of the *yang* (masculine) Viking-Rambo Jesus is now waning; a millennial march of the matrilineal, kenotic (apophatic), uterine-sapiential-Christodao in the Asian heart of the *yin* (feminine) Sage Christ is rising. Through great non-action action in her uterine tranquility and sociocosmic serenity, Christ as the Mystical-Prophetic Female will heal this fragmented, divided world torn

---

Golden Age of the Church in the Middle East, Africa, and Asia—and How it Died (New York: HarperOne, 2009).

39. Kim, *A Theology of Dao*, 8.

40. Kim is not alone in such judgments. See also the influential book Yung Hwa, *Mangoes or Bananas? The Quest for an Authentic Asian Christian Theology* (Oxford: Regnum, 1997). In common parlance "banana" is a term of derision for people of Asian heritage who have become Westernized (yellow on the outside, white on the inside) and "mangoes" refers to Asian authenticity (yellow on inside and outside).

down by the aggressive lynching of incarnated macho images and will recover the harmonious wholeness through a radical return to the pneumato-sociocosmic trajectory.[41]

Particularly notable in this passage is Kim's treatment of traditional Christological norms and principles. Not only is this kind of Christological reflection said to produce a "Western face" of Jesus, but it is so as part of a "millennial crusade" of this Christology. In this view, Christology has primarily been a form of cultural hegemony and colonization, and thus not an authentic testimony to the truth of Jesus Christ as revealed in scripture. Indeed, Kim identifies the questions of traditional Christology which focus on Christ's being as constituting an "onto-Christology" that is at once phallic and kataphatic—that is, its maleness is evident in the fact that it attempts to articulate positive knowledge about Jesus Christ.

Admittedly, there is nothing in Kim's description that is not present in the academic centers of liberation theology in the West. Indeed, Kim's work has deep roots in the progressive Western academic establishment. For our purposes, this is instructive because it is ironic that Kim's rejection of responsibility vis-à-vis Christian theological norms and principles is itself a very modern Western position. This should give one pause about claims that Chinese Catholic theology ought to stress cultural relevance and dismiss a commitment to Christian orthodoxy as hegemonic. For it is evident that Kim and much of modern liberation theology has not freed itself from subservience to a greater power, but merely one particular power. Kim seeks liberation from the proposed hegemony of Christian theological tradition, but instead submits to what Patrick Deneen has astutely called "hegemonic" liberalism.[42] Following the dictates of hegemonic liberalism, Kim reduces Christian theological tradition to a (Western) cultural moment that has passed away or should pass away in lieu of a (post)modernity that can ground truly "authentic" East Asian Christianity.

---

41. Kim, *A Theology of Dao*, 55.

42. See Patrick J. Deneen, "Hegemonic Liberalism and the End of Pluralism," in *The Church in a Pluralist Society: Social and Political Roles*, ed. Cornelius J. Casey and Fáinche Ryan (Notre Dame, IN: University of Notre Dame Press, 2019), 29–44. See also Patrick J. Deneen, *Why Liberalism Failed* (New Haven, CT: Yale University Press, 2018), 64–90.

Introduction 25

Of course, it makes good sense that Kim's commitment to post-modern liberal principles leads to a lack of developing the kind of framework of assessment I offer in this book. To cite Deneen again, what liberalism actually offers is homogeneity with the "patina" of diversity.[43] Globalism and pluralism concern the eradication of the local and cultural, not their embrace. Hence, in the end liberal Chinese Christian theology looks like all other forms of liberal theology—indeed, there are many passages in Kim's work such as that cited above that one could find in almost any modern liberal theology, with a few decorative terms switched out. In this sense, I see no reason to conclude that Kim's approach to eschew traditional Christian norms and principles gets one any closer to an "authentic" East Asian Christianity.[44] It seems rather to simply produce a liberal Christianity with an Asian face that is more conformable to the whims and dictates of the liberal order.

In this book, I too strive to help ground a theology that is culturally responsive and authentic for Chinese Christians. However, unlike Kim, I see no reason to presume that taking the traditional theological discursive norms and principles seriously endangers this work of cultural authenticity. This is not least because I reject the thesis of the liberal order that Christian theological claims are products of human culture that bear the burden of blame for problems of the "old world" that must be now made into privatized religious commitments for the sake of the common good. Rather, I hold that the theological principles of the Christian tradition are guides

---

43. Deneen, "Hegemonic Liberalism," 38: "The claim that liberal orders encourage or defend 'pluralism' and diversity should be treated with a justified skepticism, joined to a willingness to perceive in those claims a deeper formative effort to shroud a pervasive homogeneous monoculture in a patina of variety."

44. See, e.g., Robert Cummings Neville, *Boston Confucianism: Portable Tradition in the Late-Modern World* (Albany, NY: SUNY Press, 2000); Robert Cummings Neville, *Ritual and Deference: Extending Chinese Philosophy in a Comparative Context* (Albany, NY: SUNY Press, 2008); John H. Berthrong, *All Under Heaven: Transforming Paradigms in Confucian-Christian Dialogue* (Albany, NY: SUNY Press, 1994); John H. Berthrong, *Expanding Process: Exploring Philosophical and Theological Transformations in China and the West* (Albany, NY: SUNY Press, 2008); Heup Young Kim, *Wang Yang-ming and Karl Barth: A Confucian-Christian Dialogue* (Lanham, MD: University Press of America, 1996); Jung Young Lee, *The Trinity in Asian Perspective* (Nashville, TN: Abingdon Press, 1996); Hyo-Dong Lee, *Spirit, Qi, and the Multitude: A Comparative Theology for the Democracy of Creation* (New York: Fordham University Press, 2013).

to saving truth. The historical form of Christian theology has been mediated through concrete cultures and intellectual traditions, but it is deeply inaccurate to simply label these cultures as "Western" as if they were monochromatic. In reality, Christian theological tradition has always involved linguistic, cultural, and racial diversity, and there is no obvious reason to assume East Asian culture is so radically different from other human cultures that it cannot find its own place *within* the Christian tradition. However, finding the genuine place where Chinese philosophy can flourish within Catholic theological science requires a means of taking Chinese philosophy seriously as a resource for Catholic theology by submitting it to rigorous theological assessment.

Undoubtedly striking the right balance between taking Chinese philosophy seriously and being respectful to the norms and principles of the Catholic theological tradition is not easy. For Phan and Kim, the scale tips almost entirely in one direction. The late Anselm K. Min shows the other side of the problem in a recent article providing a compelling reflection on the Trinity in Aquinas compared to a triadic concept in the thought of Zhu Xi.[45] Min's analysis is concrete and respectful of the Thomistic conception of the Trinity as the norm to be applied to Confucian concepts. Yet Min also admits the shortcomings of his own approach in that he simply lacks the expertise to develop the concepts of Zhu Xi's system in their own context to such a degree that they become truly useful and able to be incorporated into Chinese Catholic theology (or Korean Catholic theology in Min's case).[46] With humility, I propose here a way to strike the right balance between being theological responsible to the tradition of Catholic theological science and being grounded in rigorous, focused analyses of Chinese philosophical traditions on their own terms. In this way, the book will at least begin to fill the lacuna in Western scholarship I have sketched above.

---

45. Min, "The Trinity of Aquinas and the Triad of Zhu Xi."
46. Min, 151.

THE NEED FOR A BETTER APPROACH:
A BROADER VIEW

The previous section sought to show why the approach for the theological utilization of Chinese philosophy that I present in this book is needed in the Western context. However, I also think my approach can benefit the development of Chinese Catholic theology in other contexts, such as mainland China and Taiwan. Describing these benefits means I must emphasize where I think my approach improves upon other tendencies and approaches in these other contexts. however, I stress that I take these other projects of building Chinese Catholic theology to be great sources of inspiration and knowledge, essential for developing Chinese Catholic theology. My argument is that inasmuch as Chinese Catholic theology entails a need to engage the theological limits and possibilities of Chinese philosophical concepts, the approach I model in this book will yield the best intellectual foundations for such a Chinese Catholic theology.[47]

To be clear, then, my argument in this book is in no way intended to circumvent or ignore the very real (and very fascinating) historical contributions made in Chinese Catholic theology, which are worthy of their own book and study to articulate properly.[48] Hence,

47. I have not here dealt with the approaches of Catholic philosophers from Taiwan such as Luo Guang and Vincent Shen who have worked out deep integrations between Neo-scholastic philosophy that incorporates Chinese thought, because their aims are more properly philosophical than theological. Luo Guang (sometimes known as Stanislaus Lo Kuang) served as bishop in Taiwan and president of Fujen Catholic University in Taiwan from 1978–1992. His most famous contribution to Taiwanese Neo-Scholasticism is *Shengming zhexue* 生命哲學, in which Luo attempted to discuss the resonances Chinese philosophical traditions and Neo-Scholastic wisdom along the axes of the "philosophy of life." See Luo Guang, *Luo Guang quanshu* 羅光全書, vols. 1–2 (Taiwan: Xuesheng shuju, 1996). Vincent Shen (Shen Qingsong) served on the faculty of University of Toronto for many years and wrote extensively on the relationship between Chinese philosophy and modern Western philosophy in particular, though out of a perspective sympathetic to Neo-Scholasticism. See among other examples, Shen, "From Gift to Law"; and Vincent Shen, *Cong Li Madou dao Haidege: kua wenhua mailuo xia de zhongxi zhexue hudong* 從利瑪竇到海德格: 跨文化脈絡下的中西哲學互動 (Taibei: Taiwan Shangwu Yinshuguan, 2014).

48. Chinese Catholic theology is underrepresented in scholarship on Chinese Christian theology, and so this is a field that is rich for tilling in the future. At the present, I will limit myself to noting that I personally have found tremendous theological value and interest in several modern Chinese Catholic writers such as Wang Changzhi, Xu Zongze, and Luo Guang, whose philosophical and spiritual works are worthy of further study for their theological attributes. Thankfully, Chloë Starr has helped shed light on Xu's contributions, at least, for English

this book does not set any foundations for Chinese Catholic theology in an historical sense. Rather, here I mean to focus solely on providing foundational intellectual principles for that can improve that aspect of Chinese Catholic theology that requires engaging with and adopting from traditional Chinese philosophies.

This book differs from other attempts in Chinese Catholic theology to address the relationship between Chinese philosophy and Catholic theology in two main respects: the emphasis on concrete, in-depth analyses of the concepts within finite textual parameters, and my use of Aquinas as a systematic framework of assessment. Above, I explained why concrete engagement with Chinese philosophical traditions is needed. As regards my use of Aquinas, while I do not suggest he is the only appropriate source for the work I offer here, he is not purely accidental to the success and importance of my analyses. This is not because of my own predilection for Aquinas—I am not really a Thomist in the technical sense of the word—but because of what he offers as a *doctor ecclesiae* and a master of theology.

To engage Aquinas's thought is, in a sense, to engage the entire theological tradition of the Catholic Church. With him we meet the priority of study of the scriptures, reverence for the Church Fathers of both the East and West, and recognition of the important contributions of early medieval thinkers such as Anselm and the fruits of monastic theology. Additionally, we find in Aquinas a persistent attention to the capacity of human reason to aid in knowing and loving God, as he constantly engages the Greek and Roman philosophical traditions in figures such as Plato, Proclus, Cicero, and of course Aristotle. And we should remember that Thomism itself is a robust tradition that has had tremendous impact on the development of official Catholic doctrine, famously at the Council of Trent and in the writings of pontiffs, such as Leo XIII and John Paul II. Both the expansive quality of Aquinas's thought and influence, and his integrative instincts to honor and love the best of pagan wisdom and incorporate it into the work of theology strikes me as the perfect combination for the work I undertake in this book. Put simply, his thought

---

readers: see Chloë Starr, *Chinese Theology: Text and Context* (New Haven, CT: Yale University Press, 2016), 100–27. For some limited examples of Chinese Catholic theology in translation, see Chloë Starr, ed. *A Reader in Chinese Theology* (Waco, TX: Baylor University Press, 2023).

Introduction 29

allows for just the sort of rigor and depth needed to test the theological possibilities of Chinese philosophical concepts, while also allowing for the kind of responsiveness and flexibility to meet the Chinese concepts on their own terms. So, while St. Thomas does not provide the only theological framework that could be used in such a project, it is hard to imagine one better suited to this project's ends.

The kind of concrete engagement with Chinese philosophy via a robust appeal to Aquinas as an instrument of theological assessment is aimed to correct the two problems that I find with Chinese Catholic theology's use of Chinese philosophical concepts. Fleshing out these problems in more detail thus clarifies the benefits of my approach. The first problem in Chinese Catholic theology is the presence of a kind of uncritical employment of Chinese philosophy. Above, I noted that this approach assumes that analogous concepts between Chinese philosophy and Catholic theology can simply be discovered and used in Chinese Catholic discourse without systematically and rigorously analyzing how these Chinese concepts do and do not resonate with Catholic teaching. To be clear, I do not find this to be a deep fault when understood in its own context. After all, when the Jesuits first entered China and when Chinese literati first began to convert to Catholicism, they were not seeking to develop a Chinese Catholic theological science. The Jesuit missionaries' task was to use whatever resources they could to promulgate the Gospel, and they were wise and correct to see Chinese intellectual traditions (especially Confucianism) as fitting vectors of transmission. On the other hand, Chinese converts to Catholicism had been steeped in Chinese intellectual traditions all their lives, and had a very limited engagement with Catholicism as an intellectual tradition. How could they do anything else but to uncritically understand the Gospel in terms and concepts immediately available to them?

Yet when we seek to develop Chinese Catholic theological science, it is evident that the uncritical application of Chinese philosophical concepts in Catholic theology results in problems that need to be addressed. Let me provide some examples to illustrate this. First, there is the example of Matteo Ricci, who shrewdly recognized that discussion of the moral law was an important way to present the Gospel in the Chinese context. Thus, Ricci offered translations of the Decalogue as a way of proving the moral character of Catholicism to the Chinese literati. In his translation of the fourth commandment to honor one's parents (Ex 20:12, "*kabed et-abikah v'et immekah*"), Ricci rendered it as "*xiaojing fumu* 孝敬父母" which literally means "giving filial reverence to one's parents."[49] As a translation that approximates the Hebrew word *kabed* in classical Chinese, *xiaojing* is not a bad choice, though one could argue *rong* 榮 and *jing* 敬 together would be better. Still, the concept of *xiao* ("filial piety") is much more central to specifically Confucian Chinese culture, as a central pillar of the family. Thus, Ricci was prudent to draw upon the weighty idea of *xiao* to communicate the meaning of the Decalogue in a Chinese context, and as a means of showing that the Gospel supports rather than dissolves Chinese moral standards.

However, there is an important conceptual disparity between the Hebrew notion of honoring one's parents and the Confucian doctrine of *xiao*. For Confucians at the time, to hear the Catholic faith involved *xiaojing* would have associated Catholicism with the standards and practices of filial reverence in the Confucian tradition, such as having children, mourning parents' deaths, and sacrificing to one's ancestors and parents.[50] At least two of these concerns—those filial duties of sacrifice and having children—were genuine sources of conflict between the Jesuit missionaries and Chinese officials and intellectuals in the late Ming and early Qing.[51] In this, the rhetorical analogy between the Decalogue and the Confucian virtue of filial piety gave way to conflict in practice, signaling that the concepts themselves were not as harmonious as we might assume.

---

49. Earlier, Ruggieri had rendered "honor one's parents" as "*ai jing* 愛敬" or "love and reverence," whereas Ricci used *xiaojing* across several publications, including the *Tianzhu Jiaoyao* 天主教要. See Tian Haihua, "Confucian Catholics' Appropriation of the Decalogue: A Case-Study of Cross-Textual Reading," in *Reading Christian Scriptures in China*, ed. Chloë Starr (London: T&T Clark, 2008), 164–67,

50. See my discussion of these aspects of *xiao* in Brown, *Balthasar in Light of Early Confucianism*, 69–100; and that in Keith N. Knapp, *Selfless Offspring: Filial Children and Social Order in Medieval China* (Honolulu, HI: University of Hawaii Press, 2005), 113–63.

51. Two concrete examples were the critiques of priestly celibacy during the Ming (see Ricci, *True Meaning*, 413–37, for a defense of celibacy in response to concerns of his Chinese interlocutors) and the Chinese Rites Controversy, which concerned differing theological opinions over whether Chinese Catholics were able to practice the rites of ancestral veneration.

Introduction

Therefore, in order to develop a conception of filial piety that fits within Catholic theological science, it would be necessary to determine the genuine points of agreement and disagreement between Confucianism and Catholicism on this score.[52] While we find some clarification about Catholicism and filial piety in Jesuit texts, we have nothing resembling a rigorous testing apparatus suited to finding the strengths and weaknesses of Chinese concepts, though this is again understandable given the challenges the missionaries themselves faced. Hence, I do not mean to condemn the Jesuits for failing to develop such readings of Chinese philosophy, but I merely note that to incorporate concepts such as *xiao* into Catholic theological science, the kind of work I model here is needed.

Another helpful example of a laudable yet incomplete theological appeal to Chinese philosophical concepts is evident in a concept utilized by both Jesuit missionaries and Chinese literati converts to Catholicism. In the late Ming, prominent writers such as Ricci and Yang Tingyun described God as the "great father-mother" (*da fu-mu* 大父母).[53] The appeal to this appellation makes tremendous sense in the intellectual context of imperial China. The terms "father" and "mother" had been classically applied to *Tian* as a source of generation and production of life, especially in the Confucian school.[54] Additionally because of the role of parents in caring for and raising their children, there was a long tradition of applying the binomial term "father-mother" to the ruler in classical Chinese thought.[55] Indeed, in the *Shengshui jiyan*, the first appeal to God as "father-mother" is offered with a political color, as it says that "the people of the six directions and the ten-thousand countries all have one Great

---

52. Tian Liang, "*Jianli Zhongguo gongjiao wenhua chuyi* 建立中國公交文化芻議," *Xinduosheng* 5, no. 26 (December 1959): 33–46. Tian's article appealed to *xiao* as a foundation for a Chinese public theology and the renewal of Chinese Catholic culture. Unlike Ricci's early appeal to *xiao*, Tian's argument involved a close reading of *xiao* in the Confucian tradition with a more sophisticated and critical eye toward the theological utility of *xiao*. In this sense, Tian is an example of how *xiao* can be developed theologically, though many Chinese Christian thinkers appeal to filial piety as a metaphor for understanding the Christian relationship with God.

53. Standaert, *Yang Tingyun*, 116–23.

54. E.g., Yang Xiong, *Yangzi fayan*, 13.2.

55. There is a clear ritual link here in ancient China in that both parents and the ruler were accorded a three-year mourning period. Additionally, there are attestations to this conception of the ruler as "father-mother" found in many texts, such as *Mengzi*, 1B:14.

Father-Mother."[56] The political shade of the concept helpfully shows how calling God "the great father-mother" is a natural outgrowth of taking divine providence and governance seriously from the Chinese intellectual context, and is a justifiable appellation.

Still, the cultural appropriateness of the appellation does not mean it is without theological problems that must be resolved. As Nicholas Standaert has noted, in the Neo-Confucian tradition, the idea of heaven and earth as "father-mother" was taken to apply to the primary causal forces in the cosmos (*qian* and *kun* 乾坤), which began the process of generation of all things through the movements of *yin* and *yang*.[57] Although writers like Yang Tingyun did not seek to apply the term "great father-mother" to *qian* and *kun* but to God alone, it is not clear how the natural duplex structure of generation implied in the "father-mother" metaphor can be applied singly to God in such a way that requires the retainment of "father-mother" and not simply "father."

On the terms of Catholic theology, this problem is illustrative. For if the generative work of God is stressed or simply included in the appellation of "great father-mother" there must be some account of how the duplex order of generation is appropriate to God. This would be very difficult to do in Catholic systematic theology given the doctrine of appropriations, which holds that the act of creation is a single act of the Trinity, and not a duplex act. One option would be the kind of creation theology found in Sergius Bulgakov which posits an activity of "Sophia" that is not properly part of the Triune God, but also not properly creation.[58] However, this resolution creates problems due to implying the need of an intermediate power in creation, which casts a shadow on the doctrine of *creatio ex nihilo*. At the very least, it is evident that describing God as "father-mother" implies a kind of conjugal or at least combinatory process of generation that is inherent in the Neo-Confucian cosmology, but which the Catholic doctrine of creation justifiably resists.

---

56. *Shengshui jiyan*, p. 5; in M. Courant, *Catalogue des Livres Chinois, Coréens, Japonais, etc.* (Paris, 1912), held in the Bibliothèque nationale de France, catalog no. Chinois, 6845. "吾六合萬國人之一大父母也."

57. Standaert, *Yang Tingyun*, 118.

58. See, e.g., Sergius Bulgakov, *The Lamb of God*, trans. Boris Jakim (Grand Rapids, MI: Eerdmans, 2008), 89–156.

Introduction   33

My point here is not that the appellation "great father-mother" is inappropriately applied to God (since I do not believe it is inapt in its original context), but that a true systematic incorporation of the idea cannot use the appellation without qualification. "Father-mother" is not as such perfectly fit to describe aspects of God that Catholic doctrine demands. Therefore, the theologian must labor to understand more carefully the actual limits and possibilities for the application of "father-mother" to God in order to find a true place and role for the concept in a Chinese Catholic theology. Therefore, the kind of tasks I provide in this book are needed as part of the process for developing appreciative and sympathetic, yet theologically rigorous, applications of Chinese philosophical concepts.

Several scholars have undertaken tasks similar to mine, including John C. H. Wu, some of whose work is available in English and who is even enjoying a bit of a renaissance of interest at present.[59] Wu's essential insight was that the main religious traditions of China—Confucianism, Daoism, and Buddhism—each were in different ways a preparation for the gospel in China. More recently, biblical theologians such as Aloysius Zhang Chunshen and Mark Fang Zhirong have contributed much to the Catholic study of Chinese philosophy, albeit through occasional essays rather than monograph projects.[60] While these authors indeed expand our understanding of relationship between Catholic theology and Chinese philosophy, however,

59. For some of Wu's most important writings touching on this subject, see John C. H. Wu, *From Confucianism to Catholicism* (Huntington, IN: Our Sunday Visitor Press, 1949); John C. H. Wu, *Chinese Humanism and Christian Spirituality* (Jamaica, NY: St. John's University Press, 1965); and John C. H. Wu, *Beyond East and West* (Notre Dame, IN: University of Notre Dame Press, 2018), originally published in 1951. I personally know of at least two doctoral dissertations currently being written on Wu's work in US institutions.

60. Much of Zhang and Fang's writings regarding Chinese philosophy have been published in a theology journal produced by Fujen 輔仁 university in Taiwan (formerly of Beijing), which is the preeminent Catholic university in Taiwan if not the Chinese-speaking world. See the following examples: Zhang Chunshen, "Jiaohui 'benweihua' de weijie 教會 (本位化) 的癥結," *Fujen daxue shenxue lunji* 33 (1977): 347–62; Zhang, "Zhongguo jiaohui de benweihua shenxue 中國教會的本位化神學"; Zhang, "Zongjiao jiaotan de shenxue jichu 宗教交談的神學基礎," *Fujen daxue shenxue lunji* 45 (1980): 328–38; Fang Zhirong, "Zhongguo ji Yiselie gu xianzhi de xun yan yu zongjiao 中國及以色列古先知的訓言與宗教," *Fujen daxue shenxue lunji* 13 (1972): 478–85; Fang Zhirong, "Rujia sixiang de tian yu shengjing de shangdi zhi bijiao 儒家思想的天與聖經的上帝之比較," *Fujen daxue shenxue lunji* 31 (1977): 14–41; Fang Zhirong, "Kongzi suofanying de Jidu mianmao 孔子所反映的基督面貌," *Fujen daxue shenxue lunji* 61 (1984): 366–74.

34 Introduction

what they lack is an approach that yields depth of analysis and a systematic rigor. For the most part, their contributions are occasional essays, and few demonstrate the level of engagement with modern sinological research needed for truly effective analyses. Additionally, these scholars also tend to develop the theological arm of their analyses in a very generalized way, employing the biblical text as the main source, and treating Catholicism and Chinese philosophy on the level of "traditions" rather than engaging concepts within the parameters of concrete texts. For example, one of the few book-length studies of Catholicism's relationship to concepts in Chinese philosophical traditions is by the Taiwanese theologian Zhao Binshi.[61] Zhao's approach is typical inasmuch as he seeks to analyze the relationship between Catholicism, Confucianism, and Daoism on the level of traditions—that is, to represent generalized forms of the positions popular in these traditions and compare these generalized pictures, much like one sees in modern comparative religions and world religions textbooks.

The problem with this approach is that to a certain degree, it prevents rigor and depth. To his credit, Zhao shows considerable strength in his approach to Confucianism, for example, by appealing to concrete examinations of the tradition's arguments regarding concepts such as "human moral nature" and "filial piety" as found in primary sources. However, Zhao's presentation of Christian theology fails to reach the same levels of sophistication. Zhao tends to refer to the scriptures as the sole textual basis upon which to compare Confucian and Christian perspectives.[62] Although this is undoubtedly helpful and fruitful, such an approach begs for a greater systemization. For it is indubitable for Catholic theological science, at least, that scripture cannot be properly accessed and understood apart from the sacred tradition that guards the meaning and interpretation of the revealed texts.

A deep and compelling theological incorporation of Chinese philosophy naturally requires a robust and well-developed account of the Christian tradition on a given issue in order to articulate how

61. Zhao Binshi, *Ru dao sixiang yu Tianzhujiao* 儒道思想與天主教 (Taipei: Guangqi Chubanshe, 1964).

62. See, e.g., Min, 168–72.

Introduction   35

this issue fits within the overall perspective of Christian doctrine and dogma. Although it is too much to say that Aquinas's theology provides *the* magisterial framework fitting for such a task, it cannot be gainsaid that he provides an exemplar of a theology that articulates (and allows for the further exploration of) the fuller meaning and relationship between topics of Christian belief. Consequently, by drawing upon a theologian such as Aquinas to furnish a framework for analyzing Chinese philosophical concepts in relation to Christian theology, one gains the ability to more and more deeply penetrate the diverse levels of interaction that are at play between Catholic theological science and Chinese philosophy.

Self-evidently, the task of Chinese Catholic theology bears a fundamentally different responsibility than Protestant theologies regarding fidelity to sacred tradition (in unity with sacred scripture) and thus in relation to the magisterial ministry of the Church that clarifies the proper interpretation of revelation. As Ramón García de Haro once observed, fidelity to the magisterium is a "condition of authenticity" for Catholic theology, which is a prominent point of distinction from Protestant theology.[63] That said, I hope the approach I offer in this book will be of value to non-Catholic Chinese Christian theologians as well, particularly since the book models a kind of systematic and concrete approach to understanding the theological promise and limitations of Chinese philosophical concepts. I have benefited from the scholarship of Protestant theologians such as He Shiming and Paulos Huang on these matters, but I believe the attempts of Protestant theologians to incorporate Chinese philosophy into a vibrant and authentic Christian theology would be improved by drawing upon the methods practiced in this volume.[64]

To give an example, I have deep sympathies with Zhao Dunhua's

---

63. Ramón García de Haro, *Marriage and the Family in the Documents of the Magisterium: A Course in the Theology of Marriage*, trans. William E. May (San Francisco, CA: Ignatius, 1993), 44.

64. He Shiming is the author of five books on Confucianism and Christianity, all of which were republished in 1999 as the following volumes: He Shiming, *Jidujiao yu ruxue duitan* 基督教与儒学对谈 (Beijing: Zongjiao Wenhua Chubanshe, 1999); He Shiming, *Jidjujiao ruxue sixiang* 基督教儒学思想 (Beijing: Zongjiao Wenhua chubanshe, 1999); He Shiming, *Zhongguo wenhua zhong zhi youshenlun yu wushenlun* 中国文化中之有神论与无神论 (Beijing: Zongjiao wenhua chubanshe, 1999): He Shiming, *Cong Jidujiao kan Zhongguo xiaodao* 从基督教看中国孝道 (Beijing: Zongjiao wenhua chubanshe, 1999); He Shiming, *Rongguan*

36   Introduction

study of the doctrine of original sin in the Christian tradition and the concept of the goodness of human nature in the Confucian tradition. (I address similar themes in chapter 4 of this book.)[65] I fully concur with Zhao that the distance between the dominant traditional Christian and Confucian conceptions of the human person vis-à-vis moral goodness is not nearly as stark as polemics in the late Ming and early Qing—or indeed, among modern intellectuals—would suggest.[66] Yet I also think that the issue requires more clarification and systematic analysis than Zhao provides. This is not least because the Confucian commitment to human moral goodness and the Christian doctrine of original sin function in close relation to a host of other commitments within each tradition. Consequently, the way particular figures understand these concepts and address intellectual problems accompanying them varies within traditions. To obtain a more accurate understanding of the points of tension or harmony between the Confucian and Christian approaches to human morality, we need concrete textual frameworks, along with a substantive theological perspective that can grant access to the complexity and interdependency of the doctrine of original sin in relation to other Christian commitments. Hence, the kind of analysis I provide here would be of service in making Zhao's argument more detailed and precise regarding where and how Confucians and Christians would agree and disagree on such issues.

In sum, I submit the following chapters as examples of a work that is sorely needed, yet too frequently left undone, especially in modern Western theology. Put simply, it is my great desire to see Catholic theological science attend to the proper place that Chinese philosophy has within the Pauline exhortation that "whatever is true, whatever is honorable, whatever is just, whatever is pure, whatever is lovely, whatever is gracious, if there is any excellences and if there

---

shenxue yu rujia sixiang 融贯神学与儒家思想 (Beijing: Zongjiao wenhua chubanshe, 1999). See n. 14 above for Huang's work.

65. Zhao Dunhua, "The Goodness of Human Nature and Original Sin: A Point of Convergence in Chinese and Western Cultures," in Ruokanen and Huang, 3–11.

66. For an excellent example of scholarship emphasizing the conflict between Chinese intellectuals and Christianity (and providing excellent coverage of the debates, albeit with little theological sensitivity), see Jacques Gernet, *China and the Christian Impact: A Conflict of Cultures*, trans. Janet Lloyd (Cambridge, UK: Cambridge University Press, 1985).

Introduction 37

is anything worthy of praise, think about these things" (Phil 4:8). I am hopeful that my analyses below prove that there is much that is true, honorable, lovely, excellent, and laudable in Chinese philosophical traditions. However, in order to arrive at seeing these features of Chinese philosophy, we must take up another Pauline admonition and "test everything; retain what is good" (1 Thes 5:21). I offer this book as a model for testing Chinese philosophy so that we might better retain its goodness.

1

A Thomistic Assessment
of the *Mengzi* on *Tian* [1]

A PROLOGUE TO A THEOLOGICAL QUESTION

In Chinese, Catholicism is known as "the teaching of the Lord of Heaven" or *Tianzhujiao* 天主教, a term derived from the name for God (*Tianzhu*) that began to be applied by Catholic missionaries and Chinese converts to Catholicism in the late Ming dynasty. [2] The term *Tianzhu* is a modification of *Tian*, which referred to the high god during the Zhou dynasty. At the beginning of the Zhou dynasty, the divine status of *Tian* seems have to been largely unquestioned; in fact, *Tian* was seen as the deity which had willed the beginning of the Zhou reign, giving the Zhou family the "Mandate of *Tian*" (*Tianming* 天命) to rule and govern the Chinese people. However, as the Zhou rulers began to suffer loss of power and the dynasty showed signs of dissolution, this forced many intellectuals to reckon with how or why *Tian* would allow such strife to befall

---

1. In this and Chapter 2, I take *Tian* 天 primarily in a theistic sense, and thus capitalize the term. However, 天 also can mean something more like "nature" or simply "the heavens" and thus has a non-theistic function, and would properly be rendered *tian*. However, in order to avoid confusion and to have uniformity in the text, I have erred here on using the capitalized version of *Tian* for all renderings of the term; readers can rely upon context to infer what meaning of *Tian* I have in mind.

2. For an account of the genesis of the term, see Jean-Pierre Charbonnier, *Christians in China: A.D. 600 to 2000*, trans. M. N. L. Couve de Murville (San Francisco: Ignatius Press, 2007), 144–45.

A Thomistic Assessment of the *Mengzi* on *Tian*   39

the chosen rulers. As a result, many thinkers began to understand and emphasize *Tian* as a kind of force behind or within the natural world, at times as something like natural law.[3] Given that *Tian* had also functioned to describe the heavens and upper reaches of the cosmos, this was not a far stretch.[4]

Although it is impossible to determine the original intent of using *Tianzhu* to describe the God of Christian revelation, many Catholic missionaries interpreted *Tianzhu* as a corrective to the inadequate theological concept of *Tian* in the Chinese tradition. Some even believed that the classical Chinese terms for the divine (*Shangdi* 上帝 and *Tian*) must be wholly dispensed with in the Christian setting.[5] The debates came to a head within the context of the Chinese Rites Controversy, when in 1693 the Vicar Apostolic of Fujian, Charles Maigrot, MEP, issued a decree stating that only *Tianzhu* should be used by Catholics.[6] Later in 1705, Charles Thomas Maillard de Tournon acted in his authority as Apostolic Visitor to meet with the Kangxi emperor in an effort to resolve the controversy. De Tournon defended Maigrot's position, arguing that *Tianzhu* helped to clarify the distinction between God and nature. Notably, the Kangxi emperor replied that *tian* is conceptually multivalent, and saw no need for a more specific term to denote God as Catholics understood him.[7] But, for better or worse, the Catholic use of *Tianzhu* was definitively settled when Pope Clement XI issued the

---

3. For an excellent account of this crisis regarding *Tian*, see Yuri Pines, *Foundations of Confucian Thought: Intellectual Life in the Chunqiu Period, 722–453 B.C.E.* (Honolulu: University of Hawaii Press, 2002), 55–88.

4. Feng Youlan 冯友兰, *Zhongguo zhexue shi* 中国哲学史, vol. 1 (Chongqing: Chongqing chubanshe, 2009), 34–35.

5. Liam Matthew Brockey, *Journey to the East: The Jesuit Mission to China, 1579–1724* (Cambridge, MA: The Belknap Press of Harvard University, 2007), 85–87. Brockey notes this was a debate within the early Jesuit missionary communities, spurred in part by experiences of some who were veterans of the Japanese missions. In the Japanese missions (which had been considered successful until Toyotomi Hideyoshi's persecution in 1587), the missionaries had preferred using transliterations of Latin terms, and advocated similar practices in China, for example, preferring the term *Dou-si* 陡斯, a transliteration of *Deus*.

6. See Ray R. Noll, ed., *100 Roman Documents Concerning the Chinese Rites Controversy (1645–1941)*, trans. Donald F. St. Sure (San Francisco, CA: Ricci Institute, 1992), 9. As cited in Nicholas Standaert, *The Fascinating God: A Challenge to Modern Chinese Theology Presented by a Text on the Name of God Written by a 17th Century Chinese Student of Theology* (Rome: Editrice Pontificia Università Gregoriana, 1995), 12.

7. Charbonnier, 260.

papal bull *Ex illa Die* (1715) and suppressed use of other Chinese terms for God.

As this brief review suggests, the career of *Tianzhu* and its preference over *Tian* in later Chinese Catholic history raises an interesting question vis-à-vis the relationship between classical Chinese philosophy and Catholic theological science.[8] Precisely how does the classical Chinese conception of *Tian* resonate or not resonate with the God of revelation? In this and the following chapter, I seek to explore this question in the concrete, offering a more rigorous and detailed account of where the true "fault lines" between *Tian* and the LORD lie, and where there are significant resonances upon which to build a robust Chinese Catholic theological science.

My first exploration of the theological contours of *Tian* proceeds via an examination of the concept in one of the most important texts of early Confucianism, the *Mengzi*.[9] Although Mengzi's conception of *Tian* is neither systematically developed nor a central theme of explication in his thought, his is still a vibrant and interesting account that is an important foundation for his philosophy.[10] Mengzi's account of *Tian* is not quite a "theology," since *Tian* is never an object of understanding for its own sake. However, the *Mengzi* does feature an "indirect" doctrine of *Tian* that is interesting, illuminating, and worthy of theological analysis.

Therefore, the primary aims of this chapter are first to exposit Mengzi's doctrine of *Tian* and then draw upon Aquinas to assess this theology in light of revealed truth about God. Given the inherently political context in which *Tian* was understood by the early Chinese, one vastly important aspect of Mengzi's *Tian* theology is the

---

8. The best study of the name of God in Chinese theology written in English is Standaert, *The Fascinating God.*

9. Standaert, *The Fascinating God.* This work provides a translation and analysis of diverse Chinese philosophical conceptions of *Shangdi* and *Tian* by a late seventeenth-century Chinese Christian named Yan Mo (dates uncertain). Yan cited passages concerning these terms from the classical texts of the Chinese tradition (*Shijing* and *Shangshu* in particular) including some from the *Mengzi* in order to argue that these classical concepts resonated with God (*Tianzhu*) inasmuch as natural concepts can (see, e.g., Standaert, *The Fascinating God*, 54).

10. Yearley, 4. Yearley juxtaposes Aquinas' "theistic cosmology" to Mengzi's "organistic cosmology" as the genesis of differences between the two. To a certain degree, throughout his important work, Yearley sees the theological aspects of Aquinas as a profound point of contrast with Mengzi, who does not, in Yearley's eyes, seem to possess a genuine theological conception of *Tian.*

A Thomistic Assessment of the *Mengzi* on *Tian*   41

providence or governance of *Tian* over the world. A second connected yet distinctive theme in Mengzi's *Tian* doctrine is the theme of the goodness of *Tian*. As I hope to show, both central themes are full of significant problems, but also great promise for developing a Chinese Catholic theology of God. In terms of method, I will first exposit Mengzi's conception of *Tian* considering the themes just mentioned, and then offer an assessment of each theme from the perspective of Aquinas's theology.

MENGZI'S *TIAN* THEOLOGY

Background and Context

As I mentioned above, it is unclear Mengzi possesses what one might justifiably call a philosophical "theology" of *Tian*. There are two reasons for this judgment. First, Mengzi was not concerned with developing an account of *Tian* such that *Tian* is seen as an object of philosophical reflection per se. Like most Warring States thinkers, Mengzi was focused on developing moral philosophy, and *Tian* is a decisively background concept supporting the structure he seeks to build. Consequently, scholars of Mengzi's thought rarely give a distinctive treatment of his understanding of *Tian*.[11] All told, much of what Mengzi seems to have believed about *Tian* was presupposed as part of the textual tradition preceding him, and little of these beliefs are explained or expanded in a way reminiscent of theological science.

Second, some contemporary scholars would dismiss the notion that Mengzi can have a *Tian* theology on the grounds that they hold Mengzi as part of a thoroughly naturalistic philosophical

---

11. For standard influential and helpful studies of the *Mengzi* in English, see Kwong-loi Shun, *Mencius and Early Chinese Thought* (Stanford, CA: Stanford University Press, 1997); Alan K. L. Chan, ed. *Mencius: Contexts and Interpretation* (Honolulu: University of Hawaii Press, 2002); Philip J. Ivanhoe, *Ethics in the Confucian Tradition: The Thought of Mengzi and Wang Yangming* (Indianapolis, IN: Hackett Publishing, 2002); Xiu Sheng Liu and Philip J. Ivanhoe, eds., *Essays on the Moral Philosophy of Mengzi* (Indianapolis, IN: Hackett Publishing, 2002). For a briefer treatment, see Bryan W. Van Norden, *Introduction to Classical Chinese Philosophy* (Indianapolis, IN: Hackett Publishing, 2011), 87–101. In each of these works, Mengzi's main concerns are presented as concerning human moral nature (*renxing*), the cultivation of virtue, et cetera. The centrality of these themes is unquestionable, but the importance of *Tian* for making sense of these topics in *Mengzi* is often overlooked.

42   Chapter 1

perspective.[12] Consequently, for many modern Western scholars in particular, Mengzi's *Tian* is in no way like the Christian or pagan *Theos*. At most, such scholars would hold, *Tian* stands for the personification of nature, and thus they would contend Mengzi's *Tian* philosophy is really a philosophy of nature, not of God.

With these two challenges, the latter is clearly more determinative than the former. For if there is reason to think of Mengzi's understanding of *Tian* as being theistic in some sense, the indirect ways that *Tian* functions in his thought can be seen to constitute a vibrant if underdeveloped and unsystematic natural theology, which is the position I take here. However, the trouble in decisively solving the second problem is that it rests not simply upon the evidence in Mengzi's thought, but the very categories used to examine it, such as "theism," "divinity," and "naturalism."[13] Put in these terms, a full-fledged defense of interpreting Mengzi as possessing a theistic worldview would necessitate dealing with the appropriateness of these categories in being used to understand a thinker like Mengzi, who does not seek to either affirm or deny that *Tian* is "god" or "divine," and for whom the very question would make little sense in these terms.[14] Indeed, if we were to ask Mengzi if *Tian* was meant to be divine or purely natural, he might well fail to understand the distinction implied by the question. This is especially true given that in modern theology and philosophy (more so the latter), the distinction between God and nature is often structured in terms of the transcendence-immanence dialectic that arose among Enlightenment Deists. While the distinction between God and the natural world is a perpetual feature of Judeo-Christian theology throughout

---

12. Esp. James Behuniak, Jr., *Mencius on Becoming Human* (Albany, NY: SUNY Press, 2005). Michael Puett provides a very helpful discussion of how Mengzi has been read as naturalistic or with an eye to transcendence, and some of the sinological problems of each attempt. It is worth noting he traces the naturalistic reading of Mengzi to Frederick Mote, though one could argue it has Chinese antecedents as well in Dai Zhen. In more recent scholarship, those advocating for a naturalistic reading of Chinese thought find support in other quarters such Xunzi or Zhuangzi more so than Mengzi. See Puett, *To Become a God: Cosmology, Sacrifice, and Self-Divinization in Early China* (Cambridge, MA: Harvard University Asia Center for the Harvard-Yenching Institue, 2002), 140–44.

13. See Brown and McLeod, chapter 2

14. Shun, *Mencius and Early Chinese Thought*, 209. In this I agree with Shun, who elects to "not try to decide whether we should describe *t'ien* [*Tian*] as a personal deity, since this depends largely on what connotations we build into the term."

A Thomistic Assessment of the *Mengzi* on *Tian*   43

its history, the juxtaposition and even opposition between God and nature is strikingly modern and cannot be assumed to have existed in the same way in Warring States China.[15]

Since this is a book about theology and not sinology, I will not attempt to give a comprehensive defense of my theological reading of Mengzi that will satisfy sinologists—that would take an entire book. For my purposes here, it is sufficient to say I have three main reasons for doing so. The first is that numerous scholars have observed that *Tian* did function as the high god of the Zhou dynasty, and in Mengzi's own time *Tian* remained an object of sacrifice.[16] In my own study of the *Mengzi* I have found nothing to suggest Mengzi was critical of the theistic conception of *Tian* that had been predominant in his own culture and in the classical texts he studied. Case in point, scholars such as Robert Eno have defended a theistic reading of *Tian*, even while underscoring that *Tian* had several meanings for Mengzi in addition to a divine meaning.[17] To cite another imminent scholar, Kwong-loi Shun has observed that because *Tian* is ascribed personal characteristics in early China, is viewed as having an ethical dimension, and is offered as something one should venerate or serve, "it is unlikely that 't'ien' [*Tian*] refers merely to an impersonal natural order."[18] Therefore, absent an explicit rejection in the text of the classical, theistic conception of *Tian*, it seems to me preferable to assume Mengzi thought about *Tian* as possessing what theological science would consider to be divine attributes.

15. See Louis Dupré, *The Enlightenment and the Intellectual Foundations of Modern Culture* (New Haven, CT: Yale University Press, 2004), 243–56.

16. See inter al. Benjamin I. Schwartz, *The World of Thought in Ancient China* (Cambridge, MA: The Belknap Press of Harvard University, 1985); Cheng Chung-ying, "Classical Chinese Views of Reality and Divinity," in *Confucian Spirituality*, ed. Tu Weiming and Mary Evelyn Tucker (New York: Crossroad,2003), 1:113–33; Michael Loewe, *Faith, Myth, and Reason in Han China* (Indianapolis: Hackett Publishing, 2005); Julia Ching, *Chinese Religions* (Maryknoll, NY: Orbis Books, 1993), esp. 1–9; Shu-Hsien Liu, "The Confucian Approach to the Problem of Transcendence and Immanence," *Philosophy East and West* 22, no. 1 (January 1972): 45–52; and Edward J. Machle, *Nature and Heaven in the Xunzi: A Study of the Tianlun* (Albany, NY: SUNY Press, 1993).

17. See e.g., Robert Eno, *The Confucian Creation of Heaven: Philosophy and the Defense of Ritual Mastery* (Albany, NY: SUNY Press, 1990), 105. Eno notes that "in the course of this single passage [*Mengzi* 5A:5], Mencius [Mengzi] employs three different notions of T'ien [*Tian*]: T'ien is a single purposive deity; it is functionally the sum of all the spirits; it is the collective will of the people."

18. Shun, *Mencius and Early Chinese Thought*, 209.

44   Chapter 1

Second, I would contend that a theological reading of Mengzi simply makes better sense of the text. In naturalistic readings of Mengzi, the ascription of something like providence to *Tian* is treated as metaphorical, rather than Mengzi's actual position.[19] The problem with this is the providential character of *Tian* is prominent in the *Mengzi*, and the text does not explain this theme away as simply a metaphor. Rather, Mengzi's reading of *Tian* and his yearning for a true king seem to be instances of a phenomenon observed by Yuri Pines (among others) that the collapse of the Zhou dynasty occasioned a real crisis for many thinkers about the doctrine of Heaven's mandate (*Tianming* 天命), which had been taken to govern the rise and fall of rulers according to the law that virtuous rulers flourish and wicked ones perish.[20] I would submit that a naturalistic reading of Mengzi makes it very difficult to see how Mengzi could take this situation as a real crisis, and thus makes little sense of his passages that touch upon *Tian's* governance. On the other hand, if we understand *Tian* in a broadly theistic sense—even if this sense was under negotiation during Mengzi's lifetime—it makes much more sense of the intellectual crisis that the fall of the Zhou dynasty caused, and which informs Mengzi's thinking on *Tian*.

Third, I err on the side of treating Mengzi as a theistic thinker here as an act of theological charity. Although those who claim Mengzi is a naturalist thinker do so in approbative manner, they also do so with the assumption that Mengzi's conception of *Tian* is naturalistic because it fails to meet particular criteria of the conception of God as articulated in the Judeo-Christian tradition, such as divine

---

19. Though speaking of Confucius, Hall and Ames offer understanding the "Mandate of Heaven"—a classically providential idea—as "constituting the causal conditions that sponsor the emergence of a particular human being, or any other phenomenon" wherein "these conditions are neither predetermined nor inexorable" (Hall and Ames, *Thinking Through Confucius*, 213). For Hall and Ames, this is understood as the function of human action to shape one's own world (see 210). It is difficult to square the *Mengzi* with this sort of utterly immanentized frame of reference, as my analysis shows.

20. See Pines and Eno, as cited above. For additional helpful discussions of how politics and *Tian* intertwined, see Julia Ching, *Mysticism and Kingship* (Cambridge, UK: Cambridge University Press, 1997), Puett, *To Become a God*, esp. 31–79 and 225–58; Michael Puett, "Following the Commands of Heaven: The Notion of *Ming* in Early China," in *The Magnitude of Ming: Command, Allotment, and Fate in Chinese Culture*, ed. Christopher Lupke (Honolulu: University of Hawaii Press, 2005), 49–69; and Scott Cook, "'*San De*' and Warring States Views on Heavenly Retribution," *Journal of Chinese Philosophy* 37 supp. (2010): 101–23.

A Thomistic Assessment of the *Mengzi* on *Tian* 45

transcendence. This strikes me as being rather poor manners. As a theologian, I am undoubtedly bound to accept the guidance of divine revelation and say that God must have the attributes ascribed to him by scripture and sacred tradition. But does this also mean that I can deny that Mengzi is speaking about the divine simply because his conception of *Tian* does not measure up to what I think correct talk about God demands? Put more positively, I am willing here to extend the courtesy to Mengzi to treat his conception of *Tian* as a real account of the divine, and not call it naturalistic simply because it fails to meet the demands of Christian orthodoxy regarding what it means for God to be God.

The question I am interested in, ultimately, is determining what Mengzi might bring to the development of a Chinese Catholic theology of God. Providing a theological assessment of his *Tian* theology is therefore needed. My approach is to first exposit Mengzi's "theology" of *Tian* according to what I consider as the three main motifs in his account, and then provide a Thomistic assessment of Mengzi's positions.[21] Although Mengzi himself did not construct his philosophy around these motifs or in service of them, he seems to express or presuppose beliefs about *Tian* that can be helpfully organized via these motifs. I should also note that in my analysis, I do not claim that Mengzi must be *consistent* in any of his beliefs about *Tian*—in fact, I see Mengzi's inconsistency as an interesting feature of his account of *Tian* that can be readily explained. So, I am not arguing Mengzi has a theology of *Tian* that systematically holds together, but he certainly has theological concerns regarding what *Tian* is like that animate his thought in important ways. These motifs will occupy the remainder of this half of the chapter and are as follows:

Tian as source of existence and order in the world;
Tian as a providential, guiding force in the world;
Tian as an exemplar and source of goodness.

21. Eno, 99–130. Eno argues Mengzi bears two main understandings of *Tian*, one prescriptive and one descriptive. Eno uses "prescriptive" to refer to those passages in which *Tian* is "invoked to urge imperatives for future action," whereas "descriptive" refers to passages "in which Ti'en [*Tian*] is invoked to explain past events" (see 102). Though helpful, I find Eno's classification of Mengzi's *Tian* theology limiting for theological analysis. By understanding Mengzi in light of theological concerns that are present in his thought I aim to better prepare for a Thomistic assessment of his text.

Tian as source of existence and order

The *Mengzi* does not contain a protology or cosmogony in terms of a creation narrative or account of the world's beginnings.[22] However, Mengzi does refer to classical protological and cosmogonic tropes that held great explanatory power for his moral doctrine. Whenever Mengzi discusses *Tian*, one of his main sources is the *Shijing*, a collection of poetry attributed to the early Zhou period.[23] Scattered throughout the *Shijing* in admittedly unsystematic ways are descriptions of *Tian* as cause of all being, and Mengzi cites a few of these passages. Significantly, Mengzi cites these teachings in the context of making other arguments, such as his defense of the goodness of human nature in Book 6A. This suggests both that Mengzi sees such protological positions as the unarticulated "fundamental philosophy" behind his moral reflections, and that there was some sense of general acceptance of these principles such that, by citing them, his conclusions might gain broader support.

The first major protological claim about *Tian* that Mengzi takes from the *Shijing* is that *Tian* is the source of creaturely life. Following the *Shijing*, Mengzi says that *Tian* "produced" (*sheng* 生) humanity.[24] Elsewhere he adds more scope, saying that *Tian* produced all things (*sheng wu* 生物).[25] Ultimately for Mengzi, this claim that *Tian* produces creaturely life is important because it entails *Tian* imbuing creaturely life with some kind of order.[26] However, at this point, I would like to briefly examine what Mengzi may have meant by *Tian*'s producing the world as part of his *Tian* theology.

22. The absence of a protology is not unique to the *Mengzi*. In fact, the general infrequency of protological discourse in early Chinese texts gave rise to a presupposition among many scholars that early Chinese had no creation narrative as such until around the eighth century. For an excellent discussion and rebuttal of this view, see Paul Goldin, "The Myth that China Has No Creation Myth," *Monumenta Serica* 56 (2008): 1–22.

23. For a general discussion of Mengzi's reading of Classical texts (including the *Shijing*), see Huang Chun-chieh, "Mencius' Hermeneutics of Classics," *Dao* 1, no. 1 (2001): 15–29.

24. *Mengzi*, 6A:6.2.

25. In context, the phrase *sheng wu* implicitly means all "things" (*wu*), which usually refers to material or formal (*xing* 形).

26. Some scholars would deny that Mengzi or any other early Chinese thinker believes in an ordered cosmos, which I grant is true in some regard, inasmuch as many Chinese thinkers saw humanity as having to complete the work of the cosmos. But there are two caveats to this claim. First, not all Chinese thinkers had the same view of what human creativity accomplished, and second, this does not necessarily entail the universe is entirely without order.

A Thomistic Assessment of the *Mengzi* on *Tian*   47

In classical Chinese, the verb *sheng* is not a unique verb associated with *Tian*, but is a general verb of reproduction (as a noun, it also means "life"). Thus, unlike the verb *barah* in the Hebrew tradition, *sheng* does not have a specific theological purpose. Notably, modern Chinese Catholics use an entirely distinctive verb of "making" to express the idea of divine creation (*chuangzao* 創造) rather than an idea associated with *sheng* or generative production.[27] In the Confucian context, *sheng* does not have a specific technical use, and therefore we can discern very little of what kind of cosmogony Mengzi has in mind with the language of *Tian* producing the world. It is semantically possible that Mengzi has in mind a strong reading of *Tian's* productive agency in the sense of *Tian* willing the world to be. One could even press the idea of *sheng* into a *creatio ex nihilo* account, though nothing in Mengzi gives warrant to suggest he thought of *Tian's* production of the world in this way.

Yet there are other ways of reading *Tian* according to the sparse language Mengzi uses that are textually appropriate. In another passage in 6A, Mengzi makes a similar protological point but uses a different verb, this time speaking of *Tian's* "condescension" (*jiang* 降) to give human beings natural abilities (*cai* 才). If we assume there is some form of convertibility between the *sheng* of 6A:6 and the *jiang* of 6A:7, this might suggest a way in which *Tian's* production of humanity should be interpreted. The Han period of Chinese thought in particular came to be dominated by an intricate theory of *qi* that depended heavily upon a conception of *Tian's* condescension. In this view, *Tian* is composed of light, pure *qi* while the earth is full of heavier, condensed *qi*. The theory would hold that *Tian's qi* "descends" (*jiang*) that is becomes heavier and more condensed to

27. The use of *zao* to describe creative generation goes back to Ricci, *True Meaning*. The first use of *chuangzao* as a binomial to describe creation seems to have been Aleni, *Wanwu zhen yuan*. In the early Jesuit literature, the missionaries often issued a defense of the existence of God via a version of Aquinas's Fifth way (see *ST* Ia, q. 2, corp.). Often, the missionaries would cite the metaphor of a king's palace (or some other construction) and say the fact of the building with its rooms, gardens, columns, et cetera, implies a craftsman who made it. Gernet helpfully observes that this metaphor actually was not very successful for many Chinese intellectuals, who understood the appeal to God as a craftsman to imply the creator is a kind of blue-collar laborer low on the social hierarchy; see Gernet, 208–9. All in all, the theological appeal to *zao* rather than *sheng* may have been a missed opportunity in developing Chinese metaphysics into the fold of Catholic theology.

48   Chapter 1

become material things. Such a theory of *qi* eventually was mythologized in the famous creation story of Pan Gu.[28]

In my view, it is anachronistic to ascribe such a theory to Mengzi in full, since there is little indication he actually possesses such a specific view of either *qi* or *Tian*.[29] Yet this interpretive possibility and its dominance in later Confucian tradition is evidence that Mengzi's protological view of *Tian* is extremely imprecise.[30] Even if one pushes for a more creation-analogous account, is unclear what kind of creator or originating force Mengzi presumes *Tian* to be.

Why, then, did Mengzi not develop his account more? I think this lack of development rests upon two reasons. First, it is unclear to what degree Mengzi would have felt the need to clarify his protological assumptions. Even a cursory reading of the *Mengzi* shows that Mengzi's positions are often tailored to the contours of specific debates. Significantly, the passages in which he mentions *Tian* are found in debates with thinkers whose fundamental philosophy bears significant similarities to Mengzi's. Concretely, in his debates with Gaozi in Book 6A and the Mohist Yi Zhi in Book 3A, both opponents are likely to accept the veracity and significance of the claim that *Tian* produced the world. One principal text that does

28. The traditional creation myth of Pan Gu (often titled *Pan Gu Kai Tian* 盤古開天) concerns Pan Gu, who was born in an egg of chaos, then burst this egg with an ax. After this, Pan Gu spent thousands of years holding up the heavens (*Tian*) and standing on the earth so they would not join together again. After the distance between the heavens and the earth were fixed, Pan Gu fell dead of exhaustion, and his body became the various physical forms of the world (rivers, mountains, animals, etc.). For a version of this story in English, see Claude Helft, *Chinese Mythology: Stories of Creation and Invention*, trans. Michael Hariton and Claudia Bedrick (New York: Enchanted Lion Books, 2007), 20–24.

29. See Behuniak, 1–21. Behuniak is confident based on citations from the *Zuo Zhuan*, the *Zhuangzi*, and the presence of the *Yijing* that the *qi* theory intimated in the text above should be presupposed when reading the Mengzi. I am less confident that particularly naturalistic theories of *qi* (primarily articulated in the Han) should be retroactively associated with Mengzi. At least, if these theories of *qi* can be ascribed to Mengzi, I see no reason why an account of *qi* that seems to involve a more theistic reading of *Tian* (such as that found in the *Chunqiu Fan Lu*) cannot be ascribed to Mengzi as well. Ultimately, Mengzi has very little to say about *qi* in a metaphysical sense (much like *Tian*) so that it is difficult to assume to what degree he would have agreed or disagreed with the picture of *qi* Behuniak ascribes to him.

30. Eventually, Zhou Dunyi 周敦頤 (1017–1073) composed his famous and influential "Essay on the Diagram on the Great Ultimate" (*Taiji tushuo* 太極圖說) which promoted a nuanced *qi*-cosmology that was accepted as standard in China at the time of the Jesuit missions. Many scholars with a naturalistic understanding of the world seem to read texts like the *Mengzi* through a lens informed by the Neo-Confucian cosmology of Zhou, which is anachronistic at best.

undermine the protology Mengzi assumes is the *Laozi*, but sadly we have no record of Mengzi engaging Daoist thought. So, it is unclear if Mengzi would have had reason to develop his *Tian* protology in more specific ways.

Second, even though the fortunes of the Zhou dynasty threatened many of the theological assumptions of Chinese intellectuals regarding *Tian* and *Tian's* Mandate, Mengzi was not primarily occupied in addressing these challenges. In a sense, Mengzi's understanding of *Tian* as universal cause of being was not really threatened in the Zhou dissolution. For Mengzi, the central point was that *Tian* had given human beings the resources for cultivating moral virtue. Mengzi shows no tendency in the least to question the veracity of this opinion. Consequently, the crisis he saw was getting rulers and others to act according to the principles of morality. Although Mengzi's philosophy is admittedly anthropocentric, this is because he thought the real problems of his age were anthropogenic.

For Mengzi, then, there was simply no need for a precise account of *Tian's* creative agency because the creative work of *Tian* was not a question with which he (or his intellectual environment) was deeply concerned. What mattered most to Mengzi was that *Tian* produced order in the cosmos, and especially a moral order. Now, some scholars such as Roger T. Ames would strongly reject my assertion here that Mengzi sees *Tian* not only as a kind of productive principle, but a principle of order.[31] Against this view, I side with the analysis of Robert Eno who argues that for Mengzi, *Tian* "is a teleological force ... and its engendering of the good *hsing* [*xing* 性] in man indicates what man's purpose, or 'final cause,' is to be."[32] It is worth noting, as Eno does, that for Mengzi the order of *Tian* is not *merely* a moral order. Mengzi also recognizes order within the larger cosmos that impacts humans, as we see in his thesis of an ordered time between reigns of sage kings.[33] Nonetheless, for Mengzi, the greatest sign of *Tian* as an ordering principle lies in the moral order of human beings.[34]

---

31. See, e.g., Roger T. Ames, "Mencius and a Process Notion of Human Nature," in Chan, *Mencius: Contexts and Interpretation*, 72–90.

32. Eno, 121.

33. See Eno, 102.

34. Luo Guang, *Zhongguo zhexuesixiang shi, xian Qin pian* in *Luo Guang Quanshu*, 6:

50   Chapter 1

In his discussion of human nature in 6A:6.l, Mengzi argues that human nature is good because of its natural endowments or "resources" (*cai*). What he means by this is that human beings have the capacities to be good—we possess the tools we need in our constituted natures to be morally good. And these endowments come from *Tian*. Specifically, Mengzi emphasizes the fact that *Tian* made human beings in such as a way as to make them able to respond to laws (*you ze* 有則) and "love admirable virtue" (*hao shi yi de* 好是懿德).[35] Consequently, *Tian* gives human beings a natural disposition to governance and order, and a loving response to admirable virtue.

For Mengzi, the emotional endowments from *Tian* are particularly important. Mengzi's moral philosophy holds that human beings are endowed with connatural emotional dispositions of the heart-mind that are the "sprouts" of moral virtue, i.e., they show we have moral capacities and even tend us toward virtue, though we must cultivate them successfully as well.[36] Consequently, it is vital for Mengzi that these emotions are structured in the human heart-mind by *Tian*. In 6A:7, Mengzi states that in good years, people are mostly good and in calamitous years they are often violent. But this is not because of a difference in what *Tian* has given them. Rather, "this difference is due to that in which their hearts have been sunk."[37]

Here we see how Mengzi seeks to dissociate *Tian*'s endowments from the human abuse of those endowments. Although human beings may fail to employ our natural endowments properly or well, *Tian* has given all these endowments to us as part of the production

---

430–31. Luo assumes the traditional lineage that Mengzi was educated by Confucius's grandson Zisi, who was said to have written the *Zhongyong*. Thus, he attempts to interpret Mengzi in light of a passage from the *Zhongyong* which holds that *xing* in its entirety is a gift of *Tian*. The assumption Luo makes regarding Mengzi's use of the *Zhongyong* is quite debatable. Wang Ping and Ian W. Johnston identify two important interpretations by Feng Youlan and Jeffrey Riegel that question the traditional Zisi authorship claim, noting that Feng believed the *Zhongyong* imitated the *Mengzi* and thus came after, and that Riegel contends the *Zhongyong* was composed record of a Han dynasty debate. See Wang Ping and Ian Johnston, trans. and ann., *Daxue and Zhongyong: Bilingual Edition* (Hong Kong: The Chinese University Press of Hong Kong, 2012), 185–89, here 187–88.

35. *Mengzi*, 6A:6.2

36. The role of emotions in Mengzi's thought is complex; for a fuller discussion, see chapter 4 below.

37. *Mengzi*, 6A:7. "其所以陷溺其心者也".

A Thomistic Assessment of the *Mengzi* on *Tian*   51

of humanity. Therefore, in Mengzi's eyes, *Tian* is the principle of what is connatural to human beings (the natural endowments making virtue possible for us) and not the misuse of these connatural capacities.

In a similar vein, Mengzi also identifies *Tian* as the source of what is connatural to humanity by focusing on the concept of *xing* 性, meaning "nature" in the sense of propensities connatural to a kind of thing.[38] In 7A:1, Mengzi says that "he who exhausts his heart-mind knows his *xing*, and he who knows his *xing* knows *Tian*."[39] Zhao Qi (the earliest commentator of the *Mengzi*) explains this as meaning that a man who knows his *xing* is one who has cultivated the virtuous sprouts of his heart-mind is able to fulfill his heart-mind in thinking and doing what is good, and by this moral "knowing his *xing*" such a man "knows the *dao* of *Tian*."[40] In this interpretation, *Tian* is not identified with human propensities as such, but rather *xing* functions as a collective term for *Tian's* endowments for human beings. Focusing on the moral capacities given from *Tian* allows insight into the most genuine account of what human beings are according to our propensities. Consequently, to know our moral capacities is to know our propensities, and this is to know *Tian* since it includes recognizing *Tian* as the source of these propensities to the good.

Similarly, *Mengzi* 7A:20 teaches that "the body and its acts are part of the *xing* given by *Tian*; it is only the sage who can act according to the body as it should be."[41] Here again, for Mengzi the one who knows *Tian*—in this case, the sage—is the one who understands humanity best. This is because human propensities and capacities come from *Tian* and have ultimate reference to *Tian*. Only the sage, who understands human propensities in the context of the endowments of *Tian*, actually employs the endowments well. In this case, Mengzi has not emphasized the capacities of the heart-mind, but has extended the principle to the body, which is nonetheless guided and directed by the heart-mind in his thought. In this way,

38. For discussion of *xing* as related to *Tian*, see Eno, 114–22.
39. *Mengzi*, 7A:1.
40. Zhao Qi, *Mengzi* 7A:1. In *Sibu congkan chu bian* 四部叢刊初編. Vol. 41 (Shanghai: The Commerical Press, 1919–1922).
41. *Mengzi*, 7A:20.

52 Chapter 1

Mengzi has made the same point in another direction: what is connatural to human beings comes from *Tian*, and thus *Tian* is an ordering principle and referent for human flourishing.

As his account of human moral emotions suggests, for Mengzi, *Tian* as source of order is clearly tied to natural capacities. Hence, Mengzi's conception of the moral emotions bears some resemblance to the principles of natural law, at least in some interpretations of the Thomistic understanding of the term.[42] Mengzi associates *Tian* with the capacities and principles of human beings—evident in his association of *Tian* with *xing* and *cai* above. More explicitly, Mengzi connects *Tian* with the kind of natural consequences of seeking or neglecting virtue in the political sphere.[43] One of the best examples of *Tianming* as natural law of governance in the *Mengzi* is on display in Mengzi's theme of ruling as "pleasing" (*yue* 悅) the hearts of the people. In 1B:17, King Xuan of Qi, who had just led his state in a successful military campaign against the state of Yan, asks Mengzi if he should "take possession" (*qu* 取) of Yan by annexing it into Qi. Xuan's own reasoning is that the victory he won was miraculously swift and overwhelming, and he thinks it clear that he did not win the victory simply because of his own military prowess—rather, Xuan is convinced that *Tian* willed this to happen. Consequently, Xuan judges that if he does not take possession of Yan, *Tian* will be displeased and visit calamities upon him.[44]

Mengzi replies by providing a principle of discernment: If the people of Yan would be pleased (*yue*) by Xuan's possession of Yan, then he should do it. If the people would not be pleased, he shouldn't do it.[45] On its face, it might appear that Mengzi is offering practical advice to displace faulty theological thinking. But actually, the broader context of Mengzi's thought shows he is offering a different theological rationale for discerning whether to take possession of Yan or not.

In his treatment of the ascension narrative of the sage-king Shun

---

42. Richard Kim, "Natural Law in Mencius and Aquinas," in *Confucianism and Catholicism: Reinvigorating the Dialogue*, ed. Michael R. Slater, Erin M. Cline, and Philip J. Ivanhoe (Notre Dame, IN: University of Notre Dame Press, 2020), 135–54.

43. See Eno, 120–30.

44. *Mengzi*, 1B:17.1.

45. *Mengzi*, 1B:17.2.

A Thomistic Assessment of the *Mengzi* on *Tian* 53

(to which I return in more detail below), Mengzi teaches that Shun was presented to *Tian* as a candidate for rule and approved because he pleased the people.[46] He does not mean that Shun succeeded in getting the people to support him politically. Rather, Mengzi means that Shun carried out administrative duties in ways that led the people to flourish, and therefore they desired Shun as their ruler. Mengzi cites a story that after Shun's predecessor had died, Shun left the ruling region in order to give way to his predecessor's son. But all the people needing a ruler—such as in the case of those seeking judgment over legal disputes—sought out Shun.

In this context, Mengzi's advice to King Xuan does not neglect theological principles for ruling, for he is offering a kind of natural law argument. *Tian*'s mandate does not primarily apply to individual rulers but to human nature, and the role of ruling corresponds to the exercise and cultivation of natural human capacities.[47] For Mengzi, *Tian* has ordained that rulers should rule with virtue and seek the moral and material flourishing of their people. Following these principles will bring success while neglecting them will bring ruin.

For Mengzi, this is what it ultimately means to "harmonize" (*shun* 順) with *Tian*: to understand and appropriately respond to the order of things given by *Tian* in the production of all things. In one passage, Mengzi states that "the one who harmonizes with *Tian* will be preserved, and he who rebels against *Tian* will perish."[48] Mengzi in this context does not see *Tian* as offering punishment per se against rebellious humans. Rather, *Tian* has produced things and given us the principles of flourishing. Therefore, to follow and harmonize with *Tian* is simply following this order and reaping the benefit of flourishing inherent in the order or principles themselves. Receiving calamities and perishing are simply the inherent consequences of failing to discern and follow the principles instilled in things by *Tian*.

As a final note to this motif in Mengzi's *Tian* theology, I should add that none of the above observations about *Tian*'s production or

---

46. *Mengzi*, 5A:5.

47. Eno, 123–30. Eno notes there is a tension in Mengzi between personal *ming* and the *ming* of the state.

48. *Mengzi*, 4A:7.1.

54 Chapter 1

ordering necessarily require Mengzi to hold to *Tian* as a "personal god." Partially, this is because the category of "personal god" seems to arise primarily in the Judeo-Christian context (i.e., under the demands of conceiving God as a person who elects and loves) and would be wholly foreign to Mengzi. But at the same time, even as Catholic theological science could not settle for the ambiguous divinity of *Tian* found in Mengzi, this does not mean Catholic theology can or should reject whatever is noble, good, and true in Mengzi's account. Ultimately, although I am convinced Mengzi had beliefs about how *Tian* had produced and ordered the world, these beliefs were either not important enough or not under enough scrutiny to play a larger role in his philosophical reflection and were not clarified in a way that theological science necessitates. Thus, the motif of *Tian*'s production and order is filled with ambiguity and a lack of clarity on matters that are very important to Catholic theological science. I will assess these issues below, but now will turn to examine the other motifs in Mengzi's *Tian* theology.

Tian as providential force of society

For an early Chinese intellectual such as Mengzi, it was almost unavoidable that the relationship between *Tian* and the political would become a major concern impacting his understanding of *Tian*. After all, the Zhou dynasty in which Mengzi lived referred to the state as "All Under *Tian*" (*Tianxia* 天下) and the term for the Zhou ruler was *Tianzi* 天子, the "Son of *Tian*."[49] As I mentioned above, scholars largely agree that during the Warring States period the way in which early Chinese intellectuals understood the nature of *Tian* was in a state of flux. Theologically, one might say that the specific doctrinal concern regarding *Tian* was that of providence—was Tian a providential force that governed the world? The world of classical China by-and-large answered yes to this question, seeing *Tian* as the cause of legitimate rulers and the cause of the downfall of

---

49. For helpful background on the evolution of the *Tianxia* concept and its significance in early Chinese thought, see Yuri Pines, "Changing Views of *Tianxia* in Pre-imperial Discourse," *Oriens Extremus* 43 (2002): 101–16; and Liu Junpin, "The Evolution of Tianxia Cosmology and Its Philosophical Implications," trans. Huang Deyuan *Frontiers of Philosophy in China* 1, no. 4 (Dec. 2006): 517–38.

A Thomistic Assessment of the *Mengzi* on *Tian*   55

illegitimate rulers. However, as the Zhou power waned despite claiming *Tian* as its supreme deity and worshipping *Tian*, this created an intellectual crisis in whether *Tian* worked in ways traditionally assumed.

As an early Confucian thinker, Mengzi dealt with the problem of *Tian*'s political providence in an additional sense. Robert Eno emphasizes that Mengzi held what are analogous to messianic beliefs: Mengzi believed he lived in an age "prophesied by numerology and manifest in the desperation of the times" during which a new sage-ruler would arise.[50] This entailed the belief that Confucian moral doctrine would be vindicated when someone, perhaps Mengzi himself, would govern the world and turn the wrongs to right.[51] As Eno notes, Mengzi utterly failed in bringing about sagely rule and knew it. Hence, he had to come to terms with how to explain why *Tian* had failed to allow the Confucian path of virtue to genuinely succeed in transforming the world.[52]

Consequently, Mengzi's view of *Tian*'s providence must be understood in the context of very serious challenges to the understanding of *Tian* in his time. The idea that *Tian* not only exhorted but rewarded moral virtue had long been a fundamental idea in Zhou and especially Confucian thought; in Mengzi's time it was becoming less coherent and convincing.[53] At times, he suggests a very strong reading of *Tian* as a providential force guiding the political fortunes of the Zhou, and at times he treats *Tian* as a more "hands-off" force, reading *ming* in this context like the Western notion of fate.[54] In this way, Mengzi's account of *Tian* is one that deals with the question of

50. Eno, 123.

51. Eno, 123. Eno argues Mengzi understood himself as the possible sage ruler.

52. Eno, 123–30. Eno notes that this failure led to a genuine shift in Mengzi's view of *Tian*.

53. See, e.g., Chao Fulin and Yongqiang Lei, "On the Origin and Development of the Idea of 'De' in Pre-Qin Times," trans. Lei Yongqiang, *Frontiers of Philosophy in China* 1, no. 2 (June 2006): 161–84. Chao and Lei argue that in the Shang period, *de* 德 (virtue) had meant receiving blessings from *Tian* (based on the homonym *de* 得) and in the Zhou period underwent stages of change, eventually coming to mean something obtained in "the inner heart" (see Chao and Lei, 183). The interiorization of the evolution of *de* is likely a consequence of the Zhou *Tian* theological crisis.

54. The former is close to what Eno calls the descriptive sense of *Tian*, which he argues is primarily historical for Mengzi, and the latter resembles what he calls the prescriptive, which is oriented toward the future and understanding *Tian* as exhorting moral virtue. By-and-large I find this distinction helpful, but some of the passages Eno might consider prescriptive seem

56 Chapter 1

whether *Tian* is a providential force or not, and I argue, the answer is not entirely clear.

While the Catholic theological tradition strongly emphasizes a distinction between providence and fate, I am not as confident such a distinction is as helpful for interpreting Mengzi.[55] Ning Chen helpfully distinguishes between two meanings of fate.[56] The first is "moral determinism," meaning that "happiness and misery are determined by a moral and personal god (or gods) who oversees human conduct, rewarding the good and punishing the wicked."[57] The second is "blind fate," which means "a person's fixed lot, which is believed to have been regulated by an impersonal and thus unapproachable power."[58] Chen's contention is that Mengzi holds to neither of these options absolutely, but unites by distinguishing between two spheres of fate, one in which humans have control to respond to the moral decrees of *Tian* and one in which they do not.[59]

For my purposes, I am less concerned with how Mengzi makes this negotiation work since that would require a detailed excursus on both fate itself and the seemingly endless debates about the metaphysics Mengzi would have presupposed.[60] My simple point is that even when Mengzi's reading of fate and destiny seems to be something like chance or fortune, it is not *simply* this, but there is almost always something like a providence that is active as well. Again, I

---

to me to espouse a strong reading of providence, as well as the inverse. Hence, I am less sure about the historical piece of his framework being an absolute classifier of Mengzi's accounts.

55. See, e.g., Augustine, *City of God*, V.8–9.

56. For other general treatments of the theme of fate in early China, see Lupke, ed., *The Magnitude of Ming*.

57. Ning Chen, "The Concept of Fate in Mencius," *Philosophy East and West* 47, no. 4 (October 1997): 495. See also Chen's additional essays on fate in early Confucianism: Ning Chen, "Confucius' View of Fate (*Ming*)," *Journal of Chinese Philosophy* 24, no. 3 (1997): 323–59, and Ning Chen, "The Genesis of the Concept of Blind Fate in Ancient China," *Journal of Chinese Religions* 25 (1997): 141–67.

58. Chen, "The Concept of Fate in Mencius," 495.

59. Chen, "The Concept of Fate in Mencius," 503.

60. Kidder Smith, "Mencius: Action Sublating Fate," *Journal of Chinese Philosophy* 33, no. 4 (Dec. 2006): 571–80. Case in point, although he does not cite Chen, Kidder Smith's interpretation of Mengzi's conception of fate rests upon the assumption of a strict non-dualism— that is, no "extra-human fatal process" (573)—would dissolve the very tension Chen observes in Mengzi's conception of fate. Contra Smith, I do not think "non-dualism" accurately captures Mengzi's view of things for reasons I have discussed above, but demonstrating this point at length would be beyond the scope of my argument here.

A Thomistic Assessment of the *Mengzi* on *Tian*   57

do not necessarily think this needs to be resolved in the *Mengzi* itself because the ambiguity between providence and fate is explicable as an outcome of the larger intellectual crises of the Zhou dynasty that Mengzi lived through. Eventually later Confucians or Catholic theologians drawing upon Mengzi would need to gain greater clarity, but I am not sure such clarity is to be found in Mengzi himself, for whom providence and fate are not clearly delineated.

As this brief aside suggests, analyzing the providential ways *Tian* works in the *Mengzi* is quite difficult. Chen has argued convincingly that for Mengzi, there are two distinct levels on which *Tian* works among humanity: the individual and the communal. *Tian* provides the individual with inalterable fate that can in no way be responded to or altered based on moral conduct. Collectively, however, morality can induce *Tian* to respond with benefits.[61] For the sake of making my analysis manageable, I will only focus here on the more or less collective or communal aspect of *Tian*, especially (or to the extent that) as *Tian* was seen to safeguard the rise and fall of ruling powers.

Mengzi's stronger reading of *Tian* as a providential force is heavily dependent upon his classical sources. One example is how Mengzi sees Tian's providence at work in the order and hierarchies of human life. In 1B:10, Mengzi approvingly cites a strong reading of *Tian's* providence from the *Shangshu* (often translated as "the Book of Documents"). The *Shangshu* states that, "when *Tian* descended to bring about the common people, it made them rulers and teachers, so that they may assist Shangdi and were preferred all over the world."[62] In this view, *Tian* not only produced the world, but specifically brought about special individuals within humanity to lead and guide the common people. Within such a view, *Tian's* providence can be seen at work in both 1) the institutions of masters/education and rulers/governance and 2) illustrious individuals who serve in these capacities.

As this passage from the *Shangshu* suggests, Mengzi's view of *Tian's* providence is predominantly tied to the intersection of socio-

---

61. Chen, "The Concept of Fate in Mencius."
62. *Mengzi*, 1B:10.4.

58 Chapter 1

political success and moral virtue. Unsurprisingly, Mengzi's strongest reading of *Tian* as providential force occurs in his treatment of the historical sage-king Shun, who Mengzi sees as both an excellent ruler and a sagacious teacher of moral virtue.[63] Specifically, in his discussion of Shun's ascension narrative, Mengzi leaves little doubt that *Tian* is an active force at work in this event.[64] He emphasizes that *Tian* indeed gave (*shou* 授) Shun the throne, and accepted Shun as Son of *Tian*. In Zhou China, the ruler was designated by the title of *Tianzi* 天子, or Son of *Tian*. In Mengzi's account, Shun's predecessor Yao presented Shun to *Tian*, and *Tian* "accepted" (*shou* 受) Shun, thus making him the rightful ruler.[65]

There are features of this account that also heavily qualify a strong providential reading of *Tian*, but I will address those below. For now, it is helpful to point out other aspects of the narrative that suggest a strong reading of *Tian* as providential force. One example is when Mengzi says that "a ruler is able to offer a successor to *Tian*, but he is unable to cause [*shi* 使] *Tian* to give the successor the empire."[66] Here, Mengzi is underscoring the fact that the appointment of a ruler to a genuine, legitimate rule is *not* the decision of the ruler himself, but rather *Tian*. *Tian* wills the legitimate ruler to reign, and this will cannot be frustrated, such that only a reign willed by *Tian* is legitimate and flourishing.

In another passage discussing Shun and the passage of the throne from ruler to elect successor, Mengzi makes a stronger version of the argument that *Tian*'s will is irresistible as regards governance.

---

63. David S. Nivison, *The Ways of Confucianism: Investigations in Chinese Philosophy*, ed. Bryan W. Van Norden (Chicago: Open Court Publishing, 1996), 305n10. Nivison suggests that the historical personages of Yao and Shun are a mythicization of real rulers. However, Nivison argues that Mengzi's own interpretation is also a questionable rereading of Shun's virtue. According to Nivison, it is likely that Shun represents a ruler who, far from being specially elected to rule by *Tian*, probably imprisoned his predecessor and banished his son. Nivison does not make a claim about whether he thinks Mengzi was aware of the "actual history" that Nivison assumes to be the case or if he is simply repeating a mythicization of the story. It is not clear to me why the mythicization should be presumed, except for in the vein of modern historical-critical exegesis which rejects any causes that appear "supernatural" as explanatory.

64. See my analysis in "'Son of Heaven': Developing the Theological Aspects of Mengzi's Philosophy of the Ruler," in *The Bloomsbury Research Handbook of Early Chinese Ethics and Political Philosophy*, ed. Alexus McLeod (London: Bloomsbury, 2019), 247–66.

65. *Mengzi*, 5A:5.

66. *Mengzi*, 5A:5.

A Thomistic Assessment of the *Mengzi* on *Tian* 59

He says that "when *Tian* gave the throne to someone who was worthy, the worthy one ruled; when *Tian* gave it to a son, then the son ruled."[67] A bit of historical background is needed to understand this claim. Classic histories held that Yao was succeeded by Shun, who was not Yao's son, and that Shun was succeeded by Yu, who was not Shun's son. This line of succession was said to be determined based on the one most worthy to rule. Yu, however, was succeeded by his son, beginning a tradition of patrilineal succession which founded the first dynasty of Chinese history, the Xia. Thus, in the context of the quote above, a disciple asks Mengzi why the shift in paradigm from worthiness to kinship. Mengzi's disciple at least seems concerned that *Tian*'s will had been overcome in the shift to patrilineal succession.[68]

In response, Mengzi argues the shift from worthiness to a patrilineal model was ordained by *Tian*. Essentially, Mengzi holds that *Tian*'s intention and will can never be foiled, and that success is not found outside of what *Tian* intends. This leads him to eventually offer a stark providential principle for understanding *Tian*: "everything is *Tian* when it is not in man's ability to do it. If it cannot be done and yet it is done, it is *Tian*. If it cannot be brought about and yet it occurs, it is from *Tian*'s mandate."[69] While this passage stops short of arguing for *Tian* as the prime mover of all things, it certainly attributes a providential activity to *Tian* in bringing about those things that are above and beyond human capacities. For Mengzi, *Tian*'s power to bring about what is impossible for man also means *Tian*'s intention is irresistible or irrepressible.

Apart from the historical context of the ancient sage-kings, partial testimonies to this strong reading of *Tian*'s providence are present elsewhere in the Mengzi. In 1B:21, Mengzi provides advice to Duke Wen of Teng who is anxious about a nascent crisis with a neighboring state. Mengzi notes the duke possesses an ambition that he might become the next head of a ruling dynasty. And so, Mengzi

---

67. *Mengzi*, 5A:6.2.

68. The shift from the model of succession via abdication to that of patrilineal succession has been a consistent theme of Confucian scholarship. One of the more influential treatments of the theme is Wm Theodore de Bary, *The Trouble with Confucianism* (Cambridge, MA: Harvard University Press, 1991), 1–2.

69. *Mengzi*, 5A:6.2.

60   Chapter 1

advises the duke to simply focus on doing what is good. Mengzi's rationale is that "the bringing about of great accomplishments such as these [i.e., becoming emperor] is due to *Tian*."[70] Put simply, the duke wastes his energies attempting to become the ruler of all under heaven—that alone is left to *Tian* to decide. All Duke Wen should do, according to Mengzi, is focus on acting in accordance with *Tian*: "stubbornly do what is good and that is all" (*qiang wei shan er yi* 彊為善而已).[71]

A final significant "strong" reading of *Tian*'s providence is found in Book 6B:35. In his passage, Mengzi discusses several men who were raised to office from socially obscure and difficult circumstances. He offers this principle that generally explains these events:

> When *Tian* is about to confer a great office on a man it first subjects his heart and will to suffering/bitterness, his bones and muscles to hard labor, his body and skin to hunger, subjects him to poverty, and makes his doings difficult. By these things, *Tian* moves his heart-mind and steels his moral nature [*xing*] and makes up for his deficiencies. For men make constant mistakes and then afterwards can change; when their hearts are besieged with difficulty, or weighed down with worries, they can afterwards work to deal with this situation.[72]

According to this passage, *Tian* actively subjects worthy men to difficult tests, not unlike the biblical Job or the evangelical accounts of Christ's temptations in the desert. Mengzi presents these hardships as divinely ordained means for forming worthy men. Although Mengzi suggests that *Tian* works to create hardships as a condition or impetus for moral flourishing, the hardships are apparently part of *Tian*'s guidance and interaction with these illustrious men.[73]

However, several passages in the *Mengzi* suggest a weaker account of *Tian*'s providence. One example is a passage appearing

---

70. *Mengzi*, 1B:21.2. "若夫成功, 則天也"
71. *Mengzi*, 1B:21.2.
72. *Mengzi*, 6B:35. "故天將降大任於是人也, 必先苦其心志, 勞其筋骨, 餓其體膚, 空乏其身, 行拂亂其所為; 所以動心忍性, 曾益其所不能; 人恒過, 然後能改; 困於心, 衡於慮, 而後作."
73. Such a view contrasts with Ning Chen's reading of fate as "impersonal" as regards the individual and unresponsive to human action. It may be that the Mengzi thinks *Tian* formerly guided illustrious men in special occasions, but no longer acts in this way. See Chen, "The Concept of Fate in Mencius."

A Thomistic Assessment of the *Mengzi* on *Tian*   61

twice in the text, which is also taken from the *Shangshu*. This passage states that "when *Tian* brings about calamities, they can be avoided, but when you bring about calamities yourself, you cannot survive them."[74] On its face, the notion that *Tian* can bring about calamities that can be avoided seems opposed to the irresistible intention of *Tian* implied in other parts of the *Mengzi*. On closer inspection, the difference between the views is not so stark. In Zhao Qi's interpretation, this passage is referring to classical stories wherein those with moral virtue were able to avoid and overcome evils allowed by *Tian* (such as demonic forces) because of their moral rectitude. In this reading, "those who cause calamities for themselves" refers to those who out of a lack of virtue brought disaster upon themselves.[75] In other words, Zhao Qi argues this saying does not indicate *Tian* wills evils or calamities as such, but merely emphasizes the importance of moral rectification.

This clarification does not entirely remove the difficulty, because it suggests a problem within Mengzi's *Tian*-theology that is never resolved.[76] In what sense is *Tian*'s will a genuine cause of things in the world? Does *Tian* actively will and guide humans to flourishing or ruin, or is *Tian* merely the source of principles that guide all things? With the ascension narrative of Shun, we get a sense of *Tian*'s robust agency. But in the passage discussed above, *Tian*'s agency has weakened somewhat into a type of ordering principle that certainly governs human life, even if not by direct engagement.

Indeed, this weaker interpretation of *Tian*'s providence is prominent in other parts of the *Mengzi*. In Book 4A:7, Mengzi says that "when the empire has the *dao*, those of small virtue serve those of great virtue, those of small nobility serve those of great nobility. When the empire does not have the *dao*, the small serve the great and the weak serve the strong. Both accord with *Tian*. The one who harmonizes with *Tian* will be preserved, and those who rebel against

---

74. *Mengzi*, 2A:4 and 4A:8.

75. Zhao Qi, *Mengzi*, comment on 2A:4.

76. Scholars have primarily resolved this issue by describing parallel theories of *Tian*. My position is that these parallel theories are not simply different meanings of *Tian* (i.e., different levels of being "*Tian*") but different and often conflicting understandings of *Tian* at the same "level." Hence, this points to theological unclarity about *Tian*, though I hope it is clear I do not find this a reason to dismiss what Mengzi says about *Tian* as unimportant.

62   Chapter 1

Tian will perish."[77] Here *Tian* is said to govern the world in a way, but not as an active force or cause. Rather, *Tian* seems to function as the source of immutable principles. "Rebelling" against *Tian* does not incur *Tian's* wrath and punishment; rather this rebellion consists of departing from the principles instilled by *Tian*, and thus incurring the consequences of such departure from the order of things. Such a reading of *Tian* is also present even in the "strong" providential account of *Tian* discussed above. In Shun's ascension narrative, Mengzi emphasizes that *Tian* gave Shun the throne, but in a way befitting *Tian*, which "does not speak."[78] That is, *Tian* did not declare through revealed texts or pronouncements that Shun was to rule. How then, does Mengzi suggest *Tian* made known its will that Shun rule? It was because Shun was employed in the daily tasks of administration and governance, including sacrifices to the spirits and caring for the needs of the common people.[79] When Shun performed these tasks with virtue and commitment, the people and the spirits were pleased. According to Mengzi, this is how we know Shun was accepted by *Tian*: because he pleased the people and the spirits with this conduct.

In this light, Mengzi's "strong" reading of *Tian's* providence appears somewhat weaker. Not only has *Tian* been silenced, but it is now at a further remove from direct agency.[80] *Tian* is still acting and apparently responding to Shun, but the agency seems more located

77. *Mengzi*, 4A:7.1.
78. *Mengzi*, 5A:5.
79. Sungmoon Kim, "Confucian Constitutionalism: Mencius and Xunzi on Virtue, Ritual, and Royal Transmission," *Review of Politics* 73, no. 3 (Summer 2011): 381–82. Kim admirably approaches 5A:5 from the view of practical politics. Kim argues that Mengzi's language of "the people" (*min* 民) in 5A:5 must be understood in light of broader tendencies in Mengzi to distinguish between "passive subjects" (the worse-off in society) and "active subjects" (i.e., nobility). Kim interprets Mengzi as meaning it is these "active subjects" who must confer legitimacy on the king, even as (and perhaps because) their own noble rank is subordinate to the institution of kingship. Hence, Kim's interpretation helpfully pushes back against the popular portrayal of Mengzi as a protodemocratic thinker in this regard.
80. A. T. Nuyen, "The 'Mandate of Heaven': Mencius and the Divine Command Theory of Political Legitimacy," *Philosophy East and West* 63, no. 2 (April 2013): 124. Nuyen offers a resolution to this problem by arguing that Mengzi "takes *tian* to be the ground of political legitimacy, its *ratio essendi*, and the well-being of the people as the reason why it is known whether a ruler has lost the mandate to rule and has to be deposed, or the *ratio cognoscendi* of political legitimacy." I would stress here that even in this view, in terms of providence, it is appropriate to call this a "weaker" view of providence.

A Thomistic Assessment of the *Mengzi* on *Tian*   63

in principles of natural law than a personal, providential deity. Consequently, one can ask whether it is right to call this Mengzi's view of *Tian's* governance "providence"? In the "weaker" forms of this reading, it seems more that Mengzi has a conception of *Tian* as providential force in the sense that *Tian* is the source of the principles governing the cosmos, and not in the sense of *Tian* actively guiding and responding to the world. As I will show below, in the Thomistic perspective both the stronger and weaker views of *Tian's* governance can be justly called views of providence; the question becomes which one best resonates with the revealed knowledge about God. For now, I will turn to exposit the last motif of Mengzi's *Tian*-theology, *Tian* as source of goodness.

Tian as source of goodness

The final aspect of Mengzi's *Tian*-theology I will analyze concerns *Tian* as source of goodness. Although I have touched on this topic previously, here I provide a fuller account. I should note that the *Mengzi* suggests that *Tian* is not simply the source of goodness but is itself good. For Mengzi, there is some measure of intent by *Tian*—at the very least in the production of creatures—to give human beings at least the natural "resources" for goodness. Consequently, goodness is also what *Tian* intends and desires for humans to be, which is ratified by *Tian's* election of moral men for leadership in human society.

Mengzi's understanding of *Tian's* goodness is significant since it qualifies how *Tian* is the source of goodness; however, it is clear that Mengzi's account emphasizes the latter. The clearest statement of *Tian* as the source of goodness is found in 6A:16. In this passage, Mengzi teaches that there is a "nobility" or "rank" (*jue* 爵) that both *Tian* and humanity possesses. The term *jue* here is best explained by reference to the human side of the analogy. Mengzi says that the *jue* of men consists in various offices, specifically those of duke, high minister, or chief counselor.[81] Here, *jue* seems to mean something bestowed on those who are judged worthy, and hence Bryan W. Van Norden renders the term as "honors."[82]

---

81. Follows translation of *Mengzi: With Selections from Traditional Commentaries*, ed. and trans. Bryan W. Van Norden (Indianapolis, IN: Hackett, 2008), 156–57.
82. Van Norden, 156–57.

64 Chapter 1

In contrast to those honors or nobility bestowed by human beings on others, *Tian*'s honors are decidedly immaterial and moral in character. According to Mengzi, *Tian*'s honors consist of "benevolence, rightness, loyalty, faithfulness, and delighting in goodness without growing weary of the effort."[83] Zhao Qi nicely summarizes this as meaning that "*Tian* honors by means of virtue, and men honor by means of wealth."[84] Here we find a rather fascinating claim. As I explained above, for Mengzi the moral virtues are given to human beings in the heart-mind as "resources" (*cai*) for cultivation—they are implicit in our moral nature (*xing*). In this passage, he is emphasizing the fact that these resources or sprouts of morality are gifts, indeed honors or nobility, from *Tian* to human beings.

As the passage continues, Mengzi expresses dismay at the fact that so often, human beings treat *Tian*'s honors as purely instrumental goods for selfish ends. He says that in the ancient times, men first sought to cultivate their *Tian*-given honors, and then human honors followed it. But in his own time, Mengzi argues, men cultivate *Tian*-honors only insofar as they bring about human honors, and then they abandon or discard the *Tian*-honors.[85] In other words, Mengzi believed men in his time cultivated moral virtue only insofar as it granted them honorable reputations, and then once they received employment, they did not care about pursuing virtue at all.

Clearly for Mengzi, cultivating the life of moral virtue is genuinely conducive to flourishing, and pursuing merely material benefit or political success falls short of true flourishing. In part, this is because *Tian* has ordained human beings to be moral: fulfilling human nature requires cultivating goodness for its own sake. As in his advice to Duke Wen of Teng, Mengzi believes the primary task of human beings is to "stubbornly do the good and that is all" at least in part because *Tian* has ennobled human beings with the resources to do what is good.

That *Tian* not only has given humanity the resources for goodness but desires human goodness is also on display in Book 4A:12. In this passage, Mengzi identified the *dao* of *Tian* with the virtue of

83. *Mengzi*, 6A:16.
84. Zhao Qi, *Mengzi*, comment on 6A:16.
85. *Mengzi*, 6A:16.

A Thomistic Assessment of the *Mengzi* on *Tian*   65

sincerity or genuineness (*cheng* 誠).[86] In general terms, sincerity was a significant virtue in early Confucianism, as it meant coming to genuinely and earnestly possess the virtuous character.[87] In the broader context of this passage, Mengzi argues that sincerity relies upon "enlightened understanding of what is good" (*ming hu shan* 明乎善).[88] As Zhao Qi's comments explain, sincerity relies upon having a rectified heart-mind, by which the good is recognized as good and (so it logically follows) loved for the sake of being good. According to Mengzi, *Tian's dao* for human beings is then to contemplate, understand, and enact what is good.

Importantly, Mengzi also sees *Tian* not only as source of goodness, but also as a kind of end of goodness. While Mengzi does not describe goodness as "pleasing" to *Tian*, he does associate goodness with *Tian's* intention. However, in one passage, Mengzi does come close to suggesting moral virtue is pleasing to *Tian* and that this is fitting to the pursuit of moral virtue. In 7A:20, Mengzi says the *junzi* 君子—a term for a virtuous and virtue-seeking gentleman in Confucianism—has three delights in life. One of them is essentially the delight of being morally upright, but Mengzi puts it in terms of *Tian*: "when raising his head, that he is not ashamed before *Tian*, and looking down, that he is not ashamed before other men—this is the second delight."[89]

Here we have an interesting dynamic conception of the relationship between *Tian* and the *junzi*. On the one hand, the person striving for moral virtue looks up (*yang* 仰) to *Tian*, in language suggestive of religious piety. The implication is that the *junzi* desires to live in *Tian's* favor, not to curry material benefit, but simply to live a life that is pleasing or in accordance with *Tian's* mandate. As Mengzi puts it, the *junzi* desires to look to *Tian* without shame, which implies that, like a father, *Tian* can be displeased by moral failure. Also, the *junzi* sees harmonizing with *Tian* as a source of delight. It is not simply his resources or gifts from *Tian* he enjoys, but the *junzi* takes

---

86. *Mengzi*, 4A:12.

87. For a helpful comparative analysis of *cheng* 誠, see Yangming An, "Western 'sincerity' and Confucian 'Cheng,'" *Asian Philosophy* 14, no. 2 (2004): 155–69.

88. *Mengzi*, 4A:12.

89. *Mengzi*, 7A:20.

66 Chapter 1

delight in knowing that he has properly discharged the gifts from *Tian*. In this looking up to *Tian*, it almost seems as if the *junzi* offers his moral virtue as a gift in response to *Tian*.

This presentation, brief though it is, ably demonstrates the three main motifs of Mengzi's account of *Tian*. At this juncture, I will now transition to assess Mengzi's conception of *Tian* in light of Christian theological science, aided by Aquinas's thought. To be clear, it is not my intention to use Aquinas's conception of God as an objective measure to test the strength of Mengzi's theology. Rather, I am interested in testing the degree to which Mengzi's theology of *Tian* can be drawn within the labor of Catholic theology as it attempts to explore and understand the revealed truths of God and humanity. Since this would require an account of how Mengzi's *Tian* does and does not resonate with the God who reveals himself in Christ Jesus, I now turn to provide such an account.

A THOMISTIC ASSESSMENT

Hopefully, the foregoing exposition of Mengzi's thought is evidence that he possesses an interesting and engaging reading of *Tian* worthy of theological engagement. Since my aim is to assess how Mengzi's account of *Tian* does and does not resonate with revealed theological science, I will turn to the work of Aquinas as a framework for assessment. Given that above I argued there are three principal motifs or themes to Mengzi's *Tian* theology, I will assess each of these themes in turn.

Assessing Mengzi's First Theme of *Tian*

Regarding the first theme of Mengzi's *Tian*-theology, one can fruitfully divide and assess two propositions that Mengzi threads together: 1) *Tian* is the source of things, and 2) *Tian* is the source of cosmic order. From the perspective of Catholic theological science, Mengzi suffers the same weaknesses regarding *Tian*'s generative agency as most early Chinese texts, since he fails to adequately distinguish divine generative causation from intramundane generation, thus failing to distinguish properly between God and the world. This does not

A Thomistic Assessment of the *Mengzi* on *Tian*　　　67

mean that Mengzi's *Tian* theology is for this reason devoid of truth about the God who reveals himself in scripture, but it does mean that Mengzi's conception of *Tian* faces a difficulty for being drawn into theological science. In Aquinas's view, it is ultimately impossible to have a thoroughly true account of God and especially his governance (which is central in Mengzi's thought) apart from an accurate understanding of creation. Indeed, for Aquinas God's governance is based upon the principle of God as creator and is an extension of his creative agency. The problem is not that Mengzi fails to have any account of creation whatsoever. Rather, the theological issue is that Mengzi's account is ambiguous as regards *Tian*'s creative agency. His account could perhaps be interpreted in terms analogous to the Christian conception of creation (or at least as not opposed to the revealed truth about God's creating the world), but Mengzi can also be interpreted in ways opposing revealed truth—that is, in naturalistic ways.

An appropriate sign of this ambiguity is in the verb Mengzi uses to describe *Tian*'s creative agency (*sheng*) which is not distinct linguistically from intramundane forms of generation. Against this, Aquinas argues that the Christian conception of "creation" (*creatio*) is *creatio ex nihilo*.[90] Thus, while Latin (like classical Chinese) features a verb that has historically been applied to inner-worldly and divine generation, Aquinas offers a theological clarification concerning the Christian understanding of divine creation, which he says can only be attributed to God.[91]

Furthermore, Aquinas teaches it is necessary for Christian theology to specify what is meant by divine creation. Aquinas emphasizes God is the first efficient cause, but not in such a way as to reduce all

---

90. See *ST* Ia, q. 45, art. 1, corp. See Gerhard May, *Creatio ex Nihilo: The Doctrine of 'Creation out of Nothing' in Early Christian Thought*, trans. A. S. Worrall (Edinburgh: T&T Clark, 2004). May observes that the doctrine of *creatio ex nihilo* was forged out of the theological battle with Gnosticism (especially Valentinianism) and took its ultimate doctrinal form in Irenaeus that became the standard for the subsequent tradition. Thus, for Aquinas, creation was fundamentally understood in terms of this doctrine.

91. John F. Wippel, "Thomas on Creatures as Causes of *Esse*," in *Metaphysical Themes in Thomas Aquinas II* (Washington, DC: The Catholic University of America Press, 2007), 172–94. Wippel argues it does not necessarily follow for Aquinas that because God is sole creator in an *ex nihilo* sense that human beings are not properly efficient causes of *esse*, or the act of being, in other things.

68   Chapter 1

divine causation to efficient causality or to make efficient causality a binary between God and natural causes. As Gaven Kerr has aptly put it, for Aquinas God's being the primary efficient cause means that God is not simply the past cause of being, but also the present—that is, the principle of actuality that maintains all things that are in being.[92] This further entails for Aquinas that God's causing the world is explicitly distinguished from the possibility of God as the material or formal cause of the world. Simply put, Aquinas holds that how one ascribes generation of the world to God is a matter of great importance, and not all ways of attributing creation to God are fitting or acceptable. Again, following Kerr, for Aquinas only those accounts of creation which show movement toward understanding creatures in light of "the complete and utter dependence of them on God" are laudable accounts.[93]

For this reason, it is appropriate to emphasize that, for Aquinas, God is the *primum* efficient cause. According to Aquinas, God causes all things to be in an efficient way as first cause, such that all things participate in him as effects participate in their causes. For Aquinas, this is the real key to the efficient causality claim about God. Aquinas often draws upon the imagery of fire heating iron in the context of creation. The key for Aquinas is that when fire heats iron, it is neither the material nor formal cause of the iron, but the efficient cause of the iron being hot. As the iron is heated, it participates in the property of being hot like the fire, though in an imperfect way. In the creation analogy, the fire would represent God's self-subsistent being which efficiently causes other being, and so created beings participate in the property of being that is enjoyed in God in a self-subsistent and perfect manner.[94]

All this is to say that for Aquinas, creation in its most proper sense refers to the emanation of all beings from the first principle

---

92. Gaven Kerr, *Aquinas and the Metaphysics of Creation* (New York: Oxford University Press, 2019), 115.

93. Kerr, 44. Kerr argues that Aquinas reads the Presocratics, Plato and Aristotle in light of this ultimate testing principle.

94. See e.g., *ST* Ia, q. 44, art. 1, corp. See also Kerr, *Aquinas and the Metaphysics of Creation*, 13. Kerr writes that God's primary efficient causality "does not consist in His being first in a linear causal chain, but in His being the primary source of the actuality, the *esse*, that all creatures have."

A Thomistic Assessment of the *Mengzi* on *Tian* 69

(God), and therefore refers to God's act of *creatio ex nihilo*.[95] This notion of creation as the unique divine act is essential to the Christian understanding of God, since God is the perfect act of Being in whom all beings participate and from whom all being emanates.[96] From the view of revealed theological science, it is deeply problematic that Mengzi's conception of *Tian* does not sufficiently account for the unique causality of *Tian* as the principle of the cosmos. It does seem that Mengzi has at least a thin conception of *Tian* as the efficient cause of the world, albeit indirectly. However, it is not clear that Mengzi's *Tian* is the principle of all being—indeed, in later Chinese cosmologies, *Tian* can even function as a material cause of the cosmos. That Mengzi's view of *Tian* is inadequate to ward off such views of God is evidence enough of the disparity between the God of revelation and *Tian* as Mengzi understood it.

Therefore, one must conclude that Mengzi's view of how *Tian* generates the world is far too undeveloped from the view of Catholic theological science. Mengzi's conception of *Tian* as source requires tremendous specification on its own terms, let alone if it is to be pressed into the service of Catholic theology. However, at the same time, Mengzi's *Tian*-theology is also not as juxtaposed to Christian cosmology as many modern Western naturalists suppose, and there is much in his account worth praising. For one, Mengzi believed *Tian* to be a cause of the world's generation, which can be plausibly taken as a kind of "seed of the Word" or a *preparatio evangelium* in the Chinese intellectual tradition. At the same time, it is only fair to note that naturalistic readings of Mengzi are not entirely inappropriate given the ambiguity of his conception of *Tian* as generative principle of the world.

From the Thomistic perspective, Mengzi's understanding of how *Tian* provides moral order to the world is much more resonant with Catholic theological science. A possible analogous principle for Aquinas to Mengzi's discussion of *Tian* as principle of order is the natural

---

95. *ST* Ia, q. 45, art. 1, corp.

96. See Norman Kretzmann, *The Metaphysics of Creation: Aquinas' Natural Theology in the* Summa Contra Gentiles *II* (Oxford: Oxford University Press, 1999), 70–100. Kretzmann stresses the significance, for Aquinas, of the claim that God is the cause of all things in a way that entails *creatio ex nihilo*—that is, not out of pre-existent matter.

law, though this theme is a source of tremendous debate in modern literature.[97] It is evident that the concept of natural law plays a great part in Aquinas's moral theology and moral anthropology more particularly. Since I address the relationship between Aquinas's theory of natural law and Mengzi's account of moral emotions in view of moral anthropology in greater detail in chapter 4, I will here focus only on those aspects of natural law that touch on divine order.

To briefly summarize the relevant points from Aquinas's presentation in the *ST*, Aquinas understands laws as "a rule and measure of acts, according to which man is induced to act or restrained from acting."[98] Since the "rule and measure" of human actions is reason, this means that God governs all things through the eternal law, by which he means the "Divine Reason's conception of things," which is not distinct from God himself.[99] The next step is to recognize that "all things participate in the eternal law in some way, namely inasmuch as they have inclinations toward their proper acts and ends due to its [the eternal law's] impression on them."[100] The term "natural law" is then a technical phrase to describe how this principle is true of human beings as rational creatures: natural law is the impression of eternal law upon our natures having to do with the inclination toward the proper acts and ends that fulfill our nature.[101]

The major difference between Aquinas and Mengzi regarding something like natural law is that although Mengzi understands the "four sprouts" in human beings as a gift from *Tian*, there is nothing analogous to the eternal law at work here.[102] That is, there is no clue

---

97. An excellent summary of the current debate about Aquinas's conception of natural law can be found in Justin Matchulat, "Thomas Aquinas on Natural Inclinations and the Practical Cognition of Human Goods: A Fresh Take on an Old Debate," *American Catholic Philosophical Quarterly* 94, no. 2 (2020): 240–43.

98. *ST* IaIIae, q. 90, art. 1, corp.

99. See *ST* IaIIae, q. 91, art. 1, corp. and ad 3.

100. *ST* IaIIae, q. 91, art. 2, corp.

101. J. Budziszewski, *Written on the Heart: The Case for Natural Law* (Downers Grove, IL: IVP Academic, 1997), 56. As Budziszewski helpfully puts it, "not everything made is subject to him in the special way called natural *law*. Natural *law* is a privilege of created *rational* beings ... because it is a finite reflection of his infinite purposes in their finite minds."

102. Kim, "Natural Law in Mencius and Aquinas,"144. Kim observes as I do above that Mengzi's moral philosophy lacks the language of legal terminology, which is significant within in Aquinas's conception of natural law. However, Kim also notes (and I agree with this assessment) that "while [Mencius] doesn't offer anything like a list of rules or obligations to live by,

A Thomistic Assessment of the *Mengzi* on *Tian*   71

in the *Mengzi* that *Tian* possesses perfect reason and that it has instilled the four sprouts in human beings as a kind of participation or even gift of this rational nature. *Mengzi* does not articulate any relationship between properties of *Tian* and properties of the moral emotions, and certainly he provides no description of human participation in *Tian*'s perfections. As Richard Kim has emphasized there is some divine foundation to Mengzi's moral thought inasmuch as Mengzi views that "human nature, endowed by Heaven, is directed toward the good, and that we 'serve Heaven' by nourishing our nature, it seems clear that Heaven at least approves of developing our nature."[103] Yet because *Tian* is never seen to *possess* the perfections it endows to human beings, it seems undeniable that Aquinas's understanding of eternal law as the foundation of natural law is at important variance with Mengzi's account of the moral emotions.

Of course, given that the natural law is a technical matter in Aquinas's thought, it may seem to some that all I have made clear here is that Mengzi's account of moral emotions cannot be deeply resonant with Aquinas's moral theology, and not necessarily Catholic theological science more broadly. However, we must consider the essential point in Aquinas's natural law theory vis-à-vis divine governance. For Aquinas, as for the Catholic tradition more broadly, the order and structure of the cosmos is reflective of the divine wisdom. As Russell Hittinger has rightly stressed, the traditional Catholic view of natural law is not that natural law posits an autonomous "sphere of 'ethics' immune from divine governance," but rather natural law is a means by which God governs the world—the law implies the lawgiver.[104] Aquinas's position that the natural law participates in the eternal law simply expresses how human nature is genuinely governed (even in its creation) by an eternal, rational, and simple God, who himself possesses the perfections in which humans analogously participate. By comparison, Mengzi's conception of *Tian* is empty of the perfections of reason that are constituent of the divine

---

he does endorse certain general rules (which always require proper moral perception for correct application)."

103. Kim, 143.

104. Russell Hittinger, *The First Grace: Rediscovering the Natural Law in a Post-Christian World* (Wilmington, DE: ISI Books, 2003), 47.

essence. Indeed, since the moral emotions have no clear rational aspect, it is unclear we can even speak of them as an expression of true *governance*, which implies not simply order, but an intellect and will for ordering things toward particular ends.[105]

While I think it is possible for the theologian to draw Mengzi's insights about *Tian* into a conception of God as perfect rational intellect, Mengzi himself makes no advances toward such a position. Indeed, as I noted above, it is possible to read Mengzi's understanding of *Tian* as an ordering principle within a naturalistic conception of the cosmos. Such a reading would not require positing *Tian* as a rational principle of order in the sense of having intellect, but only as bringing about some order in the cosmos, as a kind of principle-of-nature.[106] Ultimately, I am not convinced a naturalistic reading of Mengzi's on *Tian* is correct because of other aspects of his thought. However, even if one ultimately rejects the naturalistic interpretation of Mengzi, it is still fundamentally true that he provides no account of *Tian's* perfections—particularly of the intellect—that show how *Tian* is the cause of order in the cosmos in a rational manner. And for this reason, his account falls well short of truths that are ingredient to Catholic theological science.

Assessing Mengzi's Second Theme of *Tian*

My analysis of Mengzi's reading of *Tian* as a providential force requires assessment in two respects. On a general level, does Mengzi understand *Tian's* providence in ways that either prepare for or resonate with Catholic theological science? It is self-evident that for Catholic theological science, divine providence is primarily understood in light of revelation and salvation history. Nonetheless, be-

---

105. See Kim, "Natural Law in Mencius and Aquinas," 144. Kim rightly observes that "while we can't say that Mencius takes morality as backed by a lawgiver in precisely the same way that Aquinas does, Mencius does appeal to Heaven to at least partially justify his understanding of the goodness of human nature."

106. Mengzi himself did not articulate what sort of principle of order *Tian* happened to be. For this reason, the Neo-Confucian tradition sought to clarify that the order of the cosmos did have a source in a more or less rational cause, that there was a higher cause of order beyond *Tian* called "principle" (*li* 理). In this cosmology, *Tian* was relegated to a rather instrumental cause and more closely identified with nature itself. But Mengzi himself did not offer such a resolution. He clearly seemed to think *Tian* was responsible for a way of ordering nature, but may have intended *Tian* to be understood as the ordering principle within nature itself.

A Thomistic Assessment of the *Mengzi* on *Tian*   73

cause God's providence has effects which can be known through reason, Aquinas himself deals with Greco-Roman philosophical ideas of providence as part of theological science about divine providence.[107] If we invite Mengzi into this conversation, what would his participation produce? Out of this general engagement with Mengzi, a very specific question quickly arises. For Mengzi, as for most early Confucians, the providential aspects of *Tian* are significantly tied to the rise and fall of the political order, especially the king and rulers. Thus, assessing Mengzi's *Tian* theology especially requires assessing his thought in terms of a second more specific aspect, namely the political aspects of providence.

Let me first turn to the general aspects of divine providence. In this regard, it is helpful to collect some of the guiding principles of Aquinas's theology of divine providence before assessing the *Mengzi*. What does Aquinas take God's "providence" to mean? Divine governance is the primary subject of interest in *ST* Ia, qq. 103–5. In the initial article of these questions defending the truth of divine government of the world, Aquinas begins by citing the argument from some pre-Christian philosophers that the world was not governed, and all things occurred via chance or good fortune (*fortuito*). Aquinas rejects this, arguing that "for we see among natural things that they come to what is best for them [*melius est*], either always or more often than not, and this could not come to pass unless natural things are directed to their end through some sort of providence, and this providence is governance."[108] We see then that Aquinas capitalizes on the fact that *fortuito* does not mean merely "by happenstance" but something *fortunate* that occurs by happenstance. For Aquinas, the essential puzzle of chance is that very often things turn out well, and indeed, all things continue to go well: the sun does not go out,

---

107. For recent helpful discussions touching on the relationship between scripture, philosophy, and providence, see Jörgen Vijgen, "Job, Aquinas, and the Philosopher," in *Reading Job with St. Thomas Aquinas*, ed. Matthew Levering, Piotr Roszak, and Jörgen Vijgen (Washington, DC: The Catholic University of America Press, 2020), 42–67; and John F. X. Knasas, "Suffering and the 'Thomistic Philosopher': A Line of Thought Instigated by the Job Commentary," in *Reading Job with St. Thomas Aquinas*, 185–219.

108. *ST* Ia, q. 103, art. 1, corp.: "Videmus enim in rebus naturalibus provenire quod melius est, aut semper aut in pluribus, quod non contingeret, nisi per aliquam providentiam res naturales direigerentur ad finem boni, quod est gubernare."

74 Chapter 1

animals continue eating and reproducing, and plants continue growing. How, then do we account for the fact that, so often, things go well in our world?[109] On this basis, Aquinas will reject chance or fortune as the cause of fortuitous results. He argues instead that there must be real governance of the world, and for two reasons. First, he argues that when we observe natural phenomena, things tend to happen "for the best" (*melius est*), and therefore things must be ordered toward the good. Having argued from nature, Aquinas then makes a theological syllogism. If God is good, as the scriptures profess he is, then "it is unfitting to the highest goodness of God that He would not lead produced things to their perfection."[110]

Hence, for Aquinas the heart of the matter of divine governance is the fact that created things move toward their perfection or fulfillment. From the side of nature, the achievement of created things to generally move toward their perfection suggests a principle that ensures this is accomplished more often than not. From the opposite perspective, how could God be the highest good if he did not will the good of his creatures and in some manner guide them to flourishing?

At this juncture, it is apparent that Aquinas's conception of divine government is almost at odds with modern theological preoccupations. Ever since the Enlightenment, the problem of divine governance and providence has concerned evil (theodicy).[111] It is almost as if we moderns have completely shifted perspective from

109. Aquinas does not neglect the problem of evil despite these convictions. However, he distinguishes between what John F. X. Knasas has categorized as "natural" and "unnatural corruptions," the latter also called *quandoque* evils (occasional evils). Knasas helpfully reminds us that for Aquinas, natural corruptions (death) are part of God's ordering the world for the good. See Knasas, *Aquinas and the Cry of Rachel: Thomistic Reflections on the Problem of Evil* (Washington, DC: The Catholic University of America Press, 2013), 46–47.

110. *ST* Ia, q. 103, art. 1, corp. "... non convenit summae Dei bonitati quod res productas ad perfectum non perducat."

111. Notably, the term theodicy entered the Western lexicon through one of the most prominent Christian philosophers of the modern period, Gottfried Leibniz. As has been recently observed, "the *conditions* for a genuine theodicy are set out by Leibniz ... : a genuine theodicy must consist of a set of propositions, not just hypothetical but actually true, capable of showing the ultimate consistency of the existence of God and evil without sacrificing the attributes of God as classically defined." This quote appears in the introduction to Elmar J. Kremer and Michael J. Latzer, eds., *The Problem of Evil in Modern Philosophy* (Toronto: University of Toronto Press, 2001), 4.

A Thomistic Assessment of the *Mengzi* on *Tian*   75

Aquinas; for many of us today, the natural processes of the world do not seem to work out well most of the time. Rather, many people in our time judge that the evils, tragedies, disasters, and imperfections arising in nature far outweigh the good. Undoubtedly, it is true that Aquinas is aware of things that John Knasas has called "unnatural" or *quandoque* evils, such as these tragedies and disasters.[112] He is also aware of the Fall, through which sin has been introduced in the world and broken the order and relationships needed to effect flourishing not only for ourselves but for the world itself. Still, in the modern assessment of things, the *quandoque* evils occurring around us are the primary if not sole way that many have come to think about the problem of divine governance of the world; and more often than not, these people conclude God is a poor steward of the world's affairs.

Consequently, it is tempting to think Aquinas has a foolishly rose-tinted view of things. But we must seek to understand what he means by things working out "for the best" more often than not. When Aquinas means things tend to work out well in our world, he means in the sense of fulfilling their natures. If I plant a seed in my garden, I will tend to find a flower later. If a lion and a lioness mate under the right circumstances, there will tend to be a baby lion born from their congress. If I have a human child, it is more likely than not that she will grow up with proportionate limbs, the use of reason, and most capacities of human nature. Certainly, there are some cases in which the perfection of a particular thing does not arise, but more often than not it does; hence, we call it "typical."

For Aquinas, the goodness or perfection of a thing concerns the fulfillment and exercise of the capacities and powers proper to that thing. And if we view matters from this perspective, it is striking that more often than not, things do work well. Most of the time, flowers do flower-things, lions do lion-things, and humans do human-things well. Occasionally something like a genetic disorder disrupts the full perfection of the thing and may even choke off life that has barely just begun (as in the case of some miscarriages, for example). But these cases do not derail the cosmos's order. The fact that we

---

112. Knasas, *Aquinas and the Cry of Rachel*, 45–73, esp. 53–57.

76 Chapter 1

expect flowers to grow and humans to have their full capacities is what Aquinas means by saying things tend to work well: we generally expect things to attain to some perfection of their natural kinds.[113]

In sum, for Aquinas divine providence is not primarily seen in the "miraculous" making of things different than they otherwise would be, but precisely as the principle which allows the normal, typical course of flourishing to arise in the cosmos. And this is ultimately attributed as a quality of divine goodness, for as Aquinas says, "it is unfitting to the supreme goodness of God that the things he produces are not brought to their perfection."[114]

Therefore, Aquinas understands providence as guiding things to their proper end. But within this understanding, Aquinas is concerned with whether and how divine providence applies to particular things (especially corruptible things). Aquinas differentiates his view from one he attributes to Plato.[115] This position held to a tripartite distinction in providence: the supreme God governs over the heavenly bodies (thought to be incorruptible) and all universals; the lower gods govern all generation and corruption; and other spirits govern human actions on earth.[116] In Aquinas's view this position contains two serious problems. First, it holds that God does not govern all things. According to Aquinas, this is impossible because God is the universal cause of all being and all things have God's goodness as their proper end, and hence it must follow that all created things fall under divine providence.[117] The second problem is that this position holds God's government does not extend *immediately*

113. It is true that Aquinas recognizes that many times the flourishing of one thing (such as a lion eating) occurs at the loss of flourishing of another. He argues that this allowance of evil is part of the structure of the good of the world taken as a whole, and not considered in individual parts. This problem of the part-whole conception of God's good providence is taken up by Jacques Maritain in his Marquette Aquinas Lecture published as *Saint Thomas and the Problem of Evil* (Milwaukee, WI: Marquette University Press, 1942), 8–19. Maritain argues this tension is ultimately and only resolved for Aquinas because the world is "made for grace"— that is, that such evil must be understood in the "whole" of soteriology and not simply the cosmological whole. Consequently, Maritain stresses that for Christian theology, creation is ultimately part of the salvific economy, and thus subordinate to soteriology.

114. *ST* Ia, q. 103, art. 1, corp. "non convenit summae Dei bonitati quod res productas ad perfectum non perducat."

115. Elders, *Thomas Aquinas and His Predecessors*, 13. Elders stresses that Aquinas is likely here reading Plato through Neoplatonism.

116. *ST* Ia, q. 103, art. 6, obj. 1.

117. *ST* Ia, q. 103, art. 5, corp.

A Thomistic Assessment of the *Mengzi* on *Tian*   77

to all things. On the contrary, Aquinas argues God's providence must extend to even corruptible things in an immediate fashion because God's government is the most perfect form of government, and thus must care for even the least of things.[118]

Understanding this theme of God as the immediate cause of government is very important for the assessment of Mengzi's view of *Tian*. Aquinas readily recognizes that some natural kinds govern others: the heavenly bodies govern the change of the cosmos, parents govern children, and rulers govern people. Rather than deny these forms of governance, Aquinas's understanding of God's "immediate" providence relies upon a distinction between the design or plan of government (the *ratio gubernationis*) and the execution or performance of government (*executio gubernationis*), where the former (*ratio*) is the most proper designation for providence. This allows Aquinas to conclude that God governs all things immediately via the *ratio gubernationis* and governs through secondary causes (all other causes but God himself) in terms of the *executio gubernationis*.[119] Put differently, when creatures govern other creatures, they do so as an execution of the governmental designs of God, meaning that God truly governs, albeit often through secondary causes.[120]

It is very possible that Mengzi has something like the view of

118. *ST* Ia, q. 103, art. 6, corp.

119. *ST* Ia, q. 103, art. 6, corp.

120. The way that God can work through secondary causes was a significant problem in medieval theology and philosophy. The key problem is that secondary causes depend upon God as the first cause for their activity, and so in what sense are they truly causes? Gaven Kerr explains that Aquinas's position rests on two legs. First, Aquinas accepts that secondary or creaturely causes act via God's power as first cause, which causes their existence. But, because God's primary cause bestows being, this means that "a secondary cause acts through the power of the primary cause through utilizing its own actuality, its own *esse*, in order to act as a cause in the world" (Kerr, 95). For Aquinas, secondary causes have an integrity because they perform their actions of their own *esse* even as their ability to be causes and undertake the specific acts they perform is dependent upon the Prime cause. For discussion within the relevant Thomistic literature on secondary causality, I follow Kerr (see Kerr, 91n26) in recommending Wippel, "Thomas Aquinas on Creatures as Causes of *Esse*," 172–93, and Alfred Fredosso, "Medieval Aristotelianism and the Case against Secondary Causation in Nature," in *Divine and Human Action: Essays in the Metaphysics of Theism*, ed. Thomas Morris (Ithaca, NY: Cornell University Press, 1988), 74–118. Notably, this theme also touches upon a distinctive topic in modern Thomistic scholarship regarding God's knowledge of future contingent singulars, though in a much more specific sense than I aim to treat here. See, e.g., William Lane Craig, "Aquinas on God's Knowledge of Future Contingents," *The Thomist* 54 (January 1990): 33–79, and Theodore J. Kondoleon, "God's Knowledge of Future Contingent Singulars: A Reply," *The Thomist* 56 (1991): 117–39.

Tian's *ratio gubernationis* in mind with his "weaker" account of *Tianming*. Most generally, Mengzi views the ruler as enacting a form of governance that is subject to *Tian's* Mandate. That is, the ruler is charged with governing things so that they flourish, and he has no capacity to establish what flourishing is or is not. More particularly, although Mengzi does not tend to see *Tian* as an immediate governor in terms of execution, he does not reject the idea of *Tian* governing through a plan of government. In the ascension narrative of Shun, for example, Mengzi sees *Tian* as the source of the principles of good ruling that please the ruler's subjects. The people and the spirits seem to act as secondary causes that manifest *Tian's* Mandate. It is not quite right to say that this manifests *Tian's* will (i.e., *Tian's* desire that Shun be king), but it manifests *Tian's* plan or order—that is, that someone such as Shun who acts as he does and is virtuous should govern things. Of course, there is a limit to this analogy since the *ratio gubernationis* clearly relates to Aquinas's conception of eternal law, which I demonstrated above has no clear analog in Mengzi. Thus, Mengzi's approach does seem to include a contradiction because understanding *Tian* as governor implies *Tian* possesses some rational agency, but Mengzi himself does not apply such properties to *Tian*. But, as I noted, due to the unsystematic nature of Mengzi's account of *Tian*, such inconsistencies are not terribly surprising.

With this inconsistency aside, it might even be that Mengzi's "weaker" view of *Tianming* is the more useful one from the perspective of Catholic theological science. This is because Mengzi's weaker view allows for an articulation of the diverse secondary causes that God uses to bring about his plan for governance. Consequently, such an account allows for a greater ability to note how particular secondary causes can fail in their service to providence. The shortcoming, though, is that Mengzi's weaker account of divine governance is reliant upon a loss of confidence in *Tianming* to be effective in guiding the state into flourishing. In other words, it is not clear at all points in what sense the later Mengzi thinks *Tian's* governance applies to the concrete individual matters such as the dynastic fortunes of early China (which Mengzi seems to doubt *Tian* controls in an immediate way) rather than through establishing governing principles in the cosmos (such as the principle that the virtuous will become king).

A Thomistic Assessment of the *Mengzi* on *Tian*   79

But at the same time, Mengzi does not argue against the ability of *Tian* to govern things immediately. Indeed, Mengzi's account of individual fate could perhaps signal a kind of commitment to the immediate governance of *Tian* over individual human beings, at least. Therefore, Mengzi's view of *Tian*'s providence in general is adequately resonant with principles of theological science about God's providence to encourage the adoption of Mengzi into theological science. But what about the specific, political conception of providence in Mengzi? For Mengzi, a considerable problem is how *Tian*'s providence works. On the one hand, the Mandate of *Tian* was understood as the principle of rule, and as the force which seemed to secure the right to rule for those who are worthy of the office. Yet, *Tian* also does not proclaim or speak the Mandate, but is rather "articulated" or manifest through the hearts of those who would be ruled.[121] I noted above that it seems we can treat these perspectives as two different accounts of *Tian* providence, since Mengzi lived during a time in which the manner of *Tian*'s providence was coming into doubt amidst the decay of Zhou power, which supposedly had not lost the Mandate of *Tian* and yet had lost power all but in name. In my analysis of Mengzi's thought I offered my opinion that the weaker account of *Tian*'s providence was more likely his final position. Now I should like to raise the question of whether either of Mengzi's positions and especially his "weak" account of *Tian* providence can accord with Catholic theological science.

One might put the problem this way in terms of theological science: is it appropriate to hold that the God of Christian confession was responsible for the rise and fall of ancient Chinese monarchies, and if so in what sense?[122] Recall that for Aquinas there is a distinction between the *ratio gubernationis* which is properly called providence,

---

121. Again, we see that such a position hints at a kind of natural law theory, but without developing it in full.

122. I do not here wish to imply my acceptance of the view of many early Jesuits (including Figurist interpreters such as Joachim Bouvet, SJ) who sought to interpret Chinese history in the literal terms of the Old Testament history. Rather, I am focused on the question of whether the LORD can be said to have been concerned to govern the political fortunes of ancient China in ways that classical thinkers assumed *Tian* did. For an examination of Bouvet and his thought, see Claudia von Collani, *P. Joachim Bouvet S. J. Sein Leben und sein Werk* (Nettetal: Steyler Verlag, 1985).

80 Chapter 1

and the *executio* of this *ratio*, which can be and often is carried out by secondary causes.[123] In these terms, the monarchies of China must fall under the *ratio gubernationis*, but not necessarily have God as the executing agent of this order.

Even Mengzi's "weak" reading of *Tian* seems to agree that *Tian* possesses a kind of *ratio gubernationis*. Mengzi clearly sees *Tian* as at least the cause of ruling because good governance and virtue pleases the hearts of the people, and the people recognize such rule is good for them. Put differently, even on his weakest reading of *Tian*'s providence, Mengzi takes *Tianming* to signify that the one who should rule is the one who best enacts the virtues of good and just rulers. Consequently, there is a nod here to something like the *ratio gubernationis*, the design that governs all things. Mengzi sees *Tian* as the source of the principle of ruling—that is, the source of the principles of ruling that constitute the universal norms of ruling. From this, we can say that *Tianming* is a way that *Tian* governs through the ordering of human hearts and the fulfillment of them in happiness, which provides the foundation of good government.

Interestingly, then, because this "weaker" reading of *Tian* issues something like a distinction between the divine *ratio gubernationis* and *executio gubernationis*, it is actually more in line with Aquinas's theology of divine providence than the "stronger" account of providence detailed above. In his discussion of authority in political life, Yves Simon helpfully distinguished between various accounts of how leaders are given authority to rule. There are three in particular helpful to the present analysis of Mengzi. The first Simon notes is the "coach-driver theory," which holds that the people ruled hold their authority and designate rulers to guide them, but do not actually communicate genuine authority to them.[124] The second Simon calls "divine right" theory, of which he notes there are two important species. The first, which he argues is most properly called divine right theory, holds two premises: "that the power of the temporal ruler is directly from God," and "that God himself designates the person of

---

123. *ST* Ia, q. 103, art. 6.

124. Yves R. Simon, *Philosophy of Democratic Government* (Notre Dame, IN: University of Notre Dame Press, 1993), 146–54.

A Thomistic Assessment of the *Mengzi* on *Tian*   81

the temporal ruler."[125] Simon also describes a second species of divine right theory which is called a "designation" theory. In this theory, the designation of a ruler as king is "effected by men," but "the power of the king ... comes directly from God."[126]

Finally, Simon describes the "transmission theory," which he associates with Aquinas. The transmission theory of authority states that the people possess the authority of rule, but they both designate one to rule and "transmit to him the power given by God to the people."[127] In this view, God's government does not apply to human kingship as such, but to the natural goods of the people, who then transmit authority that God gives to them over to the king. From this, we can see that Mengzi's account of how *Tian* selects rulers is resonant with Aquinas's understanding of divine governance. For in his "weaker" account of *Tian*'s governance, Mengzi sees the happiness of the people and the spirits as the real measure and judgment of a ruler's receiving *Tianming*. While Mengzi does not explicitly have any idea that the people are given an authority by *Tian* that they pass along to a ruler, the people nonetheless are more directly responsible for the reign of a particular king than is *Tian* in terms of enacting or at least identifying the Mandate of *Tian*.[128] For Mengzi, *Tian* rather gives human beings the moral tendencies toward the good, and the inclination to be happy and discern what does and does not lead to flourishing. With these capacities, the people judge what ruler will best bring this about, and therein the chosen ruler fulfills *Tian*'s mandate that is given through the instrument of the people's wills and desires. Yet again, we see that although the full complement of intellectual commitments for something like Aquinas's theory of natural law are not clearly held by Mengzi, nonetheless there is something very much in effect like natural law at work in his thought.

125. Simon, 157.
126. Simon, 157.
127. Simon, 158.
128. Kim, "Confucian Constitutionalism," 380: "... Mencius does not seem to have in mind two separate (and distinct) sources of moral and political legitimacy of kingship—Mandate of Heaven *and* the people's acceptance. Rather, he believes the people's behavior tracks (or parallels) the will of heaven (*tian*)."

Assessing Mengzi's Third Theme of *Tian*

For those readers acquainted with Aquinas's theology, it is unnecessary to devote much space to demonstrating how Aquinas would agree with the general principle of Mengzi that God is the source and exemplar of goodness. For Aquinas, God is not only the perfect good, but he is also the cause of good in all other things. We can briefly summarize this in Aquinas's observation of the difference between how God loves the world and how love occurs within the world. Creatures, Aquinas teaches us, love things on account of some perceptible good in the beloved. God, however, bestows goodness upon that which he loves—the divine love *causes* goodness rather than recognizes it.

In broad strokes, much of what Mengzi says about *Tian* as source and exemplar of goodness is profoundly resonant with what Catholic theological science teaches about God. However, one significant difference between Mengzi and Aquinas concerns the extent to which the latter emphasizes the fact that God himself is the end that defines goodness. For Mengzi, *Tian* is certainly pleased or satisfied by moral self-cultivation, but there is no sense of "attaining *Tian*" as the form of happiness in the way that Aquinas holds.

At least a partial reason for this is that Mengzi fails to develop in greater detail what is meant by the goodness of *Tian*. For Aquinas, goodness lies in the perfection of a thing, and clearly God as pure act is the eternal actualization of what God is, and therefore God is perfectly good. Additionally, Aquinas teaches that God has a will and desires himself. This must be so because the will is ordered toward the good and, since God is the highest and most perfect good, the divine will must desire God himself, not as an end to obtain but as the end already enjoyed. From this, we see that God's exemplarity as goodness that causes goodness in other things also involves God's communication of himself as the proper end of all things that seek goodness. Hence, God communicates his goodness to creatures not only in the substantial goodness of the world, but also as the definition of happiness for all things—that is, participation in God.[129]

---

129. For an excellent study of the participation in God in Aquinas's theology, see Bernhard

A Thomistic Assessment of the *Mengzi* on *Tian*   83

An important question is whether Mengzi's view of *Tian* fails to include an account of *Tian* as the proper end of human moral action because of mere lack of interest in the question, or for reasons that indicate a genuine disparity between his *Tian* theology and Catholic theological science. That is, does Mengzi's conception of *Tian* prevent him from concluding that *Tian* can be the proper end of human moral action as the good sought?

This is a complicated question, but it seems likely that Mengzi's conception of *Tian* cannot really hold to an idea of *Tian* as ultimate end. James Behuniak's reading of Mengzi in terms of an "emergence" or "process" anthropology is valuable here. Behuniak stresses that for Mengzi, it is the process of "becoming human" that is most important for Mengzi, meaning that the "sprouts" of *Tian* do not signify the *arche* of a coherent and determined *telos*, but the initial momentum of emergence that requires human cultivation and effort to be actualized.[130] Although I agree with Robert Eno that there is more of a teleological structure to Mengzi's view than Behuniak acknowledges, it is still the case that for Mengzi, this "becoming human" is the only conception of flourishing he has in mind. A possible theological rapprochement is to understand *Tian* as a kind of personalization of the natural law, which would both explain its limitations as not being the ultimate end, and its teleological structure. Of course, this would also introduce other substantive issues that require their own analysis. For now, I will simply say it is clear from this suggestion underscores the fact that *Tian* may or may not be as robustly theistic as would be required for understanding God, though it can perhaps be applied within a more robust theological field of vision.

Put in terms of Confucian spirituality, Mengzi understands the ideal moral action to be a process of "self-cultivation" (*xiushen* 修身), the final end of which is "the development of one's Heavenly conferred nature."[131] The successful development of what *Tian* has conferred on humanity is at least attaining the status of the "moral

---

Blankenhorn, OP, *The Mystery of Union with God: Dionysian Mysticism in Albert the Great and Thomas Aquinas* (Washington, DC: The Catholic University of America Press, 2015).

130. See Behuniak, 87–90.

131. Philip J. Ivanhoe, *Confucian Moral Self Cultivation*, 2nd ed. (Indianapolis, IN: Hackett Publishing, 2000), 17. See also Philip J. Ivanhoe, "Confucian Self Cultivation and Mengzi's Notion of Extension," in Liu and Ivanhoe, *Essays on the Moral Philosophy of Mengzi*, 221–41.

84 Chapter 1

gentleman" (*junzi*) or ideally but most difficultly, the status of the "sage" (*shengren*). Ultimately, as we saw in Mengzi with the idea of pleasing *Tian*, there is a sense in which successful moral cultivation does impact the relationship with *Tian*. As Tu Weiming once put it, "the realization of the self, in the ultimate sense, is tantamount to the realization of the complete unity between humanity and Heaven."[132] But what Tu means here is unity in the sense of harmony and accord, such as that vision articulated in the *Zhongyong*.[133] One might observe that for later Confucian tradition, the *Zhongyong* came to be read in something like teleological ways, being read in terms of the metaphysical and cosmological notions of principle (*li* 理) or the Great Ultimate (*taiji* 太極). The key difference is I do not see any way in which the harmonization theme in the Confucian tradition can be seen to be something like Aquinas's understanding of "complete unity" with God, i.e., sharing in the divine life and experience eternal friendship with God. This is not to say the Confucian vision is antithetical to Catholic teleology—indeed, this theme of harmonization seems appreciably like the turn to social eschatology in twentieth century Western theology—but it does not feature a true union with God.[134]

This feature of Mengzi's thought cannot be overly surprising, however; as we saw above, it is unclear how much Mengzi distinguishes between *Tian* as divine and *Tian* as cosmic nature. This is important to the current issues of *Tian* as ultimate end because for many Chinese thinkers, there is a tendency to a form of panentheism. Consequently, human beings already share in some sense of a real sharing in *Tian* by virtue of existence—the moral unity with *Tian* would

---

132. Tu Weiming, *Confucian Thought: Selfhood as Creative Transformation* (Albany, NY: SUNY Press, 1985), 60–61.

133. See *Liji, Zhongyong*, 1. Tu's quotation is suggestive of the opening lines of the *Zhongyong*, which first describes the *dao* as "developing one's natural propensities" (*shuai xing* 率性) which ultimately (through education and focusing on the small matters of daily life), leads to the establishment of proper order in the world.

134. The best Catholic example of this strongly social conception of anthropology and salvation reacting against modern individualistic liberalism is Henri de Lubac, SJ, *Catholicism: A Study of Dogma in Relation to the Corporate Destiny of Mankind*, trans. Lancelot C. Sheppard (New York: Sheed and Ward, 1950). Another popular work touching on this theme in a more Trinitarian vein is the work of Orthodox theologian John D. Zizioulas, *Being as Communion: Studies in Personhood and the Church* (Crestwood, NY: St. Vladimir's Seminary Press, 1985).

A Thomistic Assessment of the *Mengzi* on *Tian*   85

seem to merely close the circle.[135] Within such a view of things, there is little need for an eschatological sense of God as ultimate end, or indeed that God must sought as end at all, for one does not desire what is possessed, except so far as maintain what is possessed.

In this regard, I would conclude that due to Mengzi's lack of firm distinction between *Tian* and nature, his account of *Tian* works against a conception of God as final end. But this is not overly surprising. After all, the nature of happiness is one of the most controverted and difficult questions in all classical philosophy, East or West. Thus, even if theological science may find Mengzi's view of *Tian* strongly divergent from a conception of God that serves articulating the final end of humanity in God, this doesn't remove all theological utility or fruitfulness of Mengzi's account of *Tian*. However, such aspects of Mengzi's philosophy of *Tian* show that in order to derive theological utility from Mengzi's account, there is a need to rely heavily upon the classical principles and doctrines of Catholic theological science (both natural and revealed) in order to illuminate and rectify the useful aspects of Mengzi's account.

CONCLUSION

In Chinese, the Catholic conception of God cannot help but touch on the theological limits and possibilities of *Tian*. By examining Mengzi's account of *Tian* more closely, I have endeavored to more carefully articulate what aspects of the concept of *Tian* do and do not resonate with Catholic theological science about God. Since Mengzi's account of *Tian* is a species of natural theology, it is unsurprising that on several points, his conception of *Tian* falls short of what the Catholic tradition teaches must be said about God. Yet despite this, there are significant points of harmony that are promising and fruitful for developing Catholic theological science in light of the philosophical frameworks of the Chinese traditions.

First, to those parts which fall short. One of the clear disparities between Mengzi's account of *Tian* and the Catholic account of

---

135. This strikes a notable chord of resonance with classical Stoic ethics, which held that only the possession of the virtues is able to bring about happiness. For an overview of Stoic ethics, see John Sellars, *Stoicism* (London and New York: Routledge, 2014), 107–34.

God is that Mengzi lacks a clear sense of divine creation and transcendence vis-à-vis the world. Mengzi's position has been read as both a kind of metaphysical naturalism by secular scholars, and as a kind of prefiguration of creation metaphysics by some Christian interpreters. In my opinion, Mengzi's account of *Tian* as principle of things is, at best, ambiguous. This is in itself a problem for Catholic theological science, which cannot fail to clarify how God stands in ontological and causal relationship to the world. This is especially true because many of the themes Mengzi touches upon—*Tian*'s governance, *Tian*'s gifts to humanity, et cetera—depend upon a theology of creation to develop them correctly in Catholic theological science.

At the same time, I do not think it would be an onerous task to develop an account of *Tian* as creator using Mengzi's resources as a starting point. Indeed, there are models of this kind of work already, such as when missionaries to China appealed to the *Book of Odes* and *Book of Documents* (note, these were Mengzi's sources) to argue for a pre-classical conception of creation in China. Therefore, adapting Mengzi's philosophy of *Tian* into a Catholic theology of creation is very much in the realm of possibility for future scholars.

Another important point of difference between Mengzi's account of *Tian* and Catholic theological science concerns what can be called the conceptions of natural law in both accounts. It seems unquestionable that there is something like natural law at work in Mengzi, most notably in his conception of the emotions of the heart-mind that are the sprouts of moral virtue in human beings that move us toward flourishing. However, there are also important aspects of genuine natural law accounts missing, such as the explicit reference to the rational perfections of God that ground the eternal law, in which natural law participates. For Aquinas, the idea of natural law cannot be separated from an account of the divine wisdom that promulgates this law and instills it in the human heart. Even if there are, at times, suggestions of something like eternal law in Mengzi (such as his account of *Tianming*), Mengzi himself never develops an account of *Tian*'s perfections (i.e., wisdom and goodness) that such concepts require.

A Thomistic Assessment of the *Mengzi* on *Tian*   87

Finally, it is evident that Mengzi's account of *Tian* fails to consider any way—even a natural way—that *Tian* is a proper end of human life. Even in terms of natural reason, Greek and Roman philosophers, including Aristotle, recognized that contemplation of the ultimate good was the fitting end of human action.[136] That *Tian* is not an object of contemplation or end of activity—coupled with the lack of true "theology" of *Tian* in Mengzi's thought—clearly shows that Mengzi did not write about *Tian* as God in ways that Catholic theological science requires. Indeed, at this point better than perhaps any other, we can see how the concept of *Tian* as Mengzi understands it may not even be an adequate theistic concept. Indeed, it may prove better, ultimately, to find a place for Mengzi's reading of *Tian* as a part of a theistic account of the world rather than to seek in *Tian* a way to describe God as the principle of the world.

That said, there are also several areas of Mengzi's account of *Tian* which are already quite helpful for serving Catholic theological science. Generally speaking, Mengzi possesses a robust and complex account of *Tian*'s governance that would be a tremendously fruitful resource for developing a Chinese Catholic theology on divine providence. At the very least, Mengzi provides a resource relevant to Chinese culture which is clearly concerned with and provides a basic structure for thinking about questions of divine governance, divine order, and divine will for human beings. Additionally, Mengzi's account of *Tian* contains interesting aporiae that can be helpful for Catholic theological science to examine alongside similar problems in the tradition. For example, one of the major problems Mengzi faces is accounting for how *Tian* guides both the flourishing and diminution of the Zhou dynasty, while not raising a new virtuous leader in its place. Catholic theology readily recognizes that God's governance must include in some way a guiding of the rulers of the world.[137] So how can we account for God's governance in situations like Mengzi faced? Did God as Christians understand him actively guard and guide the rulers of ancient China into virtue? Why and how did this work cease if it did?

136. See, e.g., Aristotle, *Nicomachean Ethics*, X.7–8.
137. See, e.g., Augustine, *City of God*, Books II–IV.

88 Chapter 1

More broadly and perhaps more significantly, I argued above that Mengzi provides a means to account for how God works through secondary causes in his providence. This is, I think, of substantial importance especially given what has occurred in philosophy and theology since the Enlightenment. As Louis Dupré once noted, one consequence of Enlightenment Deism was that God's causing the world came to be understood only in terms of direct efficient causality.[138] This meant that any outcome X could only be described through one efficient cause A, which had to be either God or natural. Hence, if a hurricane was determined to be caused by seasonal currents in the ocean, the Deist would conclude it was not caused by God. With Mengzi, we find a Chinese account that provides helpful resources for rejecting such a view of causality. For Mengzi observes that *Tian's* mandate can cause things (such as the transmission of rule from Yao to Shun) by working through lower order causes relating to the caused event. What is necessary, of course, is to develop more concretely an account of how Mengzi understands the relationship between secondary causes and their effects. In the case of Shun's ascension, the secondary causes of pleasing the people and the spirits are tied to the direct outcomes of the caused event that Shun became king (for if he did so, he would please the people and the spirits). How does this account of secondary causality compare to Catholic accounts? How might it correct the errors of the modern world?

I raise these questions here merely to gesture at the fruitfulness of Mengzi's *Tian* theology for Chinese Catholic theological science. Clearly, developing Mengzi's theology of *Tian* for use in a Catholic account of God and divine providence requires significant intellectual labor. But I hope this analysis proves such labor is not impossible to accomplish and would be a great benefit to theological science. But again, I should emphasize that this is only possible after taking up the work I am concerned with in this book: testing the limits and possibilities of Chinese philosophy for theological science. It is only after a rigorous and honest account of the disparity between Mengzi and Catholic theological science that the real value of Mengzi's account of *Tian* for describing the God of Jesus Christ is discernible.

---

138. Dupré, *Enlightenment and the Intellectual Foundations of Modern Culture*, 243–56.

2

A Thomistic Reading of the *Mozi* on Divine Will

Although little known to Western readers outside of sinology, the *Mozi* is one of the few texts of early China that has a modestly developed account of *Tian* as divine (though some prominent scholars have argued *Tian* in the *Mozi* is thoroughly naturalistic, a point I discuss below). More significantly, those who appreciate the theistic shape of *Tian* according to the *Mozi* note that its ethical vision is ultimately founded upon the text's account of *Tian*. In view of my aim in this book to foster the synthesis of Chinese philosophy and Catholic theological science, the *Mozi* is a text full of tantalizing possibilities for developing a genuinely Chinese Catholic theology of God.[1]

Theological readings of the *Mozi* are hard to come by; the only two book-length studies are both in Chinese and by Protestant authors.[2] Consequently, the question of the relationship between

1. Zhang Lifu 張立夫, *Jidujiao lunli yu Mozi zhi jianai lunli bijiao yanjiu* 基督教倫理與墨子之兼愛倫理比較研究 (Taipei: Changqing wenhua chubanshe, 1980), has argued Mohism is a better resource for developing Chinese Christian theology than Confucianism, precisely because of the "religious" perspective of the *Mozi*.

2. See Zhang Lifu 張立夫, and Wu Leichuan, *Mo Di yu Yesu*. Additionally, according to product summary on WorldCat, Wang Zhixin 王治心, *Mozi zhexue* 墨子哲学 (Nanjing: Jinling shenxue chubanshe, 1925), uses "the perspective of Christianity to analyze Mozi's ten primary tenets" (以基督教的观点论述墨子的十大主张). However, this work is held only by one library and is currently unavailable for loan, so I have not been able to confirm its contents firsthand.

90 Chapter 2

Catholic theological science and Mohist philosophy is basically untilled soil. There is a great need for a simple assessment and awareness of what the *Mozi* teaches about *Tian*, and how it fares in light of the normative principles and positions of Catholic theological science. Therefore, this chapter provides a theological assessment of the *Mozi*'s the conception of *Tian*'s will (*tian zhi* 天志), presented in the text as *Tian*'s intention (*tian yi* 天意). As I discuss in the appendix to this work, the text of the *Mozi* has a difficult history, and therefore I will deal below with the structure of the text and the sections of the work most explicitly relevant to my analysis here. As an introductory word, it is enough to say that in the *Mozi* both "*Tian*'s will" and "*Tian*'s intention" are used in expressing the same fundamental idea: that *Tian* loves all human beings and that *Tian*'s love for humanity is the standard, principle, or model of human moral action. In this chapter, then, I examine to what degree *Tian*'s love for humanity in the *Mozi* resonates with the Catholic understanding of divine love as articulated by Aquinas.

WORKING TOWARD A THEOLOGICAL ASSESSMENT OF THE *MOZI*

Before turning to assess the Mohist account of divine will and love from a Thomistic perspective, it is instructive to take stock of obstacles or difficulties inherent in such a task. Though I do not find these insurmountable, rehearsing them will help assure the reader that my assessment of *Mozi*'s thought remains respectful and charitable, in addition to accurate. First, it is notable that the framework of the *Mozi* is different from that animating Aquinas's thought in several vital respects. While Aquinas takes divine revelation as the norm for understanding the divine life and properties, Mohism does not base its understanding of *Tian* upon a revealed text at all. Consequently, the *Mozi* "self-identifies" as a kind of natural theology, even though the text would not use this term.[3]

---

3. Many Chinese authors perceive and describe Mohism as a "religious tradition" (*zong-jiao* 宗教), but the terminology in Chinese does not imply claims to revelation per se. Such authors (such as Zhang Lifu) merely mean to emphasize the theistic foundations of Mohism, which in Christian theology is still a kind of natural theology.

A Thomistic Reading of the *Mozi* on Divine Will   91

Consequently, the kind of theism found in the *Mozi* is not synonymous with the fundamental beliefs about God that guide Catholic theological science. For one, like *Mengzi* (see chapter 2), the *Mozi* is reticent to clearly distinguish *Tian* as divine from *tian* as natural. Although most interpreters see *Tian* in the *Mozi* as being broadly theistic, one notable scholar, Chris Fraser, has argued the *Mozi* presupposes metaphysical naturalism, such that *Tian* is just a "divinized" form of nature itself.[4] Again, many if not most scholars (especially from China) see the Mohist *Tian* as a genuinely theistic concept. Still, from the Christian perspective, even the most generous theistic reading of *Mozi's Tian* remains uncomfortably ambiguous regarding key Christian concepts such as creation.[5] Again, however, the same can be said for the views of the divine in pre-Christian Greek philosophy: these conceptions of God often fall short in vital ways of describing God as is necessary in Catholic theological science.

Along the same vein, Aquinas's discussion of the divine will and love is concerned with theological science—that is, it is aimed at understanding and articulating truth about God as the primary intellectual object of knowledge. In contrast, the *Mozi* does not articulate the properties of *Tian* solely for the sake of intellectually understanding what or who *Tian* is. Rather, the impetus of the discourse on *Tian's* properties is primarily motivated by moral problems.

Because of the moral emphasis in the *Mozi's* conception of *Tian*, we should note how the moral framework of the *Mozi* is markedly different from Aquinas. Many significant interpreters, such as Feng Youlan, have argued the *Mozi* should be classified as a utilitarian tradition, although this is a contested claim.[6] Hao Changchi, for

---

4. Chris Fraser, *The Philosophy of the Mòzǐ: The First Consequentialists* (New York: Columbia University Press, 2016), 105–6. See also, Chris Fraser, "The Mohist Conception of Reality," in Li and Perkins, *Chinese Metaphysics and Its Problems*, 69–84.

5. I am sympathetic with the reading given by Luo Guang, in which he argues for interpreting Mozi as a sophisticated religious thinker. Luo's position is against the view of writers such as Liang Qichao, who contended Mohism was religious in a superstitious sense (*mixin* 迷信) due to belief in ghosts and spirits. See Luo Guang, *Zhongguo zhexue sixiang shi: Xian Qin pian* 中國哲學思想事, 先秦偏 printed as *Luo Guang quanshu*, vol. 6 (Taibei: Taiwan Student Press, 1996), 346–54.

6. Feng, *Zhongguo zhexue shi*, 76–78. Bryan W. Van Norden, for his part, differs from the utilitarian claim by referring to Mohism as a consequentialist tradition, which has become a dominant way of describing the Mohists. See Van Norden, *Virtue Ethics and Consequentialism in Early Chinese Philosophy* (New York: Oxford University Press, 2007).

92 Chapter 2

example, has proposed that Mohism lacks the fundamental emphasis necessary to be utilitarian as the West understands it—namely, a focus on the "atomic individual" or the "I." Hao rightly notes that Mohist ethics is not based on benefitting oneself but benefitting the other, though he overplays a distinction between the Mohist "other" and the Confucian "we" focus (the latter he uses to describe Confucian familial ethics).[7] At heart, the Mohist emphasizes mutuality (*xiang* 相) of beneficial conduct, which encompasses a greater social "we." Hence, the Mohist is not purely about the "other" but about others that will love oneself as well in the bargain. However, even if Hao is correct that Mohism does not bear the individualistic aspects that make it identical to the problematic utilitarian tradition (problematic, that is, from the Christian view) of Bentham, Mill, et cetera, it still seems fair to classify it as a consequentialist moral tradition, as Bryan W. Van Norden has done.[8]

In this way, the *Mozi* represents what Martin Rhonheimer has criticized as "state of the world" ethics, which he contends are contrary not only to Thomism, but also to Catholic moral theology in general after the promulgation of *Veritatis Splendor*.[9] Thus, even if the *Mozi* is significantly distinct from problematic modern Western consequentialist theories, the text still approaches the moral life in a fundamentally different way that the Thomistic approach to virtue in particular, and perhaps the Catholic moral tradition more broadly.

This particularly matters regarding the question of divine love. For example, as I show below, Aquinas and Mozi generally agree on two propositions: that God/*Tian* wills the good of humans, and that God/*Tian* loves humanity as a consequence of willing their good. Yet within this agreement, it is not clear they agree on the nature of

---

7. Hao Changchi. "Is Mozi a Utilitarian Philosopher?" *Frontiers of Philosophy in China* 1, no. 3 (Sept 2006): 382–400.

8. See Van Norden, *Virtue Ethics and Consequentialism*, 30, and 142–49. Van Norden defines Mohism as a consequentialist tradition which claims that "we ought to maximize the goods of wealth, populousness and social order" (30). Later on, Van Norden examines his claim of Mohism as consequentialism in light of other scholars' arguments that Mohism is a form of divine command theory (145–49).

9. Martin Rhonheimer, "Norm-ethics, Moral Rationality, and the Virtues: What's Wrong with Consequentialism," in *The Perspective of the Acting Person: Essays in the Renewal of Thomistic Moral Philosophy*, ed. William F. Murphy, Jr. (Washington, DC: The Catholic University of America Press, 2008), 18–36.

A Thomistic Reading of the *Mozi* on Divine Will   93

the good willed by God/*Tian*, and how it is true that God/*Tian* wills the good for human beings. Indeed, the nature of the good and its pursuit are contested grounds on a theoretical level between consequentialist and virtue accounts of the moral life. Because the focus of this chapter concerns God's relationship to the good, this difference in perspective is intensified.

Case in point, many scholars have noted that in Mohism, the utilitarian ethic stands in some relationship to a kind of divine command theory ethical framework, though scholars dispute which one governs Mohist morality. In an influential essay, Rodney L. Taylor argued that the *Mozi* ultimately assumes a utilitarian framework but founds the understanding of utilitarian good on *Tian* wills.[10] However, as Van Norden has observed, understanding the *Mozi* as a divine command theory requires associating the *Mozi* with a particular metaphysical view of *Tian*—namely, one with a strong and definitive account of *Tian's* absolute transcendence from the world.[11] Actually, Van Norden is only partially correct here. He thinks that divine command theory requires simply a view of God as "radically transcending the world, and that the world is completely dependent on God for its creation and continued existence."[12] Divine command theory also requires a commitment to voluntarism, wherein will takes precedence over intellect. It may be true that the *Mozi* does not hold to a view of divine transcendence that can support a divine command theory account. However, it is very clear that the *Mozi* does not privilege the will over intellect or moral judgment in the way divine command theory requires.

For my purposes, the categorization of the *Mozi* as a consequentialist or divine command theory ethic are only important because they are indicators that underlying the Mohist account of *Tian* is a very different moral vision than what Aquinas holds. Ultimately, however, the various contrasts between Aquinas and Mozi— which are substantial and significant—do not preclude the possibility that there is much in the *Mozi* worthy of engagement and even

---

10. Rodney Taylor, "Religion and Utilitarianism: Mo Tzu on Spirits and Funerals," *Philosophy East and West* 29, no. 3 (1979): 337–46.

11. Van Norden, *Virtue Ethics and Consequentialism*, 149.

12. Van Norden, 149.

94   Chapter 2

approbation. But these general differences do suggest that uncovering and articulating the praiseworthy insights of the *Mozi* require a patient exegesis of the text's perspective, rather than a rush to judgment on apparent incommensurable perspectives.

THE MOHIST ACCOUNT OF
DIVINE WILL AND LOVE

As I discuss in the appendix to this volume, the *Mozi* contains several sequential chapters often called "triplets," each of which theoretically corresponds to a "core doctrine" of the Mohists. In this chapter, I will focus on one set of these triplets bearing the title "*Tian's* Will"; the chapters are entitled *Tianzhi shang, zhong, and xia* respectively (天志上, 天志中, 天志下), but are typically identified by their chapter numbers in modern editions of the *Mozi*, chapters 26–28. Most *Mozi* scholars believe that chapters 26–28 are among the youngest of the core chapters. Nicolas Standaert has argued that these chapters were likely written in response to criticisms from opponents which "boosted the need for an all-encompassing foundation" for their moral doctrines.[13] In this sense, it is appropriate to think of the Mohist view of *Tian* as a "core" tenet of the tradition. On the one hand, it was likely a very late development in the tradition, but on the other, it was probably developed precisely as a means of providing a foundational principle that gave coherence and authority to Mohist moral teachings.

Most likely, chapters 26–28 as we now have them come from different authors (or editors) and perhaps different views of *Tian's* intention. The strongest interpretation of these differences is the view of A. C. Graham, who holds that each chapter of the *Tianzhi* triplet reflects a different faction within Mohism, representing not only different but even opposed views. More recently, scholars have tended to see the chapters as written at different times as part of an ongoing tradition of Mohism, such that the triplet represents a series of emendations and clarifications within a tradition, rather than

---

13. Nicholas Standaert, "Heaven as a Standard," in *The Mozi as an Evolving Text: Different Voices in Early Chinese Thought*, ed. Carine Defoort and Nicholas Standaert (Leiden: Brill, 2013), 237.

A Thomistic Reading of the *Mozi* on Divine Will   95

divisive argumentation.[14] Most scholars believe that chapter 26 is the oldest of the triplet, though this does not necessarily mean it is to be taken as the "authentic" text written by Mozi himself. It is possible, much like the Q theory of biblical criticism, that each of the *Tianzhi* chapters were based on reported teachings of Mozi, or they may have just been produced by Mohist disciples to clarify *Mozi*'s position.

For my purposes, the authorship of the *Tianzhi* chapters and their dating is not as significant as it is for *Mozi* specialists. I do disagree with the faction theory of authorship; thus, I take chapters 26–28 to offer a coherent and complementary general Mohist view of *Tian*. Unlike many *Mozi* specialists, instead of focusing on the argument of each individual chapter, I will freely draw from each member of the triplet set in hopes of presenting a coherent view of *Tian*. My goal here is to present the logic of these chapters overall as one collated argument.

The argument of the *Tianzhi* chapters

Notably, the term *Tianzhi* which appears the title of these chapters does not appear often in the *Mozi* text. Even in chapters 26–28, the use of *Tianzhi* is rare; rather, the term *Tianyi* 天意 or *Tianzhiyi* 天之意 (both meaning *Tian*'s intention) are the primary terms used in these chapters. Ultimately, it is somewhat misleading to consider these chapters as concerned with *Tian*'s will if we expect by this a systematic analysis of the faculty of will or intention in *Tian*. In the *Mozi*, *Tian* is not the proper object of something like "theological science" but the foundational concept of a concrete moral vision. This is not to imply that *Tian* only serves a practical purpose of conforming to the Mohist moral perspective, but it is to observe that in terms of the text as a form of *scientia*, it is more oriented to moral than theological science.

The main proposition concerning *Tian* found in *Mozi* 26–28 is

---

14. See, e.g., Karen Desmet, "The Growth of Compounds in the Core Chapters of the *Mozi*," *Oriens Extremus* 45 (2005/2006): 99–118, esp. 99–105; Erik W. Maeder, "Some Observations on the Composition of the 'Core Chapters' of the *Mozi*," *Early China* 17 (1992): 27–82; and Defoort and Standaert, "Introduction: Different Voices in the *Mozi*: Studies of an Evolving Text," in *The Mozi as an Evolving Text*, 1–34.

96 Chapter 2

that *Tian* is the root of morality; the theological content of these chapters elucidates this proposition and the consequences following from it. In the opening passage of chapter 27, Mozi argues that if one desires to be righteous and benevolent (*yi* and *ren*), one cannot fail to examine the source of righteousness in particular (*suo cong chu* 所從出).[15] This observation initiates a deductive inquiry into the source of righteousness. Mozi first argues that righteousness must come from the "honorable and the wise" (*gui qie zhi zhe* 貴且知者) rather than the doltish and inferior. This is evident according to Mozi because righteousness is the "standard of excellence" (*shan zheng* 善政). Mozi does not explain why *yi* is such a standard; this is taken as self-evident in *Mozi* 27.[16] Rather, his point is that a clear standard of excellence must have its origins in what is deemed excellent rather than what we deem inferior. From this position, Mozi then asks what is to be the standard of excellence by posing the question, "Who is honorable? Who is wise?"[17] Though he does not use superlative terms, the context suggests Mozi means to ask, "who is *most* honorable and wise," and the answer he provides is *Tian*. Therefore, Mozi concludes that "righteousness is a product of *Tian*" (*yi guo zi Tian chu* 義果自天出).[18]

The *Mozi*'s argument can be syllogistically constructed as follows:

Major premise: Righteousness must come from a source of nobility and wisdom
Minor premise: *Tian* is exemplar of nobility and wisdom
Conclusion: Righteousness comes from *Tian*

In other words, *Tian* is the exemplar of the conditions (nobility and wisdom) necessary for righteousness to arise. Seemingly, the *Mozi*

15. *Mozi*, 27, 1.
16. It is notable that *yi* 義 does not appear at all in the *Fayi* 法儀 chapter of the *Mozi*, which focuses on the importance of standards or exemplars (*fa* 法) for governance and morality. The *Fayi* chapter does discuss *Tian* as a standard, but not *yi*. Standaert has theorized it is possible that the *Tianzhi zhong* is the last of the *Tianzhi* triplet to be composed, and that the *Fayi* was perhaps not among the last texts of the *Mozi* to be written (See Standaert, "Heaven as a Standard," 254–55). Thus, it is possible that the principle of *yi* as standard was meant to connect the *Tian* as standard argument with principles that Mohist opponents (notably, Confucians) would have found convincing.
17. *Mozi*, 27, 1. "然則孰為貴 孰為知"
18. Mozi, 27, 1.

A Thomistic Reading of the *Mozi* on Divine Will   97

implies that righteousness is the spontaneous fruit or result of *Tian's* "natural" (*ziran*) activity. As the term *ziran* means "immediate to the self," righteousness as a natural activity of *Tian* would mean that righteousness is how *Tian* acts. And so, *Tian* is the standard of righteousness in an exemplary way less than a source of mandate way.

It is key that the *Mozi* argues for the exemplarity of *Tian* because of the proposition that righteousness is rather self-evidently synonymous with good moral conduct. In chapter 26, Mozi argues that a standard must be passed from superiors to subordinates and thus the standard of righteousness prevailing among humanity must come from humanity's superior, *Tian*.[19] Significantly, the term the triplet uses as "standard" is *zheng* 政, which most often signifies a form of governance and rule. In this terminology, then, *Mozi's* argument makes good sense: righteousness is seen as moral excellence and human beings follow it just as they follow laws and practices instituted by their ruler. Thus, the standard of righteousness expresses the governance of the human superior and ruler, which can only be *Tian*. Again, Mozi does not mean that righteousness is the standard proclaimed by fiat or mandate of *Tian*, but rather that *Tian* is at least the formal cause of righteousness as the standard of conduct among human beings.

The key to this account of *Tian* as source of the standard of righteousness as exemplar lies in how the *Mozi* ascribes willing to *Tian*. The most general description of *Tian's* faculty of willing is the text's claim that there are things *Tian* desires (*yu*) and detests (*wu* 惡).[20] Crucially, the *Mozi* does not suggest that *Tian* desires things that increase its goodness or perfection since this is not a question the *Mozi* poses. Rather, "desire" functions here more as "approve" or "what *Tian* desires to see done." The *Mozi* makes a rather tautological move in linking *Tian's* desires with righteousness: "Be sure to do what *Tian* desires and avoid what *Tian* detests. How do we know what *Tian* desires and detests? *Tian* desires righteousness and hates unrighteousness. How do we know this? Because righteousness is the standard."[21]

19. *Mozi*, 26, 3
20. *Mozi*, 28, 2.
21. *Mozi*, 28, 2.

98 Chapter 2

If the *Mozi* stopped here, its account of *Tian*'s willing would be nearly impenetrable: *Tian* desires righteousness because it is the standard, and righteousness is the standard because *Tian* desires it. Some scholars have resolved this problem by arguing the *Mozi* ultimately possesses a divine command theory, which would lay stress on the second term of the tautology as the foundational one. However, it is not clear that the *Mozi* gives priority to this second term at all. Therefore, the best way forward is to analyze more closely what righteousness is in the *Mozi*, and then ascertain how it is related to *Tian*'s intention.

In *Mozi* 28, righteousness is defined in a consequentialist way: "when the world has righteousness it experiences order, and when it is without righteousness, it is in chaos."[22] Upon this view, "righteousness" functions as a collective term for the conditions that allow for general flourishing—that is, for the enjoyment of benefit (*li* 利) and the avoidance of disorder and chaos (*luan* 亂). Therefore, *Tian*'s intention is the exemplar (*fa* 法) of righteousness in the sense that *Tian* perpetually and reliably desires or intends the flourishing of all. Here we must consider *Mozi* 4 (entitled "*Fayi* 法儀") chapter which is often read in concert with the *Tianzhi* triplet. Both *Mozi* 4 and 26, cite a similarity between *Tian*'s intention and tools such as the carpenter's square or a wheelwright's compass.[23] As Standaert emphasizes, in the *Mozi* the standard is an objective measure for rectification. Whereas the carpenter's square is the *regula* for the art of cutting straight lines for joining wood, *Tian* is the objective measure of rectitude in the practices of morality and government. Thus, *Tian*'s intention provides an instrument for discernment of things or practices as good or bad, based on how they do or do not conform to the standard of intending mutual flourishing.[24]

For Mozi, the urgent question for human beings is whether we are willing and acting in accord with *Tian*'s intentions or not. But this raises the question of what kind of activities accord with this standard and exemplar, and thus constitute righteous morality in *Mozi*'s eyes? The *Mozi* describes how *Tian* intends or desires righteousness

22. *Mozi*, 28, 2. "天下有義則治, 無義則亂"
23. *Mozi*, 26, 7; *Mozi*, *Fayi*, 1.
24. See Standaert, "Heaven as a Standard," 264–69.

A Thomistic Reading of the *Mozi* on Divine Will   99

in two ways. First, the text provides concrete examples of things *Tian* desires—that is, what counts as righteous activity. Sometimes righteousness is described in religious acts such as ensuring the proper sacrifices to *Shangdi* and other various spirits and in seeking blessings from *Tian*.[25] Politically, the *Mozi* identifies what *Tian* despises as "when large states attack smaller for their own benefit, when a great family creates chaos for a lesser family, when the strong become tyrants over the weak, when the clever deceive the simple, and when the honorable are prideful over the lowly."[26] Ultimately, the fundamental rule or standard by which the *Mozi* judges what *Tian* desires is "loving and desiring to benefit others" (*ai ren li ren* 愛人利人).[27] Within this framework, what *Tian* desires is the flourishing of all, and thus virtuous human beings should have universal concern for all (*jian xiang ai* 兼相愛) and seek the mutual benefit of all (*jiao xiang li* 交相利).[28]

The *Mozi* therefore posits that fundamentally what *Tian* desires is the flourishing of all things and subsequently wills human beings to act with this concern for universal flourishing in mind. But why does the *Mozi* ascribe such a desire to *Tian*? The *Mozi* argues that *Tian* has a "great" or "substantial" (*hou* 厚) love for the people. As evidence for this, the *Mozi* first offers a cosmological argument: we know *Tian* loves the people because *Tian* has established the cosmos as it is, with celestial bodies to illumine and guide us, with seasons to follow, and forms of precipitation to nourish crops that humans might obtain and be enriched by the fruit of the earth.[29] *Tian*'s love and concern for human flourishing and benefit is apparent in the natural processes and resources that bring human beings flourishing and benefit. Significantly, Mozi emphasizes those natural processes and resources that are universal to human beings, though resources

---

25. *Mozi*, 26, 3. The belief in and service to spirits is a considerably important feature of the *Mozi* that heavily complicates naturalistic readings of the text. For a helpful example of scholars that attempts to assess the role of the spirits in *Mozi*'s thought, see Benjamin Wong and Hui-Chieh Loy, "War and Ghosts in Mozi's Political Philosophy," *Philosophy East and West* 54, no. 3 (July 2004): 343–63.

26. *Mozi*, 27, 3. "大國之攻小國也，大家之亂小家也，強之暴寡，詐之謀愚，貴之傲賤"

27. *Mozi*, 27, 8.

28. *Mozi*, 27, 8.

29. *Mozi*, 27, 6.

100 Chapter 2

can be stored, stolen, or managed in ways that allow only some to flourish and others not.

The *Mozi* also provides religious evidence that *Tian* loves humanity. In one passage, the text asks, "how do we know that *Tian* loves the various tribes of the empire?" The first answer is that *Tian* seeks to universally enlighten (*ming* 明) all, which is derived from the fact that *Tian* "possesses" (*you* 有) all the people universally. These claims may or may not be sharply distinct from the cosmological argument detailed above. W. P. Mei rendered *ming* as "teach," which would indicate distinction, but I argue this translation is too narrow.[30] *Ming* certainly does relate to intelligence and understanding, but its root meaning is illumination. As we saw above, the *Mozi* holds that the celestial bodies and seasons are guides of human activity, which does fall under a kind of illumination or enlightenment, but not "teaching" per se. That is, in early China, the movements of the cosmos were understood to clarify the nature of reality and how human beings fit into the cosmological picture. Consequently, *Tian*'s enlightenment of the people may simply be a circumlocution to describe how something like the natural law of the cosmos illumines our understanding. At the very least, that *Tian* "possesses" or "has" the people is consonant with the claim that *Tian* is the source of the things necessary for human flourishing, and that *Tian* desires human flourishing as part of the natural order.

However, the *Mozi* clearly departs from a purely natural order interpretation of *Tian*'s enlightenment and possession of the people when it cites a third piece of evidence that *Tian* loves all. Mozi argues such love is evident because *Tian* accepts sacrifices from all the people.[31] This argument offers that all the people clearly offer sacrifices to *Shangdi* and the spirits, and the text assumes *Tian* oversees and is pleased by this sacrificial economy. Put differently, the *Mozi* understands that the sacrifices made to *Shangdi*, the spirits, and presumably explicit sacrifices to *Tian* (which only rulers could offer) are part of human flourishing or benefit (*li*) that *Tian* desires.

A fourth and final way the *Mozi* says we can know that *Tian* loves

---

30. See ctext.org translation, taken from W. P. Mei, *The Ethical and Political Works of Motse* (London: Probsthain, 1929).

31. *Mozi*, 26, 5; *Mozi*, 28, 3.

A Thomistic Reading of the *Mozi* on Divine Will   101

humanity is because of *Tian*'s blessings and punishments. The *Mozi* posits that *Tian* loves all and works for the benefit of all, and thus is displeased when these ends are frustrated or neglected. Therefore, rulers who attempt to accrue "reward and fame" (*shang yu* 賞譽) from *Tian* by engaging in unrighteous activity (such as offensive wars against a weaker state) will not receive what he seeks but rather "severe punishment" (*zhu fa* 誅罰). Similarly, those who use unrighteous deeds to seek blessings and rewards from *Tian* will actually receive "calamity and evil" (*huo sui* 禍祟).[32]

At times, the *Mozi* describes *Tian*'s punishment of the wicked as a balm to the failures of justice exercised within human law. For example, the *Mozi* admits it is possible for a murderer of an innocent person to avoid legal recompense. This is especially true when an unrighteous act is committed by a ruler via a form of immoral war, which the Mohist tradition sees as graver than the unrighteousness of an individual's murder. Yet, the murderer cannot escape the judgment of *Tian*. For the rest of his life, the *Mozi* says, the unrighteous murderer will suffer misfortune (*bu xiang* 不祥) from *Tian*'s will in retribution for his unrighteous acts against the benefit and love of another human being.

Here we see that *Tian*'s intention is a standard of human life that can be rejected, but because it is the standard, such rejection brings consequences. According to the *Mozi*, *Tian* loves all human beings and desires our flourishing. In this way, the love and will of *Tian* is the foundation of moral righteousness: for a human to be righteous in the *Mozi* means to become an agent of this love and will of *Tian* to others. Therefore, humans face a fundamental choice vis-à-vis *Tian*'s will. We can choose to conform in harmony (*shun* 順) with *Tian*'s intention, or we can rebel against it (*fan* 反). Those who rebel will be treated by *Tian* as rebels, visited with "punitive war" (*zhu* 誅), usually taking the form of misfortune, sickness, and great calamities or suffering. Those who conform with *Tian* will be called "excellent" (*shan*) and will be praised by others not merely for being in accordance with *Tian*, but will bring about true order and benefit to all, allowing genuine flourishing to arise in the home and state.[33]

32. *Mozi*, 27, 4.
33. *Mozi*, 27, 8–9.

102   Chapter 2

A THOMISTIC ASSESSMENT OF THE
MOZI ON DIVINE WILL AND LOVE

Now that I have laid out the basic conception of divine will and love according to the *Mozi*, I turn to assess what in the *Mozi* can be appreciated, affirmed, or rejected from one working in the tradition of St. Thomas. There are three primary questions and one derivative question that a Thomistic perspective must consider and resolve in order to assess the content of the *Mozi* vis-à-vis divine will and love. They are as follows:

Is God's will in particular the source of moral standards for humanity?

Does God will the good of others and enjoin humans to will the same good?

Does God respond with punishment of those who fail or rebel against this standard?

Does God love all humanity?

In this schema, the enumerated questions are the primary areas of assessment. Question 2a derives from question 2, but requires its own analysis both because of its importance in the *Mozi* and the importance of divine judgment and punishment in the Catholic tradition. Therefore, in the remainder of this chapter, I will address these questions in order.

Divine Will as Source of Moral Standards

According to the *Mozi*, *Tian* is the exemplar of morality, primarily expressed through the concept of righteousness (*yi*). Assessing what Aquinas might make of this claim is challenging for many reasons, but chiefly due to the dissimilarity in concepts at work. Even if we make the decision to treat *Tian* and God as similar enough terms for comparison, the question is whether there is a Thomistic analog for *yi*. On the one hand, *yi* seems to accord with the Thomistic understanding of *iustitia*, the social virtue par excellence concerning giving to others what is due to them. However, Mozi also seems to use *yi* as a synecdoche for morally right actions in general—

A Thomistic Reading of the *Mozi* on Divine Will   103

that is, goodness itself. Thus, one could see the question in two ways: whether God is the exemplar of justice in particular or moral goodness in general.

A related issue concerns what the *Mozi* means by identifying *Tian*'s intention or will as the standard of righteousness. The terms describing the volitional faculty of *Tian* and human beings in the *Mozi* are not nearly as technically specific as those employed by Aquinas. "Intention" and "will" are indeed acts of the heart-mind power or organ (*xin*), but this power also performs intellectual acts in Chinese anthropology. Furthermore, unlike Aquinas who presses to define whether one can properly speak of a will in God (or intellect for that matter), the *Mozi* does not seek to establish a metaphysical ground in *Tian* for the act of willing or intending. That is, it is not clear that the *Mozi* sees *Tian* as possessing a *xin*, and therefore to what degree the act of willing and intending by *Tian* is a metaphor or a real predication.

Consequently, we may fruitfully observe that Aquinas might find the *Mozi* lacking in terms of the technical distinctions necessary to appropriately describe divine love and willing. However, Aquinas would also likely recognize that beyond this lack of theological specification in the *Mozi*, there are conceptions of the divine will and love worth engaging in this text. One of the more fruitful questions Aquinas might have seen in the *Mozi* regards the text's claim about *yi* in its most general sense of meaning "moral goodness itself." What would Aquinas make of the Mohist account that *Tian*'s will is the standard of moral goodness communicated to humanity?

From the Thomistic perspective, the claim that God is the standard of moral goodness is complicated to say the least.[34] On the one hand, Aquinas would certainly hold that God is certainly the exemplary cause of goodness in things because Aquinas defines goodness from being: calling a thing "good" is to claim both that it exists, and that it is desirable. As creatures, when we desire something, we do so because we find it capable of making us more perfect (e.g., food that allows us to sustain our lives, or wealth to allow us to procure goods

---

34. See Andrew J. Dell'Olio, *Foundations of Moral Selfhood: Aquinas on Divine Goodness and the Connection of the Virtues* (New York: Peter Lang, 2003).

104 Chapter 2

more easily and of higher quality). This conception of the good in terms of the perfection of being is dependent upon God as the exemplary cause, for God alone is truly good in the sense of having all perfections of his being pure act (see *ST* Ia, q. 6, art. 3) and by virtue of his being the cause of all other goodness such that all things bear a similitude to the divine goodness.[35]

In this sense, God is the exemplar and cause of all goodness, but does this entail the more specific idea that the divine will is the source of moral goodness?[36] We can grasp the complexity of this question from the moral anthropology of the *Prima secundae*. Aquinas says that human moral action is ordered to happiness. As creatures, humans seek goods that we do not yet possess and which will make us happy, ultimately union with God. Inasmuch as moral goodness for human beings involves seeking the unpossessed good (God) that makes us happy, it would seem that God cannot be the exemplar of moral goodness. For that would suggest God is not happy, and therefore is in motion (contradicting the notion that God is pure act) and moreover, that God has a higher good than himself that he desires to obtain (contradicting the notion that God is the *summum bonum*). For Aquinas, although morally good creatures, in their pursuit of happiness, aim to acquire goods not yet possessed, the pursuit of happiness by itself does not necessarily entail their moral goodness.Rather, for Aquinas the possession of the virtues is the true definition of moral goodness. The possession of virtue is what enables us to know and act rightly for the goods we seek. God possesses moral perfections without having to employ them for the sake of an extrinsic, unattained end.

35. *ST* Ia, q. 6, art. 4. Here, Aquinas emphasizes that the goodness of creatures is not *merely* participated goodness (as Plato would have concluded), but it is a real goodness inhering in creatures and possessed by them because they exist in substantial forms (i.e., they exist as such and have been actualized in having being, thus their existence which is their own is convertible with their goodness, which must be attributable to them and not solely through participation.

36. In modern Thomistic scholarship, much attention has been given to the issue of God's causative knowledge, and the problems some modern philosophers espy in this account. The very language of the controversy, i.e., that it concerns God's causative *knowledge* testifies to the complications of attributing God's exemplarity of goodness to an act of will *simpliciter*. See Eleonore Stump, *Aquinas* (London: Routledge, 2003), 159–87, esp. 178–82; Leo Elders, *The Philosophical Theology of St. Thomas Aquinas* (Leiden: Brill, 1990), 234–40; and John Wippel, *Metaphysical Themes in Thomas Aquinas* (Washington, DC: The Catholic University of America Press, 1984), 243–63, esp. 255–63.

A Thomistic Reading of the *Mozi* on Divine Will   105

Based on this observation, what Aquinas would make of the Mohist position that *Tian's* will is the standard of righteousness in the world? In his discussion of divine will, Aquinas first deals with the question of whether God is will (i.e., whether *voluntas* can be predicated of God as an essential attribute). The first objection in the first question of this article is instructive. This objection contends there is no will in God because, "the object of the will is the end and the good. But some other end is not to be assigned to God."[37] According to the logic of this argument, the whole purpose of the will is appetible: to move us toward that which is desirable and perfective. It is clear from *ST* Ia, q. 6, that God is the most proper appetible object, and so our wills are ordered toward God. But if God is the highest good and is the end of all other things, what need is there for him to have a will? In fact, suggesting that God has a will suggests God is not the highest good or end, for if he has a will, he must use this faculty in an appetible fashion. So, according to the terms of the objection, God cannot have a will.

In response, Aquinas argues that if there is intellect in God (which he has previously shown), then there must be will in God, for the intelligible form involves a volitional aspect.[38] The key is that Aquinas says there are two distinct functions of the will inasmuch as things tend toward their natural forms. On the one hand, the will seeks to possess goods that are not possessed that fulfill the form of the thing. On the other hand, the will is able to rest when the goods sought are possessed.[39] Consequently, within the divine will only the latter is predicable: God's will rests in what is possessed, and does not seek to possess more perfection than he has. As Aquinas puts is in one of his replies, God always has the good which is the object of his will, because the good is not distinct from his own essence. Thus, God always wills and possesses the good as he wills and possesses himself.

---

37. *ST* Ia, q. 19, art. 1, obj. 1.

38. Aquinas discusses intellect in God in *ST* Ia, q. 14, art. 1, in the language of God's having an intelligent form. For an important study of the divine will that articulates traditional loci of concern in the Thomistic tradition on this topic, see Harm J M J Goris, *Free Creatures of an Eternal God: Thomas Aquinas on God's Infallible Foreknowledge and Irresistible Will* (Leuven: Peeters, 1997).

39. *ST* Ia, q. 19, art. 1, corp.

In this sense, there is a fundamental similitude between the divine will and human morality. Human morality is seeking the good, and things are good inasmuch as they participate in the form of goodness that is exemplary in God. Moreover, human morality is aimed to the perfection of our rational form and possession of the highest good which is God. But God already performs the perfection of this moral act as his being: he is the perfect moral life because he loves and possesses the highest good in the most perfect manner. Therefore, there is also a fundamental dissimilitude between the human will's orientation to the good in this life and the divine will. God wills the good that is convertible with himself which he eternally possesses and cannot lose, whereas humans will the good as something we do not have and indeed cannot perfectly gain by our own power.

In the *Mozi*, it is not clear that *Tian* constitutes the highest good of the human appetite. Therefore, *Tian*'s desire for humans to be moral seems propositionally equal to the good that humans should will since both *Tian* and moral humans will a state of affairs in the world. Here we can see why those scholars who question whether Mohism is a divine command theory ethics have a point. For the *Mozi* seems to define the good (or righteousness) in an objective sense that governs even *Tian*'s will but is not grounded in *Tian* itself as the source of the good *Tian* wills. At most, the *Mozi* sees *Tian* as willing a good state of affairs immediately and spontaneously without fail. In contrast, because Aquinas understands goodness as convertible with being—and because God alone is the self-subsistent act of being—even the "objective" definition of the good applicable to God and creatures is founded upon God in an exemplary and dissimilar way than it is for creatures, who live out the real distinction between existence and essence.

From this, one can see that in broad terms, Aquinas can agree with Mozi that the divine will is the standard of moral rectitude. However, equating *yi* and *bonum* eventually becomes problematic. For Aquinas, divine goodness depends upon a subtle account of ontology and morality—God's self-subsistent act of being not only governs what it means to think of God's "morality" but also the appetible good itself. The *Mozi* on the contrary takes no great pains to clarify how *Tian* is the source of righteousness—it is enough that *Tian* wills righteousness in an exemplary way.

In this sense, the *Mozi* sees *Tian* as moral exemplar in that *Tian* wills what is good or righteous (*yi*). But, according to the *Mozi*, the only description of the *yi* that *Tian* wills is a temporal order of *yi* that may or may not obtain. Consequently, *Tian* wills a state of affairs that humans can successfully undermine, meaning that *Tian* does not possess what it wills. In contrast, Aquinas understands God's will as the exemplary cause of the moral good because moral goodness imitates God's loving the good which he is, and God's possession of the ultimate end, which is God himself. Certainly, Aquinas would agree that God wills a just state of affairs as part of the enactment of human flourishing, but God does not will this state of affairs as *the* good (which is God's self), but as the structure of human acts whereby we are given freedom to know, love, and pursue the good of union with God.

Therefore, Christian theological science can appreciate much of the *Mozi*'s account of *Tian*'s will, but there is a profound difference between the conception of divine will found in this text and that in Catholic theological science. Notably, the Mohist *Tian* is not necessarily opposed to the kind of ontology and morality framework one finds in Aquinas. The doctrine of *Tian*'s will in the *Mozi* appears to be capable of development to include an ontological foundation of righteousness that would furnish a more accurate conception of divine will from the view of Christian theology. Because the *Mozi* sees righteousness as tied to benefit or flourishing, there is already a way in which the moral good is indeed grounded in being—that which is righteous is that which sustains and facilitates being. Consequently, it seems possible to develop a Christian-Mohist account of *Tian*'s willing *yi* in a way that accounts for the dissimilitude between divine and human will and produces an account of God's perfect possession of himself as the standard of righteousness. Indeed, such an account might prove quite fruitful beyond the translation of Christian conceptions of the divine will into Chinese philosophical categories, and genuinely expand our understanding of this doctrine.

108   Chapter 2

Does God Will the Good of Human Beings?

One of the clearest foundational principles of the *Mozi* is that *Tian* desires the flourishing or benefit (*li*) of all human beings. In this regard, the *Mozi* broadly agrees with the principle of Catholic theological science that God loves the world. But how deep does this agreement go? Where are the inevitable points upon which the *Mozi* and Catholic theological science diverge about the divine love and will for creatures?

Answering this question requires dealing with two distinct but related questions from the perspective of Aquinas's thought: 1) does God will the good for others (outside of himself)? 2) Does God will the good for all? In the broad sense, of course, the first question is rather straightforward. After all, Aquinas recognizes the entire framework of Christian theology is ultimately dependent on accepting at least some sense in which God wills the good outside himself since the act of the Incarnation is done by God on our behalf, not his own (Jn 3:16). But in its details, it is tricky to explain how God genuinely loves and wills the good for things outside himself.

Leo J. Elders has helpfully noted that in neither Aristotle nor Plotinus is it said that God's will can be directed to imperfect beings outside of God's self.[40] In the eyes of the Greek philosophers, such a claim would impute an imperfection to God. What is the source of this difficulty? Aquinas holds that the will is ordered toward the good that is either possessed or desired. Since God is perfect goodness in himself, God wills himself first and foremost as the good that is possessed. Consequently, it does not seem that God can will anything outside of himself since nothing outside of him can be the highest good, toward which his perfect will must be directed.

Aquinas's explanation of how God wills himself *and* other things is to say that God wills himself as the end of created things.[41] In the

---

40. Elders, *The Philosophical Theology of St. Thomas Aquinas*, 251.

41. This touches inevitably upon the thorny issue of the natural desire for God in Aquinas. There is no space here to adjudicate this issue which has dominated much of contemporary Thomist thought. For treatments, see the following: Serge-Thomas Bonino, ed., *Surnaturel: A Controversy at the Heart of Twentieth-century Thomistic Thought*, trans. Robert Williams, rev. trans. Matthew Levering (Ave Maria, FL: Sapientia Press of Ave Maria University, 2009); Lawrence Feingold, *The Natural Desire to See God according to St. Thomas Aquinas and His*

A Thomistic Reading of the *Mozi* on Divine Will   109

Summa Contra Gentiles, he argues that God wills that all things desire him as the highest good. But because the divine essence cannot be multiplied, God also wills the good of things that bear a likeness to him, inasmuch as they possess wills ordered toward the good.[42] Aquinas further explains that God loves all things because they participate in him, and thus he loves himself in all things. But, for my purposes here, I wish to emphasize that Aquinas says God wills the good of non-divine things because they bear a *similitude* to God.

We see then that for Aquinas, God's willing good of things outside of himself means that God wills that other things will the good themselves. That is, Aquinas affirms that all things distinct from God, such as human beings, are genuine agents who live in pursuit of the highest good, which is God. It is helpful here to mention Aquinas's disagreement with Peter Lombard on the nature of charity. Lombard had deemed charity to be the presence of the Holy Spirit within the Christian. For Aquinas, this is incorrect because there must be a way in which charity becomes a habit through which the human subject acts. Under Lombard's position the Holy Spirit is the agent of charity for all, rather than human agents, and consequently no human being could be properly said to perform the act of charity. Additionally, Lombard's position would mean that God would become the form of a human being, which is impossible. And so instead, Aquinas argues that the Holy Spirit infuses the soul with the habit of charity such that the grace of the Spirit enables the human person to be the genuine agent of charity.[43]

In the same vein, for Aquinas God wills creatures to possess the good formally so that they are genuine possessors of the powers of understanding, desiring, and pursuing the good, and therefore genuine agents who seek and enact the good. Even in the formal sense

---

Interpreters (Ave Maria, FL: Sapientia Press of Ave Maria University, 2010); and Jacob Wood, *To Stir a Restless Heart: Thomas Aquinas and Henri de Lubac on Nature, Grace, and the Desire for God* (Washington, DC: The Catholic University of America Press, 2019).

42. SCG I.75. See also John Wippel, "Thomas Aquinas on the Axiom Our Knowledge of God and the Axiom That Every Agent Produces Something Like Itself," in *Metaphysical Themes in Thomas Aquinas II,* 152–71.

43. See Geerjtan Zuijdwegt, "'*Utrum Caritas Sit Aliquid Creatum in Anima*': Aquinas on the Lombard's Identification of Charity with the Holy Spirit," *Recherches de théologie et philosophie médiévales* 79, no. 1 (2012): 39–74.

of God's willing his creatures to be good, he wills that *we* possess goodness for ourselves—that is, for the sake of the integrity of our being. Importantly, the Thomistic view is that God wills this possession of volitional agency on the part of creatures as part of the same act by which he wills himself.[44] There is no other act of will in God for Aquinas because God's act of will must be non-composite. This is significant because God's willing the good of things outside of him is inherently ordered toward God as the good he wills all things to participate in.

In making this connection explicit, Aquinas introduces a second conception of divine goodness. On the one hand, God rests in the goodness he possesses (i.e., himself) and in this way is said to be good. Additionally, Aquinas says that the appetitive faculty of natural things is inclined to the good not only to obtain and possess it, but also to "diffuse their own proper good in other things, according to how it is possible for them."[45] In other words, it is "rule of the will" (*rationem voluntatis*) to communicate to others the good possessed in the thing willing the good. And so, Aquinas concludes, God not only possesses himself as the perfect good and rests in that goodness, but God also diffuses this goodness to other things, specifically by willing himself as the proper end of things.[46]

Aquinas adds that God's will is an efficient cause of all things.[47] This is important for two reasons. First, because Aquinas notes that God gives things being as something that God wills—in other words, God wills that we come into being, and thus wills us experience this most basic good: life itself. Second, God as first cause wills other things to be because of his own goodness, which is diffused and communicated to other things.

With this, Aquinas shows that God does indeed will his creatures' good in two ways. First, he wills them to imitate him in actuality, and thus he creates and gives them life. Second, God diffuses his goodness such that all things are inclined to God as their proper

---

44. *SCG* I.76.
45. *ST* Ia, q. 19, art. 2, corp.: "sed etiam ut proprium bonum in alia diffundat, secundum quod possibile est."
46. *ST* Ia, q. 19, art. 2, corp.
47. *ST* Ia, q. 19, art. 4, corp.

end. From this perspective, Aquinas can agree with Mozi on a general, yet very important level. God does indeed will the good of others by willing them to exist. For Mozi, the fact that the world enables human existence seemed proof of *Tian*'s will and care for all people. For Aquinas, the fact that the world exists at all is proof of God's willing there to be goodness outside of himself. Mozi, of course, does not have a conception that *Tian* wills goodness for others as it wills goodness itself.

Another aspect of *Mozi*'s view of *Tian*'s will is that it is connected to the virtue of *yi*, which, in the *Mozi*, is clearly analogous to giving others what they are due (*suum cuique*). Thus, the question "does God will the goodness of others" can be specified a bit more as "does God will justice toward others"? Aquinas undoubtedly holds that God wills that human beings be just to one another as part of the virtuous moral life inclined toward attaining God as the ultimate good. But is this based on something within God?

Aquinas explicitly discusses whether there is justice in God in *ST* Ia, q. 21, art. 1. In this article, Aquinas distinguishes between commutative and distributive justice. Commutative justice is based in economic terms and is related to paying debts or what is owed to others. Aquinas denies that this kind of justice can be found in God, for God is in debt to no one—as Creator, God is the ground of possibility for all things to be at all and needs nothing from us in a strict sense. On the other hand, distributive justice is defined as when "some governor or steward gives to each one [of his subordinates] according to their dignity."[48]

According to Aquinas, this kind of justice is found in God, because as Creator, God inclines and orders the things he makes. In the reply to objection 3 of the same article, Aquinas clearly explains how the creating God is just in a distributive sense, arguing for two distinct modes of his justice. First, God gives himself what he is due—namely, "that there should be in things what his wisdom and will have for them, and that his good be manifested."[49] In this mode of justice, it is owed to God (*debitum enim est Deo*) that things

---

48. *ST* Ia, q. 21, art. 1, corp.
49. *ST* Ia, q. 21, art. 1, ad 3.

112 Chapter 2

exist as he created them to be, and by virtue of their existence and inclination to goodness in diverse modes, these things then manifest the goodness that has been diffused from the divine goodness into them. The second mode of justice is what God "owes" to created things, which is "that they possess that which is ordered to them" (*quod habeat id quod ad ipsam ordinatur*).[50] As an example of what he means, Aquinas cites when human beings have hands. This means that for Aquinas, because God has willed his creatures to exist in particular forms (through his wisdom and self-diffusing goodness), the creatures created are "owed" the integrity of that created form—that is, they are owed the form of existence of the thing they are created to be. But, because what creatures are owed rests upon the divine will and wisdom, God cannot be their debtor. As Aquinas puts it, God cannot owe a debt to creatures because "he is not ordained to other things, but rather, they are ordered to him."[51] And so, in this respect, God's justice and goodness are convertible, though not in every respect.

Significantly, it is now clear that Aquinas's account of God's will for things outside of God has some stark and fundamental differences from what we find in the *Mozi*. For one, the *Mozi* does not evince any concern to elucidate either a robust conception of *Tian*'s perfections (though it seems to assume *Tian*'s nobility), or how such perfections would become an intellectual problem regarding how *Tian* wills for the world. The *Mozi* does not find it necessary to prove how a simple God who wills can make sense (as Aquinas does); rather, the text simply assume *Tian* wills for the world as a primary act. Moreover, the *Mozi* has no account of *Tian* willing itself, or more broadly of *Tian* as identifiable with the good. Consequently, Aquinas might readily conclude the *Mozi* fails to adequately address both divine perfections and their logical consequences in its account of divine love for the world.

More formally, Aquinas holds that God's willing material goods for material creatures is subordinate to his willing their good as the possession of God's self. For the *Mozi*, *Tian*'s will is most manifest in

50. *ST* Ia, q. 21, art. 1, ad 3.
51. *ST* Ia, q. 21, art. 1, ad 3.

A Thomistic Reading of the *Mozi* on Divine Will   113

the desire for material benefit for all creatures. In what sense, then, is the benevolence of *Tian* the same as the benevolence of the God of revelation? For God's will is manifest not only in a kind of governance of the cosmos, but in the ordering of the cosmos to himself. Specifically, the highest human good is for Aquinas decidedly *not* the benefit and flourishing in a material or even natural sense, but in the supernatural elevation of human beings to union with God. In this sense there is a tremendous disparity between what Aquinas and Mozi mean by the claim that God/*Tian* loves human beings. Although Aquinas holds that God does indeed will the material and social flourishing of things other than himself, but such willing is subordinate and found within the more fundamental idea that God wills himself as the good that all other things seek. Seeking God as the ultimate good includes and requires (to some extent) the natural flourishing of things including material and social needs. But God wills creaturely happiness in an instrumental sense, inasmuch as this happiness is ordered toward the possession of God as the ultimate good and final happiness.

Despite these serious points of disagreement, there are substantial points of agreement between Aquinas and the *Mozi* in the details of divine love, if not in the primary conception of divine love. Aquinas might justly argue the *Mozi* fails to develop an adequate theology of divine perfections, but this is not surprising given that the *Mozi* is not geared toward a theology as such but a moral account. By and large, Aquinas would likely applaud the Mohist claim that *Tian* is concerned for and wills the flourishing of creatures. Since many pagan philosophers would have had trouble concluding God loves the world, the Mohist convictions about *Tian* might even suggest the text has an instinctual insight into the truth about God. Thus, Aquinas might conclude the Mohists ideas about God's love were largely poignant, even if also recognizing they require a more adequate theological science to complete them.

Does God Love All?

The previous section demonstrated Aquinas can agree with Mozi God clearly wills the good of all things, though in a different way, namely inasmuch as they exist at all and inasmuch as they are ordained to him as their end. Additionally, God wills that all things he creates be given what they are "owed" by virtue of their created existence: whatever is befitting their existence in a particular created form. In this sense, God clearly wills or desires that creatures flourish. Here we must recognize that for humans in particular, God wills himself as our proper end, meaning he wills that he himself makes us happy. And this means in Aquinas's account that God wills what makes us happy, and wills that we be made happy by ordering us to this happiness. Most other goods we find and desire along the way toward our true happiness in God are not accidental but instrumental in this path to happiness. The human desires for food, wealth, and sex are all natural inclinations to seek and obtain something good that can a) sustain us on the path to seeking true happiness, or b) allow us to exercise the virtues necessary to reach happiness appropriate to this life (i.e., seeking holiness and self-giving love in likeness to God).

With this in mind, I would like to explore the question of whether Aquinas can agree with a further position of the *Mozi*, which holds that *Tian* loves all human beings. We saw above that according to the *Mozi*, *Tian*'s love for all is meant to justify the Mohist emphasis on care for all, neatly encapsulated in the phrase *jian ai* 兼愛. Since I discuss *jian ai* on its own in chapter 5, here I only wish to call attention to one specific complication of the term *jian ai*. It is unclear to what degree the *Mozi* understands *jian ai* to describe a certain scope of affection (i.e., the universality of love) or degree of love (e.g., some form of equal regard). The *Mengzi* contains an explanation of Mohist doctrine which seems to identity *jian ai* with "love without degrees of rank" (*ai wu chadeng* 愛無差等).[52] If this is an accurate representation of Mohist thought, it would suggest that *Tian* also loves all humanity at least "without degrees of rank"— that is, equally.

In the *Tianzhi* chapters, there is some confirmation for this view. These chapters clearly refer to those who care for others with "partiality" (*bie* 別) as contradicting *Tian*'s intention. Additionally, it is

---

52. *Mengzi*, 3A:5.

A Thomistic Reading of the *Mozi* on Divine Will   115

evident that the *Mozi* refers to *Tian*'s ordering of the cosmos for human flourishing as a sign of *Tian*'s love for humanity, which involves not only a universal but also equal quality of love (i.e., *Tian* genuinely wants all humans to flourish and have sufficient access to such goods in order to flourish). At the same time, however, the *Mozi* ascribes punishment and retribution to *Tian*. In this sense, *Tian* does not love, but rather seems to hate the wrongdoer who subverts or rebels against *Tian*'s primary intention to will the good of all equally.

So then, the question the *Mozi* seems to put to Aquinas is this: In what way can it be said that God loves all? Does God love all things outside himself, especially humans, universally? Does he love them equally, and if so in what sense? How is God's love related to God's use of punishment? Each of these questions might justify their own chapter, but I will attempt to give a sketch of how I think Aquinas might respond to these concerns.

Does God respond with punishment to those who fail or rebel against this standard?

A major premise of the *Mozi* is that *Tian* not only wills the good of humanity, but also *Tian* wills the punishment of those who obstruct the good of others in the name of self-interest. Does Aquinas also conceive of God punishing humanity for falling short of the standard of moral goodness God establishes for humankind?

We must begin with Aquinas's discussion of whether God wills evil.[53] Going back to St. Augustine, evil (*malum*) had been defined negatively, as the privation of good rather than something positive in itself. This is significant because the will is an appetitive power inclined toward the good, and evil is the negation of good. Hence, Aquinas holds it is impossible for any kind of thing has a genuine appetite for evil; nothing wills evil for its own sake. However, Aquinas argues, evil is often related to goods accidentally in the mode of accompaniment.[54] Accidental evil is a privation of some good, but as part of another good that is desired. He uses the example of a lion desiring food (the good), which can only be secured through killing

---

53. For an extensive study of Aquinas on the problem of evil with regard to God, see Brian Davies, *Thomas Aquinas on God and Evil* (New York: Oxford University Press, 2011).

54. *ST* Ia, q. 19, art. 9, corp.

116   Chapter 2

another animal (the evil). What is key, though, is that Aquinas argues that we only will accidental evils when the good we seek is a greater good than the good lost in the accidental evil.

Applying this to the divine will, Aquinas concludes that God does not will evil because he wills his own good and wills this good to others. However, because God wills his good for rational creatures endowed with their own free will, this can involve accidental evil. Aquinas's explicit example is that God wills punishment. On the one hand, God does not will the evil of sin which then bears the recompense of punishment. On the other hand, God wills what is just, and thus in his willing what is just he also wills that those who act unjustly are punished according to the standard of justice.[55]

In this example, we see that for Aquinas, God does not desire punishment. Indeed, punishment itself is strictly speaking an evil because it is not conducive to good of the one punished. To use an example from parenting: my children do not flourish when they are in time-out or made to cry from shame at a misdeed. Punishment becomes conducive to flourishing when it is applied by a prudent parent as a means of clarifying moral evil and encouraging good, flourishing behavior. Consequently, we punish our children as part of willing them good and flourishing, but the punishment itself is an accidental evil that we will to happen inasmuch as we hope to correct them when they stray from this path of flourishing. So it is with God, who does not will punishment itself as if this were a good, but wills the greater good of justice, which is a mode of true flourishing. Those who are unjust toward God or others are not flourishing, and hence God wills punishment to preserve the good of justice.

In this formulation, Aquinas explicitly affirms that God does punish, precisely as a means of just and upholding justice. But what is the nature of God's punishment? The *Mozi* sees *Tian*'s punishment as an active work of *Tian* to bring misfortune and maladies upon evildoers. Would Aquinas agree that God punishes in these ways?

For this question, it is apt to turn to Aquinas's *Commentary on Job*.[56] One of the primary themes of *Job* is the suffering of the righ-

---

55. *ST* Ia, q. 19, art. 9, corp.

56. For a recent publication exploring Aquinas's commentary on Job, see Levering, Roszak, and Vijgen, *Reading Job with St. Thomas Aquinas*. See also John P. Yocum, "Aquinas'

A Thomistic Reading of the *Mozi* on Divine Will   117

teous man.[57] In his commentary, Aquinas makes two pertinent points about divine punishment. First, he argues that God allows higher goods to order lower goods, and thus angels are part of the causal structure of punishment and reward. However, Aquinas says that God "punishes wicked men through both good and wicked angels, but he never induces good men to adversity except through wicked angels."[58] At the same time, Aquinas wants to argue in the commentary that the association of divine punishment with temporal punishment is problematic. As Aquinas sees it, each of Job's friends erroneously believe that God rewards the good with earthly prosperity (*prosperitate terrena*) and punishes the wicked with temporal adversity.[59] According to Aquinas, one of the main themes of the book is Job's conviction (with which Aquinas agrees) that "the good works of man are ordered to a future spiritual reward that comes after this life, and likewise that sinful works will be punished by future punishments."[60]

Of course, the Christian tradition cannot avoid the conclusion that God does visit evil doers with misfortune and calamity. The destruction of Sodom, the Exile, and the punishment of Ananias and Sapphira in *Acts* 5 illustrate that God can delivered temporal punishment for wickedness. I do not think Aquinas wishes to overlook these experiences due to a squeamishness about the "supernatural" explanations of these events. Rather, he is emphasizing that the true orientation of goodness and wickedness in humanity is either toward or away from our proper end. Therefore, the justice of God in distributing reward and punishment is most fittingly understood in terms of God's judgment of the soul after death, rather than during this earthly toil when conversion and reclamation are still possible for human beings.

Literal Exposition on Job," in *Aquinas on Scripture: An Introduction to His Biblical Commentaries*, ed. Thomas G. Weinandy, Daniel A. Keating, and John P. Yocum (London: T&T Clark, 2005), 21–42.

57. See Goris, "Sin and Human Suffering in Aquinas's *Commentary on Job*," in Levering et al., *Reading Job with St. Thomas Aquinas*, 161–84; and Joseph P. Wawrykow, "Human Suffering and Merit," in *Reading Job with St. Thomas Aquinas*, 220–60.

58. Aquinas, *Expositio super Iob ad Litteram*, 1.2

59. *Expositio super Iob*, 2.2

60. *Commentary on Job*, 2.2: "Sed [Iob] credebat bona opera hominum ordinari ad remunerationem spiritualem futuram post hanc vitam, et similiter peccata futuris suppliciis esse punienda."

118   Chapter 2

Aquinas discusses God's punishment in a more systematic way in the *Summa Contra Gentiles*. Aquinas holds that it is fitting that God punishes because punishment falls to those who make the laws, and God is the giver of law to humanity. Particularly pertinent to the theme of punishment is the divine law that human beings have our proper and supernatural end—we are ordered toward union with God. Because of the fact we are inclined or ordered toward this end, this means that those who live in accordance with this final good will receive it as a reward, and those who by sin depart from it will be cut off from the good as punishment.[61]

Such ultimate punishment is the "greatest" (*maxima*) punishment possible, and thus truly merits the name of punishment when considering the divine justice. However, in the *Summa Contra Gentiles*, Aquinas offers more description of the variety of punishments God allows, including temporal punishment. For Aquinas, it is not as simple as saying God visits calamity upon evildoers. Rather, he says that God knows that external goods are only in service of internal goods. And hence, there are times at which God provides and times at which he removes certain external goods from human beings. But either movement can be for the benefit of the virtuous person, either by providing needed goods to help his virtue, or removing goods that prove obstacles to his virtue. Similarly, it may be that God punishes a wicked person by providing more external goods, since that person will be incited to evil.[62]

Ultimately, God's punishment of human beings is commensurate with God's love since his love is expressed in the good he has willed for human beings. That is, God's willing himself as the highest good for all things naturally involves the justice of punishments that induce sinners or others to the kind of virtue leading to happiness. Both Aquinas and the *Mozi* would seem to agree, then, that God's justice is not opposed to God's love (or in tension with it), but a feature of that love that truly cares for creatures. However, this proposition only deals with part of the issue as it stands in Christian theology, and therefore we must deal with a supplemental problem.

61. *SCG* III.140.2–3.
62. *SCG* III.141.6.

Does God Love All Humanity?

The foregoing discussion on the relationship between punishment and love evokes an important tension in Christian theology. For the *Mozi*, *Tian*'s love of humanity is seen in the ordering of the world's natural resources towards the flourishing of all humans in equal measure. But in Christianity, God's love is seen not only in provision of goods for flourishing, but in the extension of salvation to lift humans from mere natural happiness into a supernatural happiness that is only possible because of the unmerited grace of God. Throughout Christian history, this has led to the scandal of particularity because God dispenses grace to some, persisting even when they are recalcitrant to heed his law and love (as Augustine would say about himself), and does not do the same for others. Does not God, therefore, love some sinners more than others? In the Old Testament, there is a struggle for readers to understand why God loves and elects unfaithful Israel rather than the Amalekites, whom God commands Saul to destroy, men, women, children, and livestock (1 Sm 15). In the Church, the scandal of particularity primarily concerns God's electing love which, ostensibly, reaches out to save some from the fires of hell, while allowing others to suffer eternal damnation, which all deserve, but to which not all are condemned.[63]

This naturally raises the question of whether God loves *all* his creatures or only some of them. Since this question becomes infinitely more complicated when considering non-human animals and angelic beings, I will limit my discussion here to asking whether Aquinas would say God loves all human beings, and if so, in what ways might he qualify this claim? The first step in answering this question is to prove there is love in God at all, which Aquinas does in ways I have just suggested.[64] If God has a will, there must be love

---

63. The question of limited or universal salvation is a thorny topic in Christian history that is increasingly contentious in contemporary theology. See, e.g., David Bentley Hart, *That All Shall Be Saved: Heaven, Hell, and Universal Salvation* (New Haven, CT: Yale University Press, 2019).

64. For a fuller account of God's love for the world in Aquinas, see Michael Dodds, *The Unchanging God of Love: Thomas Aquinas and Contemporary Theology on Divine Immutability* (Washington, DC: The Catholic University of America Press, 2008); and Anthony T. Flood,

in God because "the first movement of the will and of whatever appetitive power is love."[65] The will inclines to the good and desires it in the mode of love, and hence to desire to obtain or to rest in an obtained good (as God does the latter) is an act of love per se. Again, we must remember that being and goodness are convertible for Aquinas: something is good because it exists, and that it is seen as desirable or lovable. Hence, the will loves in its first act of recognizing being as lovely.

So, Aquinas concludes God does love, but God knows the good as he knows himself. Does God therefore really love things apart from himself? This is a trickier problem than we might initially think. Aquinas provides four objections to the claim that God loves all things. Two of these objections suggest that saying God loves anything apart from himself would deny some divine perfections. The first objection argues from Pseudo-Dionysius that loving involves passing into the other, which would mean God is "placed outside of himself and transferred to others" (*extra se positus, in alia transferatur*).[66] The second objection holds that if love is in God it must be eternal as God is, and thus God cannot love creatures who do not exist from eternity except as he loves them in himself. The catch for the objection is that if God loves things because they participate in himself, he is really loving himself in things and not the things per se.[67]

We can summarize these concerns as follows: it seems the conditions allowing the possibility that God loves things apart from himself cannot exist in God if he is God. For God can rest in himself in perfect simplicity, eternity, and rest. But love *ad alia* ("to the other") requires movement, desire, and the reality of the beloved. How can God truly love creatures and still be God? At best, it seems one could say that God loves things because they participate in him. But, is this really love of all things themselves, or does it mean God simply loves himself as we reflect his goodness? That is, is it that God alone

---

The Metaphysical Foundations of Love: Aquinas on Participation, Unity, and Union (Washington, DC: The Catholic University of America Press, 2018).

65. *ST* Ia, q. 20, art. 1.

66. *ST* Ia, q. 20, art. 2, obj. 1.

67. *ST* Ia, q. 20, art. 2, obj. 2.

A Thomistic Reading of the *Mozi* on Divine Will   121

is his own beloved, such that creatures are loved as instruments (i.e., as mirrors)? On the one hand, God's love of self must be a perfect form of self-love and not morally disordered narcissism since he is that which ought to be loved more than anything else. However, this does not remove the problem of how it is true that all things can be God's beloved in a genuine and not purely instrumental way.

How does Aquinas resolve this problem? We must recall that Aquinas argues earlier in the *ST* that God's goodness is the cause of goodness in all things so that the things caused by divine goodness genuinely possess goodness in themselves.[68] That is, the goodness of my being is not simply a shared or borrowed goodness, but it is a caused goodness: it subsists as part of my substantial existence. Because of this, all things that exist are good inasmuch as they exist, and because of whatever perfections they possess. Not only do things possess this goodness based on the divine exemplarity, but also the divine will because God has willed that every existing thing possesses some good, and therefore God has willed the good to all. And from this, Aquinas says it is clear God loves all things, but not as we creatures love things. The important difference is that when creature love, we love out of recognition that the beloved is lovely. As Aquinas puts it, the goodness of a thing evokes love for the thing in us (*bonitas eius ... provocat amorem*).[69] God's love, however, is causal: it "infuses and creates goodness" in the things God loves.[70]

Thus, in his reply to the objections, Aquinas emphasizes that God loves things in a way different from creaturely love. To the first, he argues that "being placed outside of oneself and passing into the other" means willing the good for what one loves and working for this good. And this God does as cause of goodness. That is, God truly does extend himself to the other in the act of creation causing real goodness to subsist in things apart from him. Thus, as cause of goodness, God can love other things while remaining within himself, whereas our love for things is not in any way causal.

To the second objection, Aquinas argues that all things are eternal in the sense that they have been in God from eternity. That is,

68. *ST* Ia, q. 6, art. 4, corp.
69. *ST* Ia, q. 20, art. 2, corp.
70. *ST* Ia, q. 20, art. 2, corp.

God has known all existents that will be, as they will be, in the divine intellect, which is eternal, and has known them in the eternal mode of the divine intellect. And in this sense, God's love has always been extended to things that God created, even before he brought them out of nothing into being.

Up to this point, God's love and willing the good for creatures is for all intents and purposes convertible with the act of creation. Although Mozi does not clearly provide a creation account, there is sufficient evidence that he considers *Tian*'s love as expressed in creative or generative agency: forming the cosmos, seeing human life as excellent, and providing in humanity the natural inclinations for food, shelter, society, and so on. It seems that Mozi stops at this level in his account of *Tian*'s love for humanity, and on this scale, concludes *Tian* has equal regard for all humanity from which the moral standard of caring for all results.

Next Aquinas deals explicitly with the question of whether God loves all equally. Aquinas knows that the account he provides of God's love for things at all would seem to conclude that God must love all things equally. Thus, lest his reader become confused about the nature of divine love, Aquinas offers an immediate clarification. If one attempts to say that God loves things differently in terms of the intensity of his love, then God does love all things equally, for God's act of love must be eminently simple. However, because loving something is to will its good, then we must deal with the obvious fact that some things receive a greater good than others. Aquinas thinks of this primarily in the different between types of creatures: irrational animals do not have the use of reason, and thus they do not possess as much good. Accordingly, Aquinas concludes that God does love some things differently than others since God wills a diversity of goodness in things. Indeed, this must be the case, for God's will is the cause of goodness in things, and thus there would not be greater or lesser goods at all unless God willed these goods, and this means God must love the things he wills to be greater or lesser goods in an unequal fashion.

For Aquinas, although God's providence means God cares for all and wills them good, he need not will every kind of good for

A Thomistic Reading of the *Mozi* on Divine Will   123

everything. Not only is this evident from the diversity of created things, but also in the diversity of excellences among particular species. For example, another person may possess a more excellent intelligence than I do or more excellent strength. Although I am a rational creature and am good by nature, I can recognize it is also good for someone to be of genius-level intelligence and rejoice in this excellence of the rational faculty, even as I do not possess it myself. That is, I can recognize the fittingness of a greater good than I possess and be thankful for this goodness. This capacity must rest, says Aquinas, on the ability of God to love and will diverse degrees of goodness to things. Thus, according to Aquinas's logic, while God loves the intellectually disabled with just as much intensity (as an act of will) as he does the intellectually gifted, God would seem to love them differently in view of the goods he willed them to possess in this life.[71]

It might be said that Aquinas has not satisfactorily resolved the problem. For although he holds that God does love all creatures with the same intensity of love, the fact that God wills different goods to different creatures seems, at a certain point, to contradict the equal intensity of divine love. As a father, I can will different goods for my

71. See Miguel J. Romero, "The Happiness of 'Those Who Lack the Use of Reason,'" *The Thomist* 80 no.1 (2016): 49–96. My point here is simply that the mentally disabled reflect a different situation from God's providential love than the person with full mental capacities (whose full use of the rational powers has been preserved, ultimately, due to providence). This insight, then, is purely with regard to the actual use of intellectual powers, and not the powers themselves or their proper end, happiness. Miguel J. Romero has shown that Aquinas, in fact, holds that those who lack the use of reason (*amentes* in Aquinas's terms) have the compliment of rational *capacities* necessary for human happiness, if not the full *operation* due to bodily constraints. As Romero puts it "Aquinas affirms that bodily impairment has no *per se* diminishing effect on the proper created subsistence and operation of the rational soul, which is the spiritual principle of the body. It follows that the rational soul of a human being who has a damaged brain retains in full her or his essential capacities and powers. Nevertheless, the body's capacity to be moved by material conditions via the external sense faculties can be impaired; likewise, the operative capacity of the internal sense organ … can be corrupted in such a way that there is *almost* no intelligible truth to abstract" (88–89). Because even the mentally incapacitated retain the full powers of the rational soul as the form of the person, the disabilities of the body do not remove either the dignity or the proper end of the rational soul. As demonstration of this, Romero notes that "according to Aquinas, a living human being who lacks the use of reason cannot but obtain some apprehension of intelligible truth. What this means I that while the biological aspect of a person's capacity to reason discursively can be profoundly hindered in its operation, short of death, the intellect cannot be absolutely impaired—incarnate human life is intellectual life for beings created in the image and toward the likeness of God" (89).

124   Chapter 2

sons with the same intensity, such as if I desire one to excel in math and another to excel at soccer. But as the goods involved become more fundamental goods, a disparity in my willing them to have different goods would become problematic. I cannot justly, it seems, will that one of my sons survives a car crash and that one of my sons perishes in a noble way—as a father, I should will both to live in equal measure.

So, while Aquinas's conception of God's differentiated love for humanity makes good sense in terms of temporal goods of intelligence, strength, and so on, it is difficult for the human mind to justify the disparity between God's willing salvation for one but not for another. Note, I have not suggested that God desires the damnation of any person. However, in Aquinas's eyes at least God does not will that everyone be saved in the same way he wills this ultimate good for some.

For students of Aquinas's thought, we are now beginning to step into the complicated world of Aquinas's theology of predestination and free will.[72] Fortunately, my purposes here do not require resolving or clarifying Aquinas on this particular matter. The foregoing is sufficient to show that Aquinas unequivocally holds as a Christian that God loves all but does not hold that God loves all equally in the aspect of all goods he wills his creatures to enjoy. Additionally, the *Mozi* does not concern itself with such differentiation of *Tian*-love for two main reasons. First, unlike Christianity, the Mohist tradition does not have a clear eschatological or even teleological form that requires an articulation of *Tian*'s love in assuring (in some sense) the actual enjoyment of goods that *Tian* wills for human beings. Second,

---

72. For a sampling of discussions of predestination that examine Aquinas's position in light of the biblical and theological tradition, see Taylor Patrick O'Neill, *Grace, Predestination, and the Permission of Sin: A Thomistic Analysis* (Washington, DC: The Catholic University of America Press, 2019), 13–67; Steven A. Long, Roger W. Nutt, and Thomas Joseph White, eds., *Thomism and Predestination: Principles and Disputations* (Ave Maria, FL: Sapientia Press, 2016); Matthew Levering, "Aquinas on Romans 8: Predestination in Context," in *Reading Romans with St. Thomas Aquinas*, ed. Matthew Levering and Michal Dauphinais (Washington, DC: The Catholic University of America Press, 2012), 196–215; Matthew Levering, *Predestination: Biblical and Theological Paths* (New York: Oxford University Press, 2011); and Harm J. M. J. Goris, "Divine Knowledge, Providence, Predestination, and Human Freedom," in *The Theology of Thomas Aquinas*, ed. Rik Van Nieuwenhove and Joseph P. Wawrykow (Notre Dame, IN: University of Notre Dame Press, 2005), 99–123.

A Thomistic Reading of the *Mozi* on Divine Will   125

the *Mozi* does not have to deal with the implications of holding that God is love itself—that is, a Trinitarian communion of love. Because Aquinas holds that the God who is perfect goodness and perfect love himself also has a love for his creation, this raises the question of how God's love toward creatures does or does not reflect the perfection communion of love that God is said to be through revelation. In this way, the difference between Aquinas and Mozi on whether God/*Tian* loves all equally is subject to differences between natural and revealed science as much as any gaps in culture or intellectual frameworks.

CONCLUSION

The forgoing analysis sheds light on the theological possibilities of the *Mozi*. Speaking generally, it is evident that although the Mohist account of *Tian* is closer to a robust theology of *Tian* than we find in the *Mengzi* (see chapter 2), it still falls short of a proper theological science (natural or revealed) of the divine nature. There are, undoubtedly, areas where the *Mozi* is a real triumph in this regard compared to Mengzi. For example, in the hands of Mozi, *Tian* is clearly more a subject or agent than in the *Mengzi*, drawing much closer to the idea of a self-subsistent God who elects, loves, and saves. At the same time, however, the subjective language about *Tian* is not so direct and clearly applied to the self-subsistent God that it rises inexorably above the level of metaphor. Hence, Chris Fraser's reading of the *Mozi* as a naturalistic tradition is not impossible given the suggestive rather than firm language regarding *Tian*'s subjectivity in the text.

To show why this matters, one can observe that from the perspective of Catholic theological science, one of the clearest weak points of the *Mozi* vis-à-vis a theology of *Tian* is that the text makes no attempt to clarify if or how *Tian* possesses a will (*zhi*) or even a heart-mind (*xin*). Consequently, the *Mozi* can make no real movement toward a theology of *Tian*'s willing *as such*. This in turn leads to a major speculative problem for the *Mozi* regarding *Tian* as an agent. For if it is unclear that *Tian* has the faculties for willing, then it is also unclear that *Tian*'s "intention" is a willed end, and not simply a circumlocution for order occurring by chance. The *Mozi* also fails to clearly articulate how *Tian* bears the perfections of a rational nature that would make the intent of *Tian* a compelling ground for what is righteous and what is not.

That said, the fact that the *Mozi* is unequivocal about the fact that *Tian* exercises love for humanity through the ordering and provision of natural goods suggests there is perhaps a latent vision of divine perfections in the Mohist account of *Tian*. Hence, it is possible to amend this account even internally to develop resources that can serve a Chinese Catholic theology of God. Since the later Mohist tradition also spent a great deal of effort clarifying logic and distinctions, it is perhaps possible (even advisable) to use the internal resources of Mohism itself to develop an account of what it would mean to predicate certain powers (such as will or heart-mind) or perfections (such as love or righteousness) of *Tian*.

Another notable aspect of the *Mozi* is that it is unambiguous that there is a liturgical element to *Tian*'s intention, that *Tian* wills sacrifices and offering. More importantly, it does not seem to me that one must interpret these sacrifices as part of a purely *do et des* cultus. Rather, the *Mozi* suggests religious sacrifice is an aspect of moral righteousness more broadly. Consequently, the Mohist account of *Tian*'s can resonate deeply with the Catholic belief that God has willed human beings to cultivate the virtue of piety—that is, to worship him.

Of course, even an appreciative reading of the *Mozi* on this point touches upon one of the fundamental issues the *Mozi* presents for theological science. Although it is laudable that the *Mozi* sees the divine as loving human beings, there is no sense that human beings ought to genuinely love the divine as the proper end and fulfillment of happiness for us. The Mohist perspective on *Tian* might be of service to Catholic theology, which seeks to proclaim God's desire to seek and save what was lost out of his love for humanity. However, the fuller soteriological shape of the Catholic tradition has no analog in the *Mozi*. One will search the *Mozi* in vain for precedents to the idea that God seeks to establish friendship with us, to adopt us

A Thomistic Reading of the *Mozi* on Divine Will 127

as his children and heirs, and to place us on the path to union with him in eternal beatitude.

It should be evident that the foregoing analysis has only touched the surface in terms of expositing the resources the Mohist tradition may hold for Chinese Catholic theology. None of the shortcomings of the *Mozi* from the view of Catholic theological science remit the very real theological utility the *Mozi* promises in its account of *Tian*'s love for human beings, *Tian*'s love as a standard for moral righteousness, and the way that the gift of natural goods expresses divine love. Undoubtedly the theologian would need to find a means to imbue such insights with the eschatological and soteriological principles of the Gospel to develop them into a proper theological language. But this is the entire purpose of this book: to show more precisely the theological possibilities of Chinese philosophy and highlight areas for development in the future.

3

A Thomistic Assessment of the Confucian Debate on *Renxing*

In the previous three chapters I drew upon philosophical concepts in early China in light of their possible use in Catholic theological science about God. I now turn to themes in moral theology, which is a more "natural ground" for Chinese philosophy than speculative theology. Whereas early Chinese natural theology was largely undeveloped and unsystematic, moral reflection in early China was a primary focus, and the moral philosophy of the Warring States period reached an exceptionally high quality of discourse. In this chapter, I provide a Thomistic assessment of a fundamentally important moral concept in early China, that of *renxing*, often translated as "human nature."

If Chinese Catholic theological science is to attempt to adopt and utilize Chinese philosophical concepts in the articulation of Catholic doctrine, such a project cannot ignore the vibrant debate on *renxing* that arose in early China between the Confucians Mengzi and Xunzi. To put it simply, Mengzi held that *renxing* was "excellent" or "good" (*shan*). Less than a century later, Xunzi would explicitly denounce Mengzi's position, and argue instead that *renxing* was "evil" or "bad" (*e* 惡). As I show below, it is not quite the case that Mengzi and Xunzi simply fall on radically opposite sides of the question of whether *renxing* is good or bad. Indeed, several

A Thomistic Assessment of the Confucian Debate on *Renxing*   129

contemporary scholars have argued that in fact, Mengzi and Xunzi do not really disagree materially, only formally, since the term *renxing* is not used the same way by both masters.[1] This is to say the debate on *renxing* in early Confucianism is not so straightforward as the propositional forms might suggest, but it had tremendous impact on Chinese thought and spurred debate within the Confucian tradition for quite some time.

My goal in this chapter is to provide a Thomistic assessment of this debate. If Aquinas had the opportunity to read Mengzi and Xunzi for himself (and had been able to understand the nuances of their positions as well as possible), with whom would he have sided? Or perhaps better, what would he have recognized as praiseworthy and blameworthy in each view of *renxing*?

The impetus for a study of the Thomistic response to *renxing* is abundantly clear from the side of Chinese philosophy. In the Chinese tradition, the debate on *renxing* was as formative as the questions of ideal forms or the problem of the One and the Many in the West. At the same time, the goodness of "human nature" is a clear area of concern in Catholic theological science. Van Norden, for example, has compared Mengzi's theory of human goodness to Augustine's arguments during the Pelagian controversy, and Aaron Stalnaker has offered a more extensive study of Augustine and Xunzi on this question.[2] The debate on *renxing*'s goodness is somewhat of a rare gift for comparative study: a question that is genuinely and obviously compelling to both early Chinese thinkers and Catholic theologians like Aquinas such that it engenders robust and meaningful

---

1. For discussion and rebuttal of this perspective, see Kim-chong Chong, "Xunzi's Systematic Critique of Mencius," *Philosophy East and West* 53, no. 2 (April 2003): 215–34. Chong addresses the position as articulated by the following scholars: D. C. Lau, "Theories of Human Nature in Mencius and Xunzi," in *Virtue, Nature and Moral Agency in the Xunzi*, ed. T. C. Kline III and Philip J. Ivanhoe (Indianapolis, IN: Hackett Publishing, 2000), 188–219; Nivison, "Xunzi on 'Human Nature,'" in *The Ways of Confucianism*, 203–14; A. C. Graham, "The Background on the Mencian Theory of Human Nature," in Liu and Ivanhoe, *Essays on the Moral Philosophy of Mengzi*, 1–63; and Paul R. Goldin, *Rituals of the Way: The Philosophy of Xunzi* (Chicago and La Salle, IL: Open Court, 1999), 11–13.

2. Bryan Van Norden, "Mencius and Augustine on Evil: A Test Case for Comparative Philosophy," in *Two Roads to Wisdom? Chinese and Analytical Philosophical Traditions*, ed. Bo Mou (Chicago and La Salle, IL: Open Court, 2001), 313–36; Aaron Stalnaker, *Overcoming Our Evil: Human Nature and Spiritual Exercises in Xunzi and Augustine* (Washington, DC: Georgetown University Press, 2006).

130   Chapter 3

analysis. It is true, of course, that Aquinas, Mengzi, and Xunzi will understand the question of *renxing*'s goodness in different ways. What Catholic theology means by "human nature" as good or evil is not quite what *renxing* means either for Mengzi or Xunzi.[3] But, while the topic requires a development of the conceptual apparatus for these thinkers, the concerns are ultimately shared.

Traditionally, Catholic theological science affirms that human nature—in its most basic sense, the species of humanity in terms of its bodily and spiritual faculties—is intrinsically good and endowed with the unique gift of the *imago dei*. Such a picture suggests an agreement with Mengzi, at least at first glance. Yet Catholicism also holds to the doctrine of original sin, which effects every human being, and has broken original justice for us all.[4] Aquinas holds it is necessary to recognize that through original sin, all human beings have real defects in the soul.[5] As he puts it, "the first sin of the first man not only deprived him of his proper and personal good—namely, grace, and the due order of the parts of the soul; he was deprived as well of a good related to the common nature," by which he means the submission of the inferior powers of the human being to reason, and the submission of reason to God.[6] In this way, the Catholic tradition holds that without divine grace (given especially through the sacrament of Baptism), human beings are unable to merit union with God. In this way, Catholic theological science might be able to be seen as more harmonious with Xunzi's account of *renxing*.[7]

3. For discussion of Theme of human nature and its particular difficulties in comparative studies, see Aaron Stalnaker, "Comparative Religious Ethics and the Problem of 'Human Nature," *The Journal of Religious Ethics* 33, no. 2 (2006): 187–224.

4. See, e.g., *Catechism of the Catholic Church* (New York: William H. Sadler, 1994), no. 375. It is worth noting that while all Christians would agree to the fact of the Fall and its deleterious effects on human beings afterwards, there is tremendous divergence between Catholic, Orthodox, and Protestant theologians concerning the way to describe and understand this doctrine.

5. For an excellent discussion of the complexity of original sin in Aquinas vis-à-vis the Latin tradition, at least, see Mark Johnson, "Augustine and Aquinas on Original Sin: Doctrine, Authority, and Pedagogy," in *Aquinas the Augustinian* (Washington, DC: The Catholic University of America Press, 2007), 145–58. Johnson contends that Aquinas intentionally departs from the Augustinian framework on original sin in order to better explain how original sin entails not just defects, but genuine culpability on the part of Adam's offspring.

6. *SCG* IV.52.6. Translation from Charles J. O'Neill, trans., *On the Truth of the Catholic Faith: Summa Contra Gentiles: Book Four: Salvation* (Garden City, NY: Image Books, 1957), 219–20.

7. See Xueying Wang, "Mengzi, Xunzi, Augustine, and John Chrysostom on Childhood

A Thomistic Assessment of the Confucian Debate on *Renxing*   131

At the least, these observations demonstrate that determining how *renxing* might be introduced into Catholic theological science means having to understand the particulars of the *renxing* debate more deeply in order to judge the theological stakes in the matter.[8] More importantly, I think it is rash to assume that Mengzi's position on *renxing* is the default that might work best with Catholic theological science. As I discuss below, there are clear features of Mengzi's account that readily square with Thomistic anthropology, but there are also resonances to be found in Xunzi. Exploring the *renxing* debate in more detail, then, should furnish better resources for the advancement of Catholic theological science along a most intriguing line of anthropological thinking. To arrive at a more detailed reading, one must first ask about how *renxing* is distinct from what Catholic theological science has traditionally meant by "human nature." Next, one must examine precisely what Mengzi and Xunzi mean by their respective claims that *renxing* is "good" (*shan*) or "bad" (*e*). Finally, one requires theological clarity about the Catholic claim that human nature is good, particularly in the context of the moral failures of human beings derived from original sin, which is not natural to us, but a defect that afflicts us on the level of nature.[9]

DISTINGUISHING *RENXING* AND "HUMAN NATURE"

In order to properly pursue a Thomistic assessment of Mengzi and Xunzi's accounts of *renxing*, it is necessary first to distinguish terms.

Moral Cultivation," 126–28. Wang notes that as regards the moral formation of children, Chrysostom's perspective is deeply resonant with Xunzi's on some points and resonant with Mengzi on other important aspects, though by-and-large she associates Chrysostom with Xunzi's perspective. Wang's argument at least provides cause to read the Mengzi/Xunzi debate carefully before predetermining which side Aquinas might fall on.

8. For a theological reading of the Confucian perspective on *renxing*, see Zhao, "The Goodness of Human Nature and Original Sin." Zhao's study assumes the Neo-Confucian interpretation of human nature as meaning "original human nature is good" in contrast with the Christian doctrine of original sin. In this chapter, I seek to go further by analyzing more closely the actual positions of Mengzi and Xunzi on the topic.

9. *SCG* IV. 52.6–7. Aquinas holds that original sin is present in us through participation in the common nature of Adam, which is corrupted due to the first sin. Hence, sin is not natural to us in the sense of what God has ordained for us, we all experience its corruptions, save for the Blessed Virgin and Jesus Christ, who were spared this corruption by the grace that rectifies the disorder of original sin.

132   Chapter 3

Because of the importance of human nature to Catholic doctrine and tradition, one might readily ask if someone such as Aquinas is required by the norms of the Catholic tradition to agree with either Mengzi or Xunzi *a priori*. That is, is there an apparent and necessary relationship between Aquinas's approach to Catholic theological science and either of these two famous positions on *renxing*?

This problem is complicated from both directions. Even if it is justifiable to assume that both Confucianism and Catholic theology are describing an objective anthropological reality—and not just an "anthropological worldview" that is purely a conceptual construction—both *renxing* and *natura* developed in the context of distinctive philosophical and theological questions. What is more, both concepts have complicated histories within their own contexts. Although it is certain that Catholicism proclaims doctrine and dogmas about the human species, it of course does not follow from this that Catholicism proclaims doctrine about *renxing* inasmuch as this concept signifies positions in the Confucian debate about humanity.

To take an historical example, Matteo Ricci discusses the Confucian opinions on *renxing* in the *Tianzhu shiyi*. There are two notable features of his discussion. First, Ricci expresses the question in terms of whether *renxing* is "fundamentally" good (*renxing qi ben shan* 人性其本善)."[10] Van Norden has stressed that the language of the "fundamental goodness" of human nature is actually not representative of Mengzi's position on humanity, but rather is an interpolation from Zhu Xi.[11] In fact, neither Mengzi nor Xunzi themselves considered the question of whether human beings are "originally" or "fundamentally" good, despite the fact that later interpreters of their thought used this category. In this respect, Ricci's reflections on *renxing* are understandably filtered through later Neo-Confucian interpretations of Mengzi, rather than the latter's original position.

More importantly, in his response to the question of *renxing*, Ricci observes that there is disagreement as to the meaning of *renxing* among Confucian texts. As I noted above, this is accurate. However, Ricci resolves this ambiguity by defining *renxing* as "the fundamental

---

10. Ricci, *True Meaning*, 349. My rendering of *ben shan* as "fundamentally good" follows that of Lancashire and Hu.

11. See Van Norden, introduction to *Mengzi*, xliii.

A Thomistic Assessment of the Confucian Debate on *Renxing*   133

essence of each category of things (*ge wu lei zhi ben ti* 各物類之本體).”[12] In this, Ricci successfully (if awkwardly) redefines the concept of *renxing* to fit the Latin conception of *natura*. Even if this is ultimately a helpful and perhaps necessary move for a theologian to make, redefining *renxing* to harmonize with the Latin *natura* is not the same as assessing the theological contours of the Confucian *renxing* on its own terms since the definition Ricci offers is alien to the view of *renxing* found in Mengzi and Xunzi.[13]

Since my goal here is to provide a Thomistic assessment of the Confucian concept of *renxing* as a prolegomenon to theological application, my procedure here will stress the differences between *natura* and *renxing*, keeping in mind that there are ways to alleviate these differences.[14] In a classic essay A. C. Graham once identified several meanings of *renxing* that help show how it is distinct from *natura*. One of them, which Graham took to be a more classical position, is that *renxing* is less about quiddity and more about the potencies of a thing. Graham argued that Mengzi's conception of *renxing* repeated the standard view before him, and this view understood *renxing* as the inclinations of human health and wellness.[15] Graham argues that Xunzi's view of *renxing* was more novel, and referred to the innate status of a thing, particularly the "untutored" morality of human beings.[16] In Xunzi's account of *renxing*, the term refers to the fact that human beings tend to have selfish desires rather than virtuous ones, and thus *renxing* concerns faculties or resources that must be made moral. Notably, Van Norden has shown that Graham's argument about the developmental conception of *renxing* that was predominant before Xunzi is inaccurate—there is evidence of a longer history of the innate conception of *renxing* in Warring States-era Confucian texts.[17] In other words, both Xunzi and Mengzi testify to

12. Ricci, *True Meaning*, 349. Translation from Hu and Lancaster.
13. For a broader discussion of how Ricci's conception of human nature differed from the Chinese tradition, see Sun Shangyang 孙尚扬, *Mingmo Tianzhujiao yu Ruxue de hudong: Yizhong sixiangshi de shijiao* 明末天主教与儒学的互动: 一种思想史的视角 (Beijing: Zongjiao wenhua chubanshe, 2013), 63–77. For related issues, see Vincent Shen, "The Aristotelian Concept of Substance Introduced by Early Jesuit Missionaries to China and Its Problems in Encountering Confucianism," in Slater, Cline, and Ivanhoe, *Confucianism and Catholicism*, 3–33.
14. E.g., Stalnaker, "Comparative Religious Ethics and the Problem of 'Human Nature,'" 195.
15. See Graham, "The Background on the Mencian Theory of Human Nature," 19.
16. Graham, 19.
17. Van Norden, *Virtue Ethics and Consequentialism*, 202–3.

134   Chapter 3

more or less "classical" conceptions of *renxing*, and this fact shows *renxing* was not univocal in meaning even in the early Chinese context.

Despite the disparity between Mengzi and Xunzi's understanding of *renxing*, there are important commonalities. Both understand *renxing* primarily in a moral sense, specifically regarding how human beings either do or do not incline to virtue. Also, both Mengzi and Xunzi would agree that *renxing* is at best a starting point for moral virtue. That is, both Mengzi and Xunzi would agree that to call *renxing* good or evil is not an ontological claim, but a moral one that determines how one goes about the cultivation of moral virtue. For Mengzi, the idea that human beings have a good *renxing* means that we can use and further cultivate our natural capacities and feelings to become virtuous. Xunzi, on the other hand, believes that *renxing* needs an extrinsic instrument (specifically rituals) to bring about proper moral formation. Either way, both Mengzi and Xunzi see *renxing* as a kind of *arche* for self-cultivation.

For those who have been formed in the Catholic tradition, the differences between the Catholic treatment of human nature and the Confucian emphasis of *renxing* are rather apparent. Briefly, most of the Catholic tradition uses human nature to describe the quiddity of the human species—that is, the qualities shared by members of the species. Specifically, as Robert Pasnau notes, Aquinas's discussions on human nature primarily concern a particular theological and philosophical question (largely informed by Aristotle), whether human nature is constituted by the soul, and, if so, in what way it is.[18] The contrast with *renxing* could not be starker at this point, for neither Mengzi or Xunzi were concerned about how to understand the relationship between the corporeal and immaterial parts of the human person, or which had primacy of nature. Aquinas himself had to face these questions in light of the classical Christian tradition, which had to define human nature through a struggle with dualistic philosophies in the Greco-Roman world, as well as the Averroistic interpretation of Aristotle that had become popular in Paris during his time.[19]

18. Robert Pasnau, *Thomas Aquinas on Human Nature: A Philosophical Study of the* Summa theologiae *Ia 75–89* (Cambridge, UK: Cambridge University Press, 2002), 7–9.

19. For discussion of Aquinas's approach to the Averroist issue, see Ralph McInerny,

A Thomistic Assessment of the Confucian Debate on *Renxing*   135

Here I should note that the soul-body question that dominates Aquinas's view of human nature is not *solely* due to the influence of Aristotle or historical contingency. It is also shaped by fundamental theological concerns of the Catholic tradition. Most significant dogmatically is the mystery of the Incarnation, which proclaims that Jesus Christ is the Word made flesh, or the union of the Trinitarian Person of the Son with human nature. Indeed, it has now become commonplace among theologians to note that fundamental anthropological concepts such "human nature" and "person" underwent significant alterations through the ecumenical councils focused on Christ. Ultimately at Chalcedon, the tradition clearly taught that the union between the divine nature and human nature did not occur at the level of nature, such that the divine and human natures were mixed. Rather, the union of divinity and humanity occurred in the Person of the Son. Additionally, the Church teaches that in the Incarnation, Jesus is "like us in every way but sin." This doctrinal formula thus requires that "human nature" be understood as kind of quiddity that is distinct from the typical subsistence of human persons in human nature alone. Put differently, Catholic theology cannot simply deal with a definition of human nature derived from moral tendencies and realities among human beings (which Mengzi and Xunzi do), but must also deal with the perfection of human nature in Christ Jesus, which must be ontologically identical with human nature, lest we deny the full humanity of Christ.

Apart from Christology there is also an eschatological concern shaping the Catholic view of human nature. From the earliest strands of the New Testaments, the Church has professed faith in both the resurrection of the dead, and the possibility of experiencing paradise or hell before the culmination of all things upon the Second Coming of the Lord (see, e.g., Luke 16:19–31 and Luke 23:39–43). Consequently, Catholic eschatology demands some account of the human person incorporating how death does not mean the absolute termination of a person, and how a person can genuinely experience the rewards or punishment for which they are ordained before the

---

Aquinas Against the Averroists: On There Being Only One Intellect (West Lafayette, IN: Purdue University Press, 1993).

136   Chapter 3

resurrection of the body at the end of time. As Christopher Conn has ably examined, this is an important reason for Aquinas's focus on the soul as definitive of human nature—Conn describes Aquinas as seeing humans as "ensouled organisms"—as an explanation for Christian eschatology.[20]

Additionally, it is worth noting that because Aquinas was a metaphysical realist, for him "human nature" also refers to the Idea of the human species as it exists in the divine intellect. In short, whereas for Mengzi and Xunzi *renxing* was primarily a moral problem, for Aquinas "human nature" is examined with a biological, quidditative, and ontological emphasis.[21] This is, of course, warranted given the arc of salvation history in the scriptures: Genesis 1:28 teaches that human beings were created in the *imago Dei*, which traditionally has been taken to mean human beings possess ontological excellence (such as rationality) that imitates the divine perfection in ways other corporeal creatures do not.[22]

Thus, the Chinese conception of *renxing* emphasizes the moral rather than quidditative aspect, whereas the Catholic view of human nature emphasizes the quidditative rather than moral. Yet this difference is not absolute. After all, the Catholic view of human nature as quidditative entails a moral component, as is evident from the Pelagian controversy. For Aquinas specifically, it is worth recalling that "morality" is essentially the way that human beings use their rational faculties (quidditative aspect) to flourish, meaning his view of human nature implicitly always involves a moral component. Likewise, the Chinese conception of *renxing* is not primarily quidditative, but

20. Christopher Conn, "Aquinas on Human Nature and the Possibility of Bodiless Existence," *New Blackfriars* 93, no. 1045 (May 2012): 324–38. See also Denys Turner, "The Human Person," in *The Cambridge Companion to the Summa theologiae*, ed. Philip McCosker and Denys Turner (Cambridge, UK: Cambridge University Press, 2016), 171 74.

21. This is warranted given the arc of salvation history in the scriptures. First, Genesis 1:28 teaches human beings were created in the *imago Dei*, which traditionally has been taken to mean human beings possess ontological excellence (such as rationality) that imitates the divine perfection in ways other creatures do not.

22. See *ST* Ia, q. 56, a. 3, corp. Aquinas also holds that angels are made in the image of God: "God's image is impressed on the nature itself of the Angel through his essence [*imago Dei est in ipsa natura Angeli impressa per suam essentiam*]." For a brief discussion of angels bearing the image of God and how it fits into Aquinas's ontology, see Serge-Thomas Bonino, *Angels and Demons: A Catholic Introduction*, trans. Michael J. Miller (Washington, DC: The Catholic University of America Press, 2016), 90–91.

A Thomistic Assessment of the Confucian Debate on *Renxing* 137

it is not without reference to quidditative aspects of the human species. Both Mengzi and Xunzi recognize that *xing* refers to types of things, and that the *xing* of a dog is not the *xing* of a cat, which is not the *xing* of a human. Indeed, both thinkers used *renxing* to talk about the special moral propensities *of humans* based on general, normative realities of human existence.

At the same time, Mengzi and Xunzi seem to differ on what *renxing* is and what the place of human *xing* is within the ethical process.[23] The question is not simply whether human *xing* is good or not, but how human *xing* can assist or hinder the process to becoming morally virtuous. A simplistic account of each thinker could be that Mengzi holds a maximalist position, attempting to say as much as possible that *xing* is never an obstacle to moral virtue, but always is fulfilled in virtue. Xunzi, taking a different view of what *xing* identifies, emphasizes the inability of *xing* to deliver moral virtue by itself, and hence he stresses the need for moral formation. Both accounts clearly touch upon quidditative or ontological emphases. They deal implicitly or explicitly with questions of what are "natural" human capacities, from whence do they come, and how can we undertake moral formation and improvement in light of what we "naturally" possess? This is all to say that, while the devil is in the details regarding Mengzi and Xunzi's accounts of *renxing* that do not map directly onto Aquinas's moral anthropology, there is nonetheless solid ground for reading across traditions to appreciably engage and assess these Confucian conceptions of human moral nature.

MENGZI ON *RENXING*

Now I will offer a brief description of Mengzi and Xunzi's theories on *renxing* before making a theological assessment. Since Mengzi precedes Xunzi historically, it is fitting to begin with his view. As I mentioned above, Mengzi's fundamental view of *renxing* is that it is "good" or "excellent." But what precisely does Mengzi mean? The primary texts for Mengzi's position on *renxing* are found in Book 6A of the *Mengzi*. There, Mengzi offers two famous arguments for why

---

23. I owe this observation to a blind peer reviewer from the Catholic University of America Press.

138 Chapter 3

renxing is good, both of which are developed as a response to another philosopher, Gaozi. Although these arguments do not exhaustively detail Mengzi's position on *renxing*, they provide an excellent point of departure.[24]

The first argument Mengzi makes for the goodness of *renxing* is in 6A:1. In this passage, Gaozi proposes that *renxing* is like a willow tree, and the virtues of benevolence and appropriateness (*ren* and *yi*) are like cups and bowls. If *renxing* is to become virtuous (benevolent and appropriate), Gaozi maintains it must undergo a process of transformation that takes the willow tree branches and applies the proper techniques to enable them to become formed and function as cups and bowls.[25] For Mengzi, the heart of the problem with Gaozi's proposition is that it suggests that moral virtue is a violent disruption of the natural outgrowth of the human person. In distinction, Mengzi holds that human beings are good because we possess fundamental feelings (*qing*), by which we become good.[26] This is a reference to a doctrine Mengzi explains in Book 2A:6. There, Mengzi describes the human heart as possessing emotional capacities that are the "sprouts" (*duan* 端) of moral virtue.[27]

Does this mean that Mengzi thinks human emotions are intrinsically good, trustworthy, and thus constitutive of moral excellence (i.e., the measure of the good)? This is a complicated question, in part because of uncertainty concerning how Mengzi understands the rational component of the four sprouts. David B. Wong has argued that Mengzi has no real distinction between reason and emotions. For Wong, this means that Mengzi does not appeal to moral judgments or justifications, but focuses on the emotional desires we experience as the source of moral motivation.[28] Wong's reading essentially makes Mengzi a robust ethical naturalist, who sees

24. For scholarship that has shaped my interpretation of Mengzi's conception of *renxing*, see note 1 above, as well as Ivanhoe, *Confucian Moral Self Cultivation*, 15–28; Ivanhoe, *Ethics in the Confucian Tradition*, 37–45; Shun, *Mencius and Early Chinese Thought*, 180–234.

25. *Mengzi*, 6A:1.1.

26. *Mengzi*, 6A:6.2.

27. See Van Norden, *Virtue Ethics and Consequentialism*, 217. There is some controversy about how to translate *duan* 端. I agree with Van Norden's resolution to the question, and thus translated *duan* as "sprouts."

28. See David B. Wong, "Is There a Distinction between Reason and Emotion in Mencius?" *Philosophy East and West* 41, no. 1 (Jan 1991): 31–44.

A Thomistic Assessment of the Confucian Debate on *Renxing* 139

emotions as the only true moral guidance we have (or, at least, the moral emotions described in 2A:6). More recently, however, Myeon-seok Kim has argued, convincingly in my view, that Mengzi's discussion of the sprout of wisdom and the heart-mind leading to it actually constitutes a positive account of moral judgment and justification.[29] Thus, Kim sees Mengzi as recognizing that the moral emotions are still buttressed and guided by the rational identification of the right from the wrong.[30] If one follows Kim, as I do, then one will hold that Mengzi believes that certain emotions are generally speaking trustworthy guides to moral conduct, provided that they are not divorced from the work of moral reason and reflection that investigates the nature of right and wrong.[31]

Although Mengzi clearly sees the emotional sprouts listed in 2A:6 as gifts from *Tian* for proper moral action, he also recognizes the inadequacy of the natural state of the moral emotions. In 6A:6, Mengzi teaches that these emotional capacities are "powers" or "resources" (*cai*) that all human beings possess.[32] Indeed, as Sarah Allan puts it, the *duan* of the human heart-mind "separates people from the birds and beasts and defines their nature."[33] Because we have these emotional capacities as resources, Mengzi argues all humans "are able to act in an excellent manner" (*keyi wei shan* 可以為善).[34] The key, however, is that these feeling are *resources* that enable virtuous behavior, but do not themselves constitute human activity as virtuous.[35] Rather, these talents or powers must be properly cultivated if they are to flower into genuine moral excellence, just as a seed contains the beginnings of being a flower or tree, yet it must be fed and watered to come to its full potential. This is what Mengzi means

29. Myeong-seok Kim, "Is There No Distinction between Reason and Emotion in Mengzi?" *Philosophy East and West* 64, no. 1 (Jan. 2014): 49–81.

30. See Kim, 62.

31. See Wong, 31–44.

32. *Mengzi*, 6A:6.2.

33. Sarah Allan, *The Way of Water and Sprouts of Virtue* (Albany, NY: SUNY Press, 1997), 113.

34. *Mengzi*, 6A:6.2.

35. Shun, *Mencius and Early Chinese Thought*, 187–90. Shun observes that in Mengzi is not readily apparent whether *xing* means "unlearned" at all times: "Even though Mencius believed that the ethical predispositions of the heart/mind involve something not acquired through learning, it is possible that what is unlearned has to be refined and nurtured by upbringing for them to develop into the form presented in some passages" (189).

140   Chapter 3

when he says the four virtues of benevolence, appropriateness, propriety, and wisdom are "not infused in us from an external source" (*fei you wai shuo wo* 非由外鑠我), but "we undoubtedly already possess them (*wo gu you zhi* 我固有之*).[36] Mengzi believes that human beings already possess what is necessary to become moral and virtuous in our hearts—these emotional powers are what make us human, instilled in us by *Tian* in the very order of human existence.

With these clarifications, one can clearly understand the first part of Mengzi's claim that *renxing* is good: *renxing* is "good" because goodness is connatural and fitting for it. For Mengzi, goodness cannot be an artificial work that human beings accomplish through some technique that transforms our *renxing*. Rather, goodness is in keeping with the flourishing of *renxing*, and indeed is what we should seek as we seek to flourish as human beings. Here we must keep in mind another of Mengzi's important positions, that regarding the presence of affective "sprouts" in the human heart. Mengzi holds that all human beings have particular affective powers in the heart-mind (*xin*) that are the incipient beginnings of virtue in us.[37] Thus, the virtues are the natural outgrowth and fulfillment of what humans possess as a matter of course. In short, for Mengzi *renxing* is naturally ordered to goodness just as it is to health: both are definitive of the flourishing of *renxing* being what it is, and not as being transformed into something else.

A second aspect of Mengzi's claim that *renxing* is good is formed in another response to Gaozi. In another passage, Gaozi argues *renxing* is like water held in a pool: it will flow in whatever way a gate is opened for it, as it has no preference for flowing to the east or west.[38] Here, Gaozi uses east and west as metaphors for good and evil. He argues that *renxing* has no natural inclination to be good or evil; it is only the conditions of human life that "open the gate" toward one way or another that determines if a human is morally good or bad.[39]

Gaozi's argument clearly counters Mengzi's principle regarding

36. *Mengzi*, 6A:6.2.
37. *Mengzi*, 2A:6.
38. In the early Chinese traditions, water was a very important metaphor for the moral life. For background, see Mark Edward Lewis, *The Flood Myths of Early China* (Albany, NY: SUNY Press, 2012), 38–47; and Allan, *The Way of Water and Sprouts of Virtue*, 29–62.
39. *Mengzi*, 6A:2.1.

A Thomistic Assessment of the Confucian Debate on *Renxing*   141

the naturalness of goodness to *renxing*, and in early China, his argument is compelling. Like modern Western democracies, Warring States China faced the problem of a great variety of cultures, practices, and moral visions, all grouped together in an uneasy political union. Whereas modern democracies have attempted to solve this problem in many cases by recourse to pluralistic relativism and secularism—often denying the existence of true moral good and evil—Gaozi locates the problem in *renxing* itself. For Gaozi there are clear norms and definitions of good and bad, but what explains that some people, even entire societies, do what is morally contemptible and others do what is praiseworthy? The answer: human beings experience no inclination to moral excellence or moral depravity; *renxing* is neutral, inclination-free, and only activated in one direction of another by social conditions that facilitate movement in one way or the other.

There is, however, a crucial weakness in Gaozi's argument regarding the lack of moral inclination in *renxing*. If *renxing* has no inclination, whence comes the judgment that good and bad are really good or bad? The only answer to this can be human artifice, but how did the original artisans of moral goodness or badness create and establish these concepts of good and bad? If they are not based in any truth about *renxing*, then not only are goodness and badness merely conventions, but there is no explanation for how they came to be created in the first place or how they are trustworthy guides.

Mengzi's response focuses on a key oversight in Gaozi's metaphor. Although it is true water has no typical tendency to flow east or west, it does naturally tend to flow down rather than up. Mengzi likens this tendency to flow down as the same tendency of human beings to move toward moral goodness—the natural properties and propensities of *renxing* are to behave in this way. At the same time, Mengzi notes that under certain conditions, both water and *renxing* can act contrary to these propensities. One can through technique and artifice dam water and force it to flow uphill. Similarly, the implication is human beings can create conditions in which human beings are habituated to incline to wickedness.[40] In a different passage,

---

40. Lewis, *The Flood Myths of Early China*, 38–42. Lewis observes that Mengzi's position in the text relates to the classical model of King Yu, who was said to bring order to the chaos

142   Chapter 3

Mengzi describes such conditions as arising when rulers do not care for their people, causing them to suffer from hunger or extreme cold: in such cases, people will turn to wicked deeds (theft, murder, etc.) to survive.[41]

For Mengzi, to say that *renxing* is "good" is to say human beings have a fundamental capacity and disposition for morality. Not only is humanity ordered toward moral excellence as part of human flourishing, Mengzi also believes we are generally disposed to follow this order. In terms of "natural development" humans tend toward goodness just as a tree tends to produce fruit or water tends to flow downhill. However, human beings are not "good" in the sense that we come into being already possessing the moral capacity to do the good as a matter of course and do so easily and infallibly. Mengzi emphasizes that social situations—in this context, the moral failure of superiors to create conditions for moral excellence—can cause us to become alienated from our own tendency to do good. In the example of the king failing to create conditions for flourishing, it seems Mengzi means to say that the good can be made arduous through social conditions, and, in such cases, requires heroic moral virtue to hold to the tendency of *renxing*.

Unfortunately, Mengzi does not precisely say how the social conditions for evil arise among beings who are naturally inclined to the good; this is a problem Xunzi exploits in his critique of Mengzi. For now, it is sufficient to see that Mengzi's claim that *renxing* is good does not mean human beings are in a state of moral excellence or that all human beings are moral praiseworthy as such. Rather, *renxing* is directed toward the good naturally, but just as not every seedling becomes a tree and not every stream flows downhill, not every human being experiences the fulfillment of his/her *renxing*'s trajectory.[42] Mengzi's point is that human beings are capable of moral cultivation of the self, and those who fail do so not because of lack of moral capacity.

---

of early China through controlling flood waters. Indeed, floods and water more generally were important metaphors for cosmic chaos in early China, including moral chaos.

41. *Mengzi*, 1A:7.

42. Allan, *Ways of Water and Sprouts of Virtue*, 42–43. Allan hypothesizes that Mengzi assumes that "the same principles informed natural and human phenomenon," and thus the appeal to water is not simply a metaphor but articulates a proper principle of human life.

A Thomistic Assessment of the Confucian Debate on *Renxing*   143

To summarize, then, Mengzi holds two distinct but complementary positions regarding *renxing* when he claims it is "good." First, he means that human beings are ordered toward moral goodness: when we cultivate moral virtue, we are fulfilling and perfecting our humanity, and, *ipso facto*, practicing moral evil is a departure from our human purpose. The second meaning Mengzi has in mind is that human beings are inclined or disposed to moral virtue, but this inclination is not infallible. Rather, due to particularly social conditions, humans can become inclined away from moral virtue and made to pursue what is morally evil. What Mengzi does not articulate, however, is how these conditions become internal principles of seeking moral evil. It seems that for Mengzi, if you place any human being in the right conditions, he or she will likely exercise the natural order to virtue and cultivate moral excellence.

XUNZI ON *RENXING*

Xunzi's position on *renxing* utilizes a different focus on *xing* than Mengzi's approach. The Tang dynasty commentator Yang Jing argues that Xunzi uses *xing* in two senses: the basic or "original" *xing* we possess by birth, which Yang calls *benxing* 本性, and the virtuous or "heavenly" *xing* we can come to possess, which Yang calls *tianxing* 天性.[43] Since Xunzi himself offers no such classification between types of *xing*, one ought not depend upon them too heavily. However, Yang's distinction is meant to point to how Xunzi's account of *renxing* is more focused on the problems of why human beings fail to become moral, whereas Mengzi seems to focus on why we should desire to be moral.

The essential observation Xunzi makes about *renxing* is that it is disordered, ugly or evil, all of which can be used to translate *e*.[44] In context, Xunzi means *renxing* is evil not as an absolute moral status

---

43. Wang Xianqian 王先谦, compiler, *Xunzi Jijie* 荀子集解, arranged by Shen Xiaohuan 沈嘯寰 and Wang Xingxian 王星贤 (Beijing: Zhonghua shuju, 2014), 420.

44. Kurtis Hagen, *The Philosophy of Xunzi: A Reconstruction* (Chicago and La Salle, IL: Open Court, 2007), 122–23. Hagen argues for two ways of understanding *e* 惡 in Xunzi's slogan: a) "problematic" and b) "crude" or "ugly." He summarizes the thrust of these renderings as follows: "For Xunzi, our original nature is ugly and detestable because it is unrefined, crude, and acting on undeveloped emotional impulses leads to undesirable consequences" (123).

144   Chapter 3

based on ontological dispositions, but rather *renxing* is evil or disordered in its "untutored" state. Unlike Mengzi, Xunzi takes *renxing* to identify solely what is innate in human beings.[45] According to Xunzi, *renxing* is initially inclined to disordered or wicked deeds, but not in such a way that it is beyond redemption or rectification; indeed, his central thesis is that because human *xing* is disordered, human goodness or excellence (*shan*) can come about through artifice (*wei* 偽).[46] The key for Xunzi, however, is that *contra* Mengzi, human beings *need* an artifice or external means to help us become effective agents to pursue goodness, and that our *xing* in and of itself is not adequate means for achieving moral cultivation.

In his initial definition of the badness of human *xing*, Xunzi identifies a disorder inherent in human life, particularly in the human will. He argues that humans are born and possess a love of benefit (*hao li* 好利), a weakness for wickedness (*ji e* 疾惡), and sensible desires. According to Xunzi, the problem is that humans act in accord with these dispositions (*shun shi* 順是), leading to negative moral acts such as robbery, theft, licentiousness and contention arise, and the curtailment of virtuous moral acts such as discourse, ritual propriety, righteousness and cultural refinement.[47]

For Xunzi, the notion of *xing* being bad is primarily a reference to the emotional dispositions and feelings of *xing*. He explicitly says that when humans follow their *xing*, this means they are acting in accordance with their emotions (*qing*), and disorder and wickedness arise from following these emotional or affective inclinations.[48] In terms of the Confucian debate on *renxing*, Xunzi found the soft underbelly of Mengzi's account of human *xing*, which claims moral emotions are the seeds of virtuous conduct, emphasizing the moral reliability of emotional response. Xunzi turns the table and argues that we do not merely experience shock or shame at things around us, but humans also are motivated to act initially by our own desires and loves. If we look at these desires that initially move the will to act, Xunzi might say, we do not see predominantly seeds of virtue,

45. See Stalnaker, *Overcoming Our Evil*, 58–60; Goldin, *Rituals of the Way*, 12–13.
46. *Xunzi, Xing e,* 1.
47. *Xunzi, Xing e,* 1.
48. *Xunzi, Xing e,* 1.

A Thomistic Assessment of the Confucian Debate on *Renxing*   145

but seeds of disorder. Thus, whereas Mengzi overlooked the emotional roots of bad desires in the human heart-mind, Xunzi gives them prominence in his moral psychology.

And so, for Xunzi it is not so much that *renxing* is intrinsically evil, but that it is synonymous with desires, and human *xing* does not provide the proper measure or rule for how to desire well. Ultimately, Xunzi emphasizes that the task of moral cultivation is to rule and order these desires, rather than act in accordance with them. As he puts it, following the inherent desires of the human heart-mind results in a return to tyranny (*bao* 暴)—a state ruled by violence, theft, and contention. But, Xunzi argues, "if there are master and models of transformation (*shi fa zhi hua* 師法之化) [to show us] the *dao* of ritual propriety and righteousness," then there will be "a return to order" (*gui yu zhi* 歸於治).[49]

Xunzi understands the "*renxing* is good" claim to mean the assertion of a moral naturalism wherein one trusts the unformed desires of the heart-mind as a guide to goodness. He rejects the cogency of such a position and argues instead that human beings do not have sound instincts for moral goodness, but rather must be formed to pursue morality. In this way, Xunzi's has the advantage over Mengzi's philosophy in ensuring the relevance of ritual propriety, a fundamental Confucian virtue. Unlike Daoists, such as Zhuangzi, who interpreted Confucian rituals as conventions that obstructed the development of natural morality, Xunzi authors a moral philosophy that sees these practices and conventions as essential to becoming good and virtuous.[50] Xunzi argues humans need rituals in order to learn how to order *renxing* in a virtuous way.

That said, Xunzi does not think that the capacities of *renxing* are an obstacle to moral goodness per se. He uses metaphors of a tree branch and dulled metal to say that even in nature, we find goods that can be used well. The key is that to use them well, they must be manipulated in some way: the stick must be straightened to become an arrow, and the stone must be ground and polished to be put to

---

49. *Xunzi, Xing e*, 1.

50. For a presentation of *Zhuangzi* that stresses the disparity between Confucianism and *Zhuangzi*, see Hans-Georg Moeller and Paul J. D'Ambrosio, *Genuine Pretending: On the Philosophy of the Zhuangzi* (New York: Columbia University Press, 2017).

146   Chapter 3

use.[51] Xunzi argues that masters and models (or laws as *fa* can mean both) are the "means of manipulation" that allow human beings to become rectified (*zheng* 正). What might be easily overlooked is Xunzi's emphasis on mastery or craftsmanship. It is not simply that humans must reform *xing* to make it effective for moral goodness. Rather, we require masters of *xing*—craftsmen of *xing* if you will—who know how to shape it, which evokes positive comparisons with Mengzi's Farmer of Song who pulled his crops' roots to "help" them grow. It takes a master to cultivate things the proper way. The difference is that Mengzi emphasized an agricultural metaphor that maintained the natural growth aspect of the good in question. Xunzi rather emphasizes goods that must be transformed to become useful for human beings. The sense is that our *xing* is like these goods: useful, but not ontologically identifiable with humanity in the fullest degree. The *xing* is, rather a "natural resource" for human flourishing that must be developed by a master craftsman if it is to be used well.

In Xunzi's eyes, the historical "master craftsmen" of human *xing* are the class of rulers called the sage kings (*shengwang* 聖王). According to Xunzi, these rulers recognized that human *xing* is naturally disordered, or "inclined to danger and unrectified" (*pian xian er buzheng* 偏險而不正). Out of this observation, came the sage-kings response: "they gave rise to ritual propriety and righteousness, instituting laws and standards in order to straighten and perfect humanity's emotional *xing* [*qingxing* 情性] and rectify it; they did this in order to compel and transform humanity's emotional nature and guide it [*dao* 導], thus this was the beginning of order and uniting with the *dao*."[52] All this is part of Xunzi's stress that moral rectification is a product of conforming to the masters and models (*shi fa*), and flows from "accumulating refinement and learning" (*ji wen xue* 積文學). And successful formation, for Xunzi, is equivalent to "being led by ritual propriety and righteousness" (*dao liyi* 道禮義).[53]

This neatly explains what Xunzi means by calling human excellence "artificial." When humans become good, it is because of formation or mastery that has transformed us away from our "natural"

---

51. *Xunzi, Xing e*, 2.
52. *Xunzi, Xing e*, 2.
53. *Xunzi, Xing e*, 2.

A Thomistic Assessment of the Confucian Debate on *Renxing*   147

dispositions or emotional inclinations. Sagehood, for Xunzi, is thus the product of "unnatural" or "artificial" principles and resources (learning, rituals, etc.), which successfully reform our innate desires into virtuous dispositions. It is worth noting that ontologically speaking, Xunzi undoubtedly holds that all human beings have one *xing*. That is, virtuous persons, such as sages, do not possess a different *xing* than do wicked people, but both have identical capacities.[54] In this sense, Xunzi's argument does have an ontological shade to it, but this is not systematically developed. For him, the commonality of human *xing* means that all human beings can become virtuous and good given the proper sagely formation.[55]

In arguing what separates the virtuous and the wicked, Xunzi argues that the wicked "follow their emotional *xing*" (*cong qingxing* 從情性) whereas the virtuous make use of artifice.[56] Xunzi often speaks of the sagely artifices as "transforming *xing*" (*hua xing* 化性). Thus, it seems plausible that Xunzi identifies *xing* predominantly with what Aquinas calls the sensible soul (setting to the side for the moment the structure of psychological unicity Aquinas presumes). That is, he explains emotions in terms of sensible desires and loves, and following these sensible desires is equivalent to following our *xing*.

Although Xunzi develops no special anthropological category to describe it, he nonetheless locates artifice in something resembling the rational powers of the human being. In a telling passage, Xunzi argues that "the sage accumulates thoughts and reflections, he studies the foundation of artifice, and by these he produces the rituals and (standards of) righteousness and gives rise to models and standards."[57] In terms of classical Chinese anthropology, Xunzi means that the work of artifice flows from the intellectual powers of the psychological principle of humanity, the heart-mind rather than the somatic powers of the same organ. Paul Goldin helpfully observes that for Xunzi, the heart-mind is capable of self-reflection, and so the heart-mind faculty is necessary to be able to free ourselves from

---

54. See *Xunzi, Xing e*, 20–21.
55. For an excellent description of Xunzi's theory of transformation, see Stalnaker, *Overcoming Our Evil*, 159–91.
56. *Xunzi, Xing e*, 16.
57. *Xunzi, Xing e*, 8.

148 Chapter 3

qingxing inclinations and begin to order them.[58] Hence, we have something like *qingxing* coming under the governance of reason (the heart-mind), though the heart-mind turns to artifice (rituals, etc.) to effect the transformation of the person.

As the *Xing e* essay develops, Xunzi increasingly turns to distinguish *xing* and artifice in a different manner. Rather than the distinction between body-mind faculties, Xunzi articulates *xing* and artifice as respective original state and transformed state of human life. Because Xunzi argues the sage kings are the origins of virtuous instruments, he faces the challenge from a disciple that can be summarized as follows: ultimately, aren't the artifice of the sages merely products of *xing*? Xunzi rejects this by comparing sages to a potter. When a potter shapes a clay pot, do we say that the shaped clay comes from his *xing*? Of course not, Xunzi concludes.[59] With this analogy, *xing* symbolizes the basic natural moral resources of human beings that give us the capacity for moral action. Artifice, then, arises as a response to *xing*—that is, a response to our natural moral state of having desires, that seeks to reform and transform these natural, incipient tendencies into virtuous behavior.

A THOMISTIC EVALUATION OF MENGZI AND XUNZI ON *RENXING*

In light of my analysis of Mengzi and Xunzi's respective positions on *renxing*, there are four areas of inquiry that form the necessary foundation of a Thomistic assessment of these accounts. First, one must assess the cosmological foundations or implications of each philosopher's *renxing* account. Second, one must assess the account each philosopher provides of the inclinations of *renxing*. This is closely related to but distinguishable from a third area that requires assessment, which is the role human emotions play in the moral theory of each philosopher. And finally, one must assess analogs to sin and their function or absence in these theories of *renxing*.

---

58. Goldin, *Rituals of the Way*, 36–37.
59. *Xunzi, Xing e*, 15–16.

The Cosmology of *Renxing*

As I noted above, Aquinas's *natura* is more ontological than moral, whereas *renxing* is the opposite. Despite this fact, *renxing* has distinctive cosmological foundations or connections in the accounts of both Mengzi and Xunzi. Therefore, the first frame of assessment I put forward from a Thomistic perspective is to ask to what degree the cosmological implications of Mengzi and Xunzi's theories of *renxing* resonate with a Christian metaphysics.

It seems fair to say that Mengzi's theory of *renxing* is more agreeable with Christian metaphysics than is Xunzi's. The work of Zhao Binshi helpfully articulates the apparent harmony between Christianity and Mengzi's view. Zhao argues that Confucians (though here he clearly follows a Mengzian trajectory) can agree with the Christian claim that "God is the foundational source of all that is beautiful and good, and therefore all that is made by Him is good (*shan*). *Renxing* is a gift of God and therefore *renxing* is also good [*shan*]."[60] However, Zhao's position depends upon identifying God with the Confucian notion of *Tian* in ways that eventually fall apart (to which critics of Christianity in the late Ming and early Qing bear witness).[61] Additionally, Zhao is in my judgment too hasty to equate the excellence of human nature follows from *Tian*'s activity in Confucianism to the Christian doctrinal claim that human nature is good follows from God's activity. Nevertheless, Zhao is on to something, though it requires some work to clarify how.

First, for Aquinas the ontological goodness of human nature is indeed a consequence of the Christian doctrine of creation. Specifically, Aquinas articulates God's creative activity in primarily in terms set down by Aristotle, but also in a manner heavily influenced by the Neo-Platonic framework of emanation he learned from Pseudo-Dionysius and Augustine.[62] Thus, for Aquinas human nature is good because it is caused by the divine goodness, and therefore

---

60. Zhao, *Ru Dao sixiang yu Tianzhujiao*, 149: "那麼天主既是全美全善的根原, 所以凡是祂所造的都是善的, 人性既是天主所賦, 所以人性亦當是善的了."

61. See Gernet, *China and the Christian Impact*, 193–247. Although I believe Gernet overstates the disparity between Catholic and Chinese thinkers regarding *Tian*, the contrast he exposits is unquestionably correct to some degree, thus complication Zhao's identification.

62. For a detailed description of how Aquinas's conception of God the creator is indebted

participates in divine goodness as a cause does an effect.[63] Strictly speaking, this is an ontological goodness because human nature is good inasmuch as being is good, though this can be taken two ways. First, human nature is good because it has been brought into being by God, who names human nature good as he creates it. Second, human nature is good because it is a kind of being that participates in life, which is in God preeminently, and does so according to the divine wisdom. As Aquinas observes in the *Summa Contra Gentiles*, the creative act of God is an instance of the principle of the self-diffusing good, since God as pure act produces things like himself— that is, bearing goodness.[64] Hence, as we saw in different ways in chapters 2 and 3 above, God's goodness is truly the proper ground and meaning of the goodness of human nature.

Human nature is also good because of our unique participation in divine goodness, namely our status as "rational animals."[65] Aquinas stresses that the human soul is animal since it is bound to corporeality, but our soul is ultimately still a rational soul. And this rational aspect is a participation in the kind of form that God is, because God is intellect and a rational form. Unlike other animals, the human being is created in the *imago Dei* and has innate faculties that imitate the divine activity of reason, though the rational soul of human beings is still directly united to the body.[66]

It must be admitted that Mengzi does not have an explicit participation metaphysics, but there is a significant analog in the terms of the divine gift that results in goodness predicated of what is created. For Mengzi, our moral emotions are not *sui generis*, but are implanted in *renxing* by *Tian* (though not, crucially, as a kind of perfection

---

to Aristotelian concepts, see also Kathryn Tanner, *God and Creation in Christian Theology: Tyranny or Empowerment* (Minneapolis, MN: Fortress, 1998), 61–76.

63. See, e.g., *ST* Ia, q. 6, art. 4, corp.

64. *SCG* I.37.5.

65. This language is taken from Aristotle. For a modern discussion of this principle, see Alasdair MacIntyre, *Dependent Rational Animals: Why Human Beings Need the Virtues* (Chicago and La Salle, IL: Open Court, 1999).

66. For an excellent discussion of Aquinas's hylomorphism in view in the conception of human beings as rational animals, see Thomas Petri, OP, *Aquinas and the Theology of the Body: The Thomistic Foundations of John Paul II's Anthropology* (Washington, DC: The Catholic University of America Press, 2016), 199–219, esp. 199–204, as well as Reinhard Hütter, *Bound for Beatitude: A Thomistic Study in Eschatology and Ethics* (Washington, DC: The Catholic University of America Press, 2019), 1–65.

A Thomistic Assessment of the Confucian Debate on *Renxing*   151

of *Tian* in which humans share). Mengzi's moral cosmology, then, is fundamentally that the moral emotions in the human heart come from *Tian* and therefore must be good; consequently, these emotions incline humanity naturally to the good and therefore one must say human *xing* is good.

Again, *renxing* is only indirectly an ontological concept, and, therefore, unlike Aquinas Mengzi does not explicitly argue the gift form *Tian* means the existence of human nature is good in itself.[67] However, Mengzi bears a striking similarity to the Mohists in his deep regard for the displacement and abuse of the common people by rulers he visits. He does seem, therefore, to think human life as such is valuable and good, though he does not explicitly take this position. And, like the Mohists, Mengzi seems to base this valuation of human life in the fact that it comes from *Tian*, though in a different way than the Mohists argue. In this way, Mengzi's position is broadly consonant with Aquinas's cosmology.

Consequently, a Thomistic reading could judge the cosmological aspect of Mengzi's view more compelling not only on its own merits, but also in light of issues in Xunzi's reading of *renxing*. To be fair, Xunzi does not set out a full cosmology or anthropology in his essay on *renxing*, and so we must draw in other resources from his thought that may or may not have weighed on his arguments about *renxing*. It is important to understand Xunzi's reading of *renxing* in light of broader cosmological debates in early China. Famously, many modern scholars have argued that early Chinese did not hold a conception of a "single, ordered universe." While I do not accept this judgment in its full signification, at the very least this claim is accurate inasmuch as it reflects Chinese thinkers who argued for a cosmology of disorder.

For many early Chinese philosophers, including Xunzi, the world was brought about by the agency of *Tian* and/or the *Dao* (depending on how one understands "agency") but not in a completely

---

67. Philip J. Ivanhoe, "Filial Piety as a Virtue," in *Filial Piety in Chinese Thought and History*, ed. Alan K. L. Chan and Sor-hoon Tan (New York: RoutledgeCurzon, 2004), 191. Ivanhoe argues it is not clear that Confucians like Mengzi would have thought existence itself to be good. I am more confident that Mengzi would not have disagreed with the Christian assertion about the goodness of human existence, which seems to me implicit in Mengzi's critique of King Xuan in 1A:7, and his failure to be concerned about the lives of his people.

152   Chapter 3

ordered, determined way.[68] Rather, things await a fuller ordering or
perfection. According to Xunzi, this order and perfection comes
about because of the work or artifice of the sages. One sees this
forcefully in Xunzi's application of the classical metaphysical "triad"
(*can* 參). Xunzi writes, "*Tian* has its seasons, the earth has its resources, and humanity has its ability to bring order (*ren you qi zhi*
人有其治).[69] Put simply, for Xunzi the uniqueness of human action lies in the response (*ying* 應) we make to what *Tian* and earth
have accomplished, by at least in part lending the cosmos order, including ourselves.

This underlying cosmology suggests that for Xunzi, goodness
is not a matter of ontology, for ontology is only the incipient resources of all things. Rather, goodness lies in proper use or employment of what is. For example, when Xunzi defines the difference between goodness and evil as concepts, he says goodness lies
in "rectifying the principle of things and peaceful governance" and
evil is "being inclined to a dangerous path and contravening [order]
for disorder."[70] In other words, goodness is a kind of activity of rectifying and bringing order. Consequently, when Xunzi says human
goodness is "artifice" he does not mean this merely instrumentally
(i.e., that goodness is brought about by sagely artifice) but also essentially: goodness is working out the proper kind of artifice.

Because of these features of Xunzi's cosmology, several com-
mentators have argued he has a naturalistic view of the world.[71] This
perspective is not entirely wrong-headed, especially when one compares Xunzi's strong association of *Tian* with "nature" and Mengzi's
more divinized conception of *Tian*. Still, I have argued elsewhere it
is not necessary to see Xunzi as a thorough naturalist, and he does
not seem to see all cosmic order as a product of human effort.[72] After
all, there is still a "pattern" (*li* 理) of rectification found in the world,

68. For discussion of the metaphysical context of Xunzi's position here, see Michael
Puett, *The Ambivalence of Creation: Debates Concerning Innovation and Artifice in Early China*
(Stanford, CA: Stanford University Press, 2001), esp. 64–73.

69. *Xunzi, Tian lun*, 2.

70. *Xunzi, Xing e*, 12.

71. The most significant English-language scholars in this camp are Hagen, *The Philosophy
of Xunzi*, and Janghee Lee, *Xunzi and Early Chinese Naturalism* (Albany, NY: State University
of New York Press, 2005).

72. See Brown and McLeod, ch. 7.

A Thomistic Assessment of the Confucian Debate on *Renxing*   153

even if Xunzi does not emphasize what kind of order and goodness exist in the world.

But, even accepting these qualifications and giving Xunzi a sort of "benefit of the doubt" regarding his metaphysics, it seems clear that from a Thomistic perspective Xunzi's account of *renxing* is less resonant with Christian doctrine than is Mengzi's. Little in Xunzi points to the participation of human nature in the divine wisdom, a participation which gives the former its essential goodness. Consequently, unlike Aquinas and Mengzi, Xunzi does not look to innate human capacities as an incipient sign of goodness—they are merely the starting point. For Aquinas, humans are made in the *imago Dei*, and, as such, the powers of our nature that reflect the perfections of the Creator are themselves good. Though not using concepts such as *imago Dei* or participation, Mengzi's cosmology does allow for an analogous consonance with the Thomistic perspective. Crucially, however, this does not allow one to conclude that Mengzi's account is for this reason more consonant with Christian doctrine than Xunzi's *tout court*. We must first press on to assess the three other important aspects of these accounts of *renxing* from a Thomist perspective.

The Moral Inclinations of *Renxing* according to Mengzi

Logically, it follows that the different understandings of *renxing* underlying Mengzi and Xunzi's philosophies lead to very different accounts of the moral inclinations of human beings. To briefly summarize from the exposition above, Xunzi associates human moral inclinations with disorder—our inclinations must be trained in order to be rectified and to be properly called "good." Mengzi, on the other hand, argues human beings are fundamentally inclined toward virtuous behavior in two senses, one on the level of moral theory, and the other on the level of moral anthropology. First, Mengzi holds that virtue is connatural and condign to *renxing*: becoming virtuous is more like a tree producing the fruit of its kind than a tree being chopped down and made into some sort of tool. In terms of moral anthropology, Mengzi holds that human beings have moral emotions in our hearts that are incipient guides to moral virtue.

154 Chapter 3

Given the specificity of Mengzi's account and the importance of it to later Confucian thought, it is helpful to assess his view of the moral inclinations of *renxing* on their own. This is actually more difficult than it might seem at first. On the one hand, Mengzi's debate with Gaozi in Book 6A:1 suggests that his conception of moral inclinations is harmonious with Aquinas's theology inasmuch as it is a kind of "morality of happiness," which holds that morality is not an external imposition on humanity that is contrary to or corrective of our nature, but rather conducive to the flourishing of human nature.[73] On the other hand, however, Mengzi's way of showing evidence that human beings are "made for virtue" is to point to the existence of the "sprouts" within us that are essentially premoral emotions that nonetheless are the incipient beginnings of virtue in us, should we cultivate them well.

In the broad schema of understanding moral goodness to be connatural and condign to the flourishing of human nature, then, Mengzi's moral anthropology has a place within Catholic theological science. But, what about in its details? Does Mengzi's moral anthropology as such resonate with what Catholic theological science must say about human beings? It seems to me that the best candidate for assessing Mengzi's moral anthropology is to compare it to Aquinas's conception of natural law.

As we saw in chapter 2 above, the comparison between Mengzi and Aquinas in the area of natural law presents major difficulties for incorporating Mengzi's thought into Catholic theological science. For one thing, the sprouts Mengzi describes are not put in terms of law, whereas for Aquinas this is very important. Although the natural law as Aquinas understands it maps onto and concerns what we might consider pre-rational feelings (such as the urge to procreate), the natural law is not simply these feelings or impulses. Rather, natural law provides guidance for human beings to discern and perform acts proper to our nature and flourishing. As Russell Hittinger has emphasized, "As a law, natural law is not 'in' nature or the human mind, but is rather in the mind of God."[74] Hence, the natural law as

---

73. For a condensed presentation of this account, see Servais Pinckaers, OP, *Morality: The Catholic View*, trans. Michael Sherwin, OP (Notre Dame, IN: St. Augustine's Press, 2003), 65–81.

74. Hittinger, 11.

A Thomistic Assessment of the Confucian Debate on *Renxing*   155

understood by Aquinas and the traditional science of Catholic theology requires both God as the lawgiver, and human beings as rational agents capable of discerning the natural law.

Mengzi's moral anthropology can somewhat account for the need of a lawgiver since the sprouts are placed in the human heart-mind by *Tian*.[75] However, the explicitly rational character of natural law is missing from Mengzi. Case in point, Mengzi clearly holds that the sprouts are the beginnings of virtues that must be cultivated: he recognizes there is a great difference between having the four sprouts and possessing good moral character. However, Mengzi is himself somewhat reticent to describe precisely what is required to transition from the sprouts to the virtues, though it is notable that Yearley reads Mengzi as holding it is reason that develops this moral character.[76] Still, Mengzi does not say or even suggest that the sprouts issue or can lead to the development of genuine precepts that guide moral activity; if Yearley is right that Mengzi sees the transition from moral sprouts to virtues as developed by reason, the nature of this rational development is left unclarified. Consequently, it is not clear that the main anthropological foundation of the virtues for Mengzi can be understood in terms of laws. Rather, for Mengzi the sprouts are signs that human beings are inclined to morality, to the recognition of good and bad, and, so it seems, that we inherently prefer the good. But he does not state things this way in terms of developing moral precepts—he rather emphasizes the sprouts as a kind of foundation for the development of ethical character.

Although Mengzi does not develop his account of the four sprouts in the direction of genuine precepts suggestive of a full-bore natural law theory à la Catholic theological science, this does not mean his understanding of the four sprouts is not consonant with natural law theory in other ways. In addition to speaking about natural law as precepts, Aquinas also discusses natural law in terms of "inclinations." In the *ST* IaIIae, q. 94, a. 2, Aquinas discusses whether there are one or many precepts of natural law and argues that there are many. During his explanation, Aquinas states that "the order of

---

75. Again, see Richard Kim, "Natural Law in Mencius and Aquinas."
76. Yearley, 58 and 62–72.

156 Chapter 3

the precepts of the natural law is according to the order of the natural inclinations.[77] Unfortunately, there is a tremendous amount of obscurity in Aquinas's account, not least concerning what precisely he intends in the first place by those inclinations that correspond to the order of natural law precepts.

According to Steven Jensen, there are three possible answers. First, inclinations might refer to "inborn emotional desires, what Aquinas would call the passions of the soul," such as the natural drive for sex. Second, Jensen says, Aquinas might mean "natural desires of the will" (the act of which is an inclination to the apprehended good). And third, Aquinas "might be referring to nonconscious inclinations," which Jensen identifies with involuntary processes, such as when the human body converts nutrients from food into energy.[78] The key according to Jensen is to recognize that, for thinkers like Aquinas, the inclinations testify to the eternal law. Thus, the discovery and knowledge of such inclinations in the human soul is what is meant by natural law.[79]

Thus, we can put the question to Mengzi's conception of *renxing* in two respects. First, do the four sprouts seem to be analogous to any of the candidates for Aquinas's understanding of inclinations listed above? And second, does Mengzi associate their mere *presence* with morality, or the discovery and knowledge of them? Put differently, is there a rational character to Mengzi's conception of the four sprouts, even if he does not articulate them as providing a link to positive precepts?

These are very fruitful questions. For in the first major presentation of the four sprouts in Book 2A:6, Mengzi does not associate them with "emotions" (*qing*) as he seems to do later in Book 6A, but rather simply calls the four sprouts kinds of a "heart-mind" (*zhi xin* 之心). According to Van Norden, Mengzi has three dominant

---

77. *ST* IaIIae, q. 94, art. 2, corp.

78. Steven J. Jensen, *Knowing the Natural Law: From Precepts and Inclinations to Deriving Oughts* (Washington, DC: The Catholic University of America Press, 2015), 44.

79. Jensen, 60: "In summary, then, God has a plan, called the eternal law, which he impresses upon creatures by way of natural inclinations. Human beings become aware of this plan through its effects, which are the natural inclinations. Humans become aware of the plan as it applies to themselves through their own natural inclinations. This knowledge is called the natural law."

A Thomistic Assessment of the Confucian Debate on *Renxing*   157

uses of *xin* in Mengzi's thought. First, its primary meaning is to refer to "the psychological faculty that thinks and that feels emotions."[80] Additionally, Van Norden notes *xin* refers to "the emotions that faculty manifests" and "any one of the four aspects of the *xin* that manifest the emotions and attitudes characteristic of Mengzi's four cardinal virtues."[81] Since the *xin* is both emotional and intellectual, it doesn't seem that the four sprouts refer to the kinds of nonconscious activities that Jensen mentions above. However, a strong case could be made that the four sprouts do refer to some conscious apprehension of the good, and even may refer to the natural inclination of the will toward the good (the second definition of inclination that Jensen offers).

But even if there may be a positive relationship between the inclinations of natural law according to Aquinas and the four sprouts of Mengzi, is there any kind of principle of discovery? Some secondary literature on Mengzi would dissuade from such a view. For example, Yearley contrasted Mengzi and Aquinas on the grounds that (in Yearley's view), Aquinas has a "discovery model" of moral virtue, whereas Mengzi has a "developmental model."[82] Philip Ivanhoe argued the same basic point, though contrasting Mengzi's development model with the discovery model of Wang Yang-ming.[83] In this contrast, the "discovery model" holds that moral cultivation involves merely discovering fixed, fully formed moral natures whereas developmental models such as Mengzi's emphasize the "development and extension of our innate, nascent moral sense."[84]

Although the developmental/discovery model distinction can be helpful, it is also terminologically misleading. For it obscures the fact that developmental models of moral cultivation can (and often do), contain aspects of discovery. Even in Mengzi's account, the innate, nascent moral capacities are discoverable. Not only that, they must be discovered and understood if we are to develop them properly. Of course, this is largely implicit in Mengzi. For example, in

80. Van Norden, *Virtue Ethics and Consequentialism*, 216.
81. Van Norden, 216.
82. Yearley, 59–60
83. Ivanhoe, *Ethics in the Confucian Tradition*, 88–108.
84. Ivanhoe, 89.

Book 2A:6, Mengzi offers a famous illustration of the four sprouts at work in the human heart-mind. He says that, "if today a man saw a small child about to fall into a well, anyone in this position would feel alarm and compassion."[85] Now Mengzi makes no assumption that because of these feelings of alarm and compassion that human beings will actually act to defend a small child.[86] His point, rather, is that these feelings are there, and a reliable guide (in part) to how we should act. And this means implicitly that for Mengzi, the discovery and articulation of the four sprouts is quite important.

Pursuant to this point, in Book 2A:2, Mengzi disputes a popular teaching of Gaozi that "what is obtained in teaching cannot be sought in the heart-mind."[87] Mengzi's rejection of Gaozi's position seems to be primarily based upon the fact that he doesn't think it is true that teaching places new things within the heart-mind to help it flourish—if it is not already in the heart-mind, doctrine cannot bring it out. However, this concerns the origination of virtue and morality, not the actual practice of it. Rather for Mengzi there is a necessary transition from the sprouts to the proper virtues. As an early Confucian, Mengzi's understanding of what is needed to develop morally is on the one hand through moral self-reflection (see e.g., 1A:7), but also the study and recitation of the classical texts of ancient China. Consequently, although Mengzi's conception of moral cultivation emphasizes development, it also requires us to "discover" that each of us possesses the beginnings of moral virtue, and then utilize rational practices and methods to develop our moral character as we need.

In this regard, Mengzi's conception of the four sprouts is broadly consonant with Aquinas's understanding of the natural inclinations that correspond to the order of natural law. A further step we could take is to compare the four sprouts the five inclinations

---

85. Mengzi, 2A:6: "今人乍見孺子將入於井, 皆有怵惕惻隱之心." The term for child used here (*ruzi* 孺子) can imply kinship relations. Thus, Mengzi's argument may be simply that we would feel anxiety and compassion for children to whom we are related—an admittedly low standard.

86. Van Norden, *Virtue Ethics and Consequentialism*, 218: "Mengzi does not say that everyone would actually *act* to save the child.... He believes that the sudden, prereflective character of the reaction suggests that it is an authentic expression of our nature."

87. *Mengzi*, 2A:2.8.

A Thomistic Assessment of the Confucian Debate on *Renxing*   159

Aquinas articulates in IaIIae, q. 94, a. 2. Here, Aquinas identifies five primary inclinations: the inclination to good, the inclination to preserve one's own being, the inclination to procreation and rearing offspring, the inclination to live in society, and the inclination to know the truth.[88] In Mengzi's discussion of the four sprouts, three of them seem to resonate with Aquinas's list, those being the heart-mind of commiseration (which leads to the virtue of benevolence and is the social virtue par excellence) that corresponds with the inclination to live in society, and the heart-mind to distinguish truth from falsehood, corresponding to the inclination to know the truth. Third, and perhaps most important, the second sprout—the feelings of shame and dislike—appears to resonate broadly with some account of the inclination to the good. Thus, both in broad terms and in some concrete applications, it seems that Mengzi's view of *renxing* does indeed resonate with important aspects of Aquinas's conception of natural law, even if the former does not formally resemble the latter in terms of furnishing precepts.

Moral Evaluation of Emotions

With this discussion of inclinations in general behind me, I can now turn to the shared ways that Mengzi and Xunzi discuss the propensities of *renxing*. Both Mengzi and Xunzi give importance to "emotions" (*qing*) in their accounts of *renxing*. This raises important questions about whether and how these accounts resonate with Catholic theological science regarding human emotions and moral development. Undoubtedly, this is a tricky question to negotiate from a Thomistic perspective. There is an obvious cultural and historical difference between the thought Aquinas and Mengzi and Xunzi. Specifically, Aquinas was heir to a long tradition (or traditions, more accurately) regarding emotions, especially the Aristotelian and Augustinian.[89] Hence, his discussion of emotions had a long gestation in the tradition before him. In contrast, Mengzi and

88. See Pinckaers, 97–109. Pinckaers refers to the third inclination as "the inclination to marry" (see 103–4).
89. For a recent study of Aquinas on the emotions, see Nicholas E. Lombardo, OP, *The Logic of Desire: Aquinas on the Emotions* (Washington, DC: The Catholic University of America Press, 2011).

160 Chapter 3

Xunzi describe emotions (more or less consonant with the term *qing*) before this concept was given systematic exposition and clarification in the Han dynasty.

This is significant because if one examines the Chinese concept of *qing* as understood in Han thought, it bears great similarity to the way Aquinas understands the emotions. Han authors typically define six *qing*: enjoyment (*xi* 喜), anger (*nu* 怒), grief (*ai* 哀), pleasure (*le* 樂), love (*ai* 愛 or *hao* 好, depending on the author), and hatred (*wu* 惡).[90] In the correlational cosmology dominant in the Han period, these *qing* were related to organ systems within the human body such as the intestines or bladder.[91] Additionally, Han-era thinkers tended to contrast the *qing* to the "five marks of *xing*" (*wu xing* 五性). In Ban Gu's *Baihu Tong*, the five marks of *xing* are described as marks of moral character: benevolence (*ren*), righteousness (*yi*), ritual propriety (*li*), wisdom (*zhi*), and trustworthiness (*xin* 信). Put simply, these systematic conceptions of *qing* within moral anthropology are not properly applicable to Mengzi and Xunzi, and one must be careful not to anachronistically read their accounts in light of later theories of *renxing* and/or emotions.

With Mengzi, one must keep in mind that he argues the *qing* of humanity are unique to the human as a species, and this is the beginning of our moral character. Significantly, in his key passage in Book 2A:6 on the four sprouts of virtue, Mengzi does not use the word *qing* or any synonyms to describe these sprouts. Rather, as I noted above, he simply associates the four qualities of commiseration, shame/dislike, humility/permissiveness, and approving/disapproving with a kind of heart-mind. However, in Book 6A:6, Mengzi does explicitly use the term *qing* to speak about the goodness of *renxing*, and it seems he has these four sprouts in mind. At the very least, the dispositions he talks about in 2A6 can by and large be seen as emotional responses, though not neatly distinguished from the intellect (which is expected, given the same organ of the heart-mind signified

90. Other texts lists four *qing* (e.g., *Liji, Zhongyong*, 1) or seven (e.g., *Liji, Liyun*, 18).

91. For background on the viewpoint of the body and its systems in early Chinese medicine that informed these thinkers, see Paul U. Unschuld, *Huang Di Nei Jing Su Wen: Nature, Knowledge, and Imagery in an Ancient Chinese Medical Text* (Berkeley: University of California Press, 2003).

A Thomistic Assessment of the Confucian Debate on *Renxing*   161

the affective and intellectual powers of the human person in Mengzi's anthropology). Therefore, it is fair to say that for Mengzi the *qing* of the human heart are spontaneously conducive to morality and are thus "spontaneous moral feelings."[92]

Xunzi sees the *qing* differently. In his account human *qing* are at best pre-moral appetites or desires that have no clear moral content apart from the support lent them by sagely artifices such as Confucian rituals. A stronger reading of Xunzi's *qing* could argue he treats human emotions as destructive of virtue. How are these two senses legitimate readings of Xunzi's position? They are both possible because on the one hand, Xunzi sees the desires or appetites of the *qing* as concerning necessary goods that should be desired in order to flourish. But on the other hand, when humans desire these goods with the "spontaneity" of the *qing*, humans seek them in a chaotic fashion that is genuinely calamitous for individual and social flourishing. Therefore, for Xunzi *qing* cannot be relied upon as incipient guides to moral rectification, but they must be corrected and transformed through Confucian practices.

With which of these two positions would Aquinas be sympathetic? Answering this question requires a brief description of Aquinas's own moral theory of the emotions. One significant Latin term Aquinas uses for what English calls emotions is *passiones*, a distinctly technical term.[93] Derived from the noun meaning "suffering" (*passio*), this term identifies emotions as something humans do not experience actively, but passively—that is, we are moved by things apart from us to have emotional responses. It is important to note that for Aquinas, the *passiones* are appetitive powers within the human soul, though they are specifically powers of the *sensitive* appetite (i.e., the *passiones* do not pertain as such to the reason or the will).[94] Within the sensible appetite Aquinas distinguishes two types

92. Ivanhoe, *Ethics in the Confucian Tradition*, 89.

93. Apart from Lombardo, 20–74, see Robert Miner, *Thomas Aquinas on the Passions: A Study of the Summa Theologiae, 1a2ae 22–48* (New York: Cambridge University Press, 2009); Peter King, "Aquinas on the Passions," in *Thomas Aquinas: Contemporary Philosophical Perspectives*, ed. Brian Davies (New York: Oxford University Press, 2002), 353–86; and Kevin White, "The Passions of the Soul (Ia IIae, qq. 22–48)," in *The Ethics of Aquinas*, ed. Stephen J. Pope (Washington, DC: Georgetown University Press, 2002): 103–15.

94. *ST* IaIIae, q. 22, art. 1–3.

162 Chapter 3

of powers bearing on the *passiones*: the irascible and concupiscible faculties.[95]

These are distinguished according to the object of these powers. The concupiscible powers are directed toward the "sensible good or evil, as this is simply understood" (*simpliciter acceptum*)—that is, whether the object in question is in itself deemed good or evil to us.[96] The irascible powers, in contrast, take as their object not simply the good or evil of a given thing, but according to its "arduous or difficult nature" (*habet rationem ardui vel difficilis*)—that is, whether a good is difficult to secure or an evil difficult to avoid. This, then, provides the ground upon which Aquinas provides his list of the *passiones* in the soul. The concupiscible *passiones* are joy (*gaudium*), sadness (*tristia*), love (*amor*), hatred (*odium*), and similar emotions, while the irascible ones are daring (*audacia*), fear (*timor*), hope (*spes*), and similar emotions.[97]

The real question needed to offer a Thomistic assessment of Mengzi and Xunzi's theories of human emotions is to ask whether or how these *passiones* play a role in human moral rectification. For Aquinas, the *passiones* are pre-moral; because the emotions are not an exercise of the rational powers, they need to be integrated within the movement of reason in order to become genuinely moral actions. However, because the human person does have rational powers, the *passiones* are moral inasmuch as humans succeed or fail at integrating them into the movement of reason. Therefore, Aquinas takes a position that suggests the emotions themselves are neither good per se nor evil per se, but are good or evil depending upon the conditions of each particular human person and her use of them.[98]

To see what is meant here, we can look more concretely at Aquinas's account of the passions in the moral life. Aquinas sees the

95. For an extensive treatment on the passions in these divisions, see Miner.
96. *ST* IaIIae, q. 23, art. 1, corp.
97. *ST* IaIIae, q. 23, art. 1, corp.
98. See Miner, 288–89. Miner argues Paul Gondreau and M. D. Chenu err when they argue (in different ways) that the passions are the subject of the virtues. Miner argues instead that, "rather than being the subjects of virtue, passions are acts whose regular, prompt occurrence according to the judgment of reason constitutes the perfection of the power from which they proceed. Without the passions, there is no prospect of perfecting the powers ... but since a virtue simply is the habitual perfection of a power, the moral virtues associated with the sensitive appetite requires the passions as the condition of their possibility."

A Thomistic Assessment of the Confucian Debate on *Renxing*   163

passions as movements in the soul, namely the movements of approach to or withdrawal from (*accessus et recessus*) a given, apprehended object.[99] With the concupiscible passions, this movement is determined by apprehension of an object, and the consequent judgment of its good or evil for the agent. For example, on a hot day I consider eating an ice cream good, therefore I am moved by passion to approach and consume the ice cream, which is to say I love it. On a cold winter day, I think eating ice cream will be more cooling and thus I do not want this effect (i.e., I account it an evil for me), and so I withdraw from it emotionally, or I hate it.[100]

Of course, others will reckon the good or evil of eating ice cream differently because of other factors. Someone who is lactose intolerant may see eating ice cream as evil in many cases I'd see it as good, and justifiably so. Similarly, a man who has overindulged on dinner may still see eating ice cream as a good even when he should not do so. Put simply, the approach or withdrawal movement of the concupiscible passions is dependent upon a prior judgment about the goodness or evil of the object in question. When this judgment is a sounds and true judgment of reason, then the decision to pursue or not pursue concupiscible goods is virtuous. That is, for a person who has a true and accurate understanding of things, these passions can be a great help on the path to flourishing. For those having an inaccurate understanding of things, these passions can be destructive of flourishing. If a person lacks a true grasp of the nature of things—for example, a person who eats ice cream and doesn't know she is lactose in tolerant—this is clearly distinct from someone with a disordered account of what is good, such as in the case of the overeater who thinks immoderate consumption is good and restraint is evil (as this is also distinct from the person who knows immoderate consumption is bad, but lacks the virtue of temperance to act according to this knowledge).

---

99. See Lombardo, 31–32. Aquinas holds that there are three types of appetites: natural appetite, sense appetite, and the will (or intellectual/rational appetite). Natural appetites are simply natural inclinations toward goods without apprehension or cognition (think of the flower bending toward sunlight). Passions are a kind of sense appetite, derived from the apprehension of sensible goods. But, as Lombardo stresses, Aquinas says that humans have all three appetites.

100. *ST* IaIIae, q. 23, art. 2.

164 Chapter 3

It is important to emphasize that for Aquinas, the concupiscible passions still follow a general rule that an object is apprehended as good or evil (bearing in mind the apprehension of good or evil of a thing occurs in different ways and at different levels) and thus when the object is apprehended as good in a certain respect, the passions move us to desire in that respect, and when the object is apprehended as evil in a certain respect, the passions move us to not desire it in that respect. In other words, Aquinas does hold that humans naturally seek what is good and are always moved to desire flourishing, much like Mengzi. However, Aquinas differs from Mengzi because the latter seems to have only an extrinsic account for how this desire for the good becomes mistaken—namely, the political or social context can act to "misdirect" the natural propensities of *renxing*. The closest Mengzi comes to arguing for an intrinsic cause of moral disorder is by implication: if the sprouts of moral goodness requires moral self-cultivation (*xiu shen* 修身) to become virtues, then *ipso facto* failure to cultivate moral rectification is a cause of moral disorder. But what Mengzi doesn't explain fully is why some fail to undergo this process of moral cultivation in the first place, except for the extrinsic reason just mentioned.

Aquinas, however, has room in his account to clarify the nature of the internal disorder that prevents the emotions from being universally conducive to flourishing. This is because the postlapsarian human intellect is frail and can misapprehend the good under either its concupiscible or irascible aspect. Key to this difference between Mengzi and Aquinas—beyond the concept of the Fall (see more below)—is that the latter more clearly separates the appetitive and intellectual powers (in this case, I mean the distinction between will and intellect), and associates the emotions with the sensible appetite. In Aquinas's account, the sensible appetite is only conducive to virtue when it is subordinate to the rational powers of the human person.

In this way, Aquinas's account bears a much more striking resemblance to Xunzi's account of *renxing* than it does Mengzi's. This is because Xunzi similarly treats the emotions or *qing* as a kind of pre-moral appetite that requires something else to order it toward

A Thomistic Assessment of the Confucian Debate on *Renxing*   165

moral virtue. In Xunzi's case, it is not the rational powers of the soul, but rather the ritual artifices of the sages which must direct the emotional powers into virtuous action. However, as I noted above, in the view of Paul Goldin this also involves a sense in which the *qing* are governed by the heart-mind, which can be analogous to the intellect and intellectual will in Aquinas (*mutatis mutandis*).

To conclude the Thomistic assessment of the account of the emotions in Mengzi and Xunzi's *renxing* theories, it is fair to say that neither account provides a genuine resonance with Aquinas on the emotions. However, between the two, Xunzi seems to stand closer to Aquinas inasmuch as he can account for the need for human emotions to be ordered by a higher principle. Yet this analysis of moral emotions in Mengzi, Xunzi, and Aquinas also sheds light on a very important topic that must be considered in a Thomistic assessment of *renxing*. Put simply, Aquinas will ultimately describe the moral disorder of human emotions within the context of sin and its impact on human nature. Can either Mengzi or Xunzi's account of *renxing* be seen to be concerned either with sin or its effects so as to resonate with the Catholic doctrine of human nature? This is the question I seek to answer in the last section of this chapter.

Sin and Human Nature

In their respective accounts of *renxing*, neither Mengzi nor Xunzi really provide a conception of human sin that is similar to the Christian doctrine. Modern Chinese Christians use the term *zui* 罪 or "crimes" for sin, which is helpful inasmuch as Mengzi and Xunzi both clearly acknowledge human ability to commit misdeeds and not merely in a legal sense. However, neither author commits himself to an account of the corruption of human nature or tendencies that then becomes a cause of wickedness. Although Xunzi holds to an idea that human moral nature is more disordered than Mengzi seems to allow, he does not posit a fall per se. Rather, as Aaron Stalnaker puts it, Xunzi does not think we are "innately prone to vice" (as Augustine does according to Stalnaker), but that we are "merely susceptible to vice, given the general tenor of our instincts."[101] For

---

101. Stalnaker, *Overcoming Our Evil*, 136.

166   Chapter 3

this reason, assessing whether Mengzi or Xunzi is more consonant with the Catholic perspective of the human person requires examining if there are aspects of the Catholic perspective regarding sin that their philosophies resemble even if the whole is not harmonious.[102]

Aquinas's presentation of the doctrine of sin has two important aspects vis-à-vis the assessment of *renxing*. First is Aquinas's basic definition of sin. In its most technical meaning, Aquinas uses sin to denote a "disordered act" (*actum inordinatum*) because it leads away from virtue, or more simply, sin is a "wicked human act" (*actus humanus malus*).[103] Sin is distinct from a vice, which is a habitual inclination away from virtue, although clearly vice is sinful.[104] Here we also benefit from recalling that for Aquinas, the Augustinian definition of wickedness as the privation of the good (*privatio boni*) is paradigmatic: evil and sin have no positive essence, but are the corruption of the good from its true nature.

Thus, on a theoretical level, Aquinas holds that human nature cannot be evil because evil has no positive being. Rather, human nature is good, but has been corrupted from its full goodness to be turned in part toward evil things. The fact that human nature is not utterly corrupt is evident in the fact that human beings still generally pursue the goods of our nature—for example, human beings are inclined to preserve our own being. However, our goodness is now a defective goodness: we have the powers and "material" needed for goodness, but the operation is debilitated for we have lost the proper order within the soul needed for flourishing (such as the governance of our sensible appetites by reason). This results in both the fact that we perform disordered acts (sin) and that we have habits that lead us to act in these ways (vice).

What is original sin, then?[105] In his illuminating discussion of the transmission of original sin, Aquinas examines previous opinions holding that the reproductive act, specifically the man's semen, was

---

102. Zhao, "The Goodness of Human Nature and Original Sin."
103. Quotes are from *ST* IaIIae, q. 71, art. 1, corp. and IaIIae, q. 71, art. 6, corp., respectively.
104. *ST* IaIIae, q. 71, art. 1, corp.
105. Original sin is, undoubtedly a complex topic within the Catholic tradition. For helpful overviews from a Thomistic perspective, see Matthew Levering, *Engaging the Doctrine of Creation: Cosmos, Creatures, and the Wise and Good Creator* (Grand Rapids, MI: Baker Academic, 2017), 227–72; and Daniel W. Houck, *Aquinas, Original Sin, and the Challenge of Evolution* (New York: Cambridge University Press, 2020), esp. 55–137.

A Thomistic Assessment of the Confucian Debate on *Renxing*   167

the way that original sin was transmitted to future generations. Aquinas rejects this position, primarily because seminal transmission can communicate certain qualities to an offspring's body and can even affect the soul in some way through bodily defects, but cannot seminally transmit guilt which is included in original sin.[106] Therefore, Aquinas argues original sin and its guilt is transmitted to each generation through human nature itself.[107] His explanation is that Adam and Eve's sin was an act of their human nature, and since they are source of all future human beings, their original sinful act affects not only their individual selves, but the nature common to all humans as well. Hence, every generation of human being born after Adam and Eve receives the loss of original justice.[108]

It is not my intention here to assess Aquinas's position on the transmission of original sin, which many have argued needs clarification and strengthening.[109] Rather, I simply wish to point out here that Aquinas clearly holds that original sin means that after the Fall, human beings receive a nature without original justice, which provides the right order to God and ourselves in order to flourish spontaneously and easily. This nature retains goodness in many respects, but it has suffered defects to the various operations and order between the operations needed to flourish.[110] Therefore, Aquinas speaks of original sin as a habit of nature (rather than the individual soul, which is a vice) and thus an "inordinate disposition of nature" (*dispositio naturae inordinata*).[111]

It is therefore crucial to understand what Aquinas means by the defects and disorder that comes upon human nature due to original sin. Aquinas rejects the possibility that original sin is like an infused habit that inclines human beings toward wicked acts.[112] That is, hab-

---

106. See *ST* IaIIae, q. 81, art. 1, corp. and ad 2–3.

107. For a discussion of how Aquinas develops his account of the guilt of original sin, see Houck, 119–23.

108. *ST* IaIIae, q. 81, art. 1, corp.

109. See Houck; also, for a helpful discussion of the broader theological literature in modern times (especially among Protestant thinkers) that has often criticized the classical doctrine of original sin, see Ian McFarland, *In Adam's Fall: A Meditation on the Christian Doctrine of Original Sin* (Malden, MA: Wiley-Blackwell, 2011), 3–28.

110. Houck, 121.

111. *ST* IaIIae, q. 82, art. 1, ad 2.

112. *ST* IaIIae, q. 82, art. 1, obj. 3. Though this argument comes from an objection, Aquinas clearly agrees with this premise of the objection.

168 Chapter 3

its that incline human beings away from virtue and the good cannot be connatural to us and therefore they must be acquired rather than infused or given by God or nature. Thus, Aquinas understands original sin as a defect of the operations of our nature that would flourish in the state of original justice.[113] For Aquinas, the powers and inclinations of human nature retain a measure of goodness, though the good is lessened because we are made susceptible to failure. For example, even after the Fall we all still retain a natural inclination to procreate and rear children, which is good for our nature. However, due to the defects caused by the loss of original justice, we are now susceptible to misusing this inclination, for example, by loving the sexual act above God or by following sexual desires apart from the guidance of reason. Hence, there is an important distinction between the "goods of nature" (*bonum naturae*)—meaning the powers and faculties of the human person—which are in no way destroyed by original sin, and the proper order and operation of these goods of nature toward our flourishing, for it is this this order which is defective in light of original sin.

Therefore, inasmuch as one intends the phrase "human nature is good" to mean that human powers are meant to serve the development of moral virtue, Aquinas could affirm that this is true, and he could agree with Mengzi's theory of *renxing*. However, Aquinas also believes the natural inclination toward the good has suffered defect due to original sin. Because the loss of original justice has left us without the proper order and relationship to God, ourselves, and others necessary to flourish, our natural inclinations are not, on their own, trustworthy guides to moral virtue, even regarding natural goods. For example, as we saw above, Aquinas holds that the human being is naturally inclined to seek the good rather than evil due to natural law. Yet he also knows that the effects of the Fall enable us to make mistakes such as when we fail to properly measure the different levels of goodness in things against higher goods (e.g., when we choose the pleasurable good of excessive eating over the higher good of health). As a result, humans do not easily live out the virtue that our powers are meant to serve. In this view of things, Aquinas

---

113. *ST* IaIIae, q. 85, art. 1, corp.

A Thomistic Assessment of the Confucian Debate on *Renxing*   169

agrees more with Xunzi's account of *renxing* inasmuch as he recognizes that our natural inclinations (such as our emotions) are not trustworthy *on their own* as a moral guide. In the state of sin, the order and relationship between our emotions and reason is defective, and we must engage in moral labor to determine when and how our emotions are leading us to or away from flourishing.

Furthering this point of connection, Aquinas is much more like Xunzi than Mengzi inasmuch as Xunzi thinks it important to qualify not only that human morality must be cultivated (as Mengzi would agree), but how it must be cultivated based on the work of an external cause of moral perfection. Significantly, scholars debate precisely how much Aquinas thinks it is possible for human beings to develop moral virtue. Some hold that Aquinas sees it as possible for humans without grace to acquire some natural virtue and thus arrive at an imperfect, yet natural happiness. Others hold that Aquinas thinks it impossible for the cultivation of moral happiness apart from grace.[114] What is clear, however, is that Aquinas certainly believes that the supreme happiness of human beings is supernatural and requires grace to be possessed. Xunzi for his part thinks that without the external artifice of the sages, humans cannot overcome the confused inclinations of our heart-mind. Clearly Xunzi's account of human nature does not have the eschatological character of Aquinas's moral theology, nor does his account explain how the sage is distinct from the natural as such—that is, Xunzi does not imply one requires a transcendent external cause in order to effect moral cultivation. Still, both agree that human moral flourishing is impossible based on the mere moral will of the individual. Rather, there must be something to direct and form us in this effort, which must come from outside of ourselves.

---

114. See David Decosimo, *Ethics as a Work of Charity: Thomas Aquinas and Pagan Virtue* (Stanford, CA: Stanford University Press, 2014), 3–8. As Decosimo has put it, this generally speaking concerns the problem of "pagan virtue"—that is, whether non-Christians (lacking grace and the supernatural virtue of charity) can genuinely act virtuously. Decosimo observes that there are traditionally two clashing approaches to Aquinas on this question, the "hyper-Augustinian" interpretation which sees pagan morality as falling entirely short of true virtue, and the "Public Reason Thomists" who hold to a stark contrast between natural virtue and supernatural virtue, holding that "what Thomas bequeaths us ... is a way of safely and justly navigating our pluralistic world and democratic politics by the deliverances of reason alone" (7).

Moreover, both Xunzi and Aquinas see rituals as keys to this process, though in significantly different ways. For Xunzi, the *li* of the sages can effect moral transformation by means of emulation and habituation toward the good. They are pedagogical practices at best. For Aquinas, the sacraments of the Church are the normal means by which God communicates grace to human beings. But this grace does not merely "teach" new things. Rather, divine grace transforms the human person, bestowing upon the human soul the form of charity and the additional virtues of faith and hope. The grace of Holy Spirit in the New Covenant becomes a habitual state and reality for the Christian which corrects our moral waywardness from the inside out, as a principle written on the heart.

CONCLUSIONS

In keeping with the goal of this book is to assess the limits and possibilities of Chinese philosophical concepts for use in Chinese Catholic theological science, there are several important insights to be gleaned from the foregoing analysis. First, I hope this analysis has shown that the Confucian discussion of *renxing* provides a complicated yet robust resource for considering human morality. Appreciating the Confucian approach to *renxing* in terms of a debate rather than a single position strikes me as fundamentally important to benefiting from these resources. For it is possible—even advisable—for the theologian to take Mengzi and Xunzi as both offering important insights about human morality that can and should be mined for theological utility.

I suggest we should recognize that Mengzi and Xunzi each have one distinctive strength from the perspective of Catholic theology. Mengzi's view seems to more clearly accord with the Catholic traditional frameworks of virtue theory and natural law. That is, Mengzi provides a better way than Xunzi for the theologian to examine how morality is condign and connatural to the human being, and how there are resources given to humanity on the level of nature itself that testify to our proper acts and ends in pursuing goodness. Thus, it is indubitable that Mengzi's perspective falls into greater harmony

A Thomistic Assessment of the Confucian Debate on *Renxing*   171

than does Xunzi's with the natural moral virtue approach in the Thomistic tradition, and this may suggest that Mengzi's philosophy is better suited to producing a Chinese Catholic moral theology.

However, Mengzi's view of *renxing* does not adequately deal with another fundamentally important problem that Catholic theology must address: the obstacles to moral flourishing that lie within the human heart. In this regard, Xunzi's strength from the theological perspective is that his account of *renxing* more clearly articulates the inadequacy of our inclinations to bring about consistent performance of the morality which is condign to our nature (including our nature elevated by grace). Rather, Xunzi provides a means to articulate and understand that the human heart-mind needs specific formation. Moreover, due to his emphasis on the extrinsic nature of sagely learning as the means of instilling virtue, Xunzi's conception of *renxing* can even be said to prepare for the entrance of divine grace, wherein the true Sage Ruler of the cosmos institutes the rituals and laws that guide and form human beings for our true flourishing.

Consequently, as I mentioned above, it does not seem wise to suggest that either Mengzi or Xunzi will better serve Chinese Catholic theology in absolute way; rather, they offer different gifts for different theological tasks. And indeed, I think both are needed. As I discussed in the introduction to this book, many theologians appeal (in broad ways) to Chinese philosophies as a way of offering resources that are more "relevant" to East Asian communities than Western ones. Generally speaking, I find this claim problematic, although it is not without some truth. As a case in point, the traditional Chinese conception of the human person uses a very different terminology for understanding the human person, one that describes human powers and faculties in different ways. Chinese anthropology, for example, has taught us to think of the central human faculty as the heart-mind, and to understand the various phenomena of human emotional and physical life by means of concepts such as *qing*, *qi*, and *yin-yang*.

Inasmuch as these conceptions of the human person accord with anthropological reality (and are not just an anthropological "language"), they cannot be merely replaced or translated into the categories of Western anthropology. For they may hold significant insights for understanding the human creature as God made us that can be lost in the process of conforming them to more standard forms of anthropological description in the Greek and Latin traditions. Therefore, the challenge of articulating a Chinese Catholic account of the human person that genuinely draws upon the anthropological language of Chinese philosophy is considerable. The above analysis, however, suggests that drawing upon concrete philosophical resources such as Mengzi and Xunzi can furnish guides for Catholic theological anthropology in negotiating these new contexts. Clearly such a project goes well beyond the scope of this book, which only seeks to prepare for the more intensive theological integration of Catholic theology and Chinese philosophy by clarifying the points of agreement and disagreement. Yet this chapter also shows that there are indeed fruitful resources for developing a Chinese Catholic anthropology in a systematic fashion.

4

A Thomistic Reading of Mohist *Jian ai*

Despite the challenges of vastly different conceptual, linguistic, and historical frameworks, there are occasions at which debates among early Chinese thinkers strike a familiar chord with debates within the Christian tradition. In this chapter, I undertake a Thomistic assessment of one side of such a debate from classical China. During the pre-Qin period, a significant debate arose between Confucians and followers of Mozi concerning whether hierarchies of affection were good for society or not. Confucians such as Mengzi defended the view that kinship relations, such as parents, naturally require a greater degree of affection and concern than more distant relations. This was embodied in concrete differences in the ritual treatment of parents when they were buried, for example. The Mohists, in contrast, held that such graded affections served to undermine the common good, and were ultimately nonsensical. The Mohists believed that affection for kin relations ought to be properly understood as a species of the more generic moral demand to care for others "broadly," a view that is linked with the term "*jian ai* 兼爱" often rendered as either "universal love" or "impartial care." This doctrine of *jian ai* has come to be perceived as the quintessential Mohist teaching, and thus it is extremely significant in the study of early Chinese thought.[1]

---

1. Cai Renhou 蔡仁厚, *Mojia zhexue* 墨家哲學 (Taipei: Dong da tushu gongsi, 1994), 66. Cai, an influential scholar, holds that the doctrine of *Tian*'s will is a foundational concept

174   Chapter 4

At the same time, in the broad Christian tradition, there is a considerable history of debate about the nature of Christian love (*caritas* or *agape*) and whether it allows for special, unique love between human beings or whether it is a form of love that treats all humans equally. In the broad Christian tradition, modern times has seen support, particularly in Protestant ranks, for conceiving of Christian love as a form of love that treats all equally, as seen in Gene Outka's definition of *agape* love as "a regard for the neighbor which in crucial respects is independent and unalterable."[2] Outka's definition bears great resemblance (unsurprising given his sources) to Anders Nygren's famous conceptualization of *agape* as the opposite of *eros*—that is, love that is not rooted in the value or goodness of the beloved, but completely from the will of the lover to love.[3] As Outka observes, this basic perspective can be found (in various degrees) among many of the most influential modern Protestant thinkers, such as Søren Kierkegaard, H. Richard Niebuhr, and Karl Barth.[4]

This is significant because in a 1988 essay, Jean Porter showed how Aquinas's view of charity is rather unamenable to the modern Protestant notion of equal regard. Essentially, Porter argued (and I agree with her assessment) that Aquinas does not believe charity can be understood as mere equal regard for neighbor, but, in fact, admits of a hierarchy of affection, including natural relations.[5] Put in these

---

(*genben guannian* 根本觀念) in the *Mozi*. According to Cai, the doctrine of *jian ai* has a special place because it is the "horizontal" (*heng* 橫) connection that relates all the Mohist doctrines to one another, but it is related to *Tian*'s will as the "vertical" or "transcendent" (*chaoyue genju* 超越根據) foundation. This distinction helps explain why most Western scholars—who tend to dismiss the existence of the vertical principles of a Chinese thought *a priori*—see the "horizontal" principle of *jian ai* as the central Mohist doctrine. For example, Fraser in *The Philosophy of the Mozi*, 158 claims that "the Mohists' arguments clearly indicate that inclusive care is based on the more fundamental norm of promoting the benefit of all"—that is, *jian ai* is a distillation of an "horizontal" ethical principle and not founded on a transcendent one, as Cai argues.

2. Gene Outka, *Agape: An Ethical Analysis* (New Haven, CT: Yale University Press, 1972), 9.

3. Anders Nygren, *Agape and Eros*, trans. Phillip S. Watson (New York: Harper & Row, 1969).

4. Outka, 9–22.

5. Jean Porter, "*De ordine caritatis*: Charity, Friendship and Justice in Thomas Aquinas' *Summa theologiae*," *The Thomist* 53 (1989): 197–213. For a similar and complementary treatment discussing Aquinas in light of equal regard concepts, see Stephen J. Pope, "The Moral Centrality of Natural Priorities: A Thomistic Alternative to 'Equal Regard,'" *The Annual of the Society of Christian Ethics* 10 (1990): 109–29.

A Thomistic Reading of Mohist *Jian ai*

terms, it might seem that the debate about "graded love" in pre-Qin China mirrors the debate about equal regard in the sense that you have disputants on each side defending the necessity and goodness of special, interested love of others as part of virtuous love (Aquinas, classical Catholicism, and early Confucians), and those defending the position of loving all equally regardless of personal significant (Mohists and modern Protestants).

It is significant that the few extant attempts of Chinese theologians to incorporate Mozi into Christian theology have come from Protestant thinkers and have focused on the concept of *jian ai*. The most famous example is that of Wu Leichuan, who in his book entitled *Mo Di and Jesus* argued that both Christ's and Mozi's ethics of care were fundamentally harmonious with that of Communism, indeed even portraying the two as "his ideal socialists."[6] More recently, Zhang Lifu argued that Mohism (rather than Confucianism) provides a helpful starting place for the inculturation of Christian ethics in the Chinese context because Mohism is similar to Christianity in advocating a "universal" (*pubian* 普遍) ethic of concern based on divine principles.[7] Thus, the recent Chinese turn to Mohism seems to partially work along the demarcations of debate I suggested above—that is, understanding Mohism as an ally in the modern Protestant conception of virtuous love of others. It is also worth noting that, on the other hand, Chinese Catholic writers such as Yang Tingyun have historically stressed the great disparity between Catholicism and Mohism on the theme of love of the other, seeing Mohism as opposed to the traditional Catholic (and Confucian) perspective.[8]

This supposition that the Mohist-Confucian debate maps easily and naturally onto the intra-Christian debates about charity piques one's curiosity. For one thing, if the *Mozi* reinforces a Protestant view of charity, then does it have any value in Catholic theology, buttressed as it is by Aquinas and other thinkers who issue a similar account of charity to his? But more deeply, to what degree can we assume that the Mohist position on *jian ai* truly is contradictory to the vision of charity that Aquinas held? Would Aquinas have rejected

6. Chu Sin-Jan, 123.
7. Zhang Lifu.
8. Yang Tingyun, *Dai Yi Xu Pian, Qu ai.*

176   Chapter 4

the Mohist position out of hand, or are there significant aspects that resonate with his perspective?

At the least, we have good reason to suspect that the apparent disparity between Aquinas's view of charity and the Mohist *jian ai* is not as great as it might seem. Because the Mohist tradition did not survive the Qin dynasty, the Mohist position was primarily understood through the lens of critics until the Qing saw a revival of interest in Mohism.[9] Thus, while *jian ai* has historically been associated with something like equal regard or affection, this view has come under scrutiny from recent scholars. Chris Fraser, for example, argues that *jian ai* should be understood as an expression of the central Mohist principle, which Fraser takes to be "promoting the benefit of all"; while he argues *jian ai* means "equal consideration of everyone's interests," he argues it does not entail "that we should feel equal or impartial love for all or that we have equal obligations to everyone, even distant strangers."[10] In a similar vein, Dan Robins has argued that *jian ai* does not involve "saying that we should abandon all particularist attachments," such as filial love for parents, which the *Mozi* recognizes is of great importance.[11] Adding more complication to the picture, Carine Defoort has shown that the doctrine of *jian ai* develops within the Mohist corpus, even suggesting it was not fully clarified in the *Mozi* itself.[12] Hence, one should not too quickly assume that the portrait of the Mohist ethic as one defending equal regard and criticizing particularism is accurate, without further scrutiny at least.

In this chapter, then, I seek a Thomistic reading of *jian ai*, based on a comparison between the Mohist concept and Aquinas's understanding of charity, focusing on charity as love of neighbor. Here I

---

9. Carine Defoort, "The Modern Formation of Early Mohism: Sun Yirang's *Exposing and Correcting the Mozi*," *T'oung Pao* 101, no. 1–3 (2015): 208–38.

10. See Fraser, *The Philosophy of the Mozi*, 158–59. It is worth noting that Fraser's interpretation of *jian ai* within the utilitarian framework is similar to the presentation in Feng, *Zhongguo zhexue shi*, 84–85.

11. Dan Robins, "Mohist Care," *Philosophy East and West* 62, no. 1 (January 2012): 60. For a similar perspective, see Fraser, *The Philosophy of the Mozi*, 158–84.

12. Carine Defoort, "The Growing Scope of 'Jian' 兼: Differences Between Chapters 14, 15, and 16 of the 'Mozi,'" *Oriens Extremus* 45 (2005/06): 119–40; and Carine Defoort, "Are the Three 'Jian Ai' Chapters About Universal Love?" in Defoort and Standaert, *The Mozi as an Evolving Text*, 35–68.

A Thomistic Reading of Mohist *Jian ai*   177

inquire into what the Thomistic perspective can and cannot appreciate about the Mohist concept. As students of Aquinas know well, a great tradition of moral theology draws upon the resources of natural philosophy to articulate the moral life under the gift of grace. To cite a relevant example, Aquinas draws heavily upon Aristotle's understanding of friendship to provide his account of the theological virtue of charity. While it would be possible and even fruitful to develop similar resources from Chinese philosophy regarding friendship for Catholic theology, it is also worth asking the broader question of what sorts of resources in early Chinese thought may serve to help articulate theological virtues such as charity in a Chinese context.[13] It seems to me that even a cursory understanding of the Mohist *jian ai* (such as that I have sketched in this introduction) suggests the concept might have theological utility for such purposes. However, making such use of *jian ai* first requires a rigorous examination and assessment of the concept, which is my focus in this chapter.

INITIAL LIMITATIONS

Before turning to the primary analysis of the chapter, taking stock of the limits and obstacles to the task is helpful. Aquinas's understanding of charity has a significant component that is not found in the Mohist doctrine of *jian ai*. For Aquinas, the most basic definition of charity is the friendship a man has with God.[14] The Mohist doctrine of *jian ai* does not draw upon the concept of friendship, but rather is developed as a reaction to the perceived predominance of self-love (*zi ai* 自愛). More importantly, Catholic doctrine holds

---

13. For readers interested in Chinese conceptions of friendship, I recommend: Timothy Connolly, "Friendship and Filial Piety: Relational Ethics in Aristotle and Early Confucianism," *Journal of Chinese Philosophy* 39, no. 1 (2012): 71–88; He Yuanguo, "Confucius and Aristotle on Friendship: A Comparative Study," *Frontiers of Philosophy in China* 2, no. 2 (2007): 291–307; Whalen Lai, "Friendship in Confucian China: Classical and Late Ming," in *Friendship East and West: Philosophical Perspectives*, ed. Oliver Leaman (Richmond, UK: Curzon, 1996), 215–50; Eric C. Mullis, "Confucius and Aristotle on the Goods of Friendship," *Dao* 9, no. 4 (2010): 391–405; Sor-hoon Tan, "Mentor or Friend? Confucius and Aristotle on Equality and Ethical Development in Friendship," *International Studies in Philosophy* 33, no. 4 (2001): 99–121; Aat Verhoorn, "Friendship in Ancient China," *East Asian History* 27 (2004): 1–32.

14. *ST* IIaIIae, q. 23, art. 1.

178   Chapter 4

charity is not a natural virtue that can be formed by effort or habituation in the will, but a gift of the Holy Spirit disposing those who receive the gift to friendship with God—though humans can cooperate with grace and thus grow in charity. In Aquinas's terminology, charity is a gift of the grace of the New Law that has God as its primary object.

As we saw previously in chapter 3, the *Mozi* has an interesting theological perspective its own right, but there are no true analogues to these major features of Christian charity to be found in the text. While *Tian* is a model for love or concern given to others (see chapter 3 above), there is no clear statement that *Tian* is the primary recipient of love and concern or that *Tian* even receives these at all. *Tian* receives sacrifices and service, but the *Mozi* does not associate these activities with love per se. Additionally, although the *Mozi* clearly understands loving others to derive from *Tian*'s love of all, it is not the case that love of others is describe as subordinate to loving *Tian*. In the *Mozi*, the relationship with *Tian* is conceived in terms of rituals and blessings rather than anything similar to the "friendship" model Aquinas has in mind.

Similarly, the love or concern that is explicated in the *Mozi* is not a supernatural gift of a divine economy. Rather, the text sees such care and concern arising as a natural obligation to care for others. Though derived from *Tian*'s love, the responsibility to love others with *jian ai* in the *Mozi* is a state of nature claim, not a state of grace. Thus, the *Mozi* describes the need to recognize the principle of loving others, but does not argue there is a new disposition needed from *Tian* in order to live out the love of others in a more perfect way. I should also add that in Mohism there is no clear articulation of care or love as a habit, though that is less important in this context than the fact that the Mohist conception of love or concern has a completely natural point of origin. From the Thomistic perspective, one could say that the Mohists see impartial care as discernible from natural law rather than as infused from the New Law.

This all suggests an observation by the influential Chinese Catholic intellectual and educator, Ma Xiangbo (1840–1939). In an essay on the Bible's relationship to human cultures written in 1916, Ma

A Thomistic Reading of Mohist *Jian ai*   179

observed that it was tempting to equate the biblical ethic—which Ma himself described as being "that you should love one another with mutual affection and love, and that is all" (該彼此相親相愛而已)—with the Mohist doctrine of *jian ai*.[15] Ma says this is not really so, arguing that in the biblical ethos, all others are my brothers or sisters in a genuine way because of the full truth of God's creative and providential love.[16] Ultimately, Christian theological science must recognize that the biblical conception of divine love and human charity as sharing in this love has a shape and perfection given only through revelation, and therefore Mozi's conception of *jian ai* will inevitably fall short of the full Christian conception of charity. Yet at the same time, it is not self-evident that Mozi's *jian ai* should be easily cast aside as a resource for understanding and articulating Christian charity.

In order to compare the two conceptions of love and concern with respect for these differences, it is important to narrow my focus. Rather than attempting to account for the entirety of Aquinas's understanding of charity, my analysis will explore his understanding of charity as love of neighbor. Clearly from the perspective of Aquinas this love of neighbor cannot be completely sundered from charity as friendship with God, and I make no pretense to disunite the two. However, I will attempt to isolate as much as possible the key principles and defining features of charity as love of neighbor as distinct from love of God, without artificially creating a *tertium quid*.

THE *MOZI* ON *JIAN AI*

The term *jian ai* appears in the titles of chapters 14–16 in the *Mozi* (*Jian ai shang, zhong,* and *xia* in Chinese).[17] In this section, I will

---

15. Ma Xiangbo, *Ma Xiangbo ji* 馬相伯集, ed. Zhu Weizheng 朱維錚 (Shanghai: Fudan Daxue Chubanshe, 1996), 186.

16. Ma Xiangbo, 186. As Ma puts it, "Only the Bible speaks of all those in the world as brothers to us in a genuine sense, because they are also made, nourished, and cherished by the Creator of all things, which cannot be found in the empty words of Huang Di, Shen Nong, the Yu or Xia" (惟《聖經》所說四海皆兄弟, 乃真兄弟, 同為造物主所生, 所養, 所愛護, 非黃, 農, 虞, 夏等空名詞).

17. Often these chapters are referenced by their chapter numbers in the *Mozi* (14, 15, and 16 respectively). For the sake of clarity, I will reference them in this chapter by the full chapter titles.

180 Chapter 4

focus on this triplet to describe the Mohist understanding of proper concern or love of neighbor. Contemporary scholars on the *Mozi* often debate what *jian ai* means and how it should be translated. Both terms involved, *jian* and *ai*, create problems to this end. The term *jian* is often used in the context of blending or combining things; hence, *jian ai* is sometimes treated as "universal love." Although the noun/verb *ai* does soundly translate as "love," it also can signify other activities or dispositions. In early China, *ai* as love was distinguished from affective dispositions such as enjoying (*le* 樂) or liking things (*xi* 喜), but it could also signify broader kinds of concern or affection than the English speaker associates with love. In addition to love, kindness, or care for another, there are other possible meanings of *ai*, leading to one translation of *jian ai* as "impartial care" or "inclusive care."[18]

While these debates about the meaning of *jian ai* are significant among contemporary sinologists, they can obscure other issues, such as whether *jian ai* as a concept bears much significance at all for the *Mozi*. Apart from its titular use, the term *jian ai* does not actually appear in the *Jian ai* triplet; the titles were applied to these chapters by a later editor. The closest one finds is the phrase "*jian xiang ai* 兼相愛" and more often "*xiang ai* 相愛" or "mutual love." At best, *jian ai* is a symbolic term standing in for the duties of care and/or affection defended across three chapters of the *Mozi*, and this in the view of a later redactor. In fact, Carine Defoort has argued recently that the *Jian ai* triplet does not even properly concern the doctrine of *jian ai* but represent steps in its formulation.[19] Consequently, understanding what *jian ai* represents requires a close examination of the specific arguments in the *Mozi*, and cannot be anticipated merely based on expected meanings of the term.

Yet even here we must pause and ask whether it is the case the *Jian ai* triplet of the *Mozi* consists of one coherent, developed teaching. Scholars of the *Mozi* largely agree that the *Jian ai* triplet reflects the sort of divisions underlying all the core chapters. However, there is not general agreement on how to parse or understand these

18. For a helpful discussion of the semantic possibilities of *jian ai* and how they have been treated by scholars, see Robins, 61–62.

19. Defoort, "Are the Three 'Jian Ai' Chapters About Universal Love?"

A Thomistic Reading of Mohist *Jian ai*   181

differences. One helpful example is Defoort, who has argued, *pace* Ding Weixiang, that the *Jian ai* triplet expresses an evolutionary development of *jian ai* that grows from an emphasis on "caring for oneself" in the first chapter, to "an unconditional type of caring for anyone else" in the final chapter.[20]

Regardless of authorship or intention, it does seem that the final editors of the *Mozi* thought the *Jian Ai* triplet was necessary as a triplet in order to articulate the Mohist idea of loving concern for others.[21] Thus, like my approach in chapter 3, it seems prudent to draw upon all three as a coherent if discursive account of necessary love and concern for others. Due to my present purposes, it is less important to attend to the unique perspectives of each account, and therefore I seek to examine these chapters collectively as an authentic and authoritative explication of *jian ai* according to the thought of Mozi. Nonetheless, compared to the *Tianzhi* triplet, the *Jian ai* triplet shows much clearer development throughout the chapters. That is, we find a genuine progression throughout the chapters. Therefore, it is prudent to analyze each chapter on its own terms, though as aspects of a larger, coherent conversation about concern for others in the Mohist tradition.

Mozi 14 opens by observing that "in order to do what is necessary to govern [*zhi* 治) the empire, the sage must undoubtedly know the origins of disorder [*luan zhi suo ziqi* 亂之所自起)."[22] That is, finding the practices that bring order to the world require an investigation (*cha* 察) into disorder and its causes. In the opinion of the author of chapter 14, the cause of disorder is not positive but negative: "disorder ... arises from the absence of mutual love" [*xiang*

---

20. Defoort, "The Growing Scope of 'Jian,'" 139. Ding's position is found in Ding Weixiang 丁为祥, "*Mojia jian ai guan de yanbian* 墨家兼爱观的演变." *Shaanxi shifan daxue xuebao* 28, no. 4 (1998): 70–76.

21. Fraser, *The Philosophy of the Mozi*, 160–61. Fraser defines the Mohist account of care (*ai*) as "being committed to or positively disposed toward a person's welfare, for that person's own sake and not as a means, such that we are attentive to the person's well-being, and, other things being equal, distinguishing something as beneficial to the person tends to move us to pursue it on the person's behalf, while distinguishing something as harmful to the person tends to move us to prevent or eliminate it." In a theological context, this definition of care seems to nicely relate to loving concern inasmuch as it resonates with Aquinas's definition of love as willing the good of another.

22. *Mozi*, 14, 1.

ai). Translating *xiang* in this case as "mutual" may be somewhat misleading inasmuch the English word "mutual" implies reciprocity.[23] The *Mozi* does not, at least initially, identify *xiang ai* in terms of exchanged or reciprocated love as such; rather, the emphasis is on how various moral subjects do or do not love another. As an illustration, the *Mozi* argues the absence of mutual love gives rise to disorder in terms of the father-son relationship. A disordered father-son relationship happens when "the son loves himself and does not love his father [*zi ai bu ai fu* 自愛不愛父) and therefore he will let his father suffer and benefit himself [*zili* 自利)."[24] Similarly, the father can be guilty of loving himself but not loving his son, and willing to see his son suffer misfortune if it benefits himself.[25]

The emphasis of the *Mozi* is not so much on whether the father and son enjoy the fruits of requited affection, but on the responsibilities of care bearing on each member of the relationship. According to the *Jian ai shang*, the cause of disorder is solipsistic care or affection that privileges oneself above others. On the one hand, a son may find himself empty of affection for his father at all, which is perhaps rare but does happen. More often, sons or fathers will love others as lesser goods and seek to benefit themselves over and against others. As a corrective to this disordered affection, the *Mozi* offers mutual love. Therefore, according to this context, it seems *xiang ai* is meant to signify extending to others the affection one has for oneself.

The *Jian ai shang* chapter extends this insight into broader social contexts. The failure to love mutually is also said to be at work in robbers and thieves who love their house and property but "do not love the houses of others," or they love their own bodies but not those of others.[26] Nobles evince the practice of loving their families or houses and not those of others, and princes can love their state and not love others. In each case, the measure of failure of affection

---

23. Robins, "Mohist Care," 61–62. Robins sees reciprocity as implied in 相愛, as least in *Mozi*, 14 and 15 though by *Mozi*, 16, he says the text moves away from situations which implicitly involve reciprocity. As I argue above, I am less certain *xiang* should be seen to imply reciprocity.

24. *Mozi*, 14, 2.

25. *Mozi*, 14, 2.

26. *Mozi*, 14, 3.

A Thomistic Reading of Mohist *Jian ai*   183

is the willingness of these moral agents to harm others through theft, bodily harm, political scheming, or offensive wars. What is key is that the lack of mutual love is attributed to the willingness to harm others for the sake of benefitting oneself or one's family, state, etc.

Therefore, *Mozi*, 14 concludes that what is needed for order is *jian xiang ai*, or "the universal practice of mutual love." The chapter defines the term as follow: "loving others as though one were loving himself" (*ai ren ruo ai qi shen* 愛人若愛其身).[27] In another formulation, it describes mutual love as "regarding" or "looking upon" (*shi* 視) others as oneself. If this simple principle were put into practice, the *Mozi* tells us, then there would be no failures in filial conduct, paternal conduct, no robber or thieves, and no disorder or wars.

At this stage, there are several important questions to pose about the account of mutual love in *Mozi*, 14. First, it is unclear what the precise scope of *jian* mutual love is. In her study of these chapters, Defoort noted that chapter 14 seems to urge an ethic of "care for others," meaning an exhortation to be concerned about others, specifically those with whom one has social congress or political relationships.[28] Inasmuch as this chapter promotes *jian ai*, this "universalizing" love is relative to moral agents. That is, *Mozi*, 14 doesn't argue that I have a duty to love or regard everyone equally in any theoretical sense, but contends I have a duty to treat those I meet in concrete relationships and experiences in a similar fashion.

But what are the precise limits or demands of this similar love? When the *Mozi* commends me to love others as I love myself, it is important to remember that it has described self-love primarily in terms of self-benefit. That is, I love myself inasmuch as I labor to bring myself good things and flourish. A plausible reading of the *Mozi* would be that having mutual love is a minimalist concept: I must not seek to harm others that I may benefit, and thus care for their benefit as I care for my own. In a minimalist sense, this kind of love is not so much "equal regard" as it is "unselfish regard" or perhaps "sympathetic regard" for others.[29]

More importantly, one should note that chapter 14 makes no

---

27. *Mozi*, 14, 4.
28. See Defoort, "The Growing Scope of 'Jian,'" 126–28.
29. Cai, *Mojia zhexue*, 41. Cai summarizes lacking mutual love as "selfishness" (*zisi* 自私).

184 Chapter 4

pretense to suggest that mutual love entails a collapsing of all forms of love and care into one universal affection for all. Rather, mutual love as a prohibition against pure self-interested activities allows for a diversity of loves to be enacted according to the species of the relationships they serve. As Dan Robins has expressed it, "Nothing in the *Mozi* sets out institutions that could replace the family without giving rise to particularist attachments, or denies the importance of family ties. The core argument is itself premised on the value of filial piety and other family virtues."[30] Thus, for the author of *Mozi*, 14, mutual love does not replace the principles of filial love and duty but actually results in them. The Mohist conception of *jian ai* does not mean to remove paternal compassion, but ensure its practice. Therefore, *jian xiang ai* in the first chapter of the triplet does not homogenize the affective relationships between human beings, but it guards against dissolving relational loves into self-concern and self-benefit.

Mozi, 15 offers a more precise and thus more controversial definition of virtuous concern for others. Like *Mozi*, 14, chapter 15 exhorts "universal mutual concern or love" (*jian xiang ai*) but adds a phrase that becomes a de facto clarification or definition of mutual love: *jiao xiang li* 交相利 or "mutual benefit." As we saw above, *Mozi* 14 can be read minimally as arguing selfish concern is an obstacle to mutual love, but this does not require thinking of care as working to promote the benefit of others; it could mean simply not leveraging others to benefit oneself. *Mozi*, 15 limits out this minimalist interpretation by arguing that mutual love involves and requires the pursuit of what will benefit or profit (*li*) others.

On the one hand, it is notable that this delineation of mutual love is dependent upon how chapter 15 interprets the "disorder" of the previous chapter. Instead of merely addressing the cause of "disorder" the scope is more specific. The author of *Mozi* 15 seeks to determine the cause of those practices or habits that "harm" (*hai* 害) the empire and promote against these causes those practices which will benefit (*li*) the empire. In this schema, mutual love is not only seen as the cause of lack of order, but it is offered as a concrete path

---

30. Robins, 64. Robins's observation cuts against the popular reading of Mohism derived from *Mengzi*, 3B:14, which says that the *jian ai* teaching makes it as though one has no father ("墨氏兼愛, 是無父也").

A Thomistic Reading of Mohist *Jian ai*   185

to the benefit of the empire.[31] This necessarily requires defining love more in terms of benefit, so as to demonstrate how mutual love actually brings about benefit on a universal or general scale. At the same time, such a move also requires articulating how mutual love and its consequences of mutual benefit comes to operate on a more general scale. Therefore, in addition to identifying mutual love with mutual benefit, the author argues for a more explicit universal scope of mutual love.

Responding to objections that mutual love and benefit is too difficult to be practicable, *Mozi*, 15 cites an historical example of enacting these principles. The text looks to the story of King Yu, who was renowned for his ability to install efficient methods of irrigating rivers when their flooding had wreaked havoc on his society.[32] According to the story as told in the *Mozi*, Yu focused on attenuating the effects of flooding rivers throughout China, addressing the particular needs of concrete situations "in order to benefit" (*yi li* 以利) various peoples spread across the empire.[33] Strikingly, the text also argues that Yu acted to control the flood waters to benefit not only the Zhou people identified as the people of the Chinese race, but also the diverse tribes of "barbarians" that lived on the outskirts of Zhou society. These peoples are often treated in early Chinese discourse as outsiders to the cultural identity of the Chinese people, and therefore were not typically seen as recipients of Zhou courtesy and concern.

Put into terms appreciable to the modern reader, *Mozi*, 15 is here suggesting that "universal" mutual love and benefit is truly that: extended to everyone. This especially significant because in the context of chapter 15, the author argues that the primary impediment to the enactment of the principles of mutual love and benefit are rulers who fail to commit to these principles. Notably, Yu was said to have been elevated to ruler after King Shun due to his resolution of the flooding catastrophes. The *Mozi* is here showing that it was Yu's

---

31. See Cai, *Mojia zhexue*, 43.

32. For the broader context of these heroic tales in Chinese history, see Kwang-chih Chang, "China on the Eve of the Historical Period," in *The Cambridge History of Ancient China: From the Origins of Civilization to 221 B.C.*, ed. Michael Loewe and Edward L. Shaughnessy (Cambridge: Cambridge University Press, 1999), 64–73.

33. *Mozi*, 15, 7.

186 Chapter 4

broad love and universal pursuit of mutual benefit that justified him as the heir to Shun's throne. Consequently, Yu serves as evidence that loving universally so as to be concerned for the benefit of all is not only practicable, but efficacious for flourishing.

Mozi, 16 is distinctive for its clearer definition of the scope of universal mutual love, by striking a contrast between *jian* and *bie* 別, a term often translated as "partiality" in this context. One product of this approach is a greater focus on action rather than affection or regard, which was the main concern of the *Jian ai shang.* The idea of regarding others as myself is shifted in the *Mozi,* 16 to "acting for others as I act for myself" (*wei bi zhe you wei ji* 為彼者猶為己).[34] Initially, all the contrast between *bie* and *jian* provides is a way of clarifying that such an attitude of caring for others as I care for myself is indeed synonymous with *jian.* Hence, *bie* neatly stands in for the cause and effects of disorder or harm within the state—indeed, *Mozi* 16 says that partiality is produced from the most significant threats to the empire.[35]

Fortunately, the chapter goes on to define the *bie* and *jian* perspectives through concrete examples. As a kind of thought experiment, chapter 16 has Mozi offer an account of two scholars (*shi* 士), each alike except for their adherence to a vision of caring in a *jian* way or caring in a *bie* way. The one who practices the love of partiality will exclaim to himself, "how it is possible for me to love my friend as I love myself or his parents as I love my parents?" Chapter 16 argues that because the scholar of partiality deems this kind of care impossible, he will watch his friend suffer hunger, cold and death, and not be moved to feed him, clothe him or bury him properly. The text ultimately asks a forceful question of its audience: which friend would you prefer? The conclusion is that even those who would theoretically reject *jian* love would nonetheless prefer a *jian*-minded friend to a *bie*-minded one.[36]

For the moment, I will set aside a logical issue in this argument, namely that it is not clear why my failure to love my friend as I love myself means I will neglect to intervene when he is danger. It might

---

34. *Mozi,* 16, 2.
35. *Mozi,* 16, 2: "吾本原別之所生, 天下之大害者也."
36. *Mozi,* 16, 4.

A Thomistic Reading of Mohist *Jian ai*   187

be the case that the *Mozi* has in mind a situation—sadly frequent in early China—where everyone in the state is in danger of hunger or cold; hence, the implication might be that I do not care for my friend when I am also in danger unless I love him as I love myself. At any rate, what the passage seems to clearly teach about the love of partiality is that it rests upon a firm, perhaps absolute distinction (*bie* can mean to separate or distinguish) between myself or what is mine, and others and what is theirs. Hence, partiality is still grounded in a kind of solipsistic pursuit of self-benefit.[37] It can, in this sense, perhaps refer to what St. Augustine meant by the felicitous phrase *incurvatus in se*, namely a movement reflecting back to the self and never traversing outward to others.[38]

However, the text also seems to go beyond seeing partiality as a solipsistic endeavor; it also takes on a meaning of treating certain others in a unique or special way. Through an approving citation of a classical text, *Mozi*, 16 associates partiality with three other significant dispositions The first is when one is being *pian* 偏, which means leaning or inclining in one direction; in this case, it suggests a kind of predisposition toward particular interested parties and the neglect of others. Second, partiality is associated with being *dang* 黨, typically used as the word for factions or parties. In other words, associating partiality with *dang* seems to mean putting the interests of members of one's own affiliation group above others. Finally, partiality is associated with the term *e* 阿, which also means favoring one over another.[39]

By associating partiality with these terms, *Mozi*, 16 suggests that partiality involves a pre-judgment that another or group of others is more deserving or needing of care. Consequently, in exhorting a *jian* kind of concern, the *Mozi* does not foreclose the necessity of choosing to help one person over another. Rather, it forecloses that such a choice depends upon a prejudgment of who should be given care

---

37. See Fraser, *The Philosophy of the Mozi*, 168. Fraser sees the *Mozi* as describing *bie* as "excluding others' interests from consideration altogether, such that we ignore their needs and do not hesitate to 'detest and injure' them."

38. For a helpful study of Augustine's conception of sin in terms of "*homo incurvatus in se*," see Matt Jenson, *The Gravity of Sin: Augustine, Luther, and Barth on homo incurvatus in se* (London: T&T Clark, 2006), 6–46.

39. *Mozi*, 16, 9.

188 Chapter 4

based on types of favoritism. This raises a helpful question: What sort of favoritism or prejudicial privilege of care are immoral according to chapter 16?

Toward the end of the chapter, *Mozi*, 16 deals explicitly with the implications of its teaching for filial piety, which was traditionally (especially in Confucianism) seen to legitimate the unique valuation of others: I should love and care for my parents in a unique and special way of service than I do others who are not my parents. Chapter 16's resolution to locating filial piety within *jian ai* involves first arguing that he who is filial desires that his parents be loved and cared for by others. Therefore, the best way to be filial is for me to love the parents of others, which will inspire them to love my parents.[40] Hence, the text offers this conclusion: "those who wish for filial service to be extended to all parents by everyone [*jiao xiao zi* 交孝子] … should he not first seek to follow the path of loving and benefiting parents of others?"[41]

This resolution suggests one of two options for how one should negotiate particular affections. On one reading, it seems the text is suggesting that particular affection can be good, and that one can regard one's parents or other particular relations in unique ways, but it is not moral or wise to treat them uniquely. A stronger reading of *ai* as affection and not just concern suggests that the person who has particular affection for his parents must realize he should have this same affection for the parents of others. Embracing the latter interpretation of *jian ai* would thus eventually terminate in denying the moral value of particular affection as well as unequal treatment of others.

At the very least, this discussion of filiality shows that the *Jian ai xia* assumes the problematic nature of all actions of partiality, even those which would strike us as natural, good, and not obviously grounded in desire for self-benefit. It is easier for the modern reader to see why political favoritism is a sign of selfish love rather than familial love. Of course, one should note that in the historical context of the *Mozi*, the distinction between politics and family were not so neat. Often rulers would elevate kinfolk to important positions or

---

40. *Mozi*, 16, 10.
41. *Mozi*, 16, 10.

A Thomistic Reading of Mohist *Jian ai*   189

advance the cause of their family line over-against the interest of the people they ruled. In other words, particular affection even within the family was a legitimate cause of social disorder in the early Chinese milieu.

Still, these kinds of difficulties do not automatically valorize the *Mozi*'s suggestions regarding *jian ai*. Other Chinese thinkers such as Mengzi offered their own critiques of the Mohist positions, not least in defense of the connaturality of filial affection and service within the family as important and in keeping with moral flourishing. For early Confucians, the notion of mutual love was seen to either absolutely or functionally cancel out the natural movement of love one feels for parents and kinfolk that stands in contrast to the lack of natural love we feel for strangers.

The question I pose in the remainder of this chapter is whether the Mohist vision of *jian ai* resonates with the doctrine of charity as Aquinas understood it. Put differently, does the Mohist conception of *jian ai* provide a helpful prefiguration of Christian charity in the Chinese milieu? Allowing that the Mohist conception of *jian ai* in its totality (inasmuch as there is a consensus between the chapters of the triplet) is unlikely to be perfectly consonant with Christian charity, I seek to ask what *aspects* of this doctrine can be affirmed about Christian charity and what will fall away. This will then help us to articulate how the *Mozi* can be used to understand and articulate Christian charity in a Chinese context. To effect such an assessment, I now turn to briefly explain charity as Aquinas understands it, so as to determine a theological "baseline" for Christian charity.

AQUINAS ON CHARITY

As is well known, Aquinas defines *caritas* as a form of Aristotelian love.[42] For Aquinas, charity is in its essence friendship with God, based on the Aristotelian model of "friendship of the virtuous" in

---

42. For significant discussions of this theme, see Guy Mansini, OSB, "Aristotle and Aquinas's Theology of Charity in the *Summa Theologiae*," in Emery and Levering, *Aristotle in Aquinas's Theology*, 121–37; Anthony Keaty, "Thomas's Authority for Identifying Charity as Friendship: Aristotle or John 15?" *The Thomist* 62 (1998): 581–601; L. Gregory Jones, "The Theological Transformation of Aristotelian Friendship in the Thought of St. Thomas Aquinas," *New Scholasticism* 61 (1987): 373–99.

which the love of friendship is conjoined with benevolence such that "we love someone so as to wish good to him."[43] Of course, it is of central importance for Aquinas that it is God rather than human beings who begin the movement of friendship. Thus, charity is a result of man's accepting the offer of mutual love from God.

Although Aquinas argues that charity is principally friendship with God, he notes this sort of friendship is impossible due to the natural power of the human will. This is a very technical proposition for Aquinas that requires some clarification. As a theological virtue, charity is a habit that is necessarily infused by grace, rather than acquired. By why can we not acquire charity? There are two aspects of Aquinas's answer that are important to our consideration of why charity admits of unequal regard for others. In his recent book, Christopher J. Malloy shows that for Aquinas, charity is friendship with God, but specifically under "the formal object of God as (supernatural) beatitude."[44] According to Malloy, this means that charity is friendship with God that that involves loving him not simply in an abstract way as "Most Noble Being," but concretely in her perfection as the Triune God; hence, friendship with God involves "Triune Beatitude."[45] This matters because Aquinas follows Aristotle in recognizing that friendship is founded upon the communication of something. With charity, there is a communication from God to man of properly divine goods—that is, the ability to share in divine beatitude. Since charity involves God's extended hand of friendship to communicate goods the human being could not attain in the order of her own nature, charity is impossible for humans to cultivate apart from the gift of grace that communicates the goods in promissory form.[46]

At the same time, some relationship to love (and friendship) in the order of nature is ingredient to charity. This leads us to ask that although charity is a supernatural kind of love of God, what is the relationship to this love vis-à-vis natural forms of love? There has been significant debate throughout the Christian tradition about

43. *ST* IIaIIae, q. 23, art. 1, corp.

44. Christopher J. Malloy, *Aquinas on Beatific Charity and the Problem of Love* (Steubenville, OH: Emmaus Academic, 2019), 108

45. Malloy, 109.

46. Malloy, 109.

A Thomistic Reading of Mohist *Jian ai*   191

how charity stands in regard to natural love. Again, as Malloy has noted, the strongest theological claim denying the positive relationship between charity and natural love is probably found in Martin Luther, who held that all natural human loving is reducible to a disordered love of self, such that "in our present condition and without grace, we are enslaved to an egocentrism and for this reason damnable in all we do."[47]

In Catholic theological science, however, the norm historically has been to understand that there is a way that human beings are able to naturally love God over self—that is, to genuinely love God as the highest good according to the order of nature.[48] This is especially so for Aquinas, who explicitly says that because of the way in which all things participate in God inasmuch as we have being, there is already a communication of goods (the goods of our nature) from God to us that forms the basis of a "natural friendship" (*amicitia naturalis*) we might cultivate with God.[49] Therefore although charity is definitively distinct from natural friendship with God due to the goods communicated within the friendship of charity, there is still a positive appraisal of the natural love for God.

Here it is apt to cite the scholastic maxim that "grace does not destroy nature but perfects it." Because grace does not remove the goods of nature but elevates them into perfection, the love of God in charity is not contrary to the natural friendship with God, but a perfection of it. And this fact makes a great difference for when we come to consider how love of neighbor fits into Aquinas's conception of charity. As Gerald J. Beyer has put it, for Aquinas love of God and love of neighbor are "ontologically" united.[50] This means that Aqui-

47. Malloy, 15.

48. Thomas M. Osborne, Jr., *Love of Self and Love of God in Thirteenth-Century Ethics* (Notre Dame, IN: University of Notre Dame Press, 2005), esp. 69–112. Osborne's study shows that between two highly contrasting theologians of the Scholastic period (Aquinas and John Duns Scotus), there was general agreement upon the fact that human beings are capable of loving God over loving self, according to the order of nature. The difference was how they arrived at the reasons for such a position. Osborne contends that for Aquinas, the natural love of God over self is based upon "a natural inclination in everything to act for the good of the universe and its species more than for its own good" (69–70).

49. *Super I Epistolam B. Pauli ad Corinthios lectura*, cap. 13, l. 4, par. 806. Also cited in Malloy, 108.

50. Gerald J. Beyer, "The Love of God and Neighbor According to Aquinas: An Interpretation," *New Blackfriars* 84, no. 985 (March 2003): 120–21.

nas understands charity to be the same act with distinctive objects: the Triune God for his own sake, and others for God's sake. Because the supernatural love of God in charity is founded on the communication of divine goods, so too the supernatural love of others is based on this communication of goods, wherein this communication of goods is what makes the essential difference between natural love of neighbors and supernatural love.

Here we must recognize the importance of the fact that the natural love of the human person is ordered in others in various degrees—there are some who are closer to us (such as kinship relations or friends) whom we love more than others. Importantly, for Aquinas this is not simply the way things are, but the proper order of things according to God's wisdom.[51] Thus, it is absurd to think that charity would communicate divine goods to human beings (according to the divine wisdom) in such a way as to nullify the previous order to things given by the divine wisdom. Rather, love of neighbor in charity must be a perfection and not extirpation of our natural, graded love.

The difference as Aquinas sees it is the principle upon which the love of others is founded. In natural love, the love of others proceeds out of love of oneself in the sense of loving others according to a kind of union or similitude with oneself.[52] By contrast, love for others in charity proceeds from friendship with God. As one might expect, the unequal ways in which we naturally love others are not simply transcribed from the natural onto the supernatural order; there are important differences in how we understand the proper differences within love of neighbor. Yet the main point I wish to underline here is that Aquinas recognizes that the fact of grades or distinction between how we love others is fitting for the order of charity.

Aquinas admits that charity requires love (*dilectio*) for all, even our enemies.[53] In this sense charity requires a universal and equal love of neighbor; but how does Aquinas see this proposition as

---

51. *ST* IIaIIae, q. 26, art. 6, corp.

52. See Malloy, 76–80.

53. See Michael Sherwin, "Aquinas, Augustine, and the Medieval Scholastic Crisis concerning Charity," in *Aquinas the Augustinian*, 181–204. Sherwin addresses the various forms of love Aquinas uses to describe charity such as *amiticia* (friendship), *complacientia* (pleasure), and *dilectio*.

A Thomistic Reading of Mohist *Jian ai*   193

consonant with the idea of graded or different love of neighbor within charity? Simply put, Aquinas holds that charity requires us to love others the same in terms the formal object of benevolence—that is, that we will for all others the exact same good: eternal beatitude, which is sharing in the divine goods communicated in charity. This is something that charity requires the Christian to earnestly desire for all, even her enemies.[54]

Yet the fact that charity enjoins the Christian to love all in terms of desiring them to share in the same good of beatitude, this love also admits of a just distinction regarding the intensity with which we love others.[55] Following Augustine, Aquinas makes a helpful distinction between loving others equally and universally in terms of benevolence (willing another's good) and loving others equally and universally in terms of benefaction (doing good deeds for another).[56] Whereas we can love others universally and equally with benevolence inasmuch as we will all the same good of beatitude, it is impossible for finite creatures to be beneficent to all equally and universally.

Thus there are clear ways in which humans must love some different than others. In broadest terms, Aquinas speaks of different "intensities" in the love of charity. While we should love all others equally inasmuch as we desire the same good end for them, Aquinas holds there are different degrees of intensity by which we love others and wish that they share in the good of eternal beatitude. Benefaction is one way we see this difference in intensity to be true. For example, as a Christian I am formed by charity to will the salvation of all fellow human beings and desire their beatitude. But as a father, I love my children and those close to me with a greater intensity and will their enjoyment of beatitude with a greater intensity. Thus, I will closely pay attention to my children's growth in the faith, attempt to catechize them carefully, form them morally, and teach them to

---

54. *ST* IIaIIae, q. 26, art. 6, ad 1.

55. See *ST* IIaIIae, q. 26, art. 7, corp.

56. See *ST* IIaIIae, q. 26, art. 6, obj. 1 and ad 1. The first objection cites a distinction between benevolence and benefaction found in Augustine, *De doctrina Christiana*, 1.28, wherein Augustine admits "but it is not possible to benefit [*prodesse*] all" (translation mine). Aquinas clarifies the meaning of this text in the reply to the objection.

194   Chapter 4

participate in the sacramental life of the Church, and do not perform analogous tasks for all children I happen to meet.

At this point, I should stress that Aquinas sees the limitation of benefaction as evidence of a genuine distinction in the intensity of charity-love. Aquinas argues that there is a necessary proportionality between the inclinations of grace and the actions we perform out of charity.[57] This means that there is a proportional relationship between the affection by which we love others in charity and the actions we undertake on their behalf out of that affection. To understand what is at stake here, we can recognize that according to some Christian thinkers such as Søren Kierkegaard, the affection of love is equally given to all (benevolence) but the effects of charity (acts of benefaction) are unequal because we cannot do good to all equally; and therefore the love of charity is always and everywhere universal and equal in intensity, and only instrumentally different.[58] However, Aquinas argues such a position wrongly detaches the inclination of charity (affection) from its action.

To see why this matters, it is helpful to refer to a modern version of this debate among Thomists. In modern moral theology, many interpreters of Aquinas, influenced by the thought of Immanuel Kant, have attempted to interpret Aquinas as holding that charity does not admit of real difference, only the difference between affect and action. Michael Sherwin has critically labeled such thinkers "theologians of moral motivation" such as Josef Fuchs and James Keenan.[59] Sherwin argues that these scholars' interpret Aquinas as holding to a form of intellectual determinism because they radically distinguish between a moral agent's moral freedom and his practical reason.[60]

---

57. *ST* IIaIIae, q. 26, art. 6, corp.

58. This position seems to be a logical conclusion of Kierkegaard's understanding of charity in Søren Kierkegaard, *Works of Love*, ed. and trans. Howard V. Hong and Edna H. Hong (Princeton, NJ: Princeton University Press, 2013), esp. 44–90. See also C. Stephen Evans, *Kierkegaard's Ethic of Love: Divine Commands and Moral Obligations* (New York: Oxford University Press, 2004), 180–222.

59. Michael Sherwin, OP, *By Knowledge & By Love: Charity and Knowledge in the Moral Theology of St. Thomas Aquinas* (Washington, DC: The Catholic University of America Press, 2005), 205–6.

60. A significant form of this view is James Keenan, SJ, *Goodness and Rightness in Thomas Aquinas' Summa Theologiae* (Washington, DC: Georgetown University Press, 1992). In this work, Keenan argues that Aquinas in the *Summa* (though not in Aquinas's earlier work) issues an important distinction between "goodness" (the subjective moral disposition or character

A Thomistic Reading of Mohist *Jian ai*   195

For these thinkers, charity is an expression or choice as a "fundamental option" that then directs the will to act in accordance with this imperative. The practical reasoning simply executes this fundamental choice of the free moral agent. Consequently, charity for such theologians at best names the fundamental option (the affect I described above) and cannot necessarily be instantiated in moral acts in a proper sense (the effects).[61]

As Sherwin observes, this position undercuts Aquinas's argument that charity is a true virtue.[62] According to Aquinas, each thing's natural inclinations "are proportionate to the acts or motion which is fitting for the nature of each thing."[63] Since our inclinations are ordered to actions or effects, it is unfitting that an inclination be universal and equal toward all others, yet unable to be effected in this way in moral acts. Since it is impossible that benefaction be genuinely universal and equal in scope, it seems unavoidable that the affection given to others in charity must be able to admit of diversity. Yet because charity is friendship with the infinite and omnipresent God, it is fitting to will such friendship universally and equally for all others; thus the difference in charity to others need not be in terms of the nature of the love of the good willed for others therein. This leaves, then, that there can be a difference of intensity within the affection of love extended to others that corresponds to the effects of charity in benefaction.[64]

Another way of stating this point is that charity must be a human act and thus comport in some way with our natural inclinations, perfecting not destroying them, such that the natural inclination to love some with different intensity is maintained within the order of charity. Admittedly, Jean Porter has argued this is not logically convincing. She observes that "just because charity cannot contradict the

---

of a person) and "rightness" (the objective moral status of his/her moral acts). According to Keenan, the Catholic moral tradition has often confused goodness and rightness, but they should be separated, and basically treated as parallel realities, such that a person's subjective goodness is a matter of fundamental option, and objective rightness is how a person may or may not succeed in enacting this fundamental option.

61. Sherwin, *By Knowledge & By Love*, 205.

62. Sherwin, 206–7.

63. *ST* IIaIIae, q. 26, art. 6, corp.: "videmus autem in naturalibus quod inclinatio naturalis proportionator actui vel motui qui convenit naturae uniuscuiusque."

64. *ST* IIaIIae, q. 26, art. 6, corp.

196 Chapter 4

rational ordering of human life, it hardly follows that it must follow it exactly. We might just as well say that charity transcends and supersedes the natural affections without destroying them."[65] Porter's ultimate point here is that the argument that charity must harmonize with the natural love is not enough, in isolation, to show that charity must admit of distinctions of intensity within charity as such (instead of within natural affections).

However, in concrete terms, charity is created by grace in the human soul in order to become the form of the virtues for the moral life unto eternal beatitude.[66] Before Aquinas, Peter Lombard had authored the opinion that the Holy Spirit is not merely the principle but the agent of love of neighbor in charity.[67] Aquinas rejected this view because it meant that the human being did not properly perform the act of charity, and so the human being was unable to actually participate in the divine love; instead, Aquinas recognizes there is a need to identify a cause of the act of charity within the human person.[68] This leads Aquinas to clarify that by grace, those who receive charity also receive a habitual form that inclines them toward the acts of charity.[69] Thus, Aquinas sees the gift of charity as involving the gift of a new habitual form in the soul that makes the human faculties of love able to share in the Trinitarian love and live *in via* toward eternal beatitude. Consequently, since charity is a supernatural virtue that is properly in the human soul as part of the human person who then can act through the virtue of charity, charity lifts up and perfects natural affections within the disposition of charity, though these retain their integrity as natural affections.

What remains for my purpose is to understand more precisely how charity is properly extended differently toward others in practice. Aquinas discusses three relationships (pertinent to this analysis at least), and probes whether they are seen as moments of fitting diversity in charity's intensity: 1) whether we should love ourselves more than others, 2) whether we should love those who are "more

65. Porter, *"De ordine caritatis,"* 201.
66. See *ST* IIaIIae, q. 23, art. 2, corp. and ad 2.
67. See Zuijdwegt.
68. Zuijdwegt.
69. *ST* IIaIIae, q. 23, art. 2, corp.

A Thomistic Reading of Mohist *Jian ai*   197

closely united with us" (*nobis coniunctiores*), and 3) whether we ought to love blood relations in a special way due to charity.

Aquinas first discusses love of self in distinction to love of others in two articles (*ST* IIaIIae, q. 26, aa.4–5). Perhaps somewhat surprisingly, Aquinas argues charity requires a greater love of self than of others. However, he does not mean by this an egocentric love of self, but what Anthony T. Flood has called "proper self-love" whereby I have self-friendship, and will myself the good of friendship with God.[70] Notably, within his account of charity as self-love, Aquinas makes an important distinction between loving oneself according to one's spiritual nature and one's bodily nature. His basic position is that through charity I should love my spiritual nature more than that of others, but not my bodily nature. His reasoning is that because friendship with God is the principle of loving anyone out of charity, this means that within the love of charity we love ourselves for God's sake: "a man loves himself out of charity as he participates in the aforementioned good" which is friendship with God.[71] Because this friendship with God is a certain kind of union in relation (*unione in ordine*) with God, we have greater cause (*potior ratio*) to love ourselves as being united with God than we have cause to love others who are associated with us in this participation.[72] In short, if I have charity and friendship with God I should love that union more than my association or companionship with others who are also friends with God.

Crucially, Aquinas thinks the love of self in charity affects what charity demands of us in service to others. Because we do not love our own life for its own sake with charity, we ought not love our body more than that of others. For our body is not ordered toward perfect happiness with God in the same way as is our spiritual

---

70. Anthony T. Flood, *The Root of Friendship: Self-love and Self-governance in Aquinas* (Washington, DC: The Catholic University of America Press, 2014), 3: "It is common self-love that I contend constitutes the basis for subjectivity. Common self-love that is directed to the true good of the person I call 'proper self-love.' Proper self-love is appropriately oriented but may not be fully actualized. 'Self-friendship' is the full actualization of proper self-love. Wicked or improper self-love perverts the relation away from the true good of the person."

71. *ST* IIaIIae, q. 26, art. 4, corp.: "homo autem seipsum diligit ex caritate secundum rationem qua est particeps praedicti boni."

72. *ST* IIaIIae, q. 26, art. 4, corp.

198   Chapter 4

nature, though our body serves this *telos*.[73] Thus, Aquinas can say that I should be willing to sacrifice my body or bodily goods for the sake of another out of charity. But at no time does charity compel me to place myself in spiritual danger in order to serve another.[74] Put concretely, charity might require me to exercise fortitude and lay down my life to save another so that she might know love and seek friendship with God. But charity could never entail that I should choose to take up a life of intentional mortal sin in the name of love so as to compel my friend to love God.

For example, let us imagine I have a friend who is contemplating committing adultery. I am fearful that my friend might make this grave mistake and put his friendship with God at risk. Therefore, out of charity (in my mind), I commit adultery and ruin my marriage in order to show my friend how destructive adultery can be to his life. Aquinas means to show us that such a sacrifice whereby I would surrender my own friendship with God (due to mortal sin and doing intrinsic evil) is not fittingly sacrificed for the sake of my friend.

Due to the rhetorical strategies of the *Mozi*, Aquinas's argument for love of self in charity will be important in the comparative section of this chapter. However, to make those comparisons well, I must press on to the other relationships Aquinas discusses. After love of self, Aquinas asks whether it is in keeping with charity for one to love others "more closely connected to us." In the objections of this article, Aquinas draws out the question in terms of whether charity compels us to love those who are "better" or "closer" to us. In this context, better means those who are more virtuous, and "closer" (*propinquiores*) means those who are part of our daily life. In a sense, those closer to us means our immediate family, but also friends, literal neighbors, coworkers, et cetera.

This question furnishes two interesting principles of differentiation in charity. First, Aquinas holds that because charity is friendship with God, this means that the intensity of love should depend in some respect upon our neighbor's own friendship with God. Thus, we should, out of charity, "wish a greater good to he who is closer

---

73. *ST* IIaIIae, q. 26, art. 5, corp.
74. *ST* IIaIIae, q. 26, art. 4, ad 2.

A Thomistic Reading of Mohist *Jian ai* 199

to God."[75] Aquinas says this follows out of the fact that charity wills that God's justice be maintained, and in such wise it is fitting to wish those who are more virtuous—such as the saints—to have a more perfect participation in beatitude.[76] In this way, charity can require me to love more (in terms of willing a greater good) St. Augustine or the unknown Christians who suffer for their faith around the world than those close to me.

Despite this, Aquinas says it is fitting that we love those near us with more intensity than those further from us. That is, I wish those near me the good in a more intense way than those I do not know, even if I might wish the latter a greater or more perfect good.[77] For example, any Christian mother whose child falls away from the faith would wish with the greatest intensity that her child return to friendship with God. The mother can also recognize that there are those who have persisted in the faith (such as those suffering for their faith) who merit a more perfect share in beatitude, such that she can wish that these good people do not linger in purgatory. But the mother would will more intensely (i.e., more frequently and with greater fervor) that her own child turn to serve and love God once more, even if she doesn't wish her child the most perfect goodness that the child has not merited through grace.[78]

Aquinas explains that this befits charity for at least two reasons. First, some of our closer neighbors are connected to us in ways that cannot be severed, like our family members. Thus, we can desire for those close to us to become good, in order to merit through friendship with God a greater happiness.[79] Second, Aquinas notes we love those close to us with more than charity-love; charity constitutes a real friendship with others, but with those close to us we also have diverse forms of natural friendship.[80] Though he does not directly use the terminology, Aquinas seems to mean here that natural friendship

75. *ST* IIaIIae, q. 26, art. 7, corp.: "ei qui est Deo propinquior maius bonum ex caritate velimus."

76. *ST* IIaIIae, q. 26, art. 7, corp.

77. *ST* IIaIIae, q. 26, art. 7, corp.

78. For example, see Augustine's reference to St. Monica's tears for her son's conversion in *Confessions*, III.

79. *ST* IIaIIae, q. 26, art. 7, corp.

80. *ST* IIaIIae, q. 26, art. 7, corp.

inasmuch as it is good is destroyed, but perfected by grace. Because charity is the form of all the other virtues, the virtuous aspects of natural friendships come to serve and contribute to charity and are not replaced by charity.[81] Consequently, the natural friendships we have with our neighbors which lead us to love them more intensely than others becomes grafted into the order of charity. And so, Aquinas sees charity as perfecting our natural friendships with special affection for others, rather than removing these friendships.

From this, it is quite easy to see how Aquinas defends special kinship love within the order of charity. Aquinas holds that the bond of kinship is a union that is more stable than others (e.g., citizenship) and touches upon our very substance. Hence, the special unique love for consanguineous relations is a virtuous love according to the order of natural goods.[82] This is because Aquinas holds that relationship of natural origin presents the closest (*magis coniuncti*) form of relationship among human beings, compared to other civil bonds.[83] Thus, charity commends us to love more those who are more closely united to us as a perfection of natural love. This means that charity likewise requires us to love more intensely our kinfolk than those not related to us. However, it should be remembered that what Aquinas means by this is specifically the wishing them the good of eternal beatitude through friendship with God.

A THOMISTIC ASSESSMENT OF *JIAN AI*

The question that I seek to answer in the remainder of this chapter is whether and how the Mohist concept resonates with the concep-

81. For a helpful discussion of the category of the infused cardinal virtues, see William C. Mattison III, *Introducing Moral Theology: True Happiness and the Virtues* (Grand Rapids, MI: Brazos Press, 2008), 326–30.

82. *ST* IIaIIae, q. 26, art. 8, corp.

83. *ST* IIaIIae, q. 26, art. 8, corp. Aquinas in this context is comparing natural blood relations to civic relationships and kinship on the battlefield between soldiers. Hence, he is referring to purely natural associations, of which blood relationships have the most stability. In the *SCG* III.123.6, observes that marriage is the greatest friendship of human beings due to the partnership of life involved therein. But, for Aquinas, it is also key to remember that marriage is a sacrament and not simply a voluntary association. Moreover, in terms of natural associations, marriage is unique because of the activities proper to it. This is simply to say that marriage does not disprove Aquinas's point when we understand his observation about the strength of natural blood relations to be specifically in distinction to other civil bonds, and not marriage.

A Thomistic Reading of Mohist *Jian ai*   201

tion of charity found in Aquinas. It is readily apparent that there are important ways that charity and *jian ai* are not completely consonant as love of neighbor. The primary difference between Aquinas's view of charity and the Mohist view of *jian ai* concerns the "species" of love. For Aquinas, charity is a distinctive species of love or dilection because of its proper object (God), which is also the same species of neighbor love in charity. Within charity, Christians should love our neighbors, but the principle of this love is the friendship with God, such that we love neighbors for God's sake. Even if one attempts to read together the *Mozi*'s chapters on the will of *Tian* with the *jian ai* chapters—which I think makes good sense—this would still not produce a similar concept to charity. At the most, the *Mozi* argues that *jian ai* is necessary because it is an imitation of how *Tian* loves and cares for all.[84] But to understand this imitation as constituting friendship with *Tian* would be a stretch indeed.

Also, the valuation of love of self in both Aquinas and the *Mozi* lead to important differences in their accounts. It is not so much whether we should love ourselves that is different between *Mozi* and Aquinas, but rather the importance of self-love in relation to the care for others. The *Mozi* exhorts *jian ai* by first recognizing the problem of selfishness and self-love. *Jian ai* is a corrective to this inasmuch as it involves extending love to others instead of unvirtuously and egocentrically loving oneself. In this way, one could say that the *Mozi* actually considers self-love as the paradigmatic love upon which is based *jian ai*—that is, self-love is the species of love that is then universalized or made *jian*.[85]

It is striking that when Aquinas speaks about loving oneself in charity, he does not refer to the natural inclinations for self-preservation, which he greatly esteems. He does not even say that we should love ourselves most in charity simply because we desire for ourselves to experience the greatest good possible for us, we should wish ourselves such good. Finally, he doesn't make the claim that we should

---

84. Again, this is the view of Cai, *Mojia zhexue*.

85. I mean here that the love one gives to one-self—willing the good and working for one's own flourishing—is paradigmatic of love or care in the *Mozi*, not self-love as a solipsistic movement. It is not selfishness that is the model, but the desire for the flourishing of the beloved.

love ourselves because we recognize God loves us so greatly (as the Mohist conception of *Tian* might allow). Rather, Aquinas teaches that charity requires self-love inasmuch as this love conforms to and flows from the desire for friendship with God—that is, there is the ecstatic desire for God as friend per se, and not simply a love for God as an instrument to my own happiness. Unlike the *Mozi*, Aquinas does not suggest charity begins with loving ourselves and is extended outward. Instead, charity begins with loving God, and we must extend this love to ourselves. Within charity, we must come to love ourselves for God's sake.

Despite the great disparities between Mozi and Aquinas regarding self- love, we can also find significant points of resonance regarding self-love. At first glance it might seem that the *Mozi* and Aquinas only disagree on the importance of self-love, since Aquinas says we must love ourselves before others due to charity and the *Mozi* sees such self-love as precisely the problem. But again, for Aquinas love of self in charity is love of self for God's own sake, and this means that we love ourselves more than others only in one respect—namely, as regards our spiritual nature. Our bodily nature, however, is not to be loved more than others by means of charity.

When the *Mozi* in all three chapters articulates a suspicion about self-love, it is always discussed in the context of the desire to benefit oneself in material ways. For the *Mozi* self-love is most evident in acts such as theft or robbery, in enriching or ennobling one family over others, or going to war with smaller states so as to use their resources. In brief, these are all materialistic and bodily goods. From this perspective, he who practices self-love as self-benefit according to the Mohist is doing the very thing Aquinas finds unfitting for charity: placing the love of one's body and bodily goods above others. For the *Mozi*, there is no clear sense in which benefit (*li*) is a spiritual, eternal good as the perfect happiness of heaven is for Aquinas. Rather, the exhortation to mutual love concerns mutuality in respect to bodily goods, precisely, it seems, to show how such goods are instrumental rather than the ultimate goods. Therefore, within these limits of condemning self-benefit as a privileging of one's own bodily goods over and against those of others, the Mohist vision of *jian ai* bears a striking resemblance to Aquinas's interpretation of charity.

Another important point of comparison between Mohism and Aquinas concerns benefaction and benevolence. The benevolence/benefaction distinction is very important to Aquinas's account of charity as love of neighbor since he is dissatisfied with holding benevolence to be universal and benefaction be limited in scope, and argues instead there must be an ordered relationship between affection and effect. Admittedly, the *Mozi* never makes a clear distinction between benevolence and benefaction in the same way Aquinas does. In part, this is because the term *ai* can mean affection and the effects of affection. As the argument progresses from *Mozi* 14 to 16, the Mohist vision of *jian ai* seems to emphasize the effects of affection (i.e., mutual benefit") as consonant with affection itself.

In this way, both Aquinas and the *Mozi* refuse to allow affection and effects be treated as utterly distinct. The Mohist account seems to treat affection and effects as so proximally related it is difficult to distinguish them. Hence, both accounts show a sensitivity to understand and articulate the integrity of love for others as constituted by both affection and effect, and to appreciate that universal affect cannot coincide with particular effect in terms of care or love.

Still, in chapters 15 and 16, the *Mozi* argues that *jian ai* must mean working out the broadest benefaction possible. While the text stops short of exhorting the impossible (namely, that we work to benefit all in the exact same way), it does point to rulers, such as King Yu, who, through the instrument of governmental authority, were able to truly seek to benefit "the world" as early Chinese understood it. For those without such a scope to care and concern via a particular office, the *Mozi* seems, at the least, to exhort us to benefit all of those with whom we have social congress.

In this sense, the *Mozi* protects the integrity of benevolence and benefaction by means of broadening the range of benefaction as much as possible. Aquinas resolves this problem in the opposite direction. Beginning with the limits of benefaction, he argues this must mean there is something in keeping with such limits in charitable benevolence itself. Thus, Aquinas argues that benevolence consists of the object (what good is wished to others) and the intensity of the act of benevolence and love. In short, rather than maintaining the integrity of affection and its effects by universalizing the effects, Aquinas suggests there is principle of gradation or distinction within the affection in terms of the dilection of the agent (and not in terms of the good wished to others in the affection of charity, which must be equally extended to all).

It is worth recognizing here that for Aquinas, the benefaction of charity is distinct from that of justice. Wishing the good for others in the loving act of charity is wishing others a good that neither I nor they can accomplish on their own. My doing good for them can at best encourage them to cooperate with divine grace and grow in charity, recognizing this is only possible the ministry of the Holy Spirit. In other words, our benefaction out of charity cannot secure the good we wish for others with charitable benevolence, that they become friends with God. This is fundamentally different for the *Mozi*, which sees mutual love and benefit as the genuine instruments by which to bring about the good we wish for others (namely, an orderly rather than a chaotic existence). This simply points out that under the respective auspices of *jian ai* and Christian charity, both the *Mozi* and Aquinas make seemingly appropriate logical moves.

The final point of comparison is that of particular affection. Aquinas has a robust account of the need for special loves within the order of charity. Not only should we love ourselves more than others, we also should love those closest to us and our kin more intensely than others. In one sense, Aquinas's argument that we should love those closest to us more than those who are distant from us is least objectionable from the Mohist perspective—after all, it seems proximity to others is part of the meaning of "universal" that the *Mozi* intends when exhorting mutual love and benefit. The more interesting question is whether there is room for the *Mozi* to agree with Aquinas on loving kin more than others.

Here one must take great care as an interpreter. If one assumes the Confucian critique of Mohism is correct—particularly that found in the *Mengzi*—it is easy to argue that the *Mozi* stands opposed to special love of kin. The traditional Confucian interpreted

A Thomistic Reading of Mohist *Jian ai*   205

the Mohist account of *jian ai* as denying the virtuousness of varying degrees of love and concern to such a point that Mengzi argues Mozi "has no father"—that is, his philosophy is unable to allow kinship relations to flourish. Kwong-Loi Shun has even argued that the *Mozi* is marked by "the absence of any appeal to the natural predisposition of human beings to have affection for others," which culminates in what Shun takes as the Mohist belief that "human beings have no natural affection for others, not even family members."[86]

Therefore, it is instructive to ask how the *Mozi* describes family love and affection within *jian ai*. In its simplest form of argument (such as in chapter 14), the *Mozi* argues that *jian ai* includes special familial love. The main problem the text attacks is solipsistic love, within which even the special love of kinship is sacrificed in the pursuit of self-benefit. Thus, the *Mozi* argues that as humans shun self-love and benefit for mutual love and benefit, this will enable us to genuinely practice those virtues consonant with special family relationships, such as filial piety and paternal compassion.

At this basic level, the *Mozi* does not necessarily understand special love to be inconsistent with *jian ai*. However, there would still be an important difference with Aquinas. This is because Aquinas specifies love of kin within charity as a legitimate difference in intensity of the same act of loving. The *Mozi* does not seem to treat filial piety and paternal compassion as different intensities of the same love-act, but rather a different species of love. Still, *Mozi*, 14 does not develop its own account of special love in enough detail to definitively say all gradation of intensity is ruled out by *jian ai*. For this reason, it seems apt to say that while the position advocated in *Mozi*, 14 falls short of agreeing with Aquinas's position, it is not in strict disagreement with Aquinas.

This stands in stark contrast to *Mozi*, 16, which explicitly attacks the principle of loving with partiality (*bie*). I argued above that in the terms of this account of *jian ai*, partiality is understood as another form of solipsistic concern. In other words, *Mozi*, 16, sees the special love of kin as modestly less selfish than the purely selfish love

---

86. Kwong-loi Shun, "Mencius' Critique of Mohism: An Analysis of 'Meng Tzu' 3A:5," *Philosophy East and West* 41, no. 2 (April 1991): 203–14, here 206.

decried in *Mozi*, 14. More importantly, chapter 16 suggests that special love of kin can actually hinder our ability to practice genuinely mutual love and benefit. The natural bonds of inclination and partiality toward our loved ones are obstacles, not paths to *jian ai*.

True enough, *Mozi*, 16, does explicitly argue that this vision of *jian ai* can still cooperate with filial piety. But in making the case for this cooperation, the author makes an illuminating logical move, asserting that the only way to ensure those I love specially are given the goods I seek for them is to love others in the same special way. At its best, this argument concedes that it is perhaps impossible to truly rid ourselves of special affection. What is clear is that regardless of this affection, we should not act as though we felt special affection for our parents. It is no difficult step to conclude the *Jian ai xia* means to suggest that ultimately, the practice of *jian ai* should mean that for practical moral purposes, there should be no special loves.

Contrary to the perspective of *Mozi*, 16, Aquinas holds that loving our kin is part of charity because charity perfects rather than destroys natural relationships. When the grace of the Holy Spirit infuses charity in Christian hearts, the natural bonds of special affection are not abrogated, but rather they become conformed to the principle of charity. In this sense, the distinctions we make between those we love are not taken away, but they are clarified and perfected. Aquinas does not mean to deny that disordered special love of parents and kin can and does happen, as he knew by personal experience. Rather, Aquinas believes that charity lifts up and properly orders the love of distinction and partiality.

CONCLUSIONS

Because the Mohist reflection on *jian ai* is developed apart from the context of revelation and the gifts of the New Law, it is unsurprising that it is ill-suited to articulating the Catholic doctrine of charity on its own. But my aim in this chapter has been to take stock of the Mohist *jian ai* from the Thomist perspective in order to discern more clearly where and how the Mohist tradition might furnish resources for Chinese Catholic theology. The above analysis

A Thomistic Reading of Mohist *Jian ai* 207

has succeeded in showing the points of significant divergence between Catholic moral thought and Mohism, as well as areas of fruitful promise.

There are three primary points of divergence of concern for the theologian. First, as I demonstrated above, it is not exactly clear what to make of the Mohist understanding of particular affections. Although some scholars such as Robins have observed that the *Mozi* does not oppose particular affections out of hand, it does not seem that the *Mozi* allows that particular affections *qua* particular affections are ingredient in the proper order of *jian ai*. While the Mohist perspective does hold that maintaining particular affections is important, it often seems this is so only because the general principle of *jian ai* includes kinfolk and friends within it. However, from the Catholic perspective found in Aquinas, particular affections for proximate relations have central importance for charity. Aquinas holds that there is an important way that charity requires maintaining a strong hierarchy of affections, whereas the *Mozi* sees *jian ai* as weakening (albeit not wholly dismantling) this hierarchy. This is particularly important in the Catholic tradition given the centrality of the family and family responsibility in Catholic moral thought.

A second area of theological concern is that the Mohist conception of *jian ai* does not clearly articulate the positive significance of self-love, whereas virtuous self-love is vitally important to Aquinas's moral vision. For inasmuch as grace perfects nature, he recognizes that charity cannot destroy our natural concern for our lives, but rather perfects it. As I mentioned above, I do not think the *Mozi* is opposed to something like the perfection of self-love; on the contrary, it is mainly critical of the disordered self-love that Aquinas himself would criticize. However, because there is less ontological emphasis in the *Mozi*, there is also a corresponding lack of care to say that self-love is good inasmuch as it is the love of the gift of being. Divine charity uplifts, transforms, and renews self-love rather than extirpating it.

This point leads to the third theological problem with the *Mozi*—namely, that *jian ai* does not seem to include *Tian* or God as an object of love. While *Tian*'s love is taken as the model or exemplar for *jian ai*, the *Mozi* does not suggest that humans ought to give this love to *Tian* as well. Thus, Aquinas's position on the primary importance of loving God even more than we love neighbors has no analog in the *Mozi*. The theological weaknesses of such a position are self-evident.

Turning to the more positive aspects of the *Mozi* from the theological perspective, it is laudable that the Mohist conception of *jian ai* understands love and care for others as being based in divine love. Although the Mohist understanding of *jian ai* resonates with the Greek conception of justice as giving others what they are due, there is an additional benefit to the Mohist position. Because the *Mozi* frames responsibilities toward others in terms of care and not simply the legal framework of justice, it makes it easier to see the relationship between the natural virtue of justice and the supernatural virtue of charity. That is, as the supernatural virtue of charity perfects our ability to care for others through a moral union with the divine love that participates in and shares this love with others, the Mohist understanding of *jian ai* can show with clarity that this virtue is the perfection rather than radical disruption of natural virtue.

The *Mozi*'s argument for *jian ai* also resonates with the fundamental Catholic understanding of the roots of "chaos" (*luan*) in the world. Though without the protological structure, the *Mozi* sees disordered self-love—solipsism, selfishness, and pride—as the root cause of malformation and thus the enemy of flourishing. Consequently, the *Mozi* successfully penetrates into how the human heart-mind is the seat of our interior disorder, through which we so often strive to organize the world for our private benefit. As the Catholic tradition readily recognizes, the sin of pride is the chief of the capital sins, for it is the one that most directly displaces God as the one to whom all love, honor, and devotion is due. It is disordered self-love that most deeply obstructs our pathway to happiness and flourishing. Only by surrendering to God do humans become capable of virtuous self-love; only by learning to deny ourselves can we learn how much we should love ourselves. That the *Mozi* testifies to this fundamental truth is itself reason to have confidence that the Mohist tradition can provide helpful means for developing systematic theological reflections that reflect the truth of Catholic doctrine.

Finally, although I mentioned above that from the Catholic perspective the *Mozi* fails to adequately consider *Tian* as an object of love, there are laudable aspects of its account of *Tian*. Specifically, the *Mozi* not only understands *Tian* as a subject of love, but also sees the moral responsibilities of human beings to be a kind of imitation of *Tian*. In this way, the Mohist conception of *jian ai* furnishes indirect accounts of love as a proper predicate and perfection of God, and of divine love as an exemplar of creaturely love. The second of these accounts indirectly suggests that the *Mozi* contains an implicit sense in which the human perfection of virtuous love is a kind of participation in the divine virtuous love. Though this falls well short of a metaphysical principle such that the Catholic tradition (or at least, Thomistic understanding of the Catholic tradition) necessitates, it is a vitally significant theological insight that suggests tremendous promise for future Chinese Catholic theological developments.

Although Catholic engagement with the *Mozi* is rare indeed, I hope my treatment here and in chapter 3 provide adequate reasons for the situation to change in the future. The *Mozi* possesses several aspects of the moral and metaphysical framework needed to fully articulate the truth of human and divine love from the Catholic perspective. Hence, the underestimated and understudied *Mozi* may well serve as an excellent and natural point of departure for the development of Catholic theological science that draws upon the frameworks and concepts of Chinese philosophy.

5

Thomistic Christology and Xunzi's *Shengren*

With this and the subsequent chapter, I now turn to analyze the theological limits and possibilities of Chinese philosophical concepts by testing their relationship to the study of Christ's person and work. Christology is undoubtedly the most difficult theological topic within which to develop a compelling and culturally genuine Chinese Catholic theology.[1] In the first place, the Incarnation of the Word is inseparable from the Jewish cultural and theological context, since the Son assumed flesh concretely in the context of Second Temple Judaism. Additionally, the development of the Church's Christological dogmas under the guidance of the Holy Spirit owes a great debt to ways that Greek philosophy had shaped the council Fathers, even as the Fathers' encounter with Christ also changed the way they considered Greek philosophical categories and doctrines. Although I would caution against specious arguments that the Greek character of Christological dogmas renders their content "irrelevant" to Chinese Catholics, it is nonetheless true the Christological application of Chinese philosophies is made more difficult for having to conform to truths explicitly articulated

---

1. For an essentially comprehensive guide to the history of Chinese depictions and accounts of Christ, see Roman Malek, SVD, ed. *The Chinese Face of Jesus Christ*, 5 vols. (Sankt Augustin, Germany: Institut Monumenta Serica/China-Zentrum, 2002–2017).

Thomistic Christology and Xunzi's *Shengren*　　211

through a different conceptual apparatus.[2] Apart from merely translating the terms of the Christological dogmas, it may seem initially that Chinese philosophies have very little to offer theological science regarding the person and work of Jesus Christ.

Such a conclusion would be erroneous, however, on two counts. First, inasmuch as Chinese philosophies entail a distinctive yet true anthropology, they implicitly offer resources for distinctive insights for theological science concerning the Son's assumption of human nature. However, given the complexity of Chinese anthropologies vis-à-vis the standard concepts of Greco-Roman anthropology, working out these distinctive insights would require a tremendous concerted effort.[3] Thus, given the limitations of this book, I will focus on the second reason the conclusion above would be erroneous. Namely, although Chinese philosophies (as with other non-Western traditions) offer a different technical philosophical anthropology, they also provide other images and concepts of human perfection that do not require a full explanation of the anthropological framework in order to be fruitfully drawn into Catholic theological science.

Consequently, in this and the following chapter I look toward the application of the Chinese conception of the sage (*shengren*) within Christological science. Undoubtedly, the moral ideal of the *shengren* was fundamental to many early Chinese traditions, especially Confucianism, and the concept is perfect example of why the task I undertake in this book of testing the theological limits and possibilities of Chinese philosophical concepts is necessary. For it is tempting to simply develop a theological narrative of Christ as a *shengren* in the name of cultural relevance or "meaningfulness," as Jonathan Y. Tan has ably done.[4] But, the rub is that Tan understands his construction

---

2. See, e.g., Kwok Pui-lan, *Introducing Asian Feminist Theology* (Sheffield, UK: Sheffield Academic Press, 2000), 88–91.

3. To give a sense of the complex task this would require, my hope is to offer such a study in the future, which would seem to depend upon making Christological application of unique anthropological concepts in Chinese philosophy such as *qi* 氣, *xin* 心 , the division of *po/hun* 魄魂 in the soul, and generally the relationship between form/corporeality (*xing* 形 and/or *ti* 體) and human nature (*xing* 性) or substance (*zhi* 質).

4. Jonathan Y. Tan, "Jesus, the Crucified and Risen Sage: Constructing a Contemporary Confucian Christology," in *The Chinese Face of Jesus Christ*, 3:1483–1513.

212   Chapter 5

of a Christology depicting Jesus as *shengren* as a departure from the "classical-universalist" and "European" Christology of the tradition to a culturally meaningful one for Chinese Christians.

To my mind, this is a flawed approach entailing two serious Christological problems. First, the Christological insights issued from such a project can claim to be valuable or meaningful only to Chinese peoples, threatening to produce merely a kind of "cultural Christ" that is simply a relativized form of Christ bearing no connection to the Christ of the Church Universal. Second, Tan's assumption serves to displace rather than complement essential images that are associated with Christ in scripture. For instance, Tan sees the image of Christ the King as essentially a product of Teutonic Christians rather than part of the biblical account of Jesus of Nazareth, despite the clear Messianic and Davidic typology the Gospel writers had in mind.[5] This displacement of scriptural images of Christ by supposedly more "culturally relevant" ones is theologically deadly not only because it risks betraying divine revelation, but also because it undermines the role of Israel in the salvific economy of Christ. While it is admirable and fruitful to make the person and message of Christ relevant to as many peoples as possible, any image of Jesus that willfully neglects his standing as part of the elect people of Israel in God's plan of salvation only serves to distort the truth of Christ.

And so, in this chapter, I seek a better way forward by testing the limits and possibilities of the *shengren* for use within Catholic Christological science, and not as a replacement for it. My approach here is to focus on one iteration of the sage depiction that I think holds great theological promise, that of Xunzi. Because Xunzi develops his account of the sage with an emphasis on the sage as a master of ritual (*li* 禮), the natural way to assess the fruitfulness of his account is to read it in light of Aquinas's treatment of Christ's priesthood. First, I present Xunzi's account of the sage in terms of his broader account

---

5. See Tan, 1485–1486. For presentations of the importance of Christ's kingship to the Gospel texts, Paul's writings, and the early Christian tradition see N. T. Wright, *How God Became King: The Forgotten Story of the Gospels* (New York: HarperOne, 2012); Julien Smith, *Christ the Ideal King: Cultural Context, Rhetorical Strategy, and the Power of Divine Monarchy in Ephesians* (Tübingen: Mohr Siebeck, 2011); Joshua W. Jipp, *Christ is King: Paul's Royal Ideology* (Minneapolis, MN: Fortress Press, 2015); and Per Beskow, *Rex gloriae: The Kingship of Christ in the Early Church*, trans. Eric J. Sharpe (Eugene, OR: Wipf and Stock, 2014).

Thomistic Christology and Xunzi's *Shengren*   213

of the role that rituals play in society. Briefly, Xunzi argues that the sages established rituals that provide order to the inherent chaos of the human heart-mind. Thus, the ritual agency of the sage produces moral perfection.

In the second part of the chapter, I present Aquinas's basic description of the nature and effects of Christ's priesthood offered in *ST* IIIa, q. 22, aa. 1–3. Aquinas shows how in Catholic theological science, Christ's priesthood grounds a very different conception of the effects of both rituals and sagehood than Xunzi could have anticipated. While both in terms of the nature of rituals performed and their soteriological effects there is significant disparity between Xunzi's *shengren* and Christ's priesthood, I also argue there are important ways that Xunzi's *shengren* can be read in a Christological way and therefore can serve the development of a Chinese Catholic Christological science. Therefore, I conclude this chapter with a series of observations regarding how Xunzi's *shengren* could be drawn into an account of Christ's priesthood, drawing upon the biblical book of Hebrews as a guide.

THE RITUAL SAGE: XUNZI ON RITUALS AND MORAL RECTIFICATION

For the purposes of the analysis of Xunzi's portrayal of the *shengren* in this chapter, I will focus on his presentation in the *Lilun* essay. Although Xunzi describes other qualities of the *shengren* in other essays of his work, one of the core features of his depiction is the sage as ritual master, which features significantly in the *Lilun*. The term *li* expresses two ideas, both rituals themselves and the virtue of ritual propriety. Early Confucians such as Xunzi understood the *li* as rituals to comprise two basic classes of acts, those called *yili* 儀禮 or "ceremonial rituals," and those called *quli* 曲禮or "rituals regarding minor things."[6] An example of *yili* would have been the various sacrifices practiced in ancient Chinese society: sacrifice to one's ancestors, civil sacrifices, and sacrifices offered by the ruler to *Tian*.

---

6. Ruiping Fan, "Confucian Ritualization: How and Why?" in *Ritual and the Moral Life: Reclaiming the Tradition*, ed. David Solomon, Ping-Cheung Lo, and Ruiping Fan (London: Springer, 2012), 143–60, here 143.

214   Chapter 5

It is important to note, however, that for Xunzi the *li* as a collection of ritual acts, liturgies, and rules are more important than particular rituals within this collection. For him, all of the rituals as taught by the Confucian tradition—including the sacrifices—were fundamental to the moral development and flourishing of society.[7]

Xunzi begins the *Lilun* with a history of the *li*: whence did the *li* come, and what was their purpose? According to Xunzi, "human beings are born and have desires, yet they do not obtain what they desire, and then they are unable to stop seeking what they desire."[8] As we saw in chapter 4 above, this touches on Xunzi's understanding of *renxing*. In the essay concerning *renxing*, Xunzi argues there are three types of desires with which humans are born: a love for profit (*li* 利), a proclivity toward hatred and viciousness, and desires of the eyes and ears bringing about a love of sound and color. According to Xunzi, if we nurture a love of profit, this will lead to contention and the taking of goods by force, and then discourse and submission will vitiate. If we follow our desires for hatred and viciousness, oppression and thievery will rise, and loyalty and fidelity will decline. Finally, if we give in to the desires of our eyes and ears, obscenity and disorder (*luan*) will arise, and *li* , appropriateness, culture, and the pattern of life will disappear.[9]

In the *Lilun*, Xunzi clearly sees the human problem as lying not in human desiring as such, but what human beings desire and in what degree. Specifically, the problem is that human desires are not

---

7. Much of the literature on this topic tends to fall into arguments that make Xunzi into a conventionalist as regards ritual; furthering this point, many scholars have argued that Xunzi sees human beings as crafting the conventions of ritual in order to create the order of the cosmos and society—see, e.g., Hagen, *The Philosophy of Xunzi*. This view is difficult to justly portray and refute in a footnote, but quite simply, I find this categorization of Xunzi is indebted to a modern dialecticism between the transcendent and immanent. I find that Xunzi perceives both a givenness to human life and the ability to "make" the world. As such, I do not think his theory of ritual is truly conventional but includes knowledge of the cosmic *dao* and using human faculties to establish ritual forms that enable humans to conform to the *dao*. In my reading, the key point is anthropological: human acts such as rituals and naming are in some measure conventional due to the faculties of the human person as an intellectual creature. Yet there is always a givenness to the faculties that gives them coherence. This is something not foreign to Christianity, we might add: Adam is allowed to name the animals, but he never thinks he causes them to exist in their particular forms.

8. *Xunzi, Lilun*, 1: "禮起於何也 曰人生而有欲欲而不得則不能無求."

9. *Xunzi, Xing e*, 1. See ch. 4 for more discussion.

Thomistic Christology and Xunzi's *Shengren* 215

aimed at concrete obtainable goods; rather, they are abstract and open-ended desires to serve one's own self-interest.[10] For example, when Xunzi speaks of the desire for "profit," he means the abstract sense of more money. For those with unformed desires, the only limiting factor that determines how much money is "enough" is one's self-interest, and so they perpetually desire more. Hence, Xunzi has a very specific notion of why desire is problematic: "if in their seeking to fulfill their desires there is no limit to their striving, then it would be impossible for people to *not* contend with one another; contention leads to disorder, and disorder to destitution."[11]

This, then, is the human condition out of which the need for *li* arises. The problem of human desire is that it is not limited or measured and has no guide or rule to channel it properly. Thus, everyone desires the same thing in the same unlimited ways and contends with others because of this desire. But Xunzi does not suggest we battle over the resources themselves; indeed, this would imply the human desire to eat was bad (though the difficult terrain of China meant this desire was not easily fulfilled). The problem is that the desires we have are innately unrestrained and unguided. Here we should bear in mind the political context of Xunzi's day in the Warring States period (see introduction for more discussion). When Xunzi uses the word "contention" (*zheng* 爭), this evokes not only squabbles between individuals, but battlefields of men contending over land and goods. More importantly, during the Warring States period the contention among the various states of the period was occurring as an attempt to grasp power away from the waning Zhou monarchy.[12] For Confucians like Xunzi, this was a disastrous

---

10. Winnie Sung, "Ritual in the *Xunzi*: A Change of the Heart/Mind," *Sophia* 51 (2012): 215. Sung argues that Xunzi understands *li* 利 in terms of "interests that pertain exclusively to the self." Thus, in her definition, Xunzi's conception of ritual is that is corrects or reforms the heart-mind that is originally aimed toward self-interest. Generally, I find Sung's position helpful and clarifying of Xunzi's thought, however I find it brings a slight complication. Self-interest cannot be a categorical problem for Xunzi; after all, he argues we should pursue becoming like sages precisely because it is best for us. Hence, I argue that *li* 利 is better understood in the sense of *excessive* possession, or trying to get as much as one can without regard for proper order or distinctions. In other words, Xunzi does not seem to me to think the desire to eat, learn, or have houseroom is problematic, but rather *how* I desire and move to acquire these things in excess.

11. *Xunzi, Lilun*, 1.

12. Mark Edward Lewis, *The Early Chinese Empires: Qin and Han* (Cambridge, MA:

216   Chapter 5

departure from the ancient traditions, culture, and form of life that was transmitted through the Zhou. The Warring States was to Xunzi an outgrowth of the human desires of pride, power, and prestige; these desires flourished in departing from the Zhou way of life, and thus led to mass disorder (*luan*). As he puts it elsewhere, "there are disordered rulers; states are not in themselves disordered."[13]

The significance of this is that Xunzi's conception of bad desires is not misanthropic, but a diagnosis of the social and political upheaval of his time; sadly, we know from experience and history that such upheaval is more the rule than exception. Of course, this upheaval is not limited to rulers; the thief is as much evidence of unlimited desire as the tyrant. Yet it is not the desires in themselves that are bad, but the fact that they are given free reign without any means to call them into order. And this is the fundamental problem of Warring States China, and any other age for that matter: unfettered desire leads to disorder.

However, Xunzi argues there was a time in the past when the rulers were not disordered and neither were the people or the state. Rather than nurturing our desires that lead to contention, there were instituted ways of redirecting, guiding, and re-forming desires to prevent disorder. These rulers were the ancient sage-kings, who are the source of ritual itself. According to Xunzi, the ancient sage kings hated disorder, and thus established *li* and appropriateness in various ways in order to "nourish people's desires and give to them what they seek." This then caused the people to have moderate desire for things, and the things were not broken apart due to the desiring.[14]

According to Xunzi, the ancient sage kings established *li* as a way to guide human flourishing. In his chapter on human moral tendencies, Xunzi compares our moral tendencies to a wooden branch, and the *li* of the sages to steam. The steam impacts the wood by reshaping it, and then it can be made straight (*zhi* 直). The ancient sage kings knew that people's desires went astray and tended to disorder, and so they established laws and rituals in order to "straighten out"

Belknap Press of Harvard, 2007), 185ff. For a more general history of the historical background of Warring States China, see Loewe and Shaughnessy, *Cambridge History of Ancient China*.

13. *Xunzi, Jundao*, 1.

14. *Xunzi, Lilun*, 1

(*jiao* 矯) people's emotional desires and help them become rectified (*zheng* 正).[15] Hence, Xunzi's famous argument is that our moral tendencies are bad, and that we are only made good through "artifice" (*wei* 偽).

One must bear in mind that for Xunzi, it is not simply ritualized behavior or just any moral artifice that makes for human flourishing.[16] Mark Edward Lewis has argued that for Confucians like Xunzi, the "dark side" of human nature was born out in mere human convention or custom (*su* 俗). The fact that human beings may ritualize behavior is not enough to make it an artifice that genuinely straightens the poor tendencies of human nature. Rather, at stake for Xunzi was the Confucian program of education and formation, whereby one learned the proper "straightening artifice" by studying the ancient texts and traditions championed in Confucianism.[17] For Xunzi, straightening (*jiao* 矯) human tendencies required a particular, Confucian education (*jiao* 教).

Therefore, Xunzi's emphasis is not on rituals in the abstract, but in the ritual practices originally set in place by the sage kings of old. To understand why this is the case, we must first understand the cosmic aspects of *li*. Xunzi argues that *li* has three roots. The first is Heaven and Earth (*Tiandi*天地), which is the root of life. Then are the forefathers and ancestors, who are the root of one's class of existence (*lei* 類). Third are the ruler and teacher, who are the root of order (*zhi*).[18] These three roots make the flourishing life possible, and it is the *li* (rituals) that are established to properly serve all three. Hence, *li* (ritual propriety) concerns the negotiation of the proper relationship between existence, history, cosmos, and present

15. *Xunzi, Xing e*, 2.

16. T. C. Kline III and Justin Tiwald, introduction to *Ritual and Religion in the* Xunzi, ed. Kline and Tiwald (Albany, NY: State University of New York Press, 2014). 3. Kline and Tiwald's edited volume is a response to scholars who argue Xunzi is antagonistic toward religious practice. Their volume defends the position that "what we find in Xunzi is *not* a critique of religious practice as such but rather a critique of certain forms of religious practice and interpretations of religious practice—the forms that treat rituals and supernatural beings as mere instruments of personal advantage and interpretations that fail to appreciate the proper function of ritual in moral cultivation."

17. Mark Edward Lewis, "Custom and Human Nature in Early China," *Philosophy East & West* 53, no. 3 (July 2003): 309–22.

18. *Xunzi, Lilun*, 3. *Zhi* 治 usually means something like "to rule" but more basically means giving order to things.

218 Chapter 5

relationships all at the same time. Such negotiations cannot be merely "constructed" on the whim of whoever might, but requires particular insight into the cosmological order *and* the human person.

For example, Xunzi speaks of the sage as one who applies the method of observing Heaven (*cha tian* 察天) and so can "ornament" (*cuo* 錯) the Earth.[19] In another essay, Xunzi describes Heaven, Earth, and Humanity as a triad of harmonious relationships. Heaven has its seasons or *kairoi* (*shi* 時), the Earth has its resources, and humanity has his order (*zhi*). In this context, Xunzi stresses that the sage "does not seek to know Heaven."[20] Xunzi does not mean by this that the sage is unconcerned about the movements of Heaven, and he doesn't seem to be advocating simple agnosticism regarding the transcendent.[21] Rather, Xunzi is arguing that the *shengren* realizes that his role is as a human being (*ren* 人) and he stands in relation to Heaven as such.[22] Only by ordering himself does the *shengren* stand in harmony with Heaven. Hence, it is implicit that the *shengren* must understanding something about Heaven and Earth in order to understand how to order human life to be in harmony with these movements.[23]

19. *Xunzi, Wangzhi*, 23. The verb *cuo* usually means to make a mistake or err but was also used to describe inlaying items with precious metal, polishing, or sharpening objects.

20. *Xunzi, Tianlun*, 3.

21. Chen Daqi 陳大齊, *Xunzi Xueshuo* 荀子學說 (Taipei: Zhonghua wenhua chuban weiyuanhua, 1954), 144. Chen contends that for Xunzi, "the *li* are not obtained from *Tian* and cannot take their model from *Tian*" (故禮義不得之於天, 亦非取法於天). He seems to imply by this that humans ought not have concern for *Tian*, but I would argue this is not the case. It seems to me that Xunzi's point is that the type of existence of *Tian* (especially in its transcendent aspects) is different from human existence, and thus it cannot be a model (*qufa* 取法) of how to flourish as a human being. Yet we can understand human flourishing in relation to *Tian*. For a good recovery of the transcendent features of *Tian* for Xunzi, see Edward Machle, "Xunzi as a Religious Philosopher," *Philosophy East and West* 26, no. 4 (1976): 443–61. Reprinted in Kline and Tiwald, *Ritual and Religion in the* Xunzi, 21–42.

22. Chung-Ying Cheng, "Xunzi as a Systematic Philosopher: Toward an Organic Unity of Nature, Mind, and Reason," *Journal of Chinese Philosophy* (2008): 9–31. Cheng contends that "the core and key notion for understanding Xunzi correctly and systematically" is precisely the relationship and distinction between humanity and Heaven (*tian* 天). As Cheng notes, this relationship is often summarized by the phrase *tianren xiangfen* 天人相分, which can be rendered as "the harmony and distinction of Heaven and humanity" (here, 13).

23. Ori Tavor, "Xunzi's Theory of Ritual Revisited: Reading Ritual as Corporal Technology," *Dao* 12 (2013): 327: "According to Xunzi ... the only method for avoiding [calamities] is first to understand the pattern and movement of Heaven and then to use this acquired knowledge to our advantage. This sort of knowledge is gained by observing the course of Heaven, Earth, and the Four Seasons empirically, recording their configuration, sequence, and

Thomistic Christology and Xunzi's *Shengren*   219

The *shengren* could then determine the *li* not simply because they were "creative individuals" but because they understood how to order human life, meaning they understood human disorder in cosmological and anthropological terms. For Xunzi, this is why it is possible that the ritual forms can be changed, but only by sages. In fact, Xunzi argues for the historical existence of at least a hundred sages, and advocates following only those closer to in time to our era. He teaches, "if you wish to observe the traces of the sage-kings, then look to the most clear of them, the most recent kings [*hou wang* 後王]."[24] This is not a commitment to progressivism, however, as the more recent is naturally superior to the past. Rather, Xunzi means that the later kings who are sages continue the trajectory of the ancient sages, but in ways that are more fitting to the disorder of the age. Xunzi claims that if one desires to know the ancient ways, one ought to observe the *dao* of the Zhou dynasty. Hence, "by means of the near you may know the far; by means of the one you may know the many [*yi jin zhi yuan, yi zhi wan* 以近知遠, 以一知萬]."[25]

We can summarize Xunzi's conception of the ritual sage in a few short propositions. First and foremost, (1) sagehood is intrinsically expressed in the formation of ritual. The wisdom of the sage is not self-contained, but flows outward in establishing and maintaining proper ritual forms and liturgies. Hence, to be a sage is inherently to be a ritual master or at least source of ritual. (2) The sage institutes ritual as a way of straightening and ordering (zhi 直 and zhi 治) the human person and community, and thus brings about human flourishing. Ritual is necessary to correct the tendency of unfettered desires to result in disorder (*luan*) social and individual. (3) Ritual forms are in themselves mutable, but only because the sage figure has knowledge of how to harmonize human life with the cosmos, and then institute that order in rituals. According to Xunzi, then, the *shengren* possesses intellectual and moral perfections that are

---

movements. Fortunately, claims Xunzi, this task was undertaken by sage rulers of antiquity, who left us their findings through a set of coded ritual prescriptions based on the patterns of the Way [*dao*] ... Rituals, argues Xunzi, are not arbitrary. They are markers, left by sages, which function as a prescriptive script, a guiding light for the rest of humanity to follow. Based on the one Way, ritual is thus depicted as the only viable method of putting the Way into practice."

24. *Xunzi, Feixiang*, 6.
25. *Xunzi, Feixiang*, 6.

220   Chapter 5

expressed in the establishment of rituals that enable human flourishing and perfection.

AQUINAS ON CHRIST'S PRIESTHOOD

To gain a proper perspective for assessing and appreciating the Christological limits and possibilities of Xunzi's ritual sage, I turn in this section to Aquinas's treatment of Christ's priesthood.[26] It is notable that although Aquinas's understanding of Christ's priesthood is clearly fixed within the bounds of the biblical images and history of priesthood, Serge-Thomas Bonino has observed that Aquinas's thought can accommodate an account of priesthood as a "natural institution" that invites analogs from non-Christian and non-Jewish traditions.[27] However, as my analysis will make clear, the application of such analogues within Aquinas's Christology must always maintain a view to the fundamental Jewish idiom of Christ's priesthood and sacrifice.

The most direct treatment Aquinas makes of Christ's priesthood is in *ST* IIIa, q. 22.[28] Jean-Pierre Torrell has helpfully shown

26. It seems this question was overlooked for a long period in Thomistic scholarship but has seen much interest recently. The most important general source for treatments on the theme of St. Thomas's view of Christ's priesthood is vol. 99 of *Revue Thomiste*. Readers with particular interest in the discussion of Christ's priesthood outside of the *Summa* should consult the following: Gilles Berceville, OP, "Le sacerdoce du Christ dans le *Commentaire de l'Épître aux Hébreux* de saint Thomas d'Aquin," *Revue Thomiste* 99 (1999): 143–58, and Martin Morard, "Sacerdoce du Christ et sacerdoce des chretiens dans le *Commentaire des Psaumes* de saint Thomas d'Aquin," *Revue Thomiste* 99 (1999): 119–42.

27. Serge-Thomas Bonino, OP, "Le sacerdoce comme institution naturelle selon saint Thomas d'Aquin," *Revue Thomiste* 99 (1999): 34–36. Bonino helpfully develops a concept of natural priesthood out of St. Thomas's discussion of religious virtue. He points out that Thomas also does not possess a general notion of priesthood, nor seems to have thought such an account necessary (see 34–35). However, Thomas's consideration of human nature allows for a development of a general account of priesthood, even an interreligious account. He evokes St. Thomas's description of marriage as a natural institution, by virtue of the fact that humans may incline to marriage but must act in free will to fulfill this good. Bonino suggests "priesthood" in general is this type of natural inclination of human nature (see 36). Similarly, I argue, through Xunzi, that "ritual sagehood" can name a type of priestly inclination of human nature, one preferable here because it allows for the union of ritual action and intellectual perfection. Regardless, as I hope to make clear, whether developing a general account of priesthood or ritual sagehood, in a Christological trajectory Christ will be the measure of these forms, which Bonino also notes (34).

28. For general discussions of Aquinas's Christology, see Dominic Legge, OP, *The Trinitarian Christology of St. Thomas Aquinas* (New York: Oxford University Press, 2016); Thomas

Thomistic Christology and Xunzi's *Shengren* 221

this is notable.[29] For one thing, Aquinas is the only one among his contemporaries to discuss this question in detail, just as he is the lone commentator on the Epistle to the Hebrews. Additionally, being q. 22, the discussion on Christ's priesthood occurs within the division of the *Tertia Pars* pertaining to identifying the person of Christ as the Incarnate Word.[30]

Following Joseph Wawrykow, it is helpful at this point to pose the following question: "what knowledge does Thomas assume or take for granted in the readers of his question?"[31] As his assumed reader would have been studying theology in the medieval university and hearing constant lectures on scripture from a *magister in Sacra Pagina* or *cursus biblicus*, Aquinas can take for granted that his reader will readily profess Jesus is the Incarnate Word, know Christ as the mediator of salvation, and know Christ's body and blood are received in the Eucharist.[32] With regard to the theme of Christ's priest-

---

Joseph White, OP, *The Incarnate Lord: A Thomistic Study in Christology* (Washington, DC: The Catholic University of America Press, 2017); Corey L. Barnes, *Christ's Two Wills in Scholastic Thought: The Christology of Aquinas and Its Historical Contexts* (Toronto: Pontifical Institute of Medieval Studies, 2012); Jean-Pierre Torrell, OP, *Le Christ en ses mystères: la vie et l'œuvre de Jésus selon saint Thomas d'Aquin*, 2 vols. (Paris: Desclée, 1999); F. Ruello, *La Christologie de Thomas d'Aquin* (Paris: Beauchsne, 1987). Additionally, see the French translation and commentary of the first part of the *ST* IIIa, qq. 1–26, in three volumes, published as Jean-Pierre Torrell, OP, ed. and trans., *Somme theologique: Le verbe incarné* (Paris: Éditions du Cerf, 2002). For a helpful general discussion of Christ's priesthood as a theological topic from a Thomistic perspective, see Matthew Levering, *Christ and the Catholic Priesthood: Ecclesial Hierarchy and the Pattern of the Trinity* (Chicago and Mundelein, IL: Hillenbrand Books, 2010), esp. 60–119.

29. See Jean-Pierre Torrell, OP, "The Priesthood of Christ in the *Summa Theologiae*," in *Christ and Spirituality in St. Thomas Aquinas*, trans. Bernhard Blankenhorn, OP (Washington, DC: The Catholic University of America Press, 2011), 127–28. Torrell's article here is a translation of his earlier essay, "Le sacerdoce du Christ dans la *Somme de théologie*," *Revue Thomiste* 99 (1999): 75–100.

30. See, e.g., John F. Boyle, "The Twofold Division of St. Thomas's Christology in the *Tertium Pars*," *The Thomist* 60 (1996): 439–47. Boyle argues contra M.-D. Chenu's claim that qq. 1–26 of the *Tertia Pars* employs a "scientific" approach to Christology while qq. 27–59 employs a "scriptural" one. Boyle argues instead that both divisions are scriptural, and the distinction between the parts arises out of the struggle to describe the Church's proclamation about Christ in keeping with the historical narrative of his life. Thomas approaches the problem by first discussing who Christ is (i.e., the Incarnate Word) and then understanding what Christ does.

31. Joseph P. Wawyrkow, "Wisdom in the Christology of Thomas Aquinas," in *Christ Among the Medieval Dominicans*, ed. Kent Emery, Jr. and Joseph P. Wawrykow (Notre Dame, IN: University of Notre Dame Press, 1999), 177.

32. Leonard E. Boyle, *The Setting of the* Summa theologiae *of St. Thomas* (Toronto: Pontifical Institute of Mediaeval Studies, 1982). Boyle argues that the *ST* was written to fill a lacuna in Dominican education for the *iuniores* of the Order. If this is the case, then these

222   Chapter 5

hood in general, Aquinas might have assumed that his reader would also know of the traditional perspectives unique to each Gospel, specifically that Luke is said to emphasize Jesus's humanity and to write particularly with an eye to Christ as priest.

In both the *Super Evangelium S. Matthaei lectura* and the *Catena aurea* on Matthew and Luke, Aquinas attributes this line of thought to St. Augustine's *De consensu evangelistarum*.[33] Aquinas appeals to Augustine to explain the divergence in position and content between Luke and Matthew's genealogies.[34] We can add to this that in his inaugural lecture at Paris, Aquinas evoked this same attribution of Christ as priest in Luke.[35] These citations are significant because they show it is reasonable that Aquinas could have assumed, or at least hoped, that his reader knew that Christ's priesthood is the central theme to one of the Gospels, and that this observation went back at least to St. Augustine. Moreover, the Council of Ephesus explicitly proclaimed that Jesus is called a "high priest and apostle," a testimony affirmed at Lateran IV.[36] Hence, while the reader might be aware that there were few treatments of Christ's priesthood like that featured in q. 22, the question itself was legitimate in view of sacred scripture and sacred tradition.

When Aquinas discusses why Luke provides Jesus's genealogy after his baptism instead of at the Gospel's beginning, he explains as follows: "Luke means to most commend the priestly persona of Christ, for the expiation of sins pertains to priesthood, and therefore

---

observations about the assumed reader are intensified since the reader will have at least taken the initial vow to join the Dominican order and would at the least have been taught scripture daily in the priory, as well as engaged in other spiritual disciplines.

33. Louis J. Bataillon, OP, "St. Thomas et les Pères: De la *Catena* a la *tertia pars*," in *Ordo Sapientiae et Amoris*, ed. C.-J. Pinto de Oliveira, OP (Fribourg: Éditions Universitaires, 1993), 15–36. Bataillon convincingly shows that the *Catenae* are heavily influential for Thomas's thought in the *Summa*, particularly in the *tertia pars*. Key to this for our purposes is that according to Bataillon, the *Catenae* are the way Thomas entered into the tradition and drew upon it for his own understanding of especially Christological matters. Hence, it is significant that the appeal to Christ's priesthood in Luke (through Augustine, no less) appears in the *Catena* in particular, since this means it functions not only as a source of an idea for Thomas, but informs his theological imagination, after he compiled them, course.

34. Cf. *Super Evangelium S. Matthaei lectura*, cap. 1, l. 2; *Catena in Lucam*, pr. It is worth noting Augustine is the first Father cited, after a citation from Isaiah and a gloss from the text.

35. Cf. *Commendatio Sacrae Scripturae*.

36. See Henry Denzinger, ed., *The Sources of Catholic Dogma*, trans. Roy J. Deferrari (Fitzwilliam, NH: Loreto, 2007), 51 and 169.

Thomistic Christology and Xunzi's *Shengren*   223

after his baptism, in which sins will be expiated, it is fitting for Luke to place the generation of Christ."[37] For Aquinas, to consider Christ's priesthood involves explicitly thinking of Christ's work to expiate sins.[38] When we consider the questions of the *ST* preceding q. 22, this is quite significant. In the opening question of the *Tertia Pars*, Aquinas discusses the fittingness of the Incarnation. After establishing the Incarnation on the principle of God's goodness and that due to sin humanity requires the Incarnation for redemption, he poses the question of whether the Incarnation would have occurred had no transgression taken place. Aquinas answers no because the tradition teaches that Christ came to effect the redemption from sin.[39]

Thus, the reader of q. 22 can be expected to know the traditional attribution of Luke as concerned with Christ's humanity via his priesthood, the link to this theme and expiation for sins, and the all-important fact that the *terminus* of the Incarnation is the salvation of sinners. The topic of Christ's priesthood is fittingly located in the course of describing Jesus's person as one who can affect such salvation as the God-man. In the first article of question 22, Aquinas contemplates whether it is fitting for Christ to be a priest. The objections have two foundations: the ontological dissonance between the priesthood and the *Verbum caro*, and the dissonance between Christ's ministry and the characteristics of the priesthood of the Old Testament. As to the first objection, it is pointed out that priests are lower than the angels, but that Christ is higher, and hence it is beneath his dignity to think him *sacerdos*.[40] The second objection argues that since Christ was not from the tribe of Levi he cannot be a

---

37. *Super Evangelium S. Matthaei lectura*, cap. 1, l. 2: "Lucas autem maxime intendit commendare in Christo personam sacerdotalem, ad sacerdotem autem pertinent expiatio peccatorum, et ideo post Baptismum, in quo fit peccatorum expiatio, convenientur a Luca ponitur Christi generatio."

38. See Matthew Levering, "Christ the Priest: An Exploration of *Summa Theologiae* III, Question 22," *The Thomist* 71 (2007): 379–417. Levering shows the soteriological thrust of q. 22 in four aspects taken from N. T. Wright—demonstrating that Christ's death is eschatological, sacrificial, sanctifying, and unitive. While we will not here explicate the soteriological aspects to this degree, my reading here presupposes the sort of rich soteriological account that Levering presents. What I wish to emphasize is that Christ's death accomplishes these things in a ritual manner, and that this is significant for understanding the person of Christ.

39. *ST* IIIa, q. 1, art. 3, corp.; cf. *Scriptum super Sententiis* III, d. 1, q. 1, a. 3, corp.

40. Significantly, this objection draws its force from the comparison between Christ and the angels in Hebrews 1:7ff.

224 Chapter 5

priest in fulfillment of the Old Testament type, and the third argues
the same by pointing to the Old Testament distinction between the
offices of lawgiver and priest.[41]

The objections in article 1 show the basic shape of concerns
Aquinas develops throughout the question. On the one hand, the
ontological concern deals with the union of God and man, and the
perfections of the latter as cause of the union. On the other, Aquinas is sensitive to scriptural harmony. The objections themselves
demonstrate interest in maintaining the rules for interpreting sacred
scripture, whereby the literal sense serves as a guide for the typological. With Christ's priesthood, the literal sense can seem at first to
rule out the typological conclusion the Church had defended since
the Council of Ephesus. Hence, for Aquinas, the question of Christ's
priesthood must be approached both in reference to the mystery of
the Hypostatic Union and in light of a proper exegesis of scripture.[42]

Matthew Levering has argued that these three objections have
the same basic theme: "the surpassing of the carnal mode of the Old
Testament by the spiritual mode of the New." Or as he also puts it,
in these objections, "a spiritual worship here seems entirely to replace cultic worship."[43] Following this, we can see Thomas's concern
for the historical narrative of Jesus's life and its link between Israel
and the Church. What *is* proper worship of God, and in what way
is the Church's liturgical life both resonant with and divergent from
Israel's? We can readily see the grave importance for ritual: if the
Church's worship is a spiritual worship that replaces the cultic, then
it is not fitting for Christ to effect salvation through the sacraments,
and hence his death would *negate* ritual life rather than enliven it.

In response, Aquinas first offers a definition of *sacerdos* as "hand-
ing over divine things to the people" (*divina populo tradit*); hence,

---

41. *ST* IIIa, q. 22, art. 1, obj. 1–3.

42. Berceville, 145–46. Berceville, though drawing upon Thomas's commentary on Hebrews, shows well what is at stake in the question of Christ's priesthood as regards an orthodox confession of the Hypostatic Union: "The attribution of priesthood to the Son of God,
the savior of all, raises, however, a theological difficulty which does not exist for the titles of
king, judge, or teacher: the notion of priesthood itself implies in effect this is an attribution of
service, and therefore inferiority." (*L'attribution du sacerdoce au Fils de Dieu, Seigneur universel,
soulève cependant une difficulté théologique qui n'existe pas pour les titres de roi, de juge ou de doc-
teur: la notion même de sacerdoce implique en effet celle de service, et donc d'infériorité.*)

43. Levering, "Christ the Priest," 384.

the priest is a "giver of sacred things" (*sacra dans*). He then identifies three divine things the priest mediates to the people: the law, prayers of the people to God, and satisfaction for sins. On the basis of these divine things Aquinas argues it is most fitting that Christ be a priest, for he is the mediator of the gift of partaking of the divine nature and effects reconciliation between the people and God.[44]

Consequently, Aquinas's response imbues the questions of the objections with an Incarnational logic, emphasizing the perfections of Christ's human nature flowing from the Hypostatic Union.[45] To the first objection he argues that Christ's dignity is higher than the angels in his human as well as divine nature because he "possesses the fullness of grace and glory" (*habuit plenitudinem gratiae et gloriae*). Yet at the same time the fullness of grace and glory is given to the human nature assumed by the Word, and hence Jesus "was conformed to the way-faring men who are constituted in the priesthood [*conformis fuit hominibus viatoribus in sacerdotio constitutis*]." Similarly, because Christ is the perfect union of Word and man, it does not matter that the Old Testament Levitical priesthood and distinction between priest and legislator are not present in him. Christ is not an instance of priesthood, but its norm and type: the Old Testament priesthood is a figure of Christ, and Christ's contains the perfect harmony of graces as legislator, priest, and king.[46]

The fruit of this first article of IIIa, q. 22, can be therefore articulated as follows: any attempt to speak of Christ as a ritual sage takes its form from the mystery of the Hypostatic Union and the perfections of grace and glory communicated therein. This is to say that

44. *ST* IIIa, q. 22, art. 1, corp.

45. Although modern Christology (Catholic and Protestant) often shows a preference for psychological portrayals of Christ rather than ontological, the Thomistic framework emphasizes the ontological foundations. For works that involve discussion of and correction of this tendency, See, e.g., White, *The Incarnate Lord*, 73–170; and Aaron Riches, *Ecce Homo: On the Divine Unity of Christ* (Grand Rapids, MI: Eerdmans, 2016). For more discussion on the place of the hypostatic union in the Christology of Aquinas and other medieval thinkers, see Corey Barnes, "Thomas Aquinas's Chalcedonian Christology and its Influence on Later Scholastics," *The Thomist* 78, no. 2 (2014): 189–217; Corey Barnes, "Christological Composition in Thirteenth-Century Debates," *The Thomist* 75 (2011); 173–206; Corey Barnes, "Albert the Great and Thomas Aquinas on Person, Hypostasis, and the Hypostatic Union," *The Thomist* 72, no. 1 (January 2008): 107–46; Michael Gorman, "Christ as Composite according to Aquinas," *Traditio* 55 (2000): 143–57.

46. *ST* IIIa, q. 22, art. 1, ad 1–3.

Christ's conception of ritual, exercise of ritual forms, and efficacy as priest is not due to training, discoveries, or charisma in a purely human sense. Rather, his ritual acts flow from his perfections of grace and glory that are the fruit of the union of Word and man.[47] With respect to Xunzi's ritual sagehood, this shows us that Christ cannot be seen as one unique instance of a priestly or ritual sage type. Instead, because he is the union of Word and man and as such possesses all human perfections and graces, Christ would have to be understood as the archetype of ritual sagehood not temporally, but essentially. Put differently, it is only when one seeks to locate an account of ritual sagehood within the historical and biblical attestation to the mysteries of Christ's life that ritual sagehood becomes a fitting category for Christological science.

After establishing that Christ is priest, article 2 poses the question of the material over which he presides as priest—that is, whether Christ can be both priest and victim. The objections here are built upon the perfections of Christ that Aquinas emphasizes in article 1. Objection 1 notes that the priestly sacrifice requires the killing of a victim and Jesus did not kill himself; hence, Jesus cannot be both priest and victim. Objection 2 similarly argues that because human sacrifice is alien to the Jewish priesthood, Christ would not have exercised his priesthood in treating himself as the victim. Objection 3 is perhaps the most enticing given its anti-Nestorian logic: since victims are consecrated to God in the act of sacrificing, Christ cannot be the victim of his priesthood because his consecration is due to his union to God and has always been a characteristic of his existence as Incarnate Word.[48]

It is very clear that Aquinas is not interested in simply ascribing priesthood to Christ, but also with understanding the logic of the sacraments, particularly the Eucharist, in which Christ is both priest and host. In his response to these objections, Aquinas begins by determining what a sacrifice is—"something that is offered to

---

47. For a discussion of this and related issues about the perfection of Christ's human nature, see White, *The Incarnate Lord*, 126–70, and 236–76; and Simon Francis Gaine, *Did the Savior See the Father? Christ, Salvation, and the Vision of God* (London: Bloomsbury T&T Clark, 2015).

48. *ST* IIIa, q. 22, art. 2, obj. 1–3.

Thomistic Christology and Xunzi's *Shengren*   227

God so that the human spirit is elevated to God"—and identifying three types of sacrifices. The first type is an offering for the remission of sin, according to Hebrews 5 and Leviticus 4:3. The second, taken from the peace offering in Leviticus 3 is an offering for the sake of being conserved in a state of grace. Third, echoing the holocaust of Leviticus 1:1–9, is the offering for being perfectly united with God.[49]

Building upon these three reasons for sacrifice, Aquinas shows how Christ's human nature confers these effects on us through his crucial sacrifice.[50] First, our sins are forever remitted (*deleta sunt*). Second, we receive the grace of salvation through him. And third, through him we have obtained the perfection of glory.[51] Now it is clear that the priest on his own power cannot have these effects; he exercises these effects as a form of mediation through the offering of a victim and its acceptance by God. In short, a pleasing sacrifice requires both an empowered mediator (*sacerdos*), but also a fitting victim sacrificed in a fitting way. Notably, even though a cow is required for all three sacrifices Aquinas mentions in Leviticus, there are different stipulations: the offering for union with God requires a male without blemish, the peace offering can be a male or female without blemish with only certain parts required for sacrifice, and the sin offering requires a young, spotless bullock.[52]

In light of this observation, Aquinas's reply to the objections focuses on why Christ is the most fitting victim for the sacrifice over which he is the official.[53] To the first, Aquinas emphasizes that Christ exercised his free will to give himself over to death, and thus he is the victim of his own priestly act. Second, however, Christ's free will is not to kill himself as a human sacrifice, but to give himself over to suffering. This is exceptionally important for it notes that Christ's place as victim of sacrifice is not simply corporeal. Rather, as

---

49. See Matthew Levering, *Sacrifice and Community: Jewish Offering and Christian Eucharist* (Malden, MA: Blackwell, 2005), 50–94; and Matthew Levering, "Aquinas on the Liturgy of the Eucharist," in *Aquinas on Doctrine: A Critical Introduction*, ed. Thomas G. Weinandy, OFM, Cap., Daniel A. Keating, and John P. Yocum (London: T&T Clark, 2004), 183–98, esp. 189–93.

50. See Levering, *Sacrifice and Community*, 115–202; Reinhard Hütter, *Aquinas on Transubstantiation: The Real Presence of Christ in the Eucharist* (Washington, DC: The Catholic University of America Press, 2019), 10–11.

51. *ST* IIIa, q. 22, art. 2, corp.

52. See Lv 1:3f, Lv 3:1f. and Lv 4:3f, respectively.

53. *ST* IIIa, q. 22, art. 2, corp.

228   Chapter 5

Aquinas shows in his use of Augustine's definition of sacrifice, man's spirit can indeed be offered to God. In the case of Jesus, his sacrifice is most essentially his surrender of himself unto suffering, i.e., his acceptance of the mission of redemption as the God-man.[54] Hence, Jesus's priestly office is exercised over the victim that is alone fitting for the ritual effects human sinners require. As to the third objection, the Leonine edition does not contain the reply, but we can construct a rough sense of what it might have been: because the Incarnation is entirely aimed toward the salvation worked out for humanity on the Cross, Jesus's humanity is from the moment of his conception con-secrated as perfect and fitting victim.

The second article therefore teaches that Christ's priesthood and thus ritual mastery is exercised in virtue of himself as the "sacred thing" given to us, in the sense that his life and especially his Passion are also the content of the rituals he performs for our salvation. With Christ, the ritual forms over which he presides concern first and foremost the mediation of his own life and reality to the Church. The "sacred things" over which he is priest is the union of God and man and the fruit of that union. To illustrate this principle at work in Aquinas's thought, we can simply point to the fact that the Church's sacraments have Christ as priest, and his Passion as that which is sig-nified in the sacraments.[55]

The emphasis on Christ as victim leads us toward the soterio-logical content of Christ's priesthood that Aquinas elucidates in ar-ticle 3. Here Aquinas considers the question of whether Christ's priesthood has the effect of expiating sins. Clearly, he will answer affirmatively, but it is important to see what is at stake. For Aquinas, it is not simply whether Christ can expiate for sins, but whether this expiation occurs in the ritual act of the Passion, with Christ acting as both priest and victim.

Answering this question requires again understanding the union

---

54. *ST* IIIa, q. 22, art. 2, ad 1–2.

55. *ST* IIIa, q. 60, art. 3. For discussion, see Hütter, *Aquinas on Transubstantiation*, 57–60; Reginald Lynch, OP, *The Cleansing of the Heart: The Sacraments as Instrumental Causes in the Thomistic Tradition* (Washington, DC: The Catholic University of America Press, 2017), 102–10; Jan-Heiner Tück, *A Gift of Presence: The Theology and Poetry of the Eucharist in Thomas Aquinas*, trans. Scott G. Hefelfinger (Washington, DC: The Catholic University of America Press, 2014), 94–162.

of the Word and man. The first objection is based on apparent limits of the *communicatio idiomatum*, arguing that because only God can forgive sins and Christ is priest according to his human nature, his *priesthood* cannot expiate sins. Hence, the objection calls into question whether Jesus's human nature (of which is predicated his priesthood) can bring about expiation of sins, or whether this must be an act of his divine nature alone. The second and third objections point again to the relationship between the priesthood of Christ and the Old Testament. Hebrews 10:1–3 teaches that the sacrifices of the Old Testament were not able to "make participants perfect" (*non potuerunt perfectos facere*) proving this due to their need to be offered again and again (*alioquin cessassent offerri*).[56] As both in the Lord's prayer where Jesus commends us to pray "forgive" us our sins in the present tense (*dimitte*) and in the daily sacrifice offered by the Church, the logic of Hebrews suggests his sacrifice is not efficacious to expiate sins. Similarly, the third objection argues that because Christ is the "lamb" he does not align with the typology of the proper victims for the sin sacrifice in the Old Testament, and hence his sacrifice does not expiate sins.

Although there is a formal distinction between the objection couched in the terms of Ephesus and the two taking a scriptural approach, the argument is basically the same. All three objections call into question the efficacy of Christ's priestly act. The importance of these objections cannot be overlooked: if Christ's expiation of sins is not mediated through his human act of priesthood, then this unravels the entire reason for the Incarnation as Thomas has laid it out. For Aquinas, this ritual act of expiating for sins is essential to the Church's testimony about who Jesus is and what he accomplishes for us. That is, the ritualness of Christ's Passion is important as a testimony to the nature and cause of the Incarnation.

---

56. For discussion of Aquinas's reading of Hebrews, see Daniel A. Keating, "Thomas Aquinas and the Epistle to the Hebrews: The 'Excellence of Christ,'" in *Christology, Hermeneutics, and Hebrews: Profiles from the History of Interpretation*, ed. Jon C. Laansma and Daniel J. Treier (London: T&T Clark, 2012), 84–99; Matthew Levering, "Blood, Death, and Sacrifice in the Epistle to the Hebrews According to Thomas Aquinas," in *So Great a Salvation: A Dialogue on the Atonement in Hebrews*, ed. John C. Laansma, George H. Guthrie, and Cynthia Long Westfall (London: T&T Clark, 2019), 120–43; Thomas G. Weinandy, "The Supremacy of Christ: Aquinas' Commentary on Hebrews," in Weinandy et al., *Aquinas on Scripture*, 223–44.

230 Chapter 5

Aquinas's response to the objections begins by arguing that expiation of sins requires cleansing sinners in two aspects: the stain of guilt (*macula culpae*) and the debt of punishment (*reatus poenae*).[57] The stain of guilt is forgiven through grace, which turns the sinner's heart toward God, and the debt of punishment is totally removed through man's making satisfaction to God. Aquinas then states that Christ's priesthood effects both forms of cleansing. Regarding the stain of guilt, Christ's priesthood communicates the grace to us that turns our hearts toward God, citing Romans 3:24–25 that it is through faith in Christ's blood that we are justified. Regarding the debt of punishment, Christ's priesthood satisfies for us completely, because he "took on our diseases and bore our sorrows" (Is 53:4).[58] For Aquinas, Jesus mediates grace to us for the redemption of sins through his blood in the ritual act of the Cross. His sacrifice communicates this grace to us and turns our hearts toward God. Also, Jesus's sacrifice fulfills the perfect offering as priest and what is offered as victim so as to be the perfect satisfaction for our sins.[59]

In the reply to objection 1, Aquinas argues that understanding the Passion as expiating sins requires understanding the mystery of the Incarnation. Because the Word is united to human nature and acts through it, Jesus Christ's human nature can work out the expiation of sins. Notice the Incarnational balance here. Aquinas not only identifies the importance of the divine nature to make Christ's sacrifice efficacious, but also that the Word enacts this salvation through

57. See Levering, *Engaging the Doctrine of Creation*, 299–304. See also Peter Karl Koritansky, *Thomas Aquinas and the Philosophy of Punishment* (Washington, DC: The Catholic University of America Press, 2012), 68–132; Stump, *Aquinas*, 427–54; Eleonore Stump, *Atonement* (New York: Oxford University Press, 2018), 39–71; and I. Howard Marshall, "The Theology of the Atonement," in *The Atonement Debate: Papers from the London Symposium on the Theology of Atonement,* ed. Derek Tidball, David Hilborn, and Justin Thacker (Grand Rapids, MI: Zondervan, 2008), 49–68.

58. For discussions of satisfaction in Aquinas's thought, see Junius Johnson, *Patristic and Medieval Atonement Theory: A Guide to Research* (Lanham, MD: Rowman and Littlefield, 2016), 133–41; Phillippe-Marie Margelidon, *Études thomistes sur la théologie de la redemption: de la grâce à la resurrection du christ* (Perpignan: Artège, 2010); Benedict M. Guevin, "Anselm and Aquinas on Satisfaction," *Angelicum* 87, no. 2 (2010): 283–90; Emmanuel Perrier, OP, "L'enjeu christologique de la satisfaction (I)" *Revue Thomiste* CIII (2003): 105–36; Perrier, "L'enje christologique de la satisfaction (II)," *Revue Thomiste* CIII (2003): 203–48; Romanus Cessario, OP, *The Godly Image: Christian Satisfaction in Aquinas* (Washington, DC: The Catholic University of America Press, 2020).

59. *ST* IIIa, q. 22, art. 3, corp.

Thomistic Christology and Xunzi's *Shengren* 231

the medium of sacrifice in the idiom of human nature (priesthood). Citing Augustine, Aquinas shows the priestly act of the Incarnate Word is efficacious in four ways: Christ is united with God as the one to whom the sacrifice is offered; Christ is united with sinners, for whom he offered the sacrifice; Christ offered it himself, and Christ was that sacrifice which was offered. Jesus's act of priesthood, then, is a product of the unique miracle of the Incarnation that allows Jesus's sacrifice to be perfect in each aspect of the sacrificial act.[60] For this reason, Christ's sacrifice is uniquely efficacious and has no need to be repeated. Aquinas clarifies that the New Law requires continual expiation for sins because of the frailty of the covenant members, not due to deficiency in the sacrifice. Unlike the Levitical priesthood with its multiple and repeated sacrifices, the Church offers the same sacrifice daily. Similarly, just as the Old Covenant featured several types of animals used in sacrifice, Jesus gives himself as the perfect lamb who was the "consummate sacrifice of all things."[61] According to Aquinas, Jesus's sacrificial act is categorically unique because he is the Incarnate Word.[62] Hence, the sacrifices of the Old Testament are consummated in him, and he is the norm for understanding the efficacy of the former rituals for communicating grace and reconciliation with God.

It is fruitful at this point to linger a moment to note the breadth of the effects of the cross to expiate sins in Aquinas's understanding.[63] Though certainly Aquinas means Christ's crucifixion expiates sin in a forensic or judicial sense, this is only one part of Christ's

---

60. *ST* IIIa, q. 22, art. 3, ad 1.

61. *ST* IIIa, q. 22, art. 3, ad 3.

62. The perfection and uniqueness of Christ's sacrifice, however, also creates intellectual problems. Two prominent ones are whether Christ's perfect will to accept his death is tantamount to the mortal sin of suicide, and also the general historical problem of consuming Christ's flesh being a form of cannibalism. Given my goals in this chapter, I don't have the space to deal with these issues as they deserve. For a recent treatment of the cannibalism question, see Brannon Hancock, *The Scandal of Sacramentality: The Eucharist in Literary and Theological Perspectives* (Cambridge, UK: James Clark and Co., 2014), 121–49. For an account of Christ's death that argues it is a form of divine suicide (though with discussion of attending issues), see Joel L. Watts, *Jesus as Divine Suicide: The Death of the Messiah in Galatians* (Eugene, OR: Pickwick, 2019).

63. For the larger context of Aquinas's thought on this question that deals with the influence of St. Anselm of Canterbury on Aquinas, see Cessario.

232 Chapter 5

victory over sin. In its simplest definition, sin is an inordinate and willful departure from the divine law.[64] Yet because the divine law is God's perfect knowledge of created things and their good and so sin is not only a departure from the good of one's own nature and perfection but also a rejection of God.[65] Consequently, the sacramental graces that expiate sin also lead human beings into human perfection; for example, Baptism allows man to be cut off from sin, which is intrinsic to human perfection.[66] For Christ to expiate our sins has intrinsically to do with enabling the perfection of the human person, especially in a moral sense.[67]

The third article of IIIa, q. 22 yields two important insights for assessing the limits and possibilities of Xunzi's ritual sage for Christological since. First, Christ's priesthood or ritual action is the unique form of expiation for sins and the cause of perfection of the human person with God. Christ's priesthood is unique in being soteriologically, teleologically, and eschatologically efficacious, because his priesthood is founded on the mystery of the Hypostatic Union. Additionally, Christ's work to expiate our sins is ritually mediated, so that the ritual form of his passion is the absolute norm for the communication of salvific and justificatory grace.

At this point, we now have sufficient grounds to assess the theological limits and possibilities of Xunzi's conception of the *shengren*. In this section, I showed that there are four general observations Aquinas makes about Christ's priesthood that can serve this analysis. Thus, it is helpful to restate them here before moving to utilize these principles as a means of assessment. They are as follows:

Any attempt to speak of Christ as a ritual sage takes its form from the mystery of the Hypostatic Union and the perfections of grace and glory communicated therein.

Christ's priesthood and thus ritual mastery is exercised in virtue of himself as the "sacred thing" given to us, in the sense that his life and especially his Passion are also the content of the rituals he performs for our salvation.

---

64. *ST* IaIIae, q. 71, art. 6.
65. *ST* IaIIae, q. 93.
66. *ST* IIIa, q. 62, art. 2.
67. Another way of seeing this is through Aquinas's conception of sacramental grace as a form of "re-creation." See Lynch, 100–102.

Christ's ritual action is the unique form of expiation for sins and the cause of perfection of the human person with God
Christ's work to expiate our sins is ritually mediated, so that the ritual form of his passion is absolute norm for the communication of salvific and justificatory grace

JESUS THE RITUAL SAGE? READING HEBREWS WITH AQUINAS AND XUNZI

Assessing the limits and possibilities of Xunzi's ritual sagehood for Christological science requires a concrete procedure. In this section, I have elected to offer my assessment through attempting to apply Xunzi's ritual sagehood to Christ's priesthood. Therefore, in this section, I will test how Aquinas's Christology and Xunzi's conception of ritual sagehood can sound together in a Chinse Catholic articulation of Christ's priesthood, drawing heavily upon the Letter to the Hebrews to elucidate the harmonies and tensions. In this vein, I therefore propose three axes upon which to test the Christological fruitfulness of Xunzi's *shengren*.

The first axis regards the fittingness of applying the title of "sage" to Christ, given the contours of *shengren* as developed above. Is it indeed fitting to the mystery of the Incarnate Word to describe it in terms of the ritual sage of Xunzi's work? For it to be apropos of Christ to call him a sage in a Xunzian sense, this would require that there is an inherent ritual "trajectory" to the Incarnation itself. That is, there is a burden to prove that one of the purposes of the Word assuming flesh is to bring about a certain ritual formation (and transformation) as befits the office of the sage.

To begin with, my analysis of Aquinas above shows that Christ's priesthood is assignable to Jesus's human nature alone, yet it is so in virtue of Christ's human life that is united with the eternal Word. Thus, in Aquinas's commentary on the Gospel of Matthew, he mentions that Matthew and Luke protect us from errors regarding Christ's fully human nature, and also discusses Luke as most focused on demonstrating Christ's priestly office and dignity.[68] Since

---

68. Cf. *Lectio super Matthaeum*, cap. 1, l. 1.

234 Chapter 5

Aquinas understands Christ's priesthood as an effect of grace that perfects the Lord's human nature, this suggests that the Incarnation itself as the Divine Word's assumption of flesh necessarily involves the assumption of the priestly office, inasmuch as it concerns human nature and its perfections. Put differently, the association of Christ's priesthood with his human nature suggests that Christ's priesthood corresponds to a connatural "religious" aspect of the human being, which can be more or less identified as a "ritual instinct."[69] As the Incarnation is aimed toward elevating humanity from sin to the perfection of union with God, Christ's priesthood is part and parcel of the awareness of the role of rituals in both our demise and our hope for salvation.

We can add to this that, from Xunzi's account of the human person, it would be impossible to imagine a person who is the union of God and man resulting in anything less than ritual sagehood. That is Xunzi understands the movement toward ritual is intrinsic to the perfection of the human person. Not only do humans spontaneously do ritualized activities, but rituals are also the necessary means by which human beings are led from disorder to virtue. As we saw above, when ritual forms are organized according to the wayward desires of the human being, they fall short of *li* and are merely customs. However, when a person with sound intellect and capacity to observe the movements of Heaven and Earth institutes ritual forms, these rituals are efficacious as *li*. Humans are by nature ritual-makers, but not all rituals are equal; only rituals formed by the sagely person who understands perfectly the human relation to the cosmos and the roots of disorder can institute or modify efficacious rituals. In other words, the fullness of human nature intrinsically requires

69. See Hütter, *Bound for Beatitude*, 265–66. Here we might helpfully appeal to the Thomistic topic of the virtue of religion. For Aquinas, the virtue of religion is aimed at giving God what He is due (though it should be noted that Xunzi's ritual sagehood lacks an explicit theological framework). As Hütter observes, for Aquinas, the virtue of religion is "a specific moral excellence that comprises a set of operations characteristic of the human being as a rational creature. It denotes both interior and exterior operations (interact acts of devotion and prayer and exterior acts of adoration, sacrifice, oblation, tithes, vows, et.) by way of which the human being renders what is due to the source of all being and life." Since Xunzi's idea of *li* similarly denotes both internal and external operations, it observes the "ritual instinct" of human beings in many ways harmonious to Aquinas's conception of religion, though without the explicit and all-important theistic object.

Thomistic Christology and Xunzi's *Shengren* 235

ritual enactment, and the more perfect the human being, the more efficacious the ritual in reforming human life and enabling human flourishing.

Admittedly, there are important aspects of Xunzi's account that do not necessarily recommend themselves to being grafted within Christological science. First, Xunzi's perspective on the importance of the ritual sage does not clearly describe the soteriological limits of rituals. In the Old Testament, on the other hand, the prophetic tradition clearly testifies to the fact that rituals and sacrifices practiced in the covenant are not in themselves sufficient to constitute fidelity or to bring about virtue. Rather, there is also the need for the Law to clarify the path to moral virtue (in both the Old and New Covenants). Of course, for Xunzi, rituals can and often do have a legal component, and he does understand sages to be sage rulers; therefore, the disparity between law and ritual in this regard is not that great. However, in the Old Testament prophets such as Amos explicitly juxtapose fidelity to the rites of Israel with the moral development of justice (cf. Amos 5:21–24), one that is apparently imitated by Christ Himself in discourse against the Scribes and Pharisees (e.g. Matthew 23:1–36). Within Xunzi's thought, there is no such clear confession about the limits of rituals for moral formation, and thus there is a deep tension with revealed theological science.

Part of the reason for this tension is that Xunzi's ritual sagehood concerns an extrinsic account of the effects of rituals. There simply is no mechanism for Xunzi to understand how ritual sagehood can act as an interior cause of transformation within the human heart in the way that is true of the sacramental ministry of Christ's priesthood. Thus, the disparity between Xunzi's sage and the theological of Christ's priesthood in this regard is fundamentally unavoidable because it signifies the difference between natural reason and reason in service to the economy of divine grace.

And so, while the fit is not perfectly square, there seems to be a robust place for Xunzi's conception of the ritual sage within Christological science. To demonstrate this further, we can look to how the Letter to the Hebrews can seem to confirm there are some aspects of Xunzi's sage in Christ. According to Hebrews, Jesus is sovereign

236 Chapter 5

over the world, and all things have been made subject to him, including those he has called to himself. Yet this sovereignty is exercised through an act of solidarity, for "he must in all things be like his brothers."[70] Now the "all things" is not the existential experience of sin, but the fullness of human nature. Consequently, for Hebrews the ultimate *telos* of Christ's assumption of full humanity is not simply solidarity with our sinful condition, but so that he might become the "faithful high priest to God" on our behalf.[71] In other words, Jesus's assumption of flesh to be like us so as to effect our salvation carries this movement toward ritual fulfillment.

Jesus's ritual sagehood is thus a condition of the fact of his full human nature, and indeed the perfections flowing from it. In the opening to the epistle, Hebrews reminds us that the Son who made purification for sin is not only seated at the right hand of the Majesty on high, but he also serves as the foundation of the world. That is, Christ inherits the world, yet as the one "through whom the world was made" and by the power of whose word the universe is upheld. When the Son assumes flesh, he does not leave behind his perfect relationship to the cosmos as Word of creation, but *expresses* this perfection by instituting the perfect rituals of salvation for the forgiveness and expiation of sins. Read in light of Xunzi's conception of the ritual sage, this can be interpreted as showing that Jesus's perfect knowledge by virtue of being united with the Word means that the natural ritual movement of human nature is, in him, truly perfect and efficacious.

Additionally, in Hebrews 12:2 Jesus is described as both the author and consummator of our faith. Although this authority of Jesus is distinct from the Levitical priesthood, it is still within the priestly genus, as that of Melchizedek (cf. 7:1ff.). Inasmuch as Christ becomes incarnate to establish and consummate the life of faith, he does so not merely on a rational or intellectual level (as Gnosticism teaches) but also ritually. Consequently, Jesus's life as author and perfecter of faith testifies to the intrinsic ritual enactment of his life and perfections, which we could justly call his ritual sagehood.

70. Heb 2:17–18.
71. Heb 2:17–18.

Thomistic Christology and Xunzi's *Shengren*   237

The second axis of application concerns whether it is fitting that Christ should be the content of the rituals he institutes. Although it is fitting from the view of Catholic theological science, I seek to use this question to test whether and how Xunzi's account of sagehood can support the proclamation of Christ's sacramental economy as the Catholic Church teaches it. It is self-evident that on its own steam, Xunzi's conception of the ritual sage cannot readily support Catholic doctrine in this matter. For as I noted above, Xunzi's understanding of ritual efficacy is essentially extrinsic. The rituals are expressive of perfections of the heart-mind that the sage alone possesses, but the sage is not the content of the rituals in any way. There simply is no analog in Xunzi's perspective for how a sage can be the source of rituals and also the content of them, in the way that Catholicism proclaims Christ to be both priest and victim whose Passion is the content of his sacramental ministry.

Indeed, this is made more difficult since Xunzi does not emphasize rituals toward *Tian* or the divine as the most important rituals. Unlike the Hebrew sacrificial cultus which has its roots in offering sacrifice for the sake of communion and praise of the One God, Xunzi's *li* do not have a clear transcendental reference. Rather, even the most quotidian things can be construed as part of the *li* instituted by ritual sages for moral transformation. While this is laudable to an extent, it also means that there is little ground for Xunzi's ritual sage to be a master in making offerings to God that are objectively efficacious for amending or perfecting the relationship with God. Consequently, there is little need for such an account of a ritual sage being the content of rituals in Xunzi's perspective.

That said, there do seem to be several ways in which Xunzi's account of ritual sagehood can be helpful in articulating why it is fitting that Christ is the content of the rituals he performs through his priesthood, though these require some labor to uncover. As we saw, Xunzi argues that the ritual forms are efficacious inasmuch as they help to straighten (*zhi* 直) or order (*zhi* 治) human desires toward the good. The term *zhi* 直 originally meant something like the carpenter's square: it signifies rectification as proper proportion and relation, and as such making something *zhi* requires a firm

238   Chapter 5

understanding of what the proper proportions should be.[72] The term *zhi* 治 is of more political etymology, usually applied to the rule of the king in governing a state. Hence, the ritual forms are like carpenter squares or laws—they are artifices by which a master of an art effects the proper proportions and relations within this art.

What Xunzi identified as bad desires ending in disorder (*luan*) corresponds to what revelation instructs us is sin, which ultimately constitutes the rejection of God and the divine law for the creature. Consequently, the *luan* of sin involves the loss of proper proportion and relationship with God, and this loss must be resolved. Now we see why it is so vital that Jesus Christ possesses perfect human united with the eternal Word, and is in himself the true perfection of the human person, since His human nature is in perfect harmony and union with God. Because the Lord is this union of God and man, he *is* the carpenter's square of Xunzi's reckoning. To put it as Aquinas does, in Jesus Christ the Word becomes flesh so as to become an example of "right doing" (*rectam operationem*): he is himself the rule and guide that can straighten and order the disordered human nature because he is the perfect union of God and man.[73]

From this, we see that inasmuch as Christ's ritual mastery is knowledge of what artifices can restore human beings to good and ordered desires, this is ritual mastery of his own being, including the ability to offer himself as the spotless victim of sacrifice to God. Aquinas juxtaposes Christ's priesthood to the ritual efficacy and mastery of the Levitical priest, who cannot produce the effects of salvation. Hebrews 5 argues this same point in terms of the priest's own shortcomings, since the priest must make sin-offerings for himself as much as for the people.[74] Consequently, the rituals over which the priest presides are external to him (given through Torah), for the purpose of expiating the sins of the people in which he himself is complicit. However, as the Incarnate Word, Jesus lived a life of

---

72. Cf. Huaiyu Wang, "Piety and Individuality through a Convoluted Path of Rightness: Exploring the Confucian Art of Moral Discretion via *Analects* 13.18," *Asian Philosophy* 21, no. 4 (Nov 2011): 395–418. Drawing upon *Analects*, 13.18, and Confucius's critique of a person known as "Upright Gong" (*zhi gong* 直躬), Wang provides one of the better discussions of the polyvalence of *zhi*, surrounding rectitude or conforming to a standard or rule.

73. *ST* IIIa, q. 1, art. 2, corp.

74. Heb 5:3.

Thomistic Christology and Xunzi's *Shengren*   239

perfect piety, obedience, and true suffering, and so wins eternal salvation for us.[75]

Later in the epistle, Hebrews speaks of the new covenant of Jesus having been founded on "better promises."[76] As Hebrews 9:12 states, "It is neither the blood of goats or calves, but with his own blood he has entered once for all into the Sanctuary and established eternal redemption." Going further, the letter argues that it is the blood of Christ that cleanses our consciences from works of death and allows us to serve the living God.[77] Because of the juxtaposition to cattle and goats used in sacrifices for purification, it seems the author of Hebrews means that the *sanguis Christi* is efficacious for our purification because unlike the old sacrifices, the God-man is able to make the perfect satisfaction for our sins.[78] What should be stressed here is that the moral perfection of Christ is ingredient in His work of satisfaction, in the sense that his moral perfection is reflective of the perfections of the Incarnation which makes the satisfaction humanity cannot make on its own.[79]

Hence Jesus's unique perfection as the straight and ordered one is the only perfect victim by whose sacrifice we are made straight and ordered. Yet there is more that shows that this efficacious sacrifice must concern the perfections of the God-man. As Incarnate Word, Jesus has the unique ability to be the sacrifice "once and for all." In the letter to the Hebrews, the efficacy of Jesus's sacrifice on the cross is described by the adjective *ephapax*, meaning it occurs

75. Heb 5:7–9.
76. Heb 8:6.
77. Heb 9:14.
78. The question of how Hebrews understands the relationship between the old covenant sacrifices and the new covenant sacrifice of Christ is profoundly controverted among scholars. For a recent entry in the debate, see Benjamin J. Ribbens, *Levitical Sacrifice and Heavenly Cult in Hebrews* (Berlin: Walter De Gruyter, 2016). For an overview of scholarly opinions, see Ribbens, 5–17. Ribbens argues for a typological interpretation of the distinction between the Levitical and Christological sacrifices according to Hebrews. He writes, "In this view [that of Hebrews], the levitical sacrifices are external rituals that themselves had no atoning efficacy. Yet, God promised that these external rituals would effect atonement and forgiveness, and they were able to be efficacious based on the sacrifice of Christ that would come later. His sacrifice would achieve atonement and forgiveness once-for-all-time, not only for the sins that would come after it but also for those that preceded it. The levitical sacrifices, therefore, were external rituals sacramentally linked to the efficacy of Christ's sacrifice, and that efficacy was proleptically applied to the levitical sacrifices" (236).
79. See *ST* IIIa, q. 1, art. 2, corp. and ad 2. Levering, *Engaging the Doctrine of Creation*, 302.

240 Chapter 5

only once. We will shortly attend to the wider ramifications of this doctrine, but here we must note that it is the body and blood of Christ which make for this sufficient sacrifice. For Hebrews, it is not Christ's priesthood alone that makes his sacrifice efficacious, as though any other sacrificial victim would carry the same effect of atonement for sins. Likewise, it is not due to his being a perfect human alone that is attributed his ability to be the perfect sacrifice.

Rather, he is the perfection of human nature in union with the eternal Word, and as such his offering is the truly perfect sacrifice. In Hebrews 9, the epistle draws a juxtaposition to the Levitical priesthood who sacrifices in the tabernacle, while Jesus made sacrifice in a tabernacle (*skenes*) "not made by human hands."[80] Though not found in Hebrews, the Fourth Gospel defines the Incarnation in similar terms, stating that when the Word became flesh, he "tabernacled" among us (*eskenosen en hemin*). Consequently, the tabernacle of Christ's sacrifice is his reality as Incarnate Word. Because this is so, even if Xunzi's logic of ritual sagehood cannot anticipate the sagehood of the Incarnate Word, it nonetheless necessarily follows that if the Incarnate Word is a ritual sage, he alone can be the content of the rituals he institutes since he is the fullness of what the rituals he institutes seeks to cultivate.

The third and final axis of my analysis here concerns whether it is fitting that Christ's passion is the single necessary ritual form for salvation. Here we touch upon an important tension not only for Xunzi but for interreligious dialogue more broadly. For Catholic teaching is that Jesus Christ is the only means to salvation. It is certainly true that, particularly in the last century or so of magisterial teaching, the Church has professed it is possible that through God's mercy, those who do not know of or unable to join with the community of the Church may receive extraordinary grace for salvation. However, this is typically construed in terms of obedience to natural law and moral virtue as a kind of implicit obedience to and union with God. Thus, in terms of ritual efficacy, the Church holds that only those practiced in the Church—which are actually acts of Christ's priesthood through clerical participation in their

80. Heb 9:11.

Thomistic Christology and Xunzi's *Shengren*   241

archetype—are genuinely efficacious for the communication of saving grace. That is, although the Christ of grace can be communicated in extraordinary ways apart from the sacraments, the Church does not hold that Christ bestows grace *via* the ritual practices or liturgies of non-Christian traditions.

This insight leads to important tensions with Xunzi's account of ritual sagehood. For, although Xunzi holds to the idea of multiple sages including more recent ones, there is still a concrete context to which he would expect ritual sagehood to conform. Namely, Xunzi would understand ritual sagehood to support and commend the same species of ritual acts that were defended by the Confucian tradition. This would include, for example, the observation of the three-years mourning period upon the event of a parent's death (see chapter 7 for discussion of this theme). And certainly, it would include the practice of ancestral sacrifice, which I should mention only became an acceptable practice for Chinese Catholics after a long and contentious period debate and reflection.[81] In other words, Xunzi would expect a ritual sage to institute rituals that conform to the classical rituals of Chinese culture. It is an understatement to say that the Catholic Church has not always found such rituals to be harmonious with Catholic faith and practice. Hence, how can Christ's priesthood be relevant to the forms of ritual sagehood Xunzi articulates?

Moreover, Xunzi's idea of the ritual sage does indeed give space for more recent sages to clarify ritual forms. But Xunzi does not for this reason see the previous sages or their rituals as dispensable per se. Rather, Xunzi's emphasis is that there is a tradition of ritual sagehood that has a coherent development over time. Thus, when we come to the Catholic understanding of Christ's priesthood, this is a fly in the ointment. For Catholicism will claim that Christ's sacrifice is a perfection and continuation of the Jewish priesthood, but it holds no necessary connection *qua* ritual tradition with non-Jewish ritual practices. Consequently, even if one were to articulate Christ

---

81. The ancestral veneration rites were officially illicit practices for Chinese Catholics after the promulgation of *Ex illa die* in 1715. This ban was overturned in 1939 under the pontificate of Pius XII, when the Congregation for the Propagation of the Faith issued *Plane compertum*. For discussion, see D. E. Mungello, ed., *The Chinese Rites Controversy: Its History and Meaning* (Nettetal: Steyler Verlag, 1994).

242 Chapter 5

in Xunzi's terms as a more recent ritual sage, it would seem that to accept Christ's ritual sagehood would inherently require diminishing the importance of Chinese ritual sages that preceded him in time. And this in turn would prompt us to ask why we should accept Christ's sagehood as the one, final authoritative ritual sagehood, when it involves the disruption of ritual tradition?

Finally, we can say that even if it is possible to show there is a continuity between Christ's ritual sagehood and classical Chinese sagehood as Xunzi understands it, this raises the problem of the unique efficacy of Christ's priesthood. From the Xunzian perspective, one could simply say that Christ's priesthood is the most recent and timely form of ritual sagehood, and that reason most applicable to us historically. But why would it follow from this that Christ's priesthood is not to be superseded, such that it is now the single necessary form of ritual sagehood?

These questions helpfully show the ways in which Xunzi's account cannot on its own attest to the centrality of Christ's priesthood, which is understandable. Yet despite these tensions, there are also resources within Xunzi's conception of ritual sagehood that can resonate with Catholic theological science, with a bit of development. Hebrews unambiguously teaches that Christ's sacrifice is sufficient "once for all" and is unrepeatable. Hebrews 6 provides insight as to why his sacrifice is unrepeateable, teaching that those who have fallen away cannot be renewed again to repentance, because this would constitute "crucifying again the Son of God for themselves."[82] It is striking that in this hypothetical situation, the lapsed would be the priests over Christ as victim. The failure of the lapsed as priests or ritual sages is coextensive with the inefficacy of any sacrifices they may offer. Conversely, the true efficacy and sufficiency of Jesus's ritual sacrifice extends from the unique perfections of the sacrificer and cannot be duplicated by human hands.

Hence, the unique efficacy of Christ's priesthood and ritual sagehood rests not on his skills, but on his unique person who is united with the Word. Following this, one can see logically why Jesus's priesthood would be sufficient according to Xunzi's conception of

82. Heb 6:6.

Thomistic Christology and Xunzi's *Shengren*   243

ritual sagehood. As Incarnate *Logos*, Jesus Christ is the union of man with the principle of man, and union of ritual sage with the principle of ritual sagehood. He is thus not merely one ritual sage among others, but the definitive norm of ritual history. As Hans Urs von Balthasar once put it, "Christ's uniqueness is so constituted as to be, in all its historical singularity, the concrete norm for the abstract norm itself."[83] Hence, as Incarnate Word, Christ is the embodiment of ritual knowledge, and his sacrifice is united and imbued with the principle of all ritual perfections.

This suggestion seems to align well with some implications of the emphasis of Hebrews on Christ's priesthood being in the Melchizedek line.[84] According to the epistle, it is of utmost importance that Melchizedek is a rather numinous figure of whom we are given no parentage or genealogy, or even dates of his life and death. He rather stands in the Old Testament as a prefiguration of the Son of God because he "remains a priest in perpetuity."[85] When the Incarnate Word acts as priest and ritual sage, he perfects the *typos* of Melchizedek in true eternity: "he remains in eternity where he has a sempiternal priesthood [*eo quod maneat in æternum, sempiterunum habet sacerdotium*]."[86] Christ's sacrifice is uniquely sufficient as the one thing necessary, then, because it is the ritual act of his eternal priesthood: "he is always living so as to intercede on our behalf."[87]

In Hebrews 9, this theme is developed again in juxtaposition to the Levitical high priest. According to the epistle, the high priest must enter the sanctuary to offer yearly sacrifice with blood that is

---

83. Hans Urs von Balthasar, *A Theology of History* (San Francisco: Ignatius, 1994), 23.

84. See Simon C. Mimouni, "Le 'grand prêtre' Jésus 'à la manière de Melchisédech dans l'Épître aux Hébreux," *Annali di Storia dell'Esegesi* 33, no. 1 (January–June 2016): 96–98. Mimouni notes that especially in a text uncovered at Qumran, Melchizedek was interpreted as a kind of messianic messenger and is even identified with God in this text. This is instructive as a reminder that the reference to Melchizedek is not simply a way of universalizing the priesthood of Christ, but is still a reference back to the Jewish cultic context. That said, there is also, as I argue above, the apparent possibility of finding in this reference room for an analogical way of describing Christ's priesthood in *terms* (not necessarily the reality) of other priestly concepts. See also Nathan Lefler, "The Melchizedek Traditions in the Letter to the Hebrews: Reading through the Eyes of an Inspired Jewish-Christian Author," *Pro Ecclesia* 16, no. 1 (2012): 73–89.

85. Heb 7:3.

86. Heb 7:24.

87. Heb 7:25.

not his own.[88] If this were the model of Jesus, he would have had to suffer over and over from the origins of the world. However, his sacrifice annuls sin because he has entered heaven and "appears now before the face of God for us."[89] Because Christ made a heavenly sacrifice of his own blood, his sacrifice is distinctive from any sacrifice before or after him, and is the perfect norm to which all sacrifices tend. Hence, Jesus's ritual mastery of his sufferings in the Passion are of a different character and efficacy; his sacrifice only needs be offered once to effect true salvation because by virtue of the sacrificer and the victim, his sacrifice has an eternal reality. Intrinsic to the eternal shape of Jesus's one, unique ritual sacrifice, Hebrews teaches that he "offers one sacrifice for sins, forever seated at the right hand of God."[90] His sacrifice is one, not to be remade, but its effects are forever accessible because Christ's ritual sagehood involves being seated "at the right hand of God" after his ascension into Heaven.[91]

According to Hebrews, then, the fundamental justification for the efficacy of Christ's ritual act is his life of perfect union as the God-man. Precisely because he is the Incarnate Word, Jesus's sacrifice is an act of ritual sagehood, but it is qualitatively different. He is *Immanuel*, and so closes the distance of being and dignity that separates God from his human creation. In the words of Xunzi, through the Incarnation, that which is far is brought to us through that which is near. Hence, Jesus's ritual act is eternally "relevant" to the situation of sinful humanity, which requires a ritual sage to straighten and order our disordered desires. It is a ritual form enacted in concrete history, but as an act of the God-man, it is perpetually timely and the

---

88. Luke Timothy Johnson, *Hebrews: A Commentary* (Louisville, KY: Westminster John Knox Press, 2006), 218. Johnson notes that this passage is demonstrative of the complex metaphorical framework employed in the epistle to the Hebrews, such that the temporal and spatial dimensions are mixed together, but also are used to indicate cosmological differences between Heaven and earth.

89. Heb 9:24–27.

90. Heb 10:12.

91. For an excellent of study of the importance Aquinas gives to this theme of Hebrews, see Denis Chardonnens, "Éternité du sacerdoce du Christ en effet eschatologique de l'eucharistie: La contribution de saint Thomas d'Aquin à un theme de théologie sacramentaire," *Revue Thomiste* 99 (1999): 159–80. For helpful discussions of the importance of the Ascension, see Douglas Farrow, *Ascension Theology* (London: T&T Clark, 2011), esp. 63–88; Matthew Levering, *Did Jesus Rise from the Dead? Historical and Theological Reflections* (New York: Oxford University Press, 2019), 185–209.

Thomistic Christology and Xunzi's *Shengren*   245

one (ritual) thing necessary. According to Hebrews and Christian teaching, moreover, his passion is also the only ritual act that is sufficient to truly correct the movement of sin, and to enable the fullness of human flourishing. Hence, there can be no other ritual form that accomplishes what Jesus's concrete Passion does; though a historical event, the ritual agency of Christ is relevant to all history after Him, such that His sagehood can never be equaled or surpassed.

CONCLUSIONS

With this observation, it is fitting to close this chapter's attempt to test the Christological limits and possibilities of Xunzi's conception of the ritual sage by applying it to reflection on Christ's priesthood. Essentially, the analysis above has shown that although there are understandable and predictable disparities between Christ's priesthood as understood in theological science and Xunzi's ritual sage, there is also a deep and profound consonance deserving further exploration. While the foregoing has made modest in-roads at building a genuinely Chinese Catholic theology of Christ's priesthood, my main task in this chapter has been to show that such tasks can be done once the consonance and dissonance between Chinese philosophy and Catholic theological science are taken into full account.

To summarize the findings from the analysis, there are several fundamental differences that prevent a simple identification with Christ as a ritual sage in the Xunzian sense. Three seem most problematic. First, is that Xunzi's understanding of the ritual sage is concrete—he has in mind a specific Chinese tradition and specific Chinese rituals that are the products of sagehood. Without a deep and subtle treatment of how Chinese rituals themselves can stand in relation to Catholic faith and practice, it is misleading to suggest Christ is a species of ritual sage such as Xunzi proclaimed. Second, Xunzi's conception of ritual efficacy is almost purely extrinsic—for him rituals are artifices created by sages to bring about moral virtue, but the rituals have no interiorization except via the heart-mind that performs them. Consequently, Xunzi's conception of ritual sage cannot be said to genuinely anticipate the sort of ritual performance

246   Chapter 5

Catholicism proclaims about Christ's priesthood. The third problem is that Xunzi's ritual sagehood lacks a definitive transcendental element, meaning it does not concern rituals which are aimed at worship of or union with the divine. In this way, Xunzi's conception of ritual sagehood does not provide even an adequate account of the natural religious impulse of human beings to desire God, which is fulfilled and perfected in Christ's priestly ministry.

That said, it is notable that there are many aspects of Xunzi's conception of ritual sagehood that seem to be confirmed in Catholic theological science. For one, Xunzi knows ritual is an essential part of the solution to human disorder. While he could not have had Christ in mind, Xunzi seems to recognize that if Christ is to save us as the Church says he does, then Christ *must* be a priest and not simply a moral teacher or miracle worker. Without the institution of rituals for our salvation, humans could not overcome our disorder.

Additionally, Xunzi recognizes that the truly efficacious and transformative rituals must come out of a kind of purified heart-mind, a perfected human nature. Clearly Xunzi could not have imagined that human nature would be joined with the divine in the person of the Incarnate Son, but he did realize that truly efficacious rituals require the perfection of human intellect and will. Inasmuch as Christ is the union of God and man, he possesses the necessary complement of perfections to enact not only efficacious rituals, but the most perfect and perfectly efficacious rituals. That is, Christ possesses the perfections that allow human beings to be truly transformed in ways that exceed in scope and efficacy the sorts of rituals Xunzi had in mind.

Thus, the concept of sagehood as Xunzi understands it is filled with Christological potential. The disparities between Xunzi's context and that of the Christian life under the grace of the New Law means that Xunzi's resources are indeed not naturally suited to explaining the mysteries of Christ. However, with patience, Xunzi's thought can serve the task of understanding and even expanding upon Christological science. Once the limits are set out, that is, the abiding possibilities of Xunzi for assisting theological science become clear.

6

Thomas's Reading of Matthew 8:21–22 and Confucian Filiality

This final chapter complements the assessment of ritual sagehood in the previous chapter by addressing another aspect of sagehood found in early Confucianism, dealing with the sage as a moral teacher (*shi* 師).[1] Although sages and teachers were not synonyms in early Confucianism—not all teachers were considered sages—teaching was explicitly or implicitly understood as a function of sages. Thus, in attempting to work through whether and how the conception of the sage in early Chinese philosophy can be of use to theological science, treating the question of Christ as teacher in a Chinese idiom is of paramount importance.

However, there is a unique set of problems that come with assessing the Christological utility of the sage-as-teacher concept. Unlike the concept of ritual sagehood in the previous chapter, the Catholic tradition has a long history of reflection on Christ as a teacher. In the scriptures, this is shaped in the specific context of Second Temple Judaism, wherein Jesus is called "rabbi" with all the implications that would hold for first century Jews.[2] In the Patristic

1. Although the *Mozi* does refer to the sages of antiquity as moral exemplars, the conception of the sage is not as refined or centrally significant as it is in Confucianism. Broadly speaking, the "sage as teacher" model could be developed in a compelling manner in conversation with Mohism, but the Confucian tradition presents more clear areas for theological integration and development, at least in my judgment.

2. Among biblical scholars, Bruce D. Chilton has offered several studies of Jesus in light

248   Chapter 6

tradition, texts such as Clement of Alexandria's classic text *Paidego-gos* ("The Pedagogue") and Augustine's *De magistro* testify to the significance of this doctrine.[3] And, of course, there is Aquinas's own prodigious account of Christ as teacher, both in the *ST* and in his commentaries on Matthew and John.[4]

Yet especially with Aquinas's account of Christ as teacher, we see why the Confucian conception of the teacher cannot be immediately and uncritically applied to Jesus. First, there are the very sources shaping Aquinas's thought—the Gospels—which emphasize the uniqueness of Christ as a teacher as the fulfillment of God's covenantal economy with Israel. For Aquinas and Catholic theological science more broadly, understanding Christ as teacher requires understanding his status as teacher within the Second Temple Jewish community specifically, and the covenantal narrative of Israel more generally. This is, indeed, part and parcel of the biblical message, as in Isaiah 2:3, which depicts the nations coming to Zion so that God "may instruct us in his ways, and we may walk in his paths. For from Zion shall go forth instruction, and the word of the LORD from Jerusalem."[5]

In addition to the essential Jewish context and character of Christ's

---

of the rabbinic context of his time, most notably Bruce Chilton, *A Galilean Rabbi and His Bible: Jesus' Own Interpretation of Isaiah* (London: SPCK and Michael Glazer, 1984), and Bruce Chilton, *Rabbi Jesus: An Intimate Biography* (New York: Doubleday, 2000). For an example of a robust Catholic theological engagement with the rabbinic identity of Jesus, examining the "Torah of the Messiah" and offering dialogue with Rabbi Jacob Neusner, see Pope Benedict XVI, *Jesus of Nazareth: From the Baptism in the Jordan to the Transfiguration*, trans. Adrian J. Walker (San Francisco: Ignatius Press, 2007), 99–127.

3. Clement of Alexandria, *Christ the Educator*, trans. Simon P. Wood, CP (New York: Fathers of the Church, Inc., 1954), and Augustine, *The Teacher*, in *Augustine: Earlier Writings*, trans. John H. S. Burleigh (Philadelphia: The Westminster Press, 1953).

4. For treatments of Aquinas on Christ the teacher, see Paweł Klimczak, *Christus magister: Le Christ maître dans les commentaires évangeliques de saint Thomas d'Aquin* (Fribourg: Academic Press, 2010); Michael S. Hahn, "Thomas Aquinas's Presentation of Christ as Teacher," *The Thomist* 83, no. 1 (2019): 57–89; J. Mark Armitage, "Why Didn't Jesus Write a Book? Aquinas on the Teaching of Christ," *New Blackfriars* 89, no. 1021 (2008): 337–53; Michael Sherwin, OP, "Christ the Teacher in St. Thomas' *Commentary on the Gospel of John*," in *Reading John with St. Thomas Aquinas: Theological Exegesis and Speculative Theology*, ed. Michael Dauphinais and Matthew Levering (Washington, DC: The Catholic University of America Press, 2005), 173–93; and Richard Schenk, "*Omnis Christi actio nostra est instruction*: The Deeds and Sayings of Jesus as Revelation in the View of Thomas Aquinas," in *La Doctrine de la revelation divine de saint Thomas d'Aquin* (Vatican City: Libereria Editrice Vaticana, 1990), 104–31.

5. Is 2:3.

Thomas's Reading of Matthew 8:21–22 and Confucian Filiality 249

teaching office, theologians such as Aquinas recognize that to talk about Jesus as teacher requires an account of the unique ontological situation of Christ as the God-man. For instance, underneath Aquinas's discussion of Christ as teacher is a robust and detailed account of the intellectual perfections of Christ, and what sort of knowledge he possesses due to the grace of the hypostatic union.[6]

To be sure, whatever resources from the Confucian teacher concept may be applied to Christ, they will have neither these essential Jewish characteristics nor a detailed account of the incarnate Son's knowledge to give them shape and meaning. Rather, the Confucian account of the teacher is developed in its own context of concerns about how to produce and guide a flourishing society. While the concerns of Confucians are often analogous to those of the Jewish and later Christian communities, they are also not simply interchangeable. And thus, the theological utility of the Confucian teacher concept must be tested to understand how it actually stands in relation to what Catholic theological science must say about Christ the teacher.

As with the previous chapter, the best way forward is to attempt a kind of concrete application of the Chinese teacher model to illuminate the theological limits and possibilities of the concept. This method does have some trade-offs in that we will necessarily omit certain aspects of the Confucian teacher from the analysis, but such trade-offs are worthwhile to achieve greater depth and clarity regarding the theological utility of the concept. Therefore, in this chapter I focus my analysis on a specific issue that arises when one attempts to apply the Confucian conception of teacher to Jesus Christ by analyzing one of the "hard sayings" of Jesus found in Matthew 8:18–22,

6. There is bountiful literature examining how Aquinas's views on Christ's knowledge are derived from his fundamental view that Christ's redemptive mission includes teaching others. See, *inter al.*, Frederick Christian Bauerschmidt, *Thomas Aquinas: Faith, Reason, and Following Christ* (Oxford: Oxford University Press, 2013), 201–7; White, "The Necessity of the Beatific Vision in the Earthly Christ," in *The Incarnate Lord*, 236–76; Gaine, *Did the Savior See the Father?* 105–58; Guy Mansini, OSB, "Understanding St. Thomas on Christ's Immediate Knowledge of God," in *The Word Has Dwelt Among Us: Explorations in Theology* (Ave Maria, FL: Sapientia Press, 2008), 45–72; Levering, *Christ's Fulfilment of Torah and Temple*, 31–50; Claude Sarassin, *Plein du grâce et de vérité: Théologie de l'âme du Christ selon Thomas d'Aquin* (Vénasque: Éditions du Carmel, 1992); Leo Scheffeczyk, ed., *Die Mysterien des Lebens Jesu und di christliche Existenz* (Aschaffenburg: Pattloch, 1984).

250 Chapter 6

where Jesus rejects the appeal of a would-be disciple to bury his father before following Jesus. With this saying, we step into a profound tension between the Confucian teacher and Christ the teacher. For if Christ is the true pedagogue for humanity—as theological science claims he is—then his teaching in Matthew 8:22 starkly conflicts with natural moral principles regarding filial love and service to parents (*xiao* 孝) that are readily observed in the Confucian tradition (by which I mean the Confucian tradition sees these as evident natural moral principles, even though early Confucians believe the demise of filial virtue was a key indicator of social and moral collapse of their own time).

From a Confucian perspective, Christ's refusal to allow a disciple to bury his parents is morally negligent. For in Confucianism, the proper burial and mourning of parents is one of the most important forms of filial service a child should offer his parent. The failure to bury and mourn one's parents properly is an extraordinary and fundamental breach of natural moral obligations in the Confucian tradition. Thus, this raises the question of whether Jesus can be seen as a teacher at all in light of the Confucian tradition, since his teachings seem to contravene the fundamental moral wisdom all sage-teachers are supposed to possess.

My approach will be to first develop in greater detail the Confucian problem raised by Matthew 8:18–22. Then, I seek to use Aquinas' own reading of Matthew 8:18–22 to provide solutions to the problems raised from a Confucian perspective. By means of my analysis of Aquinas, the points of dissonance and resonance between the Confucian and Catholic perspective are brought into greater relief, so that we can see more clearly where the real differences lie between the Confucian teacher and Christ the teacher and thus build effectively toward a Chinese Catholic Christology.

THE CONFUCIAN PROBLEM
WITH MATTHEW 8:18–22

As I noted above, from a Confucian perspective Matthew 8:21–22 is not simply difficult, but it seems on its face to be a deviant teaching. The reason for this lies in the provisions for mourning in the early

Confucian concept of *xiao* 孝 or filial piety. Put simply, the family was a key locus of moral responsibility and formation in early Confucianism, and for this reason, *xiao* was considered fundamental to moral rectitude. In the *Analects*, Confucius defines *xiao* as, "when your parents are alive, serve them by means of ritual propriety (*li* 禮); and when your parents pass away, bury them with ritual propriety and sacrifice to them with ritual propriety."[7] Although Confucians considered ancestral sacrifice as the ultimate act of filial devotion, proper execution of mourning rites (*sang* 喪) was the penultimate act.

Keith Knapp has demonstrated the extent to which the Confucian emphasis on proper mourning became a unique conception of filial devotion in the early Chinese context. Going back to the Shang dynasty, ancestral sacrifice to distant ancestors was the typical understanding of *xiao*. As China transitioned into the Warring States period, however, early Confucians began to shift filial devotion toward more recent forebears, especially one's parents, as the proper object. This meant not only an increased emphasis on moral aspects of filial piety, such as obedience, with regard to living parents, but also a new emphasis on burial and mourning as vehicles of filial love.[8]

In the early Confucian tradition particularly, proper mourning was defined by several concomitant aspects. Proper burial was a clear necessity, by which early Confucians meant a timely burial with the appropriate liturgy and material used in internment. The clearest example of proper burial guidelines are stipulations regarding coffins. Early Confucianism argued a proper burial for one's father, for example, required two coffins, whereas parents burying a child only needed to use one.[9] Notably, the *Liji* has a clear case of arguing this regulation is an ideal that requires material resources not everyone will have; thus, this standard can be met dispositionally, if one cannot meet it materially.[10] Yet, early Confucians saw

---

7. *Analects* 2.5.

8. Keith Knapp, "The *Ru* Reinterpretation of *Xiao*," *Early China* 20 (1995): 195–222.

9. The ideal burial of parents involved an inner coffin and an outer coffin, which was decorated ornately. There is archaeological evidence suggesting that early Chinese decorated outer coffins as a way of warding off evil spirits from disrupting the deceased.

10. *Liji, Tangongxia*, 172.

252 Chapter 6

such cases as extraordinary, and those having the means to provide a ritually proper burial for his parent was obliged to do so.

Proper mourning was also of great importance. On the one hand, children were expected to grieve (*ai* 哀), in the sense of the emotional experience of bereavement. On the other hand, mourning was expected to be conducted according to concrete ritual practices. Most generally, the proper mourning period was defined as three years, though early Confucianism defined this as a period of 25 months, rather than three full years. During this three-year period, children at mourning (importantly, adults and not adolescents) were expected to refrain from public work and labor. Additionally, mourners were expected to avoid rich fare, wear simple clothes, and eat abstemiously, to the point of becoming weak enough to require use of a cane for support. There were important qualifications for going through these aspects of the mourning rites, not unlike Catholic allowances for the Eucharistic fast or Muslim allowances for observing Ramadan.[11] But despite these allowances, proper filial mourning was clearly defined and an expected practice except in severely extenuating circumstances.

For early Confucians, mourning was not merely a cultural norm or expectation. In fact, the Confucian position on mourning rites, their proper performance, and their significance was hotly debated in early China. Unlike ancestral sacrifices which were cultural norms, Confucians had to make arguments for why mourning was important, and why the Confucian version of the rites were the best to practice. To put it generally, early Confucians believed that proper mourning was both necessary to moral rectification and helpful for moral self-cultivation. In order to demonstrate these benefits of proper mourning, it is helpful to look at Confucian defenses of the most debated aspect of their mourning rites, the three-year mourning period.

The early Confucian tradition identifies three primary benefits to having children mourn according to the rules articulated by Confucians: proper mourning allows for children to reciprocate parental

---

11. Generally speaking, the mourning rites were held to apply to healthy males. Children, the sick, or in rare cases one might imagine the very aged son would not be required to undergo the ascetical aspects of mourning rites, which could threaten their lives.

Thomas's Reading of Matthew 8:21–22 and Confucian Filiality   253

care; these rules provide proper limits and form to the mourning experience so that it can be virtuous; and proper mourning allows the fulfillment or full expression (*jin* 盡) of filial affection. Regarding the first benefit, in *Analects* 17.21, Confucius has a debate with his disciple Zaiwo about the length of the mourning period. Zaiwo argues one year would be sufficient. Confucius's response takes several steps, but the one of most immediate importance to this chapter is his argument that a moral gentleman would be unable to feel at ease (*an* 安) after only a year. Confucius later adds what can be seen as an elaboration of this point: "a child is born and for three years, he is not removed from his parents' care ... did Yu [Zaiwo's personal name] not have three years of love from his parents?"[12]

Here, Confucius suggests that the three-year mourning period enacts a reciprocation between parents and child. Just as we all are given love and nourishment by our parents at the beginning of our lives, so too we "owe" them this kind of love and care at their deaths. Confucius seems to mean that loving our parents properly while they are alive results in a natural inclination to mourn for them in a way that corresponds to what they did for us. In this sense, reciprocation is not simply repaying a debt one-for-one, but rather attempting to do for another what they have done for the agent.[13]

Importantly, according to this passage from Confucius the person of high moral standing will feel this need to reciprocate naturally. Hence, to perceive the need to mourn for one's parents and seek to do it properly is part and parcel with the pursuit of moral rectification. We might put it this way: if I find myself moved to mourn my parents only a brief time and then can be at rest, Confucius would likely conclude it is my moral rectification that is at issue. Something has gone wrong within my heart-mind (*xin* 心). Perhaps, as this passage suggests, I have failed to accurately understand my parent's love

---

12. *Analects* 17.21. The word I have translated as "care" is *huai* 懷, which typically means "bosom" or "chest." Legge renders the phrase as "leaving his parent's arms" which is a decent English rendering. The concept of physical closeness does seem important in the original, but I think "care" more clearly establishes an affective component, which is suggested later on when Confucius describe these three years as "love" (*ai*).

13. Cf. Liu Xiang, *Shuo Yuan, Xiuwen*, 22. A stronger reading of reciprocation as repayment is evident in in this text, which argues "the three-year period was established in order to repay the kindness of one's parents" (故制喪三年, 所以報父母之恩也).

254   Chapter 6

and concern. Or, more generally, I may be seen as having failed to cultivate an awareness of my filial duties toward my parents. Regardless of the specific way one might articulate it, early Confucians would agree that failure to mourn properly for one's parents is indicative of deeper moral disorder.

For this reason, the first moral benefit of mourning (i.e., facilitating reciprocity between children and parents) leads to the second moral benefit (i.e., moral formation that facilitates the flourishing life). One way the mourning practices are seen as morally important is in an objective or exemplary way. According to the *Xiaojing* (*Classic of Filial Piety*), the mourning practices express the natural feelings of filial grief. However, whenever a leader in society mourns for his parents (particularly the sage-king in the context of the *Xiaojing*), his mourning "instructs the people" (*jiao min* 教民) and "manifests to the people" (*shi min* 示民) important moral principles.[14] Specifically, by not fasting in dangerous ways, the ruler teaches the people that "one ought not injure the living for the sake of the dead."[15] Also, the ruler's observation of the three-year mourning period shows the people that mourning has an end (*zhong* 終), after which one should return to one's duties.[16]

In addition to the exemplary model of moral formation, early Confucians also argued that the mourning rites provided an internal or practical principle of moral formation. That is, some early Confucians believed that proper mourning rites were, in and of themselves, morally formative practices that help one to become capable of living a flourishing life. Undoubtedly, one early Confucian thinker who articulated the most developed account of the moral formation impact of the rites *per se* was Xunzi.[17] In the previous chapter, we saw the basics of Xunzi's philosophy of ritual and the anthropological positions underlying it. For the purposes of this chapter, I will not

14. *Xiaojing*, 18.

15. *Xiaojing*, 18: "教民無以死傷生." Literally, this passage reads "teaching the people that they should not injure the living by means of the dead." Since this doesn't make great sense in English, I have rendered *yi* 以 as "for the sake of" in keeping with the intention of the passage, which is to say that the goal of the rites is not to end life through the process of mourning the dead, but to give proper honor and respect to the dead.

16. *Xiaojing*, 18.

17. For a discussion of Xunzi's view of mourning, see Hagen, *The Philosophy of Xunzi*, 105–11.

Thomas's Reading of Matthew 8:21–22 and Confucian Filiality   255

rehearse Xunzi's broad ritual framework, but only treat his reading of filial mourning rites as an example of his approach at work. As a brief reminder, for Xunzi, rituals are a necessary path to rectification. Specifically, he would say we need the rites as advocated and taught by the Confucian tradition in order to transform our disordered morality into genuine goodness. As he puts it at one point, "if a man simply pursues rituals and righteousness, he will obtain both; if he pursues what comes from emotions and his natural inclinations, he will lose both."[18] For Xunzi, rituals and righteousness are paired concepts, indeed he often speaks of them together in the compound phrase *liyi* 禮義.[19] Relying on our natural emotions or inclinations will not bring about moral rectification. In contrast, rituals are the only the only thing that will order (*zhi* 治) moral human agency.

The mourning rites are part of this structure, and therefore facilitate moral rectification and righteousness. Xunzi speaks of the mourning rites as "the means by which the living ornament the dead" (*yi sheng shi si* 以生飾死). The word for "ornament" shows an aesthetic sensibility in keeping with Xunzi's broader moral perspective. He does not mean merely here the fact that in mourning we provided material ornamentation and devices to celebrate the deceased (coffins, clothing, etc.). Rather, for Xunzi ornamentation carries an implication of fulfillment, in this context, the full exercise of the responsibilities the living have toward the dead.

Xunzi says that rituals are a prudent and cautious way of governing both the living and the dead. Building on this point, he argues that life is the beginning a man while death is his end, and from this "the end and beginning together are good, and the conclusion of a man's way [*dao*]."[20] In other words, there is a sacredness to death just as there is to life: both together encompass the allotment of a person. Hence, Xunzi argues that the moral person "reveres the beginning and is cautious with the end, treating the end and beginning as if they are the same."[21] If we are to value life, we must also

---

18. *Xunzi, Lilun,* 4.
19. See Sung, "Ritual in the *Xunzi,*" 211–26.
20. *Xunzi, Lilun,* 17.
21. *Xunzi, Lilun,* 17.

256   Chapter 6

value death and respond to it properly. This is the way of true moral rectification in Xunzi's eyes, for life and death are inextricable from one another.

In this sense, then, mourning is for Xunzi a sign of moral rectification, the moral "instincts" of a person. Those who mourn properly do so because of their accurate moral perception about the balance of life and death. For this reason, Xunzi utters a harsh condemnation for those who do not seek to mourn properly: "there are those who are extravagant with the living and stingy toward the dead—this is giving reverence to those with knowledge and being arrogant toward those without it, and this in turn is the way of a treacherous person, and a heart of manifold betrayal."[22] In short, failure to have concern for the dead equal to concern for the living is a sign of wickedness and depravity, and is in fact abandoning the way of flourishing.

In this we see the mourning rites can signify moral rectification and disposition, much like Confucius's position in *Analects* 17.21 above. However, Xunzi goes beyond signification to argue the mourning rites effect moral transformation. According to Xunzi, the three-year mourning period enables us to "measure our emotions" (*cheng qing* 稱情) and "establishing the proper pattern" (*li wen* 立文).[23] This internal formation by the three-year mourning period enables further moral formation consisting of "forming the multitude" (*shi qun* 飾群) and distinguishing between "close and distant relations" (*qin shu* 親疏), as well as between "what is valuable and what is worthless" (*gui jian* 貴賤). In each of the latter moral formations, Xunzi means that the person undertaking the three-year mourning period learns to "differentiate" properly (*bie* 別). We can extrapolate from this that proper mourning helps us to perceive the different values others have to us, and gives us the resources to treat them accordingly.

It is clear from the instrumental sense of the passage that Xunzi's argument regarding the three-year mourning period is dependent upon his larger theory of human nature—namely, that it needs the

22. *Xunzi, Lilun*, 17.
23. *Xunzi Jijie*, 361. Zheng Kangcheng 郑康成 explains this as meaning "measuring human emotions in their lightness and heaviness [i.e., the matter of their significance or importance] and establishing the rites" (称人之情轻重而制其礼也).

Thomas's Reading of Matthew 8:21–22 and Confucian Filiality   257

refinement that comes from rituals. However, note that Xunzi does not merely think that the three-year mourning is a good subjective measure of training moral individuals—in his broader discussion of mourning as a general good, he describes these rights as both "ornamenting the dead" (*shi si* 飾死) and "ornamenting our grief for the dead" (*shi ai* 飾哀).[24] With this, we should emphasize Xunzi's initial point that human beings have "emotions" (*qing*) that must be given form and order if we are to flourish with these emotions. In the three-year mourning period, two successive steps occur: first, the emotions are taken stock of and "measured," and then the emotions are refined.

An important question that follows is this: What does Xunzi mean by "measuring" the *qing* that are then refined through the ritual process? Xunzi claims that among all things living on Heaven and earth, those that have blood and *qi* undoubtedly have intelligence (*zhi* 知), and because of their intelligence these creatures "do not fail to love their own kind" (*mo bu ai qi lei* 莫不愛其類).[25] Demonstrating his point, Xunzi describes how birds and beasts linger where they have lost companions. Establishing this universal rule, he then concludes that "among the creatures having blood and *qi*, none have more intelligence than human beings, and therefore, human beings will love their parents until the end of their lives without ceasing."[26]

For Xunzi, this then suggests that the emotional dispositions or *qing* lying behind the three-year mourning period are anthropologically founded—such *qing* are marks of being human. Expanding this point, Xunzi contends that those who can forget their parents' death in one day are not even at the dignity of birds and beasts.[27] In this way, then, Xunzi argues that the three-year's mourning allows a confirmation and expression of the very human *qing* of loving one's own kind. This period is necessary for our *qing* to be genuinely human, and so rise to the level of those creatures animated by blood and *qi* and marked by the greatest intelligence or reason. To avoid or abbreviate this mourning would still "measure" the *qing* of the mourner,

24. *Xunzi, Lilun*, 23.
25. *Xunzi, Lilun*, 26.
26. *Xunzi, Lilun*, 26.
27. *Xunzi, Lilun*, 27.

258 Chapter 6

but this measure would decisively suggest the mourner falls short of genuinely human *qing*.

In a famous debate with the Mohist Yi Zhi, Mengzi makes a complementary observation. In *Mengzi* 3A5, Mengzi says that in the ancient past people did not bury their dead at all, but merely left them in a ditch on the road. However, when they returned to the spot they saw animals chewing on the carcasses. Mengzi says that the survivors then broke out in sweat because "their heart moved to their faces and eyes" (i.e., they were filled with emotional responses that made them cry and grimace) and therefore they ran to get shovels and baskets bury the dead properly.[28] Though serving a different purpose, Mengzi's example helps to show how Confucians believed that the emotion of grief was connatural to humans and that this grief necessarily required expression in proper burial and mourning.

Referring back to Xunzi's perspective, he would note that while it is true human beings have a kind of emotional foundation that begs for expression in mourning, this doesn't mean that these emotions are themselves inerrant guides to proper conduct. Hence, the three-year period and the other Confucian rites of mourning give these emotions their proper refinement. Xunzi, suggests two primary ways that the mourning rites refine the expressions of grief, in the complementary aspects of intensity and time. Regarding intensity, Xunzi contends that the three-year mourning period enables us to "extend our pain to its fullest extent" (*suoyi wei zhi tong ji* 所以為至痛極). The fulfillment or exhaustion of grief is necessary, according to Xunzi because if we fail to exhaust our grief, then it is impossible for us to return to our duties to the living well. Xunzi thus sees grief as a pain we will feel that is an obstacle to other forms of flourishing. Instead of subduing this grief or allowing it to pervade (pollute?) other pursuits within our lives, Xunzi argues we need the three-year period in order to completely focus on the full expression of this grief.

Within this argument, Xunzi seems to be holding two things together. First, he does delineate the formative importance of the particular rituals within the three-year period. For example, he contends that abstaining from rich food, wearing shabby clothing, emaciating

---

28. *Mengzi*, 3A5.

Thomas's Reading of Matthew 8:21–22 and Confucian Filiality   259

oneself, and so on serve to "fully ornament our pain" (*zhi tong shi* 至痛飾). And so, for Xunzi the three-year mourning includes a coherent set of practices that enable the proper and full expression of grief. At the same time, Xunzi does not merely advocate undertaking these specific rituals on their own; rather, he contends they must be undertaken in the context of the three-year mourning period in order to serve their formative purpose. This means that for Xunzi, the three-year period is not merely important for conservation of the traditional form of these essential rites. Rather, Xunzi finds the three-year period does important work in how the rites accomplish the proper formation and agency.

This emphasis on intensity leads neatly into the fact that Xunzi also sees the three-year period as providing a proper space and time for which to mourn with intensity, and setting down the proper limits of this grief. In Xunzi's reading of the three-year mourning period, emphasis falls on the fact that the three-year mourning period brings to completion the expression of grief, and so it should end. Xunzi on several occasions in his essay describes the three-year mourning period and then adds the clarifying phrase in the following formula: "*san nian zhi sang, er shi wu yue er bi* 三年之喪, 二十五月而畢." I argue we should interpret this phrase as meaning, essentially, "the three-year mourning period—that is, mourning for 25 months and then stopping." With this formula, Xunzi is not only clarifying what Confucians meant by the "three-year mourning period," he is also offering a reminder that these practices have a temporal terminus. In short, the three-year mourning period makes sense as a ritual formative practice for Xunzi only if we remember that there must be a time where the pain and grief of mourning—the emotions that need to be organized—stop.

At this juncture, it is clear that early Confucians saw mourning rites as key to moral flourishing for three primary reasons. First, mourning allowed the expression of care and devotion to parents in a way that appropriately mirrored or reciprocated for parents' care of children in their youth. Second, the mourning rites allowed for the expression of natural emotions that are inherent in humanity and are signs of moral rectification. Third, the mourning rites form and shape these emotions so that when we do mourn, we do so virtuously. There is obviously much more than can be said about the Confucian esteem of mourning rites themselves, but these three points are sufficient to raise serious questions about Matthew 8:21–22.

Simply put, from a Confucian perspective it is scandalous and puzzling that Jesus can be the true Master and Lord and yet refuse to support a would-be disciple who wishes to bury his father. First, Jesus seems to deny his hopeful follower something that is not only permissible, but profoundly virtuous: the ability to fully and properly discharge his duties toward his father. Why would Jesus not welcome and indeed celebrate such a one as his disciple? Second, Jesus seems to deny the disciple the ability to do what he is by nature compelled to do. This suggests that Jesus's moral teaching undermines or negates rather than fulfills and perfects natural moral virtue. And third, Jesus's refusal to allow the disciple to bury his father seems to prefer having the man cut himself off from clearly important and helpful resources for increasing in moral virtue. If we imagine the man does as Jesus asks, neglects burying his father and follows Jesus, do we expect that he does not continue to feel the pangs of bereavement as he follows? Are these emotions not thus left in the disorder that befalls us absent of proper rituals that guide us into moral rectification? Put more sharply, does Jesus not seem to abandon the man to his own disorder, rather than direct him toward resources that would relieve him and help him grow in virtue?

AQUINAS AND MATTHEW 8:18–22

Through the exposition in the previous section, the Confucian conception of the teacher (in this case, as a defender of filial virtue) does not readily agree with the Christian claim that Jesus is the Rabbi for all of humanity. However, it is not yet clear how the disparity between the two can be breached, if at all. For example, since there is no analog of the three-year mourning period in the Catholic context, how does the logic centered around this ritual practice square with Catholic theological science? Are the Confucian principles of filial mourning consonant with Christ's teaching despite the apparent contradiction, or are they incommensurable? If there is a

Thomas's Reading of Matthew 8:21–22 and Confucian Filiality 261

consonance between these two teachings, where is it, and how deep does it go?

Thus, it is necessary to develop a more adequate theological account of Matthew 8:18–22 to better judge how the Confucian conception of the teacher of *xiao* stands in relation to Christ's teaching. I should note here that turning to Aquinas is fruitful because unlike many contemporary biblical scholars, Aquinas would seem to have deep sympathies with the kinds of concerns we see in Confucianism, and takes them seriously. In this sense, Aquinas's interpretation of Christ's teaching seeks a balance between his robust Christology and his ethical naturalism.[29]

In contrast, a number of modern biblical scholars by-and-large approach Matthew 8:18–22 with the aim of maintaining the "difficulty" of the passage and resisting what they perceive to be attempts by the tradition to make Christ's teaching more amenable to ancient society. Martin Hengel offered a paradigmatic interpretation in *The Charismatic Leader and His Followers* when he argued Matthew 8:21–22 demonstrates Jesus's resistance to follow both the mandates of the Torah (the fourth commandment) as well as the practice of "works of love" that were accepted as part of Jewish piety.[30] As others have observed, Hengel's interpretation is cause for disquiet as it "seems to follow along familiar supersessionist lines of a law-gospel polarity."[31] At the very least, such modern interpretations of Matthew 8:21–22 seem all too willing to accept a picture of Jesus as abrogating the ritualistic aspects of Torah as part of his messianic mission.

More interesting is why Hengel thinks Jesus means to move past the demands of Torah and Jewish piety. According to Hengel, the interpretive key for Matthew 8:21–22 is familiar to all students of modern biblical criticism: it is the theological background of the "imminent kingdom of God."[32] According to Hengel, Jesus's teachings in Matthew 8:18–22 has everything to do with the demands of the

29. For a still helpful description of how Aquinas's thought involves ethical naturalism, see Ralph McInerny, "Naturalism and Thomistic Ethics," *The Thomist* 40, no. 2 (April 1976): 222–42.

30. Martin Hengel, *The Charismatic Leader and His Followers*, trans. James Grieg (New York: Crossroad, 1981), 8–15.

31. Markus Bockmuehl, "'Let the Dead Bury Their Dead' (Matt. 8:22/Luke 9:60): Jesus and the Halakhah," *Journal of Theological Studies* 49, no. 2 (Oct. 1998): 553–81, here 555.

32. Hengel, 13.

262 Chapter 6

eschatological mission inaugurated by Christ, which necessitates radical discipleship. Such a vision of Christ's words as signaling the radical in-breaking of the Kingdom of God is prevalent in much of the previous generation of modern scholarship, such as the work of Ulrich Luz and Rudolf Schnackenberg.[33]

What I wish to emphasize here is that such scholarly perspectives are imbalanced inasmuch as they seek to diminish the natural moral concerns of Matthew 8:18–22 and resolve it by appealing to simply a supernatural principle that overwhelms and completely overshadows the natural. Such a theological perspective provides little hope for finding a way to appreciatively read Confucian thought so as to measure its theological utility since in such a perspective, Confucianism can at most function as a kind of non-Jewish stand-in for the ethic that is superseded in Christ. Of course, the theological analysis of Chinese philosophy requires an a priori judgment about the nature of theological science—namely, that is stands in a positive relationship to natural reason. As I have made the commitment in this book to give a positive reading of natural reason, I will not argue for such a point here. I simply mean to note that once one makes such a commitment, it is evident that the approach of Hengel and others to Matthew 8:18–22 is left wanting, and an interpretive framework sympathetic to the natural moral concerns in Matthew 8:18–22 is needed.

For these reasons, it is fitting to turn to Aquinas not only because of the structure of this book, but also because of the resources he provides in addressing this specific problem. For Aquinas is much more sensitive than are many modern readers to the scandal of Jesus's teaching. Unlike the modern interpreters discussed above, Aquinas believes with the breadth of the Christian tradition that Jesus came as wisdom incarnate, to lead us into the truth of God and the path of moral flourishing that perfects rather than destroys or replaces nature. That is, he finds it possible to recognize the radical

---

33. Ulrich Luz, *Matthew: A Commentary*, trans. Wilhelm C. Linss, vol. 2, Hermeneia (Minneapolis, MI: Fortress Press, 1989), 8–20; Rudolf Schnackenberg, *The Gospel of Matthew*, trans. Robert R. Barr (Grand Rapids, MI: Eerdmans, 2002), 84. For his part, Schnackenberg observes the following in regard to Mt 8:21–22: "With the great prophets, Jesus violates law and pious custom—not, however, as a prophetic sign but rather as a result of unconditional discipleship for the sake of the Reign of God ... An original testimonial to Jesus' radicalism!"

Thomas's Reading of Matthew 8:21–22 and Confucian Filiality   263

proclamation of Christ's kingdom while also connecting this proclamation to natural moral principles. Put differently, Aquinas's interpretation is better suited to testing how the Confucian conception of the sage-teacher can and cannot be squared with Catholic theological science.

Unlike the other chapters in this book, I will not primarily draw on the *ST* to analyze Aquinas's reading of Matthew 8:18–22, but rather on his commentary on Matthew's Gospel. In analyzing Aquinas's exegesis, one must remember that he adopts the scholastic strategy of *divisio textus*.[34] This strategy describes the themes of a book of scripture by assigning different roles to each part of the text. Sometimes these are thought to be on the intent of the author, but more often, Aquinas assigns these divisions based on the logic of central claims in a given text. Each textual division Aquinas makes builds a helpful albeit complicated framework that aids in the proper interpretation of a given passage.

So, the initial question one must ask about Aquinas's reading of Matthew 8:21–22 is this: How does he locate it within the *divisio textus*? First, it is located within the larger section of Matthew 3–20. According to Aquinas, chapters 1–2 narrate Christ's entrance into the world (*ingressu*), 3–20 tell of his "procession" (*processu*) through the world, and 21–28 teach about Christ's departure (*egress*).[35] In this context, Christ's "procession" best means Christ's ministry and form of life as he proclaims the Kingdom of God. Indeed, Aquinas says that Matthew basically identifies Christ's procession with his teaching, and uses Christ's doctrine as the formal cause of the Gospel, with Matthew 3–4 preparing for Christ's teaching (through his baptism and temptation), and his teaching beginning at chapter 5.[36]

---

34. For recent discussions of Aquinas' approach to reading the scriptures, see *inter al.* Randall B. Smith, *Aquinas, Bonaventure, and the Scholastic Culture of Medieval Paris: Preaching, Prologues, and Biblical Commentary* (Cambridge, UK: Cambridge University Press, 2020); Randall Smith, *Reading the Sermons of Thomas Aquinas: A Beginner's Guide* (Steubenville, OH: Emmaus Academic Press, 2016); Pim Valkenberg, "Scripture," in McCosker and Turner, *The Cambridge Companion to the Summa theologiae*, 48–61; Piotr Roszak and Jörgen Vijgen, eds., *Reading Sacred Scripture with Thomas Aquinas: Hermeneutical Tools, Theological Questions, and New Perspectives* (Turnhout: Brepols, 2015); and Matthew J. Ramage, *Dark Passages of the Bible: Engaging Scripture with Benedict XVI and Thomas Aquinas* (Washington, DC: The Catholic University of America Press, 2013), esp. 92–113.

35. *Super Evangelium S. Matthaei lectura*, cap. 1, l. 1, 11.

36. *Super Evangelium S. Matthaei lectura*, cap. 3, l. 1, 241.

264 Chapter 6

Significantly, Aquinas argues there are three parts of Christ's doctrine: when Christ sets down the teaching (*ponitur doctrina Christi*); when the power of his teaching is demonstrated; and the end to which the teaching leads (*finis ad quem perducit*). The setting down of Christ's teaching occurs preeminently in Matthew 5–7, but Aquinas identifies it more generally with the content of Matthew 5–12.[37] Thus, Aquinas understands Matthew 8:21–22 as part of the statement of Christ's doctrine. Aquinas is sensitive to the fact that the passage occurs just after the Sermon on the Mount material. In a sense, Aquinas identifies Matthew 5–7 with the most proper form of Christ setting down his doctrine, and he sees Matthew 8–10 as confirming these teachings through miracles.[38] As Aquinas puts it, "it could seem the Lord was speaking out of arrogance, and therefore he commends his authority by signs."[39] These signs or miracles are instruction about Christ's authority that reveal himself as the authoritative teacher, and thus are properly instructive in their own right.

The last contextual clarification needed before turning to Matthew 8:21–22 in earnest is to note that for Aquinas, Jesus works two kinds of signs in chapters 8–9. In general, Jesus performs signs which free human being from dangers (*periculis*). Matthew 8 focuses on bodily dangers, such as the fever of St. Peter's mother-in-law, leprosy, and the calming of the sea. Within these signs, Aquinas distinguishes two different dangers. He argues that in Matthew 8:1–22, Jesus "sets down [*ponit*] signs that liberate human beings from dangers coming forth from intrinsic causes."[40] Hence, it is notable that Matthew 8:19–22 in particular is caught up in a transition point in which Jesus is moving from liberating people from intrinsically caused dangers (i.e., within themselves, concerning their bodies), to extrinsic dangers (the storm on the sea). Aquinas reads Matthew 8:18 as meaning Jesus that had already entered the boat—the setting for the storm beginning in 8:23. And so, in a sense, 8:19–22 is a slight *coda* to the theme of intrinsic dangers from which humans need to be liberated.

---

37. *Super Evangelium S. Matthaei lectura*, cap. 5, l. 1, 396.

38. *Super Evangelium S. Matthaei lectura*, cap. 5, l. 1, 396. See also *ST* IIIa, q. 42–43, esp. q. 43, art. 1, corp.

39. *Super Evangelium S. Matthaei lectura,*, cap. 8, l. 1, 680.

40. *Super Evangelium S. Matthaei lectura*, cap. 8, l. 1, 680: "… ponit signa quibus homines liberantur a periculis provenientibus ex intresecis causis."

Thomas's Reading of Matthew 8:21–22 and Confucian Filiality   265

Aquinas does not explicitly say the following, but it seems nonetheless accurate about his position: the intrinsic dangers dealt with in Matthew 8:19–22 are of a different sort than those found in Matthew 8:1–18. In the first part of Matthew 8, the intrinsic dangers faced are illness, the privation of health and wellness. Jesus performs miracles that literally restore the patients to health, and remove the dangers. With 8:19–22, we do not find signs per se; no miracles are performed here, and no obvious liberation, at least not in light of 8:1–18. This is because the intrinsic dangers of 1–18 concern the body, whereas the dangers of 19–22 concern the soul. Matthew 8:19–22 sets down moral dangers that we face. Although there is no clear liberation in terms of restoration or transformation in these passages, this is consonant with the divine nature: God does not liberate us purely in an extrinsic sense, but in an intrinsic moral sense as well, making us free to pursue goodness. Because we possess free will even in the state of sin, human beings can reject our own liberation. And so in Matthew 8:19–22, Jesus perceives the intrinsic dangers of two men and works to save them from these dangers, by demonstrating to them the moral dangers they face.

Now I can proceed to a focused analysis of Matthew 8:21–22. One clear benefit of Aquinas's exegesis of this passage is that he suggests it is impossible to really understand and the content of Matthew 8:21–22 without reference to 8:19–20. Not only does 8:19–20 immediately precede vv. 21–22, the former also provides a moral problem that Aquinas believes the latter builds upon. Therefore, our analysis of 8:21–22 should properly begin with the contrast Aquinas sees in 8:19–20. According to Aquinas, Matthew 8:19 tells of one who attempted to "force himself upon" Jesus, whereas 8:21–22 concerns clarifying something to another disciple. In other words, from the outset, Aquinas would have the reader note that there is a great moral difference between the one turned away in vv. 19–20 and the one turned away in vv. 21–22.

Matthew 8:19–20 concerns the story of a scribe who comes to Jesus and says, "Master I will follow you wherever you go," and Jesus rebuffs the man (*repulit*). Aquinas, steeped in the tradition's exegesis of the passage, identifies a serious moral problem in the scribe's

266   Chapter 6

statement that makes his rejection fitting. First, Aquinas says the scribe calls Jesus "Master," but "true disciples call him 'Lord.'"[41] This is for Aquinas a sign that the scribe has an inadequate view of Jesus and thus seeks to follow him for improper reasons. First, Aquinas argues the man had the intention of simony inasmuch as he "desired to follow him [Jesus] out of wicked intentions [*mala intentione*], because he had heard that signs had been done; he [the scribe] desired to follow in order to also perform signs, as is said of Simon Magus."[42] Additionally, Aquinas cites Chrysostom as arguing that the scribe asked to follow Jesus not out of devotion but out of pride, by considering himself worthy to follow and thus of greater dignity than others (*reputabat se digniorem aliis*).[43]

In each of these aspects of Matthew 8:19, we see clearly that Aquinas considers the scribe's desire to follow Jesus to be fraudulent. The scribe therefore symbolizes the internal dangers of impiety, pride, and greed, in this case by considering God as an instrument by which to procure desired goods. The scribe does not represent a failure of discipleship, but rather a more general and pervasive moral failure; the failure to understand the nature of the good and to love it properly.

This is vital because Aquinas considers the case described in Matthew 8:21–22 to be a massive moral improvement in many regards. As Aquinas notes, the man in 8:21 calls Jesus "Lord," whereas the other called him "Master"; thus Aquinas associates the second man with a genuine devotion to Jesus lacking in the scribe. Moreover, Aquinas argues that the scribe came to Jesus in order to follow him in a deceitful manner—the scribe desired to associate with Christ to serve his own selfish gains. But Aquinas says, "the other [the scribe] used deceit, but this one uses piety [*pietatem*] because there was the precept to honor one's parents."[44] With this brief description, Aquinas acknowledges that the moral virtue of the son is much greater than that of the scribe, and his desire to bury his father is evidence of this difference. It should be apparent that such

41. *Super Evangelium S. Matthaei lectura*, cap. 8, l. 3, 718.
42. *Super Evangelium S. Matthaei lectura*, cap. 8, l. 3, 718.
43. *Super Evangelium S. Matthaei lectura*, cap. 8, l. 3, 718.
44. *Super Evangelium S. Matthaei lectura*, cap. 8, l. 3, 718.

Thomas's Reading of Matthew 8:21–22 and Confucian Filiality 267

a judgment from Aquinas can only follow upon his recognizing the desire to bury one's father as an act of virtue. Specifically, he associates it with the commandment to honor one's father, even though the commandment does not specifically state internment as a proper means of honoring one's father.[45] Aquinas rather readily assumes that the son who wishes to bury his father possesses a virtuous habit of piety.

Here arises the interesting problem of comparing Matthew 8:19–20 and 8:21–22. If we accept Aquinas's reading of Matthew 8:19–20, then it was fitting for the scribe be rejected as a disciple because he was duplicitous. It is not problematic that Jesus denies a wicked man a share in his kingdom, unless that wicked man repents and turns away from his wickedness. But what of the virtuous man, who recognizes Jesus as Lord and has a heart shaped by natural virtue and the divine law? Why would Jesus not simply allow him the time? Why give him the either/or: "follow me" or bury your father?

For Aquinas, the key lies not in the object of the man's request— that he bury his father— but the context of the man's request. The would-be disciple already brings to Jesus this very either/or situation: should I follow Jesus or bury my father? In this sense the man gives evidence of an internal struggle, whereby he knows two goods and does not know which one must take precedence over the other. Aquinas argues that Jesus tells the man to "follow me" in order to teach him that "the one who wishes to follow Christ should not give up following for the sake of some temporal activity."[46] That is, the problem for the would-be disciple was not that he desired something that was unvirtuous or un-beneficial. The problem is that in his very request to Jesus to delay his commitment to Jesus, the man was attempting to relativize the good of following Jesus, and subordinate it to the good of burying his father.

In addition, Aquinas assumes that Jesus could tell the son "let the dead bury their own dead" because "there were others who were able to bury [the father]."[47] Notably, the text gives no clear indica-

---

45. *ST* IIaIIae, q. 32, art. 2, corp. Aquinas here lists burying the dead as one of the corporal works of mercy.

46. *Super Evangelium S. Matthaei lectura*, cap. 8, l. 3, 721.

47. *Super Evangelium S. Matthaei lectura*, cap. 8, l. 3, 721.

268   Chapter 6

tion of this situation. On the one hand, Aquinas is drawing upon an assumption in the tradition. However, this begs the question of why is the tradition (and Aquinas) willing to make such an assumption? Certainly, by the time of Aquinas, burying the dead was recognized as one of the seven corporal works of mercy, and hence Aquinas and the earlier tradition clearly see an inherent value in the rites of internment and mourning for parents.[48]And so, Aquinas is arguing that Jesus does not call for the abandonment of such rites, but rather locates their goodness in relation to the vocation and desire to follow Christ.

Pursuant of this point, Aquinas next notes that "it can happen, as it often does, that he who is impeded by one business quickly runs into another, for one matter draws another."[49] Here Aquinas is pointing out that the would-be disciple is actually asking something very imprudent. Perhaps it would be possible to delay following Jesus and return as soon as the internment was finished. However, more often than not, the process of mourning itself draws one into matters that would have made following Jesus more difficult. Aquinas mentions the economic concern of a will, which is not solely the concern of the greedy. Upon a parent's death, there are always estates to be settled, and goods collected and distributed. More significantly, the *memoriam* component of mourning is inescapably a challenge to the vocation of following. The internment of one's parent certainly inspires reflection on memories, on the parent's form of life, practices, and places of rest and leisure. One can readily imagine the difficulty of persisting in the promise to follow Jesus once the son entered the home of his late beloved father: How could he leave all and follow when now, more than ever, his heart calls for him to stay and take care of his late father's home and family?

In other words, in this half of his interpretation of Matthew 8:21–22, we see clearly that Aquinas deeply values the moral importance of mourning. He indeed honors it, and recognizes the profound goods of mourning the dead. But Aquinas would have us see that just like all other temporal goods, mourning can become an obstacle

---

48. *ST* IIaIIae, q. 32, art. 2, corp. and ad 1. See, also e.g., John Chrysostom's comment at *Catena Aurea in Matthaeum*, l. 6.

49. *Super Evangelium S. Matthaei lectura*, cap. 8, l. 3.

Thomas's Reading of Matthew 8:21–22 and Confucian Filiality   269

to following Jesus in certain contexts. When the moral choice is between committing to following Jesus or delaying one's vocation for even a great good such as mourning one's parents properly, the kingdom takes precedence.

This leads neatly to the more difficult aspects of Aquinas's interpretation. He argues that in saying "let the dead bury their own dead," Christ issues four lessons (*documenta*). The first is that, "one who is called to the state of perfection should not regard his fleshly father with inordinate affection."[50] This lesson has essentially two parts. On the one hand, the father of earthly generation is revered with respect to the Father of all who is in Heaven. Through the revelation of Christ's teaching, that is, humanity is instructed that God is not merely a creator, but the true Father who is owed filial piety and devotion. Consequently, the revelation of God as Father establishes the bounds of proper affection for earthly fathers. Though we should undoubtedly give our fathers genuine love and reverence, this affection occurs within the orientation of the heart to praise and revere the Father in Heaven.

Second, Aquinas argues that Jesus instructs us that "the affection of kinship is removed between the faithful and infidels."[51] It should be apparent that this explanation seems to be precisely the kind of Christian message that is disturbing today to many informed by the Christian tradition. So, one should proceed with care to understand Aquinas precisely. First, Aquinas emphasizes that the affection of kinship (*germanitatis affectus*) is lost between believers and unbelievers. Here Aquinas cites Luke 14:26, where Jesus says his disciples must "hate" (*odit*) their fathers and mothers. Does Aquinas think Jesus is advocating disciples to withdraw affection as a consequence of discipleship? No. Rather, Aquinas notes this loss of affection occurs "when one's father or mother removes one from God" (*ubi pater et mater retrahunt a Deo*).[52] By this, Aquinas means a situation when a parent would seek to dissuade a child from following Christ (not unlike Aquinas's own experience in the castle of Roccasecca,

50. *Super Evangelium S. Matthaei lectura*, cap. 8, l. 3.
51. *Super Evangelium S. Matthaei lectura*, cap. 8, l. 3. See also Hilary's comment in *Catena Aurea in Matthaeum*, l. 6.
52. *Super Evangelium S. Matthaei lectura*, cap. 8, l. 3.

270 Chapter 6

where his family held him captive in hopes of having him abandon the Order of Preachers). In other words, Aquinas seems to conclude the loss of kinship affection is a result of one choosing the Gospel in the case of a parent opposing or proving an obstacle to choosing the Gospel.

Consequently, Aquinas means that those who choose to follow Jesus will incur the loss of affection by their parents if the parents do not live in accordance with the Gospel. This is not narrow dogmatism, for Aquinas sees the Gospel as not only a set of religious doctrines, but the true path to flourishing and happiness. Hence, it is not that the Christian seeks to abandon familial relations and affection when pursuing the Gospel. It is rather that, as the Lord says in John's Gospel, "the world will hate you because of me."[53] Therefore, when one faces the situation of parents who would "remove him from God" by either explicitly opposing the decision to follow Christ or by inducing him to a form of life incompatible with the Gospel, this does indeed become a cause of lost affection. But this is not because of the problem of the Christian faith per se; it is rather due to the hardness of human hearts not to conform to the true way of flourishing: the Gospel of Jesus Christ.

The third lesson of Jesus, according to Aquinas, is that one should not memorialize the unbelieving dead among the celebration of the saints.[54] Aquinas's position seems to extend the logic of lesson 1 above. If God is our Father in heaven to whom all filial piety is due in its highest form, then the saints are true kin with Christians, though by spirit and not blood. Because this is kinship that is truly ordered toward flourishing and the good (i.e., union with God), it is also a higher kinship that orders our actions regarding the mourning and burial of unbelievers when they die. After all, Aquinas states in the *ST* that burial is an act on behalf of the dead since it allows that the deceased "may live in the memory of man whose respect he forfeits [*honor dehonestatur*] if he remain without burial."[55] Because burial concerns the memorial honor of the dead, the practice of burial has an implicit dependence upon understanding what

53. Jn 15:19.
54. *Super Evangelium S. Matthaei lectura*, cap. 8, l. 3.
55. *ST* IIaIIae, q. 32, art. 3, ad 1. Translation via Aquinas Institute.

it honorable and not. While Christians should clearly act with mercy toward the dead, bury non-believers, and honor what is honorable and virtuous to remember in them, we must also reserve special honor for that which is most honorable in human life: the faithful following of Christ unto eternal beatitude.

The fourth and final lesson Aquinas says Jesus teaches through Matthew 8:21–22 is the lesson that "all who live outside of Christ are dead, because he himself is life, as Gregory taught."[56] This phrase does not precisely line up with a citation of Gregory the Great in the *Catena Aurea in Matthaeum*, we do find a citation that states the following: "the dead also bury the dead, when sinners protect sinners. They exalt sinners with their praises, hide the dead under a pile of words."[57] The citation from Gregory here clearly relates to a spiritual interpretation of the passage—that is, that those who live outside of Christ are weighed down by sin and do not live in keeping with the principle of true life, Jesus Christ himself. Hence, Aquinas seems to mean that Jesus simply teaches us how sin serves as an obstacle to prevent us from seeking true flourishing. Inasmuch as the desire to bury one's father over following Christ represents the way that sin obstructs our pursuit of living in right relation with God, this desire is a sign of death rather than life. Here again, the point is not that there is anything morally problematic about the burial of one's father per se, only when this desire is placed in competition with the desire and willingness to follow Christ.

A THOMISTIC RESOLUTION

Now that we have seen both the Confucian account of mourning and Aquinas's interpretation of Matthew 8:21–22, it is appropriate to consider precisely what Confucian mourning might ask of Matthew 8:21–22 and to show how Aquinas resolves these problems. The reason for this is that, by working toward a resolution of the problems, the actual tensions and limits between the Confucian perspective and Catholic theological science regarding Christ as teacher will

---

56. *Super Evangelium S. Matthaei lectura*, cap. 8, l. 3.
57. *Catena aurea in Matthaeum*, cap. 8, l. 6.

become clearer. For example, although many Christian exegetes would wish to point out that there are others who would bury the son's father (so the burial would still be carried out), this resolution would not be convincing from the Confucian perspective. In Confucianism, the proper burial of one's parent is a moral obligation, not simply to ensure it happens, but to perform the service oneself if at all possible. Hence, the practical issue of ensuring the dead are buried is not the primary point of tension between Confucianism and Catholic theological science, but rather the moral problem of the son's natural obligations to bury and mourn for his parents properly. For this moral issue more directly concerns the perfections of Christ *qua* sage-teacher, which primarily concerns me here.

In my view, there are three main problems the Confucian tradition poses for understanding Matthew 8:21–22 to be a teaching of a sage. The degree to which Aquinas can be used to resolve these problems therefore furnishes an excellent gauge of how much the Confucian tradition can or cannot serve Christological science. And so, the first problem is that according to the Confucian tradition, there is a natural moral obligation to mourn a father's death, arising from the love a son has for his parents. Confucius emphasized this affection as manifest in the inability of the moral person to feel "at rest" (*an* 安) until he had mourned his father for three years due to the care he received from his father. Xunzi described it as the natural love of kinship and kind that is found even among beasts. In other words, Confucianism teaches that our genuine connections of affection and concern for our blood relations are part and parcel of being human. If we ignore or do not cultivate proper affection for our parents, this is not simply a family crisis, it is a failure of human morality as such.

This is vital because Confucianism sees mourning as the natural expression or extension of this natural affection for parents. For the Confucian tradition, the idea that one could genuinely love and care for a parent, but fail to mourn his or her death, is nonsensical: proper affection for parents inherently leads the morally upright person to mourn his or her parents' deaths. Consequently, when Jesus obstructs the filial son's desire to bury his father, it seems to a Confucian perspective that the Lord is either a) denying the validity

Thomas's Reading of Matthew 8:21–22 and Confucian Filiality 273

of the son's natural affection for his parents being manifest in mourning and internment, or b) suggesting proper mourning is not inherent to human moral rectitude and, therefore, unimportant.

To resolve this problem, one must first determine whether Catholic theological science can agree with the Confucian position that the desire to mourn is a natural moral obligation, and if so, how does this natural obligation fit within the hierarchy of goods as clarified by revelation? Aquinas's interpretation provides help in both respects. First, in juxtaposing the filial son in Matthew 8:21 with the scribe in Matthew 8:19, Aquinas argues the former is more virtuous than the latter. Significantly, the only evidence for such a conclusion in the text is the son's request to bury his father. Consequently, Aquinas interprets Jesus as recognizing that the son who wishes to bury his father requests something typically in keeping with moral virtue: it is in keeping with natural law to desire to mourn one's father properly. Indeed, Aquinas takes great steps to ensure his reader that Christ does not consider burying and mourning parents immoral, improper, or unimportant. Aquinas undoubtedly believes that dead parents should be buried and not have their bodies left on the roadside to rot. Thus, the son's perception that he should properly mourn and bury his father is both accurate and a testament to his moral character as one who wishes to follow the Way, the Truth, and the Life.

But if Aquinas seems to admit that burying one's father is a natural moral obligation that ought typically to be done, why does his interpretation not conclude that Christ's teaching is problematic? As the analysis above shows, Aquinas's interpretation emphasizes that the tension in the passage stems not from the goods of burial and mourning per se, but rather the context of this request—that is, in the request for discipleship. The son makes his request to the Lord in terms of wanting to follow and serve Him, and offers the burial of his father as an impediment to this task. Thus, the desire to bury his father in this context seems to express moral ambiguity regarding his desire to follow Christ. But discipleship is the principle of the good life itself, the path to full happiness and flourishing, and when there is a fork in the road, one must choose following Christ over any other temporal good.

274 Chapter 6

Now this does provide a resolution, though perhaps not as compelling from the Confucian perspective as it is from the Christian one, since it rests upon understanding Christ's Gospel to be what the Church professes it to be: the true path to ultimate happiness and flourishing. Logically, it holds together, but requires judgments about the terms involved. Consequently, this points out a helpful way that the Confucian sage-teacher and Christ as teacher stand in tension. For although it is possible in Confucianism to articulate higher goods than parents, there is a deep reluctance to do so. Moreover, the idea that a sage in the Confucian understanding would see following *himself* as the higher good than mourning practices is profoundly absurd. Finally, the way that early Confucianism understood the cosmos and processes of life meant that it was much harder to separate and juxtapose service to parents, on the one hand, and service to higher goods on the other.

And so, one must understand why Christ is justified to make following him a higher good than burying parents, which requires insight into the cosmology of revealed science. As we saw above, the Confucian understanding of the mourning rites as a natural obligation is tied to parents' generative agency. As the *Xiaojing* puts it, "our bodies—bones, hair, and skin—are received from our parents; if one does not dare to injure or harm [this gift], this is the beginning of filial piety."[58] Our parents mediate life to us, and because of this gift, there naturally arises love, care, and concern in human beings for our parents. At the same time, as I discussed in chapters 2 and 3, early Chinese often perceived *Tian* to be generative (producing life or *sheng* 生), while Earth produced form (*xing* 形) and so the generative agency of *Tian* was not primarily understood in the sense of creation per se, but the confluence of agency to bring about life, which is formally imitated (and not just materially repeated) in parental generation. Consequently, many early Confucians interpreted *Tian* as producing life for material creatures, but not as the sole source and ground of the order of the cosmos and all the goods therein.

That said, Confucianism is aware of the fact that very often, moral goods cannot be pursued in concert, but we must decide which good orders others. Pursuant to this problem, early Confucians

58. *Xiaojing*, 1.

Thomas's Reading of Matthew 8:21–22 and Confucian Filiality   275

by-and-large rejected the idea that filial piety to parents was indicative of the good as such and could never be altered for the pursuit of more important goods. Rather, early Confucians—Xunzi chief among them—argued that following the *dao* of moral righteousness was a higher good than typical acts of filial piety, such as obeying parents' commands. As Xunzi puts it, if a parent commands me to do something that does not lead to their flourishing, I have the obligation to do the opposite.[59]

The tension between Confucianism and Christ's teaching on this score, then, is quite specific. Given the importance of parents as those who mediate life, it is never clear in the Confucian tradition what moral goods would be so great as to legitimize breaking the proper burial and mourning obligations. Theoretically, it is possible for a higher good to exceed the obligations to bury and mourn parents, but it is practically uncertain what it would be. And this is because Confucianism does not understand obligations to *Tian*, for example, to stand in contrast with the obligations to parents, since parents are the means of life's mediation. Catholic theological science, on the other hand, holds that the Creator God is a distinctive creative agent from parents, and as such is owed forms of obedience and service that are distinct from those owed parents.

To put the point more sharply, through Jesus Christ we learn that paternity is truly and deeply part of the divine life, indeed we learn that the Father is an eternal Person within the Triune life of God.[60] From the view Catholic theological science, devotion owed to God is ultimately a species of filial obligation that, while not necessarily in a dialectical relationship with filial obligation to parents, stands in distinction to the filial obligations owed parents.[61] This distinction is of a sufficient degree that if the obligations to one's parents come into conflict with the obligation toward God—as they do in the question of discipleship for the would-be follower—the filial obligations to God supersede those to parents. From this it is straightforward to

59. *Xunzi, Zi Dao*, 1–2. A similar position can be found in the Zengzi tradition in the *Da Dai Liji, Zengzi Shi Fumu*, 1.

60. See *ST* Ia, q. 32, art. 1, corp.

61. The application of filial piety to God within the Christian tradition is a standard tope of Chinese Catholic theological literature. See, e.g., Tian Liang 田良. "*Jianli Zhongguo gongjiao wenhua chuyi* 建立中國公交文化芻議." *Xinduosheng* 5, no. 26 (December 1959): 33–46.

276   Chapter 6

say that since Jesus is the God-man, following him is a direct form of filial piety to the Creator that supersedes (when in conflict) the natural moral obligations to one's parent.

Thus, in a certain degree, early Confucians could heartily agree that the moral goods of filial piety can conflict with higher goods, and that in such circumstances, choosing the *dao* is better than strictly following the norms of filial piety. However, it is only the principle of the Incarnation and the theology of the Creator that allow one to see why Christ is a true sage (and not a deviant sophist) in Matthew 8:18–22. For it is not simply that following Jesus is a higher good than filial piety, but that following Jesus is a better and higher fulfillment of the demands of filial piety because it is piety given to God. This goes beyond fulfilling the norms of filial piety toward our earthly fathers. The latter is still good, virtuous, and important, but it simply is not the highest good. Yet because Confucianism lacks an analogous conception of *Tian* or another divine figure as an intentional, creative, and paternal agent of generation, it is not clear from the perspective of Confucian tradition that the obligations to *Tian* can rise to be such a higher good as to supersede the natural obligations toward deceased parents.

The second chief problem the Confucian perspective raises regarding Christ as sage-teacher is that early Confucians argue that the mourning rites shape and order mourning properly so that our mourning is virtuous. Even without these rites, Confucianism assumes humans would still mourn their parents. The problem is that we would mourn in ways that impede our flourishing. For example, perhaps we would become so consumed by grief that we would fail to eat properly, care for ourselves or care for our living family for months. Perhaps we will attempt to ignore our grief and avoid the pain of mourning only to see our relationships with our friends and loved ones suffer or break apart. Perhaps we will never be able to move past the loss we have experienced, and become caught in an endless cycle of grief and despair. There are, we must admit, many perils that come from losing loved ones and Confucians argue that proper mourning allows us to face them well.

The Confucian perspective leads, then, to a fascinating problem

Thomas's Reading of Matthew 8:21–22 and Confucian Filiality   277

with Matthew 8:21–22. If filial grief is a natural and unbidden response to a parent's death, then if the son were to follow Jesus without burying his father, he would still be in a state of mourning. Would not the son be better served by Jesus telling him to go, mourn, and heal? Why does Jesus deny him the very means by which he might become able to flourish? Is Jesus's teaching just set at an incommensurable variance with the Confucian tradition on the nature of moral virtue? Clearly at face value, the sage-status of Jesus's teaching in Matthew 8:21–22 is at least dubious from the Confucian perspective.

Fortunately, Aquinas's interpretation of this passage provides two insights that the Confucian position on rituals and moral virtue is to be found within Christ's teaching. First and significantly, Aquinas is sensitive to the problem of mourning and the proper order or shape of mourning. He suggests we consider a concrete example of how we can morally negotiate the dangers that can arise from mourning: "if we saw another person excessively affected [*affectum nimis*] at his father's death, he would be prohibited from burying him on account of the danger."[62] In context, Aquinas means that the sadness of the son would be too much for him to bear and thus he'd be genuinely unable to withstand the internment of his father. Here, Aquinas notes that we should be moved by a parent's death, but it is also possible that we mourn in problematic ways that can prevent us from flourishing.

Second, Aquinas suggests that the mourning process is not itself a foolproof guide to moral flourishing. After all, burying one's father properly requires attention to material, economic, and diverse other considerations. It can be that one who seeks to mourn properly actually finds the process a source of never-ending affairs so that the mourning does not stop in a timely fashion, or truly does consume other obligations we have to other relations. Put differently, it may be the case that mourning rites ideally help us understand what it means to mourn and bury our parents in virtuous ways. However, it seems to logically follow from Aquinas's treatment that unless we possess sufficient virtue beforehand (in this case, the implication is the virtue of fortitude), we can fall into other moral dangers (such

62. *Super Evangelium S. Matthaei lectura*, cap. 8, l. 3.

278 Chapter 6

as failing to end our grief) even as we seek to do the virtuous act of mourning and burying a loved one.

A third problem the Confucian perspective raises for reading Matthew 8:21–22 as an expression of Christ the sage-teacher concerns the way that the natural moral obligations of filial mourning promote a broader moral consciousness. According to Xunzi, human flourishing involves not just respecting and ordering ourselves toward the living, but also the dead. Without caring for the dead well, we are stingy, and "small people" (*xiaoren* 小人) in Confucian parlance. Therefore, mourning rites can militate against a tyrannical materialism, perhaps of the very kind that threatens contemporary Western society: the dictatorship of the present, which treats the dead as either insignificant or impediments to flourishing. Instead, Xunzi at least advocates for the practice of the traditional mourning rites as a means to gaining and maintaining a proper view of what has come before, and not privilege the present moment at the expense of the past.

This problem touches upon one of the apparently irresolvable conflicts between Christ the teacher and the Confucian sage-teacher. As we saw in chapter 6, the Confucian tradition would understand the sage to connect human beings with the traditional practices and insights of the Chinese intellectual tradition. Clearly, Jesus has no expressed concern to unite his teachings with those of the sages of Chinese antiquity. Thus, whatever measure of retrospective moral formation one can find in Jesus's teachings, it certainly does not refer to the classical Chinese context, which is the implicit expectation of Confucian sages. While this is a considerable complication, it seems fair to recognize that the Incarnation involved the condescension to human weakness, which includes the fact that human beings are all part of concrete, particular cultural traditions. That Christ was bound not to all cultures but to the Jewish people is due to the divine economy for our salvation, which worked through the Hebrew people first and then diffused to the nations. Consequently, the question we should really ask is whether Jesus is such a sage-teacher as to be concerned about the sort of retrospective moral formation expected of the Confucian sage, or if he would dismiss these concerns and thus break from the Confucian sage image entirely.

Thomas's Reading of Matthew 8:21–22 and Confucian Filiality   279

Undoubtedly this problem is rather knotty, since how one resolves it touches upon important other theological presuppositions. For example, from the Confucian perspective, it might seem that by making a distinction between following in the way of the kingdom and burying one's father, Jesus also accepts the tyranny of the present, even if this present is ultimately virtuous (i.e., the trajectory toward his hour on the cross). However, in Catholic theological science, such a conclusion is not warranted since following Christ is the greatest good, that fulfills rather than abolishes the Law and the Prophets (Mt 5:17). From the Confucian perspective, then, it may seem at first that Christ's teaching involves the risk that we might become "small people" (*xiaoren*) in pledging allegiance to this life that causes us to willfully lose our perspective and standing within a tradition. However, when one accepts the truth of the Gospel and takes up the path of following Christ, it is self-evident (in Catholic theological science) that such loss of perspective and standing is not a result of following Jesus as such.

Here we see it is especially helpful to have Aquinas as an interlocutor for this book, since his approach furnishes helpful resources for seeing why Christ's doctrine does not entail a radical disaffiliation from traditions and history per se. For example, Aquinas emphasizes the moral virtue of the son's desire to bury his father. It is significant that, again, in his discussion of burial as a corporal work of mercy, Aquinas emphasizes burial's relationship to remembering and honoring the dead.[63] Much like early Confucians, Aquinas understands burial to be an important part of retrospective formation that helps us become virtuous. Yet, Aquinas also recognizes (as early Confucians do) that commemoration and honor are not ultimate goods, but rather dependent goods. Without submitting our hearts to the ultimate good (God), we cannot properly commemorate and honor our parents, or our tradition more broadly. The commemoration and honoring of our parents and our tradition can come to function in idolatrous ways for us if we do not maintain our connection with the principle of goodness and nobility itself, God. Hence, Christ's teaching does not lead us into a myopia that dispels the importance of the

63. *ST* IIaIIae, q. 32, art. 2, ad 1.

past, but into the proper perspective through which we can rightly love and honor that which came before us.

Neither Christ nor Aquinas suggest abandoning mourning itself or suggest abandoning mindfulness of the past and duties to what has come before us. Rather, Christ has reoriented the memorial aspect of mourning to become more perfect. This is ultimately because, as Catholic theological science recognizes, through Christ's sacrifice on the cross, resurrection, and ascension into Heaven "death has been swallowed up in victory."[64] Consequently, in mourning for the dead we not only engage in retrospective honor, but we also look toward the fulfillment of God's faithful promises wherein those who die in grace will find true beatitude. Mourning the dead in the Catholic faith is also an occasion to recall the work of Christ and the promises of his grace, and a reminder that the close of this mortal life is not the end.

Aquinas's' reading of Matthew 8:21–22 helps us say that Christ's teaching does not at all disregard the past. Rather, it injects something heretofore absurd to consider about the past and the dead: genuine hope. Hope that those who cleave to God and have fallen asleep in death shall awake, and, through God's grace, find true, eternal happiness. For this reason, Catholic theological science might say that Christ the sage enables a truer love and devotion to what has come before us. This is because for the one whose parents, ancestors, and other loved ones (including the saints) pass unto death in a state of grace, these loved ones are not *mere* memories maintained by our acts of commemoration, but they are alive in Christ, enjoying the reward of happiness.[65] Because of the wonders of divine grace, life in the kingdom does not resign us to abandoning the past, but facilitates genuine and full honorable communion with those who come before us, and provides a genuine, full, and accurate recognition of the virtue and nobility of those loved ones for whom we mourn on the way to our own eternal rest in God.

64. 1 Cor 15:54.
65. See *SCG* IV.92.

CONCLUSIONS

It should be now evident that although the desire to develop more "culturally relevant" resources for Chinese Catholic Christology is a good and just desire, the actual work of building such a Chinese Catholic Christology requires much care and scholarly patience. The concept of the Confucian sage is an example of both the immense fecundity of turning to Chinese philosophical concepts for Christological reflection, and the difficulty of doing so responsibly. For though it may be tempting and rhetorically effective to describe Christ in terms of the Confucian *shengren*, the actual applicability of this title is complex. Thus, in the analysis above, I have endeavored to test the theological limits and possibilities of the Confucian conception of sagehood by attempting to apply it to Jesus Christ.

On the one hand, the foregoing analysis has shown where the genuine differences between Catholicism and Confucianism lie on the theme of the sage as a moral teacher. Most basically, there is a fundamental cultural difference that cannot be dispensed with. The Jewish rabbi cannot be the same as the Confucian sage because both concepts presuppose a connection to an actual, particular tradition of instruction and ritual practices that cannot merely be replaced one for the other. The fact that Jesus was not Chinese and did not explicitly concern himself with connecting his teaching to the historical shape of Chinese antiquity understandably weakens our ability to understand him as a sage from the Confucian perspective, as does the inability of the Confucian tradition to articulate the place of the moral sage within the covenantal economy of Israel.

However, at the same time, this problem merely points out that the application of the sage title to Jesus must be analogous in important ways. And so, it is also worth remembering we have seen in the above analysis several points at which the application breaks down. For one thing, there are several fundamental characteristics of Jewish and Christian theology that do not have an adequate analog in the Confucian tradition. Namely, the theological commitments of God the Creator and the eschatological telos of the world are implicit structures that make sense of the claim that Christ is a kind of sage-teacher. As the Confucian tradition lacks these doctrines in a robust way, there is no way from the Confucian tradition itself to understand Christ as a genuine sage. Rather, one would have to adopt the principles of revealed science regarding these matters in order to understand how Christ's sagehood is what the Church claims it is.

Additionally, it is evident that the doctrine of the Incarnation makes all the difference in understanding Christ as a sage teacher. Without understanding Jesus as the God-man, it is quite frankly absurd to think that one would follow him as a sage-master following the principles of the Confucian tradition. For it is only in light of the mystery of the Incarnation that it makes sense to see Christ as sage in the way that his teaching requires (i.e., as a higher good than natural moral obligations).

This is quite significant. For as I mentioned in the previous chapter, some theologians, such as Kwok Pui-lan and Jonathan Y. Tan, have argued that the traditional Christological teachings about Christ's nature are "irrelevant" to the Chinese mind, and thus should be replace for more "native" and "relevant" categories. My analysis here demonstrates that any attempt to articulate Christ apart from the traditional doctrines regarding Christ's nature is doomed to failure. For it is precisely the truth communicated and safeguarded by these doctrines—that Jesus Christ is the Word made flesh (Jn 1)—that is necessary to make Christ relevant to non-Western categories at all. Solely on Confucian terms and without the background of traditional Christological dogmas, the claim that Jesus is a sage is laughable, and shows how deeply irrelevant Jesus would be, were he not the Living God who dwelled among us (Jn 1:14).

All this admitted, the foregoing analysis has also revealed a deep consonance between Christ the teacher and the Confucian sage. For like a traditional Confucian sage, Jesus Christ understands what is necessary for moral flourishing. According to Aquinas, Christ recognized the inherent moral virtue of burying one's father, and could recognize it as laudable. Consequently, Aquinas would have us see that Christ's sagehood is such that it does not destroy our natural moral obligations. Rather, his teaching leads us into perfection so that we can actually perform these obligations in a way conducive

Thomas's Reading of Matthew 8:21–22 and Confucian Filiality   283

to flourishing. Moreover, Aquinas shows us that Christ the teacher is also sensitive to the fact that practices like burying and mourning constitute kinds of moral formation. Although Jesus does not reject the positive moral formation of the mourning rites, his teaching concerns the more perfect context of moral formation that gives new life to our moral practices. In this way, Christ genuinely fulfills and perfects the expected work of the Confucian sage-teacher: He leads his followers into the path of wisdom and truth that perfects the moral life.

Here we see at once the moment of clearest convergence and divergence between Christ the teacher and the Confucian sage. As a sage-teacher, Christ is concerned with establishing and illuminating the proper context needed to develop and practice (graced) moral virtue. Just like the Confucian sage, Christ is concerned with calling attention to the practices and formative beliefs that allow us and our society to move toward happiness. The difference is that Christ is himself the proper context in which moral virtue can be truly perfected. Yet the key is that once this context of discipleship is provided, this means that all the previous moral practices and contexts receive new life. By being brought into the Christologically-determined drama of salvation, the Christian returns to cultural practices with a new, more perfect sense of how these practices fit within the path to happiness. Hence, Christ the sage-teacher can well be seen to support many Confucian sage teachings regarding mourning, but it is only after the illuminating light of revelation that the goodness and truth of these Confucian teachings become clear.

Can the Church, then, rightly speak of Christ the sage-teacher? It seems to me not only that we can, but that we must, for Christ is all the things that the Confucian sage is meant to be: a guide to wisdom, flourishing, and ritual practices. Yet clarifying what this means and unpacking the significance of this attribution for Christological science is a larger problem, although a joyous burden to be sure. Now that the true Christological limits and possibilities of the Confucian sage concept are clear, the more important work of articulating more deeply how Christ fulfills the sage-ideal can and should be taken up.

A Brief Conclusion

The goal of this book has been to provide a concrete model for assessing the theological possibilities and limitations of Chinese philosophical concepts. As I mentioned in the work's introduction, this book intentionally lacks a comprehensive scope. There are a tremendous variety of important and interesting Chinese texts and concepts deserving of theological attention that I have left untouched that would be of tremendous value for building a robust and faithful Chinese Catholic theology. Yet I have accepted this limitation of the book in order to produce what I think is truly valuable in the foregoing chapters—namely, the demonstration of the kind of rigorous depth and attention needed to bring Chinese philosophical concepts into the service of Catholic theological science. That is, the chapters hold together as exemplifying a better way of developing a robust, responsible, and vibrant Chinese Catholic theology, even if they do not spell out what such a theology must or would look like.

In my view, the work I have undertaken in this book has been necessary because of shortcomings in extant theological scholarship that seeks to use Chinese philosophical concepts without first offering a rigorous analysis of the theological limits and possibilities of the terms. Hopefully, it is now clear that my critique has a double edge. While I applaud the interest in Chinese philosophical concepts that lies behind the avidity for the expeditious theological application of these ideas, I would argue that applying them in theology without proper preparation diminishes both theological science

A Brief Conclusion   285

and the interpretation of Chinese philosophical texts. Put simply, a deep and abiding reverence for Chinese philosophies ought to make one cautious about simply instrumentalizing them for the sake of a contemporary theological bent. Similarly, a deep and abiding reverence for Catholic theological science ought to make one recognize that the intellectual resources of the Catholic tradition are not simply denominations of mental currency that can be exchanged haphazardly with other concepts and traditions. Rather, a Catholic theology that is both honest with itself as a form of Catholic theological science and seeks to be culturally relevant by appealing to Chinese philosophies must advance with care and precision.

Therefore, my argument in this book has not simply been to offer theological analyses of Chinese philosophical concepts, but to offer an approach that models the kind of care and precision the task demands. My appeal to Aquinas as a resource for theological analysis has been a choice for convenience and precision, and I have endeavored to promote the virtues of trying to think like Aquinas in my analyses. While Aquinas does not provide the sole possible means of making the kind of assessments I try to make here, I do think his perspective provides tremendous assistance. I hope the foregoing chapters demonstrate that Aquinas's theological synthesis and deep respect for the fruitfulness of natural reason provide an inestimably helpful lens from which to assess and articulate the true standing of Chinese philosophical concepts vis-à-vis Catholic theological science. Although Aquinas's theological approach is well-defined, technical, and a tradition unto itself, it can accommodate a wide range of analogous perspectives and principles in early Chinese texts without having to translate them into Aquinas's system per se. Thus, Aquinas's approach has allowed the analyses in this book to have genuine theological depth while maintaining the integrity of Chinese philosophical concepts on their own.

Ultimately, this book deals with a theological prolegomenon. It is not Chinese Catholic theology as such, but rather an important step I believe whole-heartedly is needed for grounding Chinese Catholic systematic theology (or indeed any theology seeking to incorporate pre-Christian Chinese or non-traditional sources). In this way, the chapters of the book have not effected the theological integration I believe is possible and necessary, but have merely issued an aide to the process. My great hope is that the book's sober measure of the ways Chinese philosophy does and does not accord with Catholic theological science will inspire others to recognize the great opportunity that lies ahead for integrating Chinese thought into Catholic theology. Put differently, although I have tried to be honest and rigorous about the ways Chinese thought does not resonate with the principles and norms of Catholic theological science, I hope the reader is more convinced of the true possibilities and fruitfulness of engaging Chinese philosophy, and developing Catholic theology along the axes of concepts such as *tian, renxing, jian ai,* and *shengren,* as well as many others.

It is fitting, then, to conclude the book with an exhortation. There is a tremendous need for theologians to seek to understand how the traditions of Chinese philosophy can be employed in service to the saving Gospel of Jesus Christ. I believe and hope that the method of assessment I have promoted in this book will be of use to theologians who currently labor at building a Chinese Catholic theology in various intellectual contexts, with whose work I often have deep sympathies. To these friends and co-laborers, I must reiterate that my aim here has been to provide what I believe is a better approach to engaging and assessing Chinese philosophical concepts for the sake of application in Chinese Catholic theology. I am convinced that the sort of work I provide in this book is essential to producing a Chinese Catholic theology that is robust, intellectually compelling, culturally relevant, and steadfastly faithful to Catholic theological principles, and offer it as help along the way for those already engaged in excellent and fruitful service.

However, given my own intellectual context, my main concern in this book has been the improvement of Chinese Catholic theology written in Western languages. To this point, the relevant literature is dominated by scholars who trade in an unremitting and unfruitful dialectic between cultural relevance and orthodoxy, seeking to leverage Chinese philosophy to unseat traditional theological science and its concepts. Rather than inviting Chinese philosophy to become a friend of God by becoming engrafted into the true Vine (see Jn 15:1–17), many scholars today seek to remove the branches God has drawn to himself and replace them with what they deem to be more beautiful or relevant members.

Animating this book is my belief that that we should not accept such a dialectic or the deeply problematic theology it engenders. The Chinese philosophical traditions deserve a better, more rigorous assessment from the perspective of Catholic theological science. The Catholic theological tradition deserves better than theological approaches that treat the beauty, goodness, and truth of our tradition with easy contempt in the name of cultural relevance. And finally, Chinese Catholics deserve and are owed a better, more intellectually compelling and faithful theology than much of what is available to them in Western languages.

Therefore, I conclude with a word to those who likewise yearn for a better Chinese Catholic theology, who desire to discover a genuine and abiding harmony between the traditions of Chinese reason and that of Catholic faith, and who refuse the false dichotomy with which we have so often been presented between drinking deeply from the font of Chinese wisdom or from that well of Living Water that brings eternal life. I can do no better in this exhortation than to quote from the Living Water Himself, who nourishes and perfects our appeal to Chinese philosophy rather than destroys it. "At the sight of crowds, his heart was moved with pity for them because they were troubled and abandoned, like sheep without a shepherd. Then he said to his disciples, 'The harvest is abundant, but the laborers are few; so ask the master of the harvest to send out laborers for his harvest'" (Mt 9:36–37).

Appendix
Introduction to Early Confucianism and Mohism

———:———

Because of the amount of work of contextualization needed to understand the purposes of this volume in the introduction, I have elected to give background to the texts I examine in this appendix rather than the main corpus of the book. Therefore, this appendix serves to introduce the larger context of the texts and concepts I have analyzed in the book for those who need it or desire to build on their background knowledge of early Chinese philosophy by appealing to relevant literature.

There are many capable books providing overviews of classical Chinese philosophy; here I will only provide the briefest treatment needed to appreciate the historical and philosophical context of the texts I have analyzed in the book.[1] The foregoing chapters have engaged two of the most significant traditions of early Chinese

---

1. For those seeking a general introduction to early Chinese philosophy, I recommend the following (the first two due to influence in the field, and the latter due to the sheer excellence of the text): Schwartz, *The World of Thought in Ancient China*; Angus C. Graham, *Disputers of the Tao: Philosophical Argument in Ancient China* (Chicago and La Salle, IL: Open Court, 1989); Van Norden, *Introduction to Classical Chinese Philosophy*. Another influential if dated overview text is the recently reprinted classic Feng Youlan 馮友蘭, *Zhongguo zhexue shi* 中国哲学史, vol. 1 (Chongqing: Chongqing chubanshe, 2009), also available in English translation as Fung Yu-lan, *A History of Chinese Philosophy*, vol. 1, *The Period of the Philosophers* (*From the Beginnings to Circa 100 B.C.*), 2nd ed., trans. Derk Bodde (Princeton, NJ: Princeton University Press, 1952). Also recommended is the anthology of classical philosophical texts available as Philip J. Ivanhoe and Bryan W. Van Norden, eds., *Readings in Classical Chinese Philosophy*, 2nd ed. (Indianapolis, IN: Hackett Publishing, 2005).

thought, the Confucian and Mohist school. For my purposes in this book, "early" Chinese thought is basically synonymous with the period sinologists refer to as the "pre-Qin period" of Chinese history—that is, that falling before 221 BC (the founding of the Qin dynasty). More specifically, the texts I have engaged are all essentially from the Warring States period (475–221 BC), which largely falls within the period known as the Eastern Zhou (770–256 BC).[2]

During this period of Chinese history, the ruling dynasty of the age, called the Zhou dynasty, was falling apart. The dissolution of the political power of the Zhou also gave rise to (or, in some readings was preceded by) a decay in morality, religion, and propriety. Consequently, Warring States philosophical thinking arose in response to cultural crisis, and therefore took on a particular character. Namely, it was marked primarily by a concern for practical philosophy (especially moral and political philosophy) and yielded little abiding and sustained interest in speculative philosophical questions, such as metaphysics. This is not to say that Warring States philosophers were not concerned with speculative questions entirely, or that they did not have presuppositions that equate to positions on speculative matters. Still, by-and-large, Warring States thinkers focused on the "way of humanity" (*rendao* 人道) rather than the "ways of Heaven" (*tiandao* 天道).

The Warring States period was extremely fecund with regard to philosophical development, even earning the moniker "the period of One Hundred Schools" (*zhuzi baijia* 諸子百家) for the florid variety of philosophical schools and thinking occurring at the time. As this appellation suggests, the Warring States period produced several schools and texts worthy of engagement for the sake of Christian theological science. To name but a few I have not engaged in this book, texts such as the *Zhuangzi*, *Gongsunlongzi*, and the *Shangjun shu* all would be rich interlocutors for Christian theology.[3] For this

2. In my view, the best single general discussion of the place of philosophy in the Warring States context is David S. Nivison, "The Classic Philosophical Writings," in Loewe and Shaughnessey, *The Cambridge History of Ancient China*, 745–812.

3. The *Zhuangzi* is one of the most important texts of the Daoist tradition, perhaps the earliest, famous for its views on epistemology and language. The *Gongsunlongzi* is a text from the School of Names tradition (*Mingjia* 名家), which focuses on issues of naming reality. It is particularly famous as the locus of the "White Horse Discourse" (*Baima lun* 白馬論), which

Introduction to Early Confucianism and Mohism   291

book, however, I elected to focus on a few representative texts from Confucianism (*Rujia*) and Mohism (*Mojia*). My rationale for selecting these schools and the specific texts within is explained in more detail in the introduction to the volume; at the present, I will merely provide more background on significant issues relevant to each tradition.

The Confucian tradition is the most well-known of early Chinese traditions, by reputation if not content.[4] Strictly speaking, "Confucianism" is a misleading term for the school for two reasons.[5] First, because the name of the tradition in Chinese is not derived from Confucius but rather the term *Ru* meaning "literati." Second, because Confucius (or Kongzi as he is known in Chinese), was not the founder of the school, but indeed was himself a member of a *Ru* tradition that preceded him. Thus, many sinologists refer to Confucianism as "Ruism." However, I do not find the term "Confucianism" especially problematic so long as the proper historical caveats are kept in place, and I have retained use of this term.

Apart from being a tradition that celebrates Confucius as a sage, what exactly is Confucianism? Early Confucianism was a comprehensive intellectual tradition founded on study and interpretation

---

has been read by some as a favorable analog to Platonic philosophical discourse. The *Shangjun shu* is a central text from the Legalist school (*Fajia* 法家), which is famous for its vision of the structuring all the practices of a state for the purpose of supporting war, and suppressing the cultivation of virtue (*de* 德) in the common people. The *Zhuangzi* is partially available in English in several forms, most recently in Brook Ziporyn, ed. and trans., *Zhuangzi: The Essential Writings with Selections from Traditional Commentaries* (Indianapolis, IN: Hackett Publishing, 2009). The *Shangjun shu* has been recently made available in an updated translation as Yuri Pines, ed. and trans. *The Book of Lord Shang: Apologetics of State Power in Early China* (New York: Columbia University Press, 2017). For *Gongsunlongzi*, a translation of the White Horse Discourse is available in Ivanhoe and Van Norden, *Readings in Classical Chinese Philosophy*, 363–38.

4. There are several admirable introductions to Confucianism. I recommend Paul R. Goldin, *Confucianism* (Durham: Acumen, 2011); Xinzhong Yao, *An Introduction to Confucianism* (New York: Cambridge University Press, 2000); and Daniel K. Gardner, *Confucianism: A Very Short Introduction* (Oxford: Oxford University Press, 2014).

5. See Lionel Jensen, *Manufacturing Confucianism: Chinese Traditions and Universal Civilization* (Durham, NC: Duke University Press, 1997). Although Jensen mistakenly attributes the term Confucianism to the Jesuits, his work is a reminder of the complexities and sometimes problems that arise from using the term. I find that as long as one makes a proper qualification about the background of the Confucian terminology, it is acceptable to use Confucianism to identify the Ru tradition. For a sound rebuttal of Jensen's argument vis-à-vis the Jesuit origins of "Confucianism," see Nicholas Standaert, SJ, "The Jesuits Did NOT Manufacture 'Confucianism,'" *East Asian Science, Technology, and Medicine* 16 (1999): 115–32.

292   Appendix

of a set of classical texts from the early centuries of the Zhou dynasty.[6] Over time, the school began to accept and treat other texts by later *Ru* as important, foundational texts. At least symbolically, the chief of these texts to later Confucians was the *Analects* (*Lunyu*), traditionally attributed to Confucius. It is worth noting, however, that almost no scholars today hold that the *Analects* were actually composed by Confucius, and it is evident the text underwent an extended compilation process.[7] Also highly valued was the *Liji*, a compendium of books and essays describing, interpreting, and commenting upon the ritual practices of classical China. Eventually, the Song dynasty scholar Zhu Xi would offer a now-standard list of the Confucian "canon," called the Four Books: the *Analects*, the *Mengzi*, the *Da Xue* ("Great Learning"), and the *Zhongyong* ("Doctrine of the Mean"), the latter two of which were original single chapters contained within the *Liji*.[8]

Confucianism is often described as a "humanistic philosophy," which is unfortunately misleading since in the West, humanism often has irreligious or atheistic connotations. It is better to see the Confucian tradition as focused on classical learning and drawing upon this learning to help guide humanity to flourishing. Most early Confucians believed that the classical texts and traditions of ancient China were exemplars of flourishing, and so they sought guidance from ritual texts and the moral examples of ancient sages, and encouraged governing based on these models and texts. While these tasks necessarily concerned humanity such that there is little to no speculative theology in the Confucian tradition, it is erroneous to conclude theological matters were insignificant to Confucians.

6. The Zhou dynasty is generally listed as lasting from 1046–256 BC, with the Western Zhou dynasty referring to the earlier part (because the capital was able to be located in the Western part of Zhou holdings). The Western Zhou is usually said to cover 1046–770 BC and the Eastern Zhou lasted from 771–256 BC.

7. The most significant and influential argument for the composition of the *Analects* is E. Bruce Brooks and A. Taeko Brooks, *The Original Analects: The Sayings of Confucius and His Successors* (New York: Columbia University Press, 1998), esp. 201–48, for their argument regarding the composition of the text. Another theory of an even longer compositional history to the *Analects* can be found in Michael Hunter, *Confucius Beyond the Analects* (Leiden: Brill, 2017).

8. A helpful volume with parts of these texts and featuring comments from Zhu Xi can be found in Daniel K. Gardner, ed. and trans. *The Four Books: The Basic Teachings of the Later Confucian Tradition* (Indianapolis, IN: Hackett Publishing, 2007).

Introduction to Early Confucianism and Mohism   293

Rather, one might fairly observe that the problems early Confucians faced and attempted to resolve were not primarily speculative theological problems, but moral and political ones.

A final introductory word about Confucianism concerns the two Confucians who feature prominently in this book, Mengzi (327–289 BC) and Xunzi (300–230 BC). Mengzi and Xunzi are undoubtedly the two most important Confucian thinkers from the Warring States period, and both had immense effect on the later tradition through the texts bearing their names. One of the most significant and lasting impacts of each scholar was their participation in a debate about whether human moral nature is good or bad—a debate I analyzed at length in chapter 3. For the sake of background knowledge, it is only important to note that in the debate about human moral nature, Mengzi and Xunzi testify to the variety of Confucian thought. What differentiates their positions is, in the end, not only different interpretations of basic concepts (such as *renxing*), but also different emphases regarding which aspects of the Confucian tradition are most fundamental.

The second tradition I engage in this book is the Mohist tradition, which is one of the least familiar schools of Chinese thought for non-specialists.[9] Unlike Confucianism, the Mohist school did not survive as a coherent tradition after the Qin dynasty.[10] Also unlike these other schools, the Mohist tradition is primarily retained in one central text, called the *Mozi*, named after the founder of the school, Mo Di.[11] Even in China, there was little deep interest in the *Mozi* until a Mohist revival began slowly during the late Ming dynasty (AD 1368–1644).[12] It is unclear precisely why the Mohist school

9. There are not many introductions to the *Mozi* that a non-specialist would find manageable, apart from treatments in the general introductions mentioned above on p. 329, n. 1. An exception to this is Fraser, *The Philosophy of the Mòzǐ*.

10. See Paul R. Goldin, "Why *Mozi* is included in the *Daoist Canon*: Or, why there is more to Mohism than utilitarian ethics," in *How Should One Live? Comparing Ethics in Ancient China and Greco-Roman Antiquity*, ed. R. A. H. King and Dennis R. Schilling (Berlin: De Gruyter, 2011), 63–91.

11. As the *Mozi* is less well known than other texts examined in this volume, it is helpful to point to some extant translations of the text. See Burton Watson, *Mozi: The Basic Writings* (New York: Columbia University Press, 2003); Ian Johnston, *The Mozi: A Complete Translation* (Hong Kong: Chinese University Press, 2010).

12. Defoort, "The Modern Formation of Early Mohism," 209n1. Defoort reminds that the *Mozi* was not *entirely* forgotten before the Ming, but the text was not a significant part of

294 Appendix

did not survive the Qin. The Qin rulers did embrace the Legalist philosophy and banned other philosophical schools, as evidenced by the famous "burning of the books" from that period. But the Qin was itself short-lived and Confucianism, Daoism, and other movements were able to flourish after this period. Perhaps Mohism did not survive because of internal weaknesses. For example, A. C. Graham has argued that by the third century BC, the Mohist school had split into three distinct branches, each of which rejected the others as heretical.[13]

Whatever the reason, the Mohist tradition is now mainly a historical phenomenon, though it has been resuscitated somewhat in modern times. Carine Defoort has observed how an edition of the *Mozi* produced by the Qing scholar Sun Yirang not only facilitated a revival of interest in Mohism, but also irrevocably shaped how modern scholars approach the text.[14] After the dissolution of Qing dynasty, interest in Mohism has steadily grown in China. A theologically relevant example of this is the work of Wu Leichuan, who attempted to offer Mozi (and Jesus) as a kind of proto-socialist reformer.[15] All that is to say, even if Mohism is not today a lived tradition, it has become a revitalized object of philosophical and ethical interest among sinologists and Chinese intellectuals alike.

Little is known for certain about Mozi himself—scholars have speculated that he was originally a merchant or laborer, or perhaps a former convict.[16] The text of the *Mozi* probably reflects Mozi's own thought, though it is difficult to ascertain precisely when and where this is the case because the book features distinctive layers of Mohist interpretation that show considerable development of concerns and

---

the intellectual landscape. For further discussion of the history of Mohist and its reception in China, see Zheng Jiewen 郑杰文, *Zhongguo Moxue tongshi* 中國墨學通史 (Beijing: Renmin chubanshe, 2006); Qin Yanshi, *Mozi yu Mojia xuepai* 墨子與墨家學派 (Jinan: Shangdong wenyi chubanshe, 2004).

13. Graham, *Later Mohist Logic, Ethics and Science* (Hong Kong: The Chinese University Press, 1978), 3.

14. Defoort, "The Modern Formation of Early Mohism."

15. Wu, *Mo Di yu Yesu*. For a description and analysis of this work, see Chu Sin-jan, *Wu Leichuan: A Confucian-Christian in Republican China* (Hong Kong: Peter Lang, 1995), 123–51.

16. The theory that Mozi may have been a former convict is based in part on the fact that Mo 墨 can mean ink, and possibly is a name of derision for one who was tattooed. In Zhou China, tattoos were a form of punishment for some crimes.

Introduction to Early Confucianism and Mohism   295

themes that suggest different historical periods. It is possible and fruitful to tease out theories about the composition of the text, but these are at best provisional guides to interpreting it. Thus, in this book, I will analyze the *Mozi* by often speaking of the positions as belong to the man Mozi, but this is only for the sake of convenient prose— where it is important to distinguish between the text and the man, I do so clearly in my analysis.

Despite the historical collapse of Mohism and the difficulties of ascertaining the original core text of the *Mozi*, the tradition and text still holds much value for the kind of speculative theological readings I offer in this book. For one, as Chris Fraser has noted, the *Mozi* offers a profoundly different account of the social problems plaguing the Zhou dynasty than other schools.[17] Mohism was perhaps alone among Warring States schools which championed the needs and cause of the common people, the *min* 民 (though Confucians like Mengzi showed a great concern for the common people as well). As a clan-based society, a typical assumption of early Chinese intellectual elites was that human society required a hierarchical arrangement in order to function well. Later, stories such as the creation myth of Nu Wa suggest that such hierarchical arrangement was due to divine ordinance and was based on essentialist kind of differences between nobility and the common people.[18] The Mohist school strongly questioned the legitimacy of such views. While stopping short of a full-throated egalitarianism, the *Mozi* does defend a robust view of human society based on the equal regard for all human beings, and ordered toward *universal* human flourishing, material and otherwise.

In terms of doctrinal matters, scholars often describe the Mohist school as being organized around ten primary teachings, many of which bear on significant concerns for Christian theological science. These ten doctrines have historically seen as central teachings because of the structure of the *Mozi*, which features ten so-called "core chapters." The core chapters are composed of three-chapter sets all with the same title, hence they are often called core triplets. Much

17. Fraser, *The Philosophy of the Mozi*, 5–17.

18. Discussion of this story can be found in Lihui Yang and Deming An with Jessica Anderson Turner, *Handbook of Chinese Mythology*, 67–69.

of contemporary scholarship on the *Mozi* concerns the composition and dating of the triplet chapters. A. C. Graham set the terms for modern discussion when he identified the triplets as being authored by three distinct sources he termed Y, H, and J, based on grammatical features in these texts.[19] Graham's own analysis was that the Y-text was the oldest and purest, and the J-set was the latest.[20]

Hopefully, my analyses in chapters 2 and 4 have demonstrated that the *Mozi* possesses one of the more robustly theologically-inclined moral perspectives in early China. Likely due to the historical failure of Mohism, the tradition is often overlooked for its theological possibilities in Chinese Christian literature. By embracing engagements with the tradition here, I seek to show how Mohism provides a tremendous resource for the development of Chinese Catholic systematic theology, even if it has no actual practitioners today.

19. Angus C. Graham, *Divisions in Early Mohism Reflected in the Core Chapter of Mo-tzu* (Singapore: Institute of East Asian Philosophies, 1985).

20. For a helpful summary and response to Graham's argument, see Desmet, "The Growth of Compounds in the Core Chapters of the *Mozi*," esp. 99–105. Also helpful in this regard is Maeder, "Some Observations on the Composition of the 'Core Chapters' of the *Mozi*," 27–82.

Bibliography

Aleni, Giulio, SJ [Ai Rulüe 艾儒略]. *Wanwu zhen yuan* 万物真原. Printed as Zheng Ande, *Mingmo Qingchu Yesuhui sixiang wenxian hui bian* 明末清初耶稣会思想文献汇编. Vol. 8.

Allan, Sarah. *The Way of Water and Sprouts of Virtue.* Albany, NY: State University of New York Press, 1997.

Ames, Roger T. "Mencius and a Process Notion of Human Nature." In Chan, *Mencius: Contexts and Interpretation,* 72–90.

An Yangming. "Western 'sincerity' and Confucian 'Cheng'" *Asian Philosophy* 14, no. 2 (2004): 155–69.

Aquinas, Thomas. *Expositio super Iob ad litteram.* Vol. 26, Leonine Edition. Rome: 1965.

———. *Glossa continua supera Evangelia (Catena Aurea).* 2 vols. Edited by A. Guarienti. Turin: Marietti, 1953.

———. *Summa Theologiae.* Vols. 13–20 of *Latin/English Edition of the Works of St. Thomas Aquinas.* Translated by Laurence Shapcotes, OP. Lander, WY: The Aquinas Institute for the Study of Sacred Doctrine, 2012.

———. *Summa Contra Gentiles.* 4 vols. Edited by C. Pera, P. Marc, and P. Caremello. Rome: Marietti, 1961–1967.

———. *Super I Epistolam B. Pauli ad Corinthios lectura.* In *Super Epistolas S. Pauli lectura.* Vols. 1–2. Edited by Raphael Cai. Turin: Marietti, 1952.

———. *Super Evangelium S. Matthaei lectura.* Edited by Raphaelis Cai. Rome: Marietti, 1951.

Aristotle. *Nicomachean Ethics.* Revised ed. Translated and edited by Roger Crisp. Cambridge: Cambridge University Press, 2014.

Armitage, J. Mark "Why Didn't Jesus Write a Book? Aquinas on the Teaching of Christ." *New Blackfriars* 89, no. 1021 (2008): 337–53.

Augustine. *City of God.* Translated by G. R. Evans. New York: Penguin, 2014.

Balthasar, Hans Urs von. *A Theology of History.* San Francisco: Ignatius, 1994.

Barnes, Corey L. "Albert the Great and Thomas Aquinas on Person, Hypostasis, and the Hypostatic Union," *The Thomist* 72, no. 1 (January 2008): 107–46.

298 Bibliography

———. *Christ's Two Wills in Scholastic Thought: The Christology of Aquinas and Its Historical Contexts.* Toronto: Pontifical Institute of Medieval Studies, 2012.

———. "Christological Composition in Thirteenth-Century Debates," *The Thomist* 75 (2011): 173–206.

———. "Thomas Aquinas's Chalcedonian Christology and its Influence on Later Scholastics," *The Thomist* 78, no. 2 (2014): 189–217.

Bataillon, Louis J., OP. "St. Thomas et les Pères: De la *Catena* a la *tertia pars.*" In *Ordo Sapientiae et Amoris*, edited by C.-J. Pinto de Oliveira, OP, 15–36. Fribourg: Éditions Universitaires, 1993.

Bauerschmidt, Frederick Christian. *Thomas Aquinas: Faith, Reason, and Following Christ.* Oxford: Oxford University Press, 2013.

Behuniak, James, Jr. *Mencius on Becoming Human.* Albany, NY: State University of New York Press, 2005.

Benedict XVI. *Jesus of Nazareth: From the Baptism in the Jordan to the Transfiguration.* Translated by Adrian J. Walker. San Francisco: Ignatius Press, 2007.

Berceville, Gilles, OP. "Le sacerdoce du Christ dans le *Commentaire de l'Épître aux Hébreux* de saint Thomas d'Aquin." *Revue Thomiste* 99 (1999): 143–58.

Berthrong, John H. *All Under Heaven: Transforming Paradigms in Confucian-Christian Dialogue.* Albany, NY: State University of New York Press, 1994.

———. *Expanding Process: Exploring Philosophical and Theological Transformations in China and the West.* Albany, NY: State University of New York Press, 2008.

Beskow, Per. *Rex gloriae: The Kingship of Christ in the Early Church.* Translated by Eric J. Sharpe. Eugene, OR: Wipf and Stock, 2014.

Beyer, Gerald J. "The Love of God and Neighbor According to Aquinas: An Interpretation." *New Blackfriars* 84, no. 985 (March 2003): 116–32.

Bidlack, Bede Benjamin. *In Good Company: The Body and Divinization in Pierre Teilhard de Chardin, SJ and Daoist Xiao Yingsou.* Leiden: Brill, 2015.

Blankenhorn, Bernhard, OP. *The Mystery of Union with God: Dionysian Mysticism in Albert the Great and Thomas Aquinas.* Washington, DC: The Catholic University of America Press, 2015.

Bockmuehl, Markus. "'Let the Dead Bury Their Dead' (Matt. 8:22/Luke 9:60): Jesus and the Halakhah." *Journal of Theological Studies* 49, no. 2 (Oct. 1998): 553–81.

Bonino, Serge-Thomas, OP. *Angels and Demons: A Catholic Introduction.* Translated by Michael J. Miller. Washington, DC: The Catholic University of America Press, 2016.

———. "Le sacerdoce comme institution naturelle selon saint Thomas d'Aquin." *Revue Thomiste* 99 (1999): 33–57.

Bonino, Serge-Thomas, OP, ed. *Surnaturel: A Controversy at the Heart of Twentieth-century Thomistic Thought.* Translated by Robert Williams. Revised translation by Matthew Levering. Ave Maria, FL: Sapientia Press of Ave Maria University, 2009.

Boyle, John F. "The Twofold Division of St. Thomas's Christology in the *Tertium Pars.*" *The Thomist* 60 (1996): 439–47.

Bibliography

Boyle, Leonard E. *The Setting of the* Summa theologiae *of Saint Thomas*. Toronto: Pontifical Institute of Mediaeval Studies, 1982.

Brockey, Liam Matthew. *Journey to the East: The Jesuit Mission to China, 1579–1724*. Cambridge, MA: The Belknap Press of Harvard University Press, 2007.

Brooks, E. Bruce, and A. Taeko Brooks, eds. and trans. *The Original Analects: The Sayings of Confucius and His Successors*. New York: Columbia University Press, 1998.

Brown, Joshua R. *Balthasar in Light of Early Confucianism*. Notre Dame, IN: University of Notre Dame Press, 2020.

———. "A Catholic Spirituality of Non-action: Rereading Hans Urs von Balthasar with the *Daodejing*." *Communio* 49 no. 1 (Spring 2022): 80–108.

———. "'Son of Heaven': Developing the Theological Aspects of Mengzi's Philosophy of the Ruler." In *The Bloomsbury Research Handbook of Early Chinese Ethics and Political Philosophy*, edited by Alexus McLeod, 247–66. London: Bloomsbury, 2019.

Brown, Joshua R., and Alexus McLeod. *Transcendence and Non-naturalism in Early Chinese Thought*. London: Bloomsbury, 2020.

Budziszewski, J. *Written on the Heart: The Case for Natural Law*. Downers Grove, IL: IVP Academic, 1997.

Bulgakov, Sergei. *The Lamb of God*. Translated by Boris Jakim. Grand Rapids, MI: Eerdmans, 2008.

Burns, Jeffrey M., Ellen Skerret, and Joseph M. White, eds. *Keeping Faith: European and Asian Catholic Immigrants*. Maryknoll, NY: Orbis Books, 2000.

Cai Renhou 蔡仁厚. *Mojia zhexue* 墨家哲學. Taipei: Dong da tushu gongsi, 1994.

Catechism of the Catholic Church. New York: Willam H. Sadler, 1994.

Cessario, Romanus, OP. *The Godly Image: Christian Satisfaction in Aquinas*. Washington, DC: The Catholic University of America Press, 2020.

Chan, Alan K. L. ed. *Mencius: Contexts and Interpretation*. Honolulu: University of Hawaii Press, 2002.

Chang, Kwang-chih. "China on the Eve of the Historical Period." In Loewe and Shaughnessy, *The Cambridge History of Ancient China*, 37–73.

Chao Fulin and Yongqiang Lei. "On the Origin and Development of the Idea of 'De' in Pre-Qin Times." Translated by Lei Yongqiang. *Frontiers of Philosophy in China* 1, no. 2 (June 2006): 161–84.

Charbonnier, Jean-Pierre, MEP. *Christians in China: A.D. 600 to 2000*. Translated by M. N. L Couve de Murville. San Francisco: Ignatius Press, 2007.

Chardonnens, Denis. "Éternité du sacerdoce du Christ en effet eschatologique de l'eucharistie: La contribution de saint Thomas d'Aquin à un theme de théologie sacramentaire." *Revue Thomiste* 99 (1999): 159–80.

Chen Daqi陳大齊. *Xunzi Xueshuo* 荀子學說. Taipei: Zhonghua wenhua chuban weiyuanhua, 1954.

Chen Ning. "The Concept of Fate in Mencius." *Philosophy East and West* 47, no. 4 (October 1997): 495–520.

———. "Confucius' View of Fate (*Ming*)," *Journal of Chinese Philosophy* 24, no. 3 (1997): 323–59.

———. "The Genesis of the Concept of Blind Fate in Ancient China," *Journal of Chinese Religions* 25 (1997): 141–67.

Cheng Chung-ying. "Classical Chinese Views of Reality and Divinity." In *Confucian Spirituality*, vol. 1, edited by Tu Weiming and Mary Evelyn Tucker, 113–33. New York: Crossroad, 2003.

———. "Xunzi as a Systematic Philosopher: Toward an Organic Unity of Nature, Mind, and Reason." *Journal of Chinese Philosophy* (2008): 9–31.

Chilton, Bruce D. *A Galilean Rabbi and His Bible: Jesus' Own Interpretation of Isaiah*. London: SPCK and Michael Glazer, 1984.

———. *Rabbi Jesus: An Intimate Biography*. New York: Doubleday, 2000.

Ching, Julia. *Chinese Religions*. Maryknoll, NY: Orbis Books, 1993.

———. *Mysticism and Kingship*. Cambridge: Cambridge University Press, 1997.

Chong, Kim-chong. "Xunzi's Systematic Critique of Mencius" *Philosophy East and West* 53, no. 2 (April 2003): 215–34.

Chow, Alexander. *Chinese Public Theology: Generational Shifts and Confucian Imagination in Chinese Christianity*. New York: Oxford University Press, 2018.

———. *Theosis, Sino-Christian Theology and the Second Chinese Enlightenment: Heaven and Humanity in Unity*. New York: Palgrave-MacMillan, 2013.

Chu, Cindy Yik-yi, ed. *Catholicism in China, 1900–Present*. New York: Palgrave-Macmillan, 2014.

Chu Sin-jan. *Wu Leichuan: A Confucian-Christian in Republican China*. Hong Kong: Peter Lang, 1995.

Chua, Jude Soo Meng. "Nameless Dao: A Rapprochement Between the *Tao-Te Ching* and St. Thomas Aquinas' Metaphysics of Unlimited Being." *Journal of Chinese Philosophy* 30, no. 1 (March 2003): 99–113.

Clark, Anthony E. *China's Saints: Catholic Martyrdom during the Qing (1644–1911)*. Bethlehem, PA: Lehigh University Press, 2011.

Clement of Alexandria, *Christ the Educator*. Translated by Simon P. Wood, CP. New York: Fathers of the Church, Inc., 1954.

Clooney, Francis X., SJ, ed. *The New Comparative Theology: Thinking Interreligiously in the 21st Century*. London: T& T Clark, 2010.

———. *Theology After Vedanta: An Experiment in Comparative Theology*. Albany, NY: State University of New York Press, 1993.

von Collani, Claudia. *P. Joachim Bouvet S. J. Sein Leben und sein Werk*. Nettetal: Steyler Verlag, 1985.

Conn, Christopher. "Aquinas on Human Nature and the Possibility of Bodiless Existence." *New Blackfriars* 93, no. 1045 (May 2012): 324–38.

Connolly, Timothy. "Friendship and Filial Piety: Relational Ethics in Aristotle and Early Confucianism." *Journal of Chinese Philosophy* 39, no. 1 (2012): 71–88.

Cook, Scott. "'San De' and Warring States Views on Heavenly Retribution," *Journal of Chinese Philosophy* 37 supp. (2010): 101–23.

Craig, William Lane. "Aquinas on God's Knowledge of Future Contingents." *The Thomist* 54 (January 1990): 33–79.

Bibliography

301

Dauphinais, Michael, Barry David, and Matthew Levering, eds. *Aquinas the Augustinian*. Washington, DC: The Catholic University of America Press, 2007.

Davies, Brian, OP, ed. *Thomas Aquinas: Contemporary Philosophical Perspectives*. New York: Oxford University Press, 2002.

———. *Thomas Aquinas on God and Evil*. New York: Oxford University Press, 2011.

de Bary, Wm Theodore. *The Trouble with Confucianism*. Cambridge, MA: Harvard University Press, 1991.

de Lubac, Henri, SJ. *Catholicism: A Study of Dogma in Relation to the Corporate Destiny of Mankind*. Translated by Lancelot C. Sheppard. New York: Sheed and Ward, 1950.

Decosimo, David. *Ethics as a Work of Charity: Thomas Aquinas and Pagan Virtue*. Stanford, CA: Stanford University Press, 2014.

Defoort, Carine. "Are the Three 'Jian Ai' Chapters About Universal Love?" In Standaert and Defoort, 35–68.

———. "The Growing Scope of 'Jian' 兼: Differences Between Chapters 14, 15, and 16 of the 'Mozi.'" *Oriens Extremus* 45 (2005/6): 119–40.

———. "The Modern Formation of Early Mohism: Sun Yirang's *Exposing and Correcting the Mozi*." *T'oung Pao* 101, no. 1–3 (2015): 208–38.

Defoort, Carine, and Nicholas Standaert, SJ, eds. *The Mozi as an Evolving Text: Different Voices in Early Chinese Thought*. Leiden: Brill, 2013.

———. "Introduction: Different Voices in the *Mozi*: Studies of an Evolving Text." In *The Mozi as an Evolving Text: Different Voices in Early Chinese Thought*, 1–34.

Dell'Olio, Andrew J. *Foundations of Moral Selfhood: Aquinas on Divine Goodness and the Connection of the Virtues*. New York: Peter Lang, 2003.

Deneen, Patrick J. "Hegemonic Liberalism and the End of Pluralism." In *The Church in a Pluralist Society: Social and Political Roles*, edited by Cornelius J. Casey and Fáinche Ryan, 29–44. Notre Dame, IN: University of Notre Dame Press, 2019.

———. *Why Liberalism Failed*. New Haven, CT: Yale University Press, 2018.

Denzinger, Henry, ed. *The Sources of Catholic Dogma*. Translated by Roy J. Deferrari. Fitzwilliam, NH: Loreto, 2007.

Desmet, Karen. "The Growth of Compounds in the Core Chapters of the *Mozi*." *Oriens Extremus* 45 (2005/2006): 99–118.

Ding Weixiang 丁为祥. "*Mojia jian ai guan de yanbian* 墨家兼爱观的演变." *Shaanxi shifan daxue xuebao Zhexue shebui kexueban* 28, no. 4 (1998): 70–76.

Dodds, Michael J., OP. *The Unchanging God of Love: Thomas Aquinas and Contemporary Theology on Divine Immutability*. Washington, DC: The Catholic University of America Press, 2008.

Dupré, Louis. *The Enlightenment and the Intellectual Foundations of Modern Culture*. New Haven, CT: Yale University Press, 2004.

Elders, Leo J., SVD. *The Philosophical Theology of St. Thomas Aquinas*. Leiden: Brill, 1990.

302 Bibliography

————. *Thomas Aquinas and His Predecessors: The Philosophers and the Church Fathers in His Works*. Washington, DC: The Catholic University of America Press, 2018.

Emery, Gilles, OP, and Matthew Levering, eds. *Aristotle in Aquinas's Theology*. New York: Oxford University Press, 2015.

Eno, Robert. *The Confucian Creation of Heaven: Philosophy and the Defense of Ritual Mastery*. Albany, NY: State University of New York Press, 1990.

Evans, C. Stephen. *Kierkegaard's Ethic of Love: Divine Commands and Moral Obligations*. New York: Oxford University Press, 2004.

Fan, Ruiping. "Confucian Ritualization: How and Why?" In *Ritual and the Moral Life: Reclaiming the Tradition*, edited by David Solomon, Ping-Cheung Lo, and Ruiping Fan 143–60. London: Springer, 2012.

Fang Zhirong 房志榮, SJ. "Kongzi suofanying de Jidu mianmao 孔子所反映的基督面貌." *Fujen daxue shenxue lunji* 61 (1984): 366–74.

————. "Rujia sixiang de tian yu shengjing de shangdi zhi bijiao 儒家思想的天與聖經的上帝之比較." *Fujen daxue shenxue lunji* 31 (1977): 14–41.

————. "Zhongguo ji Yiselie gu xianzhi de xun yan yu zongjiao 中國及以色列古先知的訓言與宗教." *Fujen daxue shenxue lunji* 13 (1972): 478–85.

Farrow, Douglas. *Ascension Theology*. London: T&T Clark, 2011.

Fazzini, Geralomo, ed. *The Red Book of the Chinese Martyrs*. San Francisco: Ignatius, 2009.

Feingold, Lawrence. *The Natural Desire to See God according to St. Thomas Aquinas and His Interpreters*. Ave Maria, FL: Sapientia Press of Ave Maria University, 2010.

Feng Youlan 冯友兰. *Zhongguo zhexue shi* 中国哲学史. Vol. 1. Chongqing: Chongqing chubanshe, 2009.

Fingarette, Herbert. *Confucius: The Secular as Sacred*. New York: Harper & Row, 1972.

Fraser, Chris. "The Mohist Conception of Reality." In Li and Perkins, *Chinese Metaphysics and Its Problems*, 69–84.

————. *The Philosophy of the Mòzǐ: The First Consequentialists*. New York: Columbia University Press, 2016.

Fredosso, Alfred. "Medieval Aristotelianism and the Case against Secondary Causation in Nature." In *Divine and Human Action: Essays in the Metaphysics of Theism*, edited by Thomas Morris, 74–118. Ithaca, NY: Cornell University Press, 1988.

Flood, Anthony T. *The Metaphysical Foundations of Love: Aquinas on Participation, Unity, and Union*. Washington, DC: The Catholic University of America Press, 2018.

————. *The Root of Friendship: Self-love and Self-governance in Aquinas*. Washington, DC: The Catholic University of America Press, 2014.

Fung Yu-lan, *A History of Chinese Philosophy*. Vol. 1, *The Period of the Philosophers (From the Beginnings to Circa 100 B.C.)*. 2nd ed. Translated by Derk Bodde. Princeton, NJ: Princeton University Press, 1952.

Bibliography 303

Gaine, Simon Francis. *Did the Savior See the Father? Christ, Salvation, and the Vision of God*. London: Bloomsbury T&T Clark, 2015.

García de Haro, Ramón. *Marriage and the Family in the Documents of the Magisterium: A Course in the Theology of Marriage*. Translated by William E. May. San Francisco: Ignatius, 1993.

Gardner, Daniel K. *Confucianism: A Very Short Introduction*. Oxford: Oxford University Press, 2014.

————, ed. and trans. *The Four Books: The Basic Teachings of the Later Confucian Tradition*. Indianapolis, IN: Hackett Publishing, 2007.

Gernet, Jacques. *China and the Christian Impact: A Conflict of Cultures*. Translated by Janet Lloyd. Cambridge: Cambridge University Press, 1985.

Goldin, Paul R. *Confucianism*. Durham: Acumen, 2011.

————. "The Myth that China Has No Creation Myth." *Monumenta Serica* 56 (2008): 1–22.

————. *Rituals of the Way: The Philosophy of Xunzi*. Chicago and La Salle, IL: Open Court, 1999.

————. "Why *Mozi* is included in the *Daoist Canon*: Or, why there is more to Mohism than utilitarian ethics." In *How Should One Live? Comparing Ethics in Ancient China and Greco-Roman Antiquity*, edited by R. A. H. King and Dennis R. Schilling, 63–91. Berlin: De Gruyter, 2011.

Goris, Harm J. M. J. "Divine Knowledge, Providence, Predestination, and Human Freedom." In Nieuwenhove and Warykow, *The Theology of Thomas Aquinas*, 99–123.

————. *Free Creatures of an Eternal God: Thomas Aquinas on God's Infallible Foreknowledge and Irresistible Will*. Leuven: Peeters, 1997.

————. "Sin and Human Suffering in Aquinas's *Commentary on Job*." In Levering, Roszak, and Vijgen, *Reading Job with St. Thomas Aquinas*, 161–84.

Gorman, Michael. "Christ as Composite according to Aquinas." *Traditio* 55 (2000): 143–57.

Graham, Angus C. "The Background on the Mencian Theory of Human Nature." In Liu and Ivanhoe, *Essays on the Moral Philosophy of Mengzi*, 1–63.

————. *Disputers of the Tao: Philosophical Argument in Ancient China*. Chicago and La Salle, IL: Open Court, 1989.

————. *Divisions in Early Mohism Reflected in the Core Chapter of Mo-tzu*. Singapore: Institute of East Asian Philosophies, 1985.

————. *Later Mohist Logic, Ethics and Science*. Hong Kong: The Chinese University Press, 1978.

Guevin, Benedict M. "Anselm and Aquinas on Satisfaction," *Angelicum* 87, no. 2 (2010): 283–90.

Hagen, Kurtis. *The Philosophy of Xunzi: A Reconstruction*. Chicago and La Salle, IL: Open Court, 2007.

Hahn, Michael S. "Thomas Aquinas's Presentation of Christ as Teacher." *The Thomist* 83, no. 1 (2019): 57–89.

Hall, David L., and Roger T. Ames. *Anticipating China: Thinking Through the*

Narranves of Chinese and Western Culture. Albany, NY: State University of New York Press, 1995.

———. *Thinking through Confucius*. Albany, NY: State University of New York Press, 1987.

———. *Thinking from the Han: Self, Truth, and Transcendence in Chinese and Western Culture*. Albany, NY: State University of New York Press, 1998.

Hancock, Brannon. *The Scandal of Sacramentality: The Eucharist in Literary and Theological Perspectives*. Cambridge: James Clark and Co., 2014.

Hao Changchi. "Is Mozi a Utilitarian Philosopher?" *Frontiers of Philosophy in China* 1, no. 3 (Sept. 2006): 382–400.

Hart, David Bentley. *That All Shall Be Saved: Heaven, Hell, and Universal Salvation*. New Haven, CT: Yale University Press, 2019.

He Shiming 何世明. *Cong Jidujiao kan Zhongguo xiaodao* 从基督教看中国孝道. Beijing: Zongjiao wenhua chubanshe, 1999.

———. *Jidujiao ruxue sixiang* 基督教儒学思想. Beijing: Zongjiao Wenhua chubanshe, 1999.

———. *Jidujiao yu ruxue duitan* 基督教与儒学对谈. Beijing: Zongjiao Wenhua Chubanshe, 1999.

———. *Rongguan shenxue yu rujia sixiang* 融贯神学与儒家思想. Beijing: Zongjiao wenhua chubanshe, 1999.

———. *Zhongguo wenhua zhong zhi youshenlun yu wushenlun* 中国文化中之有神论与无神论. Beijing: Zongjiao wenhua chubanshe, 1999.

He Yuanguo. "Confucius and Aristotle on Friendship: A Comparative Study." *Frontiers of Philosophy in China* 2, no. 2 (2007): 291–307.

Helft, Claude. *Chinese Mythology: Stories of Creation and Invention*. Translated by Michael Hariton and Claudia Bedrick. New York: Enchanted Lion Books, 2007.

Hengel, Martin. *The Charismatic Leader and His Followers*. Translated by James Grieg. New York: Crossroad, 1981.

Hittinger, Russell. *The First Grace: Rediscovering the Natural Law in a Post-Christian World*. Wilmington, DE: ISI Books, 2003.

Houck, Daniel W. *Aquinas, Original Sin, and the Challenge of Evolution*. New York: Cambridge University Press, 2020.

Huang Chun-chieh. "Mencius' Hermeneutics of Classics" *Dao* 1, no. 1 (2001): 15–29.

Huang, Paulos. *Confronting Confucian Understandings of the Christian Doctrine of Salvation: A Systematic Analysis of the Basic Problems in the Confucian-Christian Dialogue*. Leiden: Brill, 2009.

———. "A Response to Professor He Guanghu: Different Reactions to the Similarities between Christianity and Traditional Chinese Religions." In Ruokanen and Huang, *Christianity and Chinese Culture*, 70–84.

Hütter, Reinhard. *Aquinas on Transubstantiation*. Washington, DC: The Catholic University of America Press, 2019.

———. *Bound for Beatitude: A Thomistic Study in Eschatology and Ethics*. Washington, DC: The Catholic University of America Press, 2019.

Hunter, Michael. *Confucius Beyond the Analects*. Leiden: Brill, 2017.

Bibliography

Ivanhoe, Philip J. *Confucian Moral Self Cultivation*. 2nd ed. Indianapolis, IN: Hackett Publishing, 2000.

———. "Confucian Self Cultivation and Mengzi's Notion of Extension." In Liu and Ivanhoe, *Essays on the Moral Philosophy of Mengzi*, 221–41.

———. *Ethics in the Confucian Tradition: The Thought of Mengzi and Wang Yangming*. Indianapolis, IN: Hackett Publishing, 2002.

———. "Filial Piety as a Virtue." In *Filial Piety in Chinese Thought and History*, edited by Alan K. L. Chan and Sor-hoon Tan, 189–202. New York: Routledge-Curzon, 2004.

———. Review of *Thinking Through Confucius*. *Philosophy East and West* 41, no. 2 (1991): 241–54.

Ivanhoe, Philip J., and Bryan W. Van Norden, eds. *Readings in Classical Chinese Philosophy*. 2nd ed. Indianapolis, IN: Hackett Publishing, 2005.

Jenkins, Philip. *The Lost History of Christianity: The Thousand-Year Golden Age of the Church in the Middle East, Africa, and Asia—and How it Died*. New York: HarperOne, 2009.

Jensen, Lionel. *Manufacturing Confucianism: Chinese Traditions and Universal Civilization*. Durham, NC: Duke University Press, 1997.

Jensen, Steven J. *Knowing the Natural Law: From Precepts to Inclinations to Deriving Oughts*. Washington, DC: The Catholic University of America Press, 2015.

Jenson, Matt. *The Gravity of Sin: Augustine, Luther, and Barth on Homo incurvatus in se*. London: T&T Clark, 2006.

Jipp, Joshua W. *Christ is King: Paul's Royal Ideology*. Minneapolis, MN: Fortress Press, 2015.

John Paul II. *Fides et ratio*. Encyclical Letter. September 14, 1998. www.vatican.va/

Johnson, Junius. *Patristic and Medieval Atonement Theory: A Guide to Research*. Lanham, MD: Rowman and Littlefield, 2016.

Johnson, Luke Timothy. *Hebrews: A Commentary*. Louisville, KY: Westminster John Knox Press, 2006.

Johnson, Mark. "Augustine and Aquinas on Original Sin: Doctrine, Authority, and Pedagogy." In Dauphinais, David, and Levering, *Aquinas the Augustinian*, 145–58.

Johnston, Ian, trans. *The Mozi: A Complete Translation*. Hong Kong: Chinese University Press, 2010.

Jones, L. Gregory. "The Theological Transformation of Aristotelian Friendship in the Thought of St. Thomas Aquinas." *New Scholasticism* 61 (1987): 373–99.

Justin Martyr. *Dialogue with Trypho*. In *Saint Justin Martyr: The First Apology, The Second Apology, Dialogue with Trypho, Exhortation to the Greeks, Discourse to the Greeks, The Monarchy or the Rule of God*, 147–368. Translated by Thomas B. Falls. Washington, DC: The Catholic University of America Press, 1965.

Keating, Daniel A. "Thomas Aquinas and the Epistle to the Hebrews: The 'Excellence of Christ.'" In *Christology, Hermeneutics, and Hebrews: Profiles from the History of Interpretation*, edited by Jon C. Laansma and Daniel J. Treier, 84–99. London: T&T Clark, 2012.

Bibliography

Keaty, Anthony. "Thomas's Authority for Identifying Charity as Friendship: Aristotle or John 15?" *The Thomist* 62 (1998): 581–601.

Keenan, James, SJ. *Goodness and Rightness in Thomas Aquinas' Summa Theologiae.* Washington, DC: Georgetown University Press, 1992.

Kerr, Gaven. *Aquinas and the Metaphysics of Creation.* New York: Oxford University Press, 2019.

Kierkegaard, Søren. *Works of Love.* Edited and translated by Howard V. Hong and Edna H. Hong. Princeton, NJ: Princeton University Press, 2013.

Kim, Heup Young. *A Theology of Dao.* Maryknoll, NY: Orbis Books, 2017.

———. *Wang Yang-ming and Karl Barth: A Confucian-Christian Dialogue.* Lanham, MD: University Press of America, 1996.

Kim, Myeong-seok. "Is There No Distinction between Reason and Emotion in Mengzi?" *Philosophy East and West* 64, no. 1 (Jan. 2014): 49–81.

Kim, Richard. "Natural Law in Mencius and Aquinas." In Slater, Cline, and Ivanhoe, *Confucianism and Catholicism*, 135–54.

Kim, Sungmoon. "Confucian Constitutionalism: Mencius and Xunzi on Virtue, Ritual, and Royal Transmission." *Review of Politics* 73, no. 3 (Summer 2011): 371–99.

King, Peter. "Aquinas on the Passions." In Davies, *Thomas Aquinas: Contemporary Philosophical Perspectives*, 353–86.

Klancer, Catherine Hudak. *Embracing Our Complexity: Thomas Aquinas and Zhu Xi on Power and the Common Good.* Albany, NY: State University of New York Press, 2016.

Klimczak, Paweł. *Christus magister: Le Christ maître dans les commentaires évangeliques de saint Thomas d'Aquin.* Fribourg: Academic Press, 2010.

Kline, T. C. III, and Justin Tiwald, eds. *Ritual and Religion in the Xunzi.* Albany, NY: State University of New York Press, 2014.

Knapp, Keith N. "The *Ru* Reinterpretation of *Xiao*," *Early China* 20 (1995): 195–222.

———. *Selfless Offspring: Filial Children and Social Order in Medieval China.* Honolulu: University of Hawaii Press, 2005.

Knasas, John F. X. *Aquinas and the Cry of Rachel: Thomistic Reflections on the Problem of Evil.* Washington, DC: The Catholic University of America Press, 2013.

———. "Suffering and the 'Thomistic Philosopher': A Line of Thought Instigated by the Job Commentary." In Levering, Roszak, and Vijgen, *Reading Job with St. Thomas Aquinas*, 185–219.

Kondoleon, Theodore J. "God's Knowledge of Future Contingent Singulars: A Reply." *The Thomist* 56 (1991): 117–39.

Kortiansky, Peter Karl. *Thomas Aquinas and the Philosophy of Punishment.* Washington, DC: The Catholic University of America Press, 2012.

Kremer, Elmar J., and Michael J. Latzer, eds. *The Problem of Evil in Modern Philosophy.* Toronto: University of Toronto Press, 2001.

Kretzmann, Norman. *The Metaphysics of Creation: Aquinas' Natural Theology in the* Summa Contra Gentiles *II.* Cambridge: Cambridge University Press, 1999.

Bibliography 307

Kwok Pui-lan. *Introducing Asian Feminist Theology.* Sheffield: Sheffield Academic Press, 2000.

Lai, Whalen. "Friendship in Confucian China: Classical and Late Ming." In *Friendship East and West: Philosophical Perspectives,* edited by Oliver Leaman, 215–50. Richmond, UK: Curzon, 1996.

Lau, D. C. "Theories of Human Nature in Mencius and Xunzi." In *Virtue, Nature and Moral Agency in the Xunzi,* edited by T. C. Kline III and Philip J. Ivanhoe, 188–219. Indianapolis, IN: Hackett Publishing, 2000.

Lee, Erika. *At America's Gates: Chinese Immigration during the Exclusion Era, 1882–1943.* Chapel Hill: University of North Carolina Press, 2003.

Lee, Hyo-Dong. *Spirit, Qi, and the Multitude: A Comparative Theology for the Democracy of Creation.* New York: Fordham University Press, 2013.

Lee, Janghee. *Xunzi and Early Chinese Naturalism.* Albany, NY: State University of New York Press, 2005.

Lee, Jung Young. *A Theology of Change: A Christian Concept of God in an Eastern Perspective.* Maryknoll, NY: Orbis Books, 1979.

————. *The Trinity in Asian Perspective.* Nashville, TN: Abindgon Press, 1996.

Lee, Sang H. *From a Liminal Place: An Asian American Theology.* Minneapolis, MN: Fortress Press, 2010.

Lefler, Nathan. "The Melchizedek Traditions in the Letter to the Hebrews: Reading through the Eyes of an Inspired Jewish-Christian Author." *Pro Ecclesia* 16, no. 1 (2012): 73–89.

Legge, Dominic OP. *The Trinitarian Christology of St. Thomas Aquinas.* New York: Oxford University Press, 2016.

Levering, Matthew. "Aquinas on the Liturgy of the Eucharist." In *Aquinas on Doctrine: A Critical Introduction,* edited by Thomas G. Weinandy, OFM Cap., Daniel A. Keating, and John P. Yocum, 183–98. London: T&T Clark, 2004.

————. "Aquinas on Romans 8: Predestination in Context." In *Reading Romans with St. Thomas Aquinas,* edited by Matthew Levering and Michael Dauphinais, 196–221. Washington, DC: The Catholic University of America Press, 2012.

————. "Blood, Death, and Sacrifice in the Epistle to the Hebrews According to Thomas Aquinas." In *So Great a Salvation: A Dialogue on the Atonement in Hebrews,* edited by John C. Laansma, George H. Guthrie, and Cynthia Long Westfall, 120–43. London: T&T Clark, 2019.

————. *Christ and the Catholic Priesthood: Ecclesial Hierarchy and the Pattern of the Trinity.* Chicago: Hillenbrand Books, 2010.

————. "Christ the Priest: An Exploration of *Summa Theologiae* III, Question 22." *The Thomist* 71 (2007): 379–417.

————. *Christ's Fulfillment of Torah and Temple: Salvation According to Thomas Aquinas.* Notre Dame, IN: University of Notre Dame Press, 2002.

————. *Did Jesus Rise from the Dead? Historical and Theological Reflections.* New York: Oxford University Press, 2019.

————. *Engaging the Doctrine of Creation: Cosmos, Creatures, and the Wise and Good Creator.* Grand Rapids, MI: Baker Academic, 2017.

308   Bibliography

———. *Predestination: Biblical and Theological Paths.* New York: Oxford University Press, 2011.

———. *Sacrifice and Community: Jewish Offering and Christian Eucharist.* Malden, MA: Blackwell, 2005.

———. *Scripture and Metaphysics: Aquinas and the Renewal of Trinitarian Theology.* Malden, MA: Wiley-Blackwell, 2004.

Levering, Matthew, Piotr Roszak, and Jörgen Vijgen, eds. *Reading Job with St. Thomas Aquinas.* Washington, DC: The Catholic University of America Press, 2020.

Lewis, Mark Edward. "Custom and Human Nature in Early China." *Philosophy East & West* 53, no. 3 (July 2003): 309–22.

———. *The Early Chinese Empires: Qin and Han.* Cambridge, MA: Belknap Press of Harvard, 2007.

———. *The Flood Myths of Early China.* Albany, NY: State University of New York Press, 2006.

Li Chengyang, and Franklin Perkins, eds. *Chinese Metaphysics and Its Problems.* New York: Cambridge University Press, 2015.

Liu Junpin. "The Evolution of Tianxia Cosmology and Its Philosophical Implications." Translated by Huang Deyuan. *Frontiers of Philosophy in China* 1, no. 4 (Dec. 2006): 517–38.

Liu Shu-Hsien. "The Confucian Approach to the Problem of Transcendence and Immanence." *Philosophy East and West* 22, no. 1 (January 1972): 45–52.

Liu Xiu Sheng, and Philip J. Ivanhoe, eds. *Essays on the Moral Philosophy of Mengzi.* Indianapolis, IN: Hackett Publishing, 2002.

Lombardo, Nicholas, OP. *The Logic of Desire: Aquinas on Emotion.* Washington, DC: The Catholic University of America Press, 2010.

Long, Steven A., Roger W. Nutt, and Thomas Joseph White, OP, eds. *Thomism and Predestination: Principles and Disputations.* Ave Maria, FL: Sapientia Press, 2016.

Loewe, Michael. *Faith, Myth, and Reason in Han China.* Indianapolis: Hackett Publishing, 2005.

Loewe, Michael, and Edward Shaughnessy, eds. *The Cambridge History of Ancient China: From the Origins of Civilization to 221 B.C.* Cambridge, UK: Cambridge University Press, 1999.

Luo Guang 羅光. *Luo Guang quanshu* 羅光全書. 42 vols. Taiwan: Xuesheng shuju, 1996.

———. *Shengming zhexue* 生命哲學. In *Luo Guang quanshu*, vol. 1–2.

———. *Zhongguo zhexue sixiang shi, xian Qin pian* 中國哲學思想事, 先秦偏. In *Luo Guang quanshu.* Vol. 6.

Lupke, Christopher, ed. *The Magnitude of* Ming: *Command, Allotment, and Fate in Chinese Culture.* Honolulu: University of Hawaii Press, 2005.

Luz, Ulrich. *Matthew: A Commentary.* Vol. 2. Translated by Wilhelm C. Linss. Hermeneia. Minneapolis, MI: Fortress Press, 1989.

Lynch, Reginald, OP. *The Cleansing of the Heart: The Sacraments as Instrumental*

Causes in the Thomistic Tradition. Washington, DC: The Catholic University of America Press, 2017.

Ma Xiangbo 馬相伯, *Ma Xiangbo ji* 馬相伯集. Edited by Zhu Weizheng 朱維錚. Shanghai: Fudan Daxue Chubanshe, 1996.

Machle, Edward J. *Nature and Heaven in the Xunzi: A Study of the Tianlun.* Albany, NY: State University of New York Press, 1993.

MacIntyre, Alasdair. *After Virtue: A Study in Moral Theory.* 3rd ed. Notre Dame, IN: University of Notre Dame Press, 2007.

————. *Dependent Rational Animals: Why Human Beings Need the Virtues.* Chicago and La Salle, IL: Open Court, 1999.

————. "Incommensurability, Truth and the Conversation between Confucians and Aristotelians about the Virtues." In *Culture and Modernity: East-West Philosophic Perspectives,* edited by Eliot Deutsch, 104–23. Honolulu, HI: University of Hawaii Press, 1991.

————. "Once More on Confucian and Aristotelian Conceptions of the Virtues: A Response to Professor Wang," In *Chinese Philosophy in an Era of Globalization,* edited by Robin R. Wang, 151–62. Albany, NY: State University of New York Press, 2004.

————, "Questions for Confucianism: Reflections on Essays in *Comparative Study of Self, Autonomy, and Community.*" In *Confucian Ethics: A Comparative Study of Self, Autonomy, and Community,* edited by Kwong-loi Shun and David B. Wong, 195–210. Cambridge: Cambridge University Press, 2004.

Maeder, Erik W. "Some Observations on the Composition of the 'Core Chapters' of the *Mozi.*" *Early China* 17 (1992): 27–82.

Malek, Roman, SVD, ed. *The Chinese Face of Jesus Christ.* 5 vols. Sankt Augustin, Germany: Institut Monumenta Serica/China-Zentrum, 2002–2017.

Malloy, Christopher J. *Aquinas on Beatific Charity and the Problem of Love.* Steubenville, OH: Emmaus Academic, 2019.

Mansini, Guy, OSB. "Aristotle and Aquinas's Theology of Charity in the *Summa Theologiae.*" In Emery and Levering, *Aristotle in Aquinas's Theology,* 121–37.

————. *The Word Has Dwelt Among Us: Explorations in Theology.* Ave Maria, FL: The Sapientia Press, 2008.

Margelidon, Phillippe-Marie. *Études thomistes sur la théologie de la redemption: de la grâce à la resurrection du christ.* Perpignan: Artège, 2010.

Maritain, Jacques. *Saint Thomas and the Problem of Evil.* Milwaukee, WI: Marquette University Press, 1942.

Marshall, I. Howard. "The Theology of the Atonement." In *The Atonement Debate: Papers from the London Symposium on the Theology of Atonement,* edited by Derek Tidball, David Hilborn, and Justin Thacker, 49–68. Grand Rapids, MI: Zondervan, 2008.

Matchulat, Justin. "Thomas Aquinas on Natural Inclinations and the Practical Cognition of Human Goods: A Fresh Take on an Old Debate." *American Catholic Philosophical Quarterly* 94, no. 2 (2020): 239–71.

Mattison, William C. III. *Introducing Moral Theology: True Happiness and the Virtues.* Grand Rapids, MI: Brazos Press, 2008.

May, Gerhard. Creatio ex Nihilo: The Doctrine of 'Creation out of Nothing' in Early Christian Thought. Translated by A. S. Worrall. Edinburgh: T&T Clark, 2004.

McCosker, Philip, and Denys Turner, eds. The Cambridge Companion to the Summa theologiae. Cambridge: Cambridge University Press, 2016.

McFarland, Ian. In Adam's Fall: A Meditation on the Christian Doctrine of Original Sin. Malden, MA: Wiley-Blackwell, 2011.

McInerny, Ralph. Aquinas Against the Averroists: On There Being Only One Intellect. West Lafayette, IN: Purdue University Press, 1993.

———. "Naturalism and Thomistic Ethics." The Thomist 40, no. 2 (April 1976): 222–42.

Mei, W. P. The Ethical and Political Works of Motse. London: Probsthain, 1929.

Mimouni, Simon C. "Le 'grand prêtre' Jésus 'à la manière de Melchisédech dans l'Épître aux Hébreux." Annali di Storia dell'Esegesi 33, no. 1 (January–June 2016): 79–105.

Min, Anselm Kyongsuk. "The Trinity of Aquinas and the Triad of Zhu Xi: Some Comparative Reflections." In Word and Spirit: Renewing Christology and Pneumatology in a Globalizing World, 151–70. Berlin: Water De Gruyter, 2014.

Miner, Robert. Thomas Aquinas on the Passions: A Study of the Suma Theologiae, 1a2ae 22–48. New York: Cambridge University Press, 2009.

Moeller, Hans-Georg and Paul J. D'Ambrosio. Genuine Pretending: On the Philosophy of the Zhuangzi. New York: Columbia University Press, 2017.

Morard, Martin. "Sacerdoce du Christ et sacerdoce des chretiens dans le Commentaire des Psaumes de saint Thomas d'Aquin." Revue Thomiste 99 (1999): 119–42.

Mullis, Eric C. "Confucius and Aristotle on the Goods of Friendship." Dao 9, no. 4 (2010): 391–405.

Mungello, D. E. ed. The Chinese Rites Controversy: Its History and Meaning. Nettetal: Steyler Verlag, 1994.

Neville, Robert Cummings. Boston Confucianism: Portable Tradition in the Late-Modern World. Albany, NY: State University of New York Press, 2000.

———. Ritual and Deference: Extending Chinese Philosophy in a Comparative Context. Albany, NY: State University of New York Press, 2008.

Ng, Peter Tze Ming. Chinese Christianity: An Interplay Between Local and Global Perspectives. Leiden: Brill, 2012.

Nivison, David S. "The Classic Philosophical Writings." In Loewe and Shaughnessey, The Cambridge History of Ancient China, 745–812.

———. The Ways of Confucianism: Investigations in Chinese Philosophy. Edited by Bryan W. Van Norden. Chicago and La Salle, IL: Open Court Publishing, 1996.

Noll, Ray R. ed. 100 Roman Documents Concerning the Chinese Rites Controversy (1645–1941). Translated by Donald F. St. Sure. San Francisco, CA: Ricci Institute, 1992.

Nuyen, A. T. "The 'Mandate of Heaven': Mencius and the Divine Command Theory of Political Legitimacy," Philosophy East and West 63, no. 2 (April 2013): 113–26.

Bibliography

Nygren, Anders. *Agape and Eros*. Translated by Phillip S. Watson. New York: Harper & Row, 1969.

O'Neill, Charles J., trans. *On the Truth of the Catholic Faith: Summa Contra Gentiles: Book Four: Salvation*. Garden City, NY: Image Books, 1957.

O'Neill, Taylor Patrick. *Grace, Predestination, and the Permission of Sin: A Thomistic Analysis*. Washington, DC: The Catholic University of America Press, 2019.

Osborne, Thomas M., Jr. *Love of Self and Love of God in Thirteenth-Century Ethics*. Notre Dame, IN: University of Notre Dame Press, 2005.

Outka, Gene. *Agape: An Ethical Analysis*. New Haven, CT: Yale University Press, 1972.

Pasnau, Robert. *Thomas Aquinas on Human Nature: A Philosophical Study of the Summa theologiae Ia 75–89*. Cambridge: Cambridge University Press, 2002.

Perrier, Emmanuel OP. "L'enjeu christologique de la satisfaction (I)" *Revue Thomiste* CIII (2003): 105–36.

———. "L'enjeu christologique de la satisfaction (II)," *Revue Thomiste* CIII (2003): 203–48.

Petri, Thomas OP. *Aquinas and the Theology of the Body: The Thomistic Foundations of John Paul II's Anthropology*. Washington, DC: The Catholic University of America Press, 2016.

Phan, Peter C. *Being Religious Interreligiously: Asian Perspectives on Interfaith Dialogue*. Maryknoll, NY: Orbis Books, 2004.

———. "Betwixt and Between: Doing Theology with Memory and Imagination." In *Journeys at the Margin: Towards and Auto-Biographical Theology in Asian-American Perspective*, ed. Phan, Peter C., and Jung Young Lee. Collegeville, MN: The Liturgical Press, 1999, 113–34.

———. *Christianity with An Asian Face*. Maryknoll, NY: Orbis Books, 2003.

———. "Catholicism and Confucianism." In *Catholicism and Interreligious Dialogue*, ed. James L. Heft, SM, 170–87. New York: Oxford University Press, 2017.

———. "Inculturation of the Christian Faith in Asia through Philosophy: A Dialogue with John Paul II's *Fides et Ratio*." In *Christianity with an Asian Face*, 47–71.

Pinckaers, Servais, OP. *Morality: The Catholic View*. Translated by Michael Sherwin, OP. South Bend, IN: St. Augustine's Press, 2001.

Pines, Yuri, ed. and trans. *The Book of Lord Shang: Apologetics of State Power in Early China*. New York: Columbia University Press, 2017.

———. "Changing Views of *Tianxia* in Pre-imperial Discourse" *Oriens Extremus* 43 (2002): 101–16.

———. *Foundations of Confucian Thought: Intellectual Life in the Chunqiu Period, 722–453 B.C.E.* Honolulu, HI: University of Hawaii Press, 2002.

Pope, Stephen J. "The Moral Centrality of Natural Priorities: A Thomistic Alternative to 'Equal Regard.'" *The Annual of the Society of Christian Ethics* 10 (1990): 109–29.

Bibliography

Porter, Jean. "*De ordine caritatis*: Charity, Friendship and Justice in Thomas Aquinas' *Summa theologiae*." *The Thomist* 53 (1989): 197–213.

Puett, Michael J. *The Ambivalence of Creation: Debates Concerning Innovation and Artifice in Early China*. Stanford, CA: Stanford University Press, 2001.

———. "Following the Commands of Heaven: The Notion of *Ming* in Early China." In Lupke, *The Magnitude of* Ming, 49–69.

———. *To Become a God: Cosmology, Sacrifice, and Self-Divinization in Early China*. Cambridge, MA: Harvard University Asia Center, 2002.

Qin Yanshi 秦彦士. *Mozi yu Mojia xuepai* 墨子與墨家學派. Jinan: Shangdong wenyi chubanshe, 2004.

Ramage, Matthew J. *Dark Passages of the Bible: Engaging Scripture with Benedict XVI and Thomas Aquinas*. Washington, DC: The Catholic University of America Press, 2013.

Ratzinger, Joseph Cardinal. *Truth and Tolerance: Christian Belief and World Religions*. Translated by Henry Taylor. San Francisco: Ignatius Press, 2004.

Ribbens, Benjamin J. *Levitical Sacrifice and Heavenly Cult in Hebrews*. Berlin: Walter De Gruyter, 2016.

Ricci, Matteo, SJ. *The True Meaning of the Lord of Heaven*. Edited by Edward J. Malatesta. Translated by Douglas Lancashire and Peter Hu Kuo-chen. St. Louis, MO: Institute of Jesuit Sources, 1985.

Riches, Aaron. *Ecce Homo: On the Divine Unity of Christ*. Grand Rapids, MI: Eerdmans, 2016.

Rhonheimer, Martin. "Norm-ethics, Moral Rationality, and the Virtues: What's Wrong with Consequentialism." In *The Perspective of the Acting Person: Essays in the Renewal of Thomistic Moral Philosophy*, edited by William F. Murphy, Jr., 18–36. Washington, DC: The Catholic University of America Press, 2008.

Robins, Dan. "Mohist Care." *Philosophy East and West* 62, no. 1 (January 2012): 60–91.

Romero, Miguel J. "The Happiness of 'Those Who Lack the Use of Reason.'" *The Thomist* 80, no. 1 (2016): 49–96.

Roszak, Piotr, and Jörgen Vijgen, eds. *Reading Sacred Scripture with Thomas Aquinas: Hermeneutical Tools, Theological Questions, and New Perspectives*. Turnhout, Belgium: Brepols, 2015.

Ruello, Francis. *La Christologie de Thomas d'Aquin*. Paris: Beauchsne, 1987.

Ruggieri, Michele, SJ (Luo Mingjian 罗明坚). *Tianzhu shengjiao shilu* 天主圣教实录. Printed as Zheng Ande, *Mingmo Qingchu Yesuhui sixiang wenxian hui bian* 明末清初耶稣会思想文献汇编. Vol. 1.

Ruokanen, Miikka, and Paulos Huang, eds. *Christianity and Chinese Culture*. Grand Rapids, MI: Eerdmans, 2010.

Sarassin, Claude. *Plein du grâce et de vérité: Théologie de l'âme du Christ selon Thomas d'Aquin*. Vénasque: Éditions du Carmel, 1992.

Scheffeczyk, Leo, ed. *Die Mysterien des Lebens Jesu und di christliche Existenz*. Aschaffenburg: Pattloch, 1984.

Schenk, Richard OP. "*Omnis Christi actio nostra est instruction*: The Deeds and Sayings of Jesus as Revelation in the View of Thomas Aquinas." In *La Doctrine*

Bibliography

313

de la revelation divine de saint Thomas d'Aquin, edited by Leo J. Elders, 104–31. Vatican City: Libereria Editrice Vaticana, 1990.

Schnackenberg, Rudolf. *The Gospel of Matthew*. Translated by Robert R. Barr. Grand Rapids, MI: Eerdmans, 2002.

Schwartz, Benjamin I. *The World of Thought in Ancient China*. Cambridge, MA: Harvard Belknap, 1985.

Sellars, John. *Stoicism*. London and New York: Routledge, 2014.

Shen, Vincent [Shen Qingsong 沈清松]. "The Aristotelian Concept of Substance Introduced by Early Jesuit Missionaries to China and Its Problems in Encountering Confucianism." In Slater, Cline, and Ivanhoe, *Confucianism and Catholicism*, 3–33.

———. *Cong Li Madou dao Haidege: kua wenhua mailuo xia de zhongxi zhexue hudong* 從利瑪竇到海德格: 跨文化脈絡下的中西哲學互動. Taibei: Taiwan Shangwu Yinshuguan, 2014.

———. "From Gift to Law: Thomas's Natural Law and Laozi's Heavenly *Dao*." *International Philosophical Quarterly* 53, no. 3 (September 2013): 251–70.

Shengshui jiyan 聖水紀言. M. Courant, *Catalogue des Livres Chinois, Coréens, Japonais, etc.* (Paris, 1912), held in Bibliothèque Nationale de France, catalog no. Chinois, 6845.

Sherwin, Michael, OP. "Aquinas, Augustine, and the Medieval Scholastic Crisis concerning Charity." In Dauphinais, David, and Levering, *Aquinas the Augustinian*, 181–204.

———. *By Knowledge & By Love: Charity and Knowledge in the Moral Theology of St. Thomas Aquinas*. Washington, DC: The Catholic University of America Press, 2005.

———. "Christ the Teacher in St. Thomas' *Commentary on the Gospel of John*." In *Reading John with St. Thomas Aquinas: Theological Exegesis and Speculative Theology*, edited by Michael Dauphinais and Matthew Levering, 173–93. Washington, DC: The Catholic University of America Press, 2005.

Shun, Kwong-loi. *Mencius and Early Chinese Thought*. Stanford, CA: Stanford University Press, 1997.

———. "Mencius' Critique of Mohism: An Analysis of 'Meng Tzu' 3A:5." *Philosophy East and West* 41, no. 2 (April 1991): 203–14.

Simon, Yves R. *Philosophy of Democratic Government*. Notre Dame, IN: University of Notre Dame Press, 1993.

Slater, Michael R., Erin M. Cline, and Philip J. Ivanhoe, eds. *Confucianism and Catholicism: Reinvigorating the Dialogue*. Notre Dame, IN: University of Notre Dame Press, 2020.

Slingerland, Edward G. *Mind and Body in Early China: Beyond Orientalism and the Myth of Holism*. New York: Oxford University Press, 2019.

Smith, Julien. *Christ the Ideal King: Cultural Context, Rhetorical Strategy, and the Power of Divine Monarchy in Ephesians*. Tübingen: Mohr Siebeck, 2011.

Smith, Kidder. "Mencius: Action Sublating Fate," *Journal of Chinese Philosophy* 33, no. 4 (Dec. 2006): 571–80.

Smith, Randall B. *Aquinas, Bonaventure, and the Scholastic Culture of Medieval*

Paris: Preaching, Prologues, and Biblical Commentary. Cambridge: Cambridge University Press, 2020.

———. *Reading the Sermons of Thomas Aquinas: A Beginner's Guide*. Steubenville, OH: Emmaus Academic Press, 2016.

Stalnaker, Aaron. "Comparative Religious Ethics and the Problem of 'Human Nature." *The Journal of Religious Ethics* 33, no. 2 (2006): 187–224.

———. *Overcoming Our Evil: Human Nature and Spiritual Exercises in Xunzi and Augustine*. Washington, DC: Georgetown University Press, 2006.

Standaert, Nicholas, SJ. and Adrian Dudink, eds. *Chinese Christian Texts from the Roman Archives of the Society of Jesus*. Vol. 1 Taipei: Taipei Ricci Institute, 2002.

———. *The Fascinating God: A Challenge to Modern Chinese Theology Presented by a Text on the Name of God Written by a 17th Century Chinese Student of Theology*. Rome: Editrice Pontificia Università Gregoriana, 1995.

———. "Heaven as a Standard." In Defoort and Standaert, *The Mozi as an Evolving Text*, 237–69.

———. "The Jesuits Did NOT Manufacture 'Confucianism.'" *East Asian Science, Technology, and Medicine* 16 (1999): 115–32.

———. *Yang Tingyun, Confucian and Christian in Late Ming China: His Life and Thought*. Leiden: Brill, 1988.

Starr, Chloë. *Chinese Theology: Text and Context*. New Haven, CT: Yale University Press, 2016.

———, ed. *A Reader in Chinese Theology*. Waco, TX: Baylor University Press, 2023.

Stump, Eleonore. *Aquinas*. London and New York: Routledge, 2003.

———. *Atonement*. New York: Oxford University Press, 2018.

Sturgeon, Donald, ed. *Chinese Text Project: A Dynamic Digital Library of Premodern Chinese*. Digital Scholarship in the Humanities, 2019. https://ctext.org.

Sun Shangyang 孙尚扬.*Mingmo Tianzhujiao yu Ruxue de hudong: Yizhong sixiangshi de shijiao* 明末天主教与儒学的互动: 一种思想史的视角. Beijing: Zongjiao wenhua chubanshe, 2013.

Sung, Winnie. "Ritual in the *Xunzi*: A Change of the Heart/Mind." *Sophia* 51 (2012): 211–26.

Tan, Sor-hoon. "Mentor or Friend? Confucius and Aristotle on Equality and Ethical Development in Friendship." *International Studies in Philosophy* 33, no. 4 (2001): 99–121.

Tanner, Kathryn. *God and Creation in Christian Theology: Tyranny or Empowerment?* Minneapolis, MN: Fortress Press, 2005.

Tavor, Ori. "Xunzi's Theory of Ritual Revisited: Reading Ritual as Corporal Technology." *Dao* 12 (2013): 313–30.

Taylor, Rodney. "Religion and Utilitarianism: Mo Tzu on Spirits and Funerals." *Philosophy East and West* 29, no. 3 (1979): 337–46.

Tian Haihua. "Confucian Catholics' Appropriation of the Decalogue: A Case-Study of Cross-Textual Reading." In *Reading Christian Scriptures in China*, edited by Chloë Starr, 163–80. London: T&T Clark, 2008.

Bibliography

315

Tian Liang 田良. "*Jianli Zhongguo gongjiao wenhua chuyi* 建立中國公交文化芻議." *Xinduosheng* 5, no. 26 (December 1959): 33–46.

Tiedemann, R. G., ed. *Handbook of Christianity in China*. Vol. 2, *1800–Present*. Leiden: Brill, 2010.

Tong, John H. "The Church from 1949 to 1990." In *The Catholic Church in Modern China: Perspectives*, edited by Edmond Tang and Jean-Paul Wiest, 7–27. Maryknoll, NY: Orbis Books, 1993.

Torrell, Jean-Pierre, OP. *Le Christ en ses mystéres: la vie et l'œuvre de Jésus selon saint Thomas d'Aquin*. 2 vols. Paris: Desclée, 1999.

———. "Le sacerdoce du Christ dans la *Somme de théologie*." *Revue Thomiste* 99 (1999): 75–100. Translated by Bernard Blankenhorn, OP, as "The Priesthood of Christ in the *Summa Theologiae*." In *Christ and Spirituality in St. Thomas Aquinas*, translated by Bernhard Blankenhorn, OP. Washington, DC: The Catholic University of America Press, 2011.

———. *Saint Thomas d'Aquin: L'homme et son oeuvre*. Paris: Éditions du Cerf, 1993.

———, ed. and trans. *Somme théologique: Le verbe incarné*. Paris: Éditions du Cerf, 2002.

Tu Weiming. *Confucian Thought: Selfhood as Creative Transformation*. Albany, NY: State University of New York Press, 1985.

Tück, Jan-Heiner. *A Gift of Presence: The Theology and Poetry of the Eucharist in Thomas Aquinas*. Translated by Scott G. Hefelfinger. Washington, DC: The Catholic University of America Press, 2014.

Turner, Denys. "The Human Person." In McCosker and Turner, *Cambridge Companion to the Summa theologiae*, 168–80.

Unschuld, Paul U. *Huang Di Nei Jing Su Wen: Nature, Knowledge, and Imagery in an Ancient Chinese Medical Text*. Berkeley: University of California Press, 2003.

Valkenberg, Pim. "Scripture." In McCosker and Turner, *The Cambridge Companion to the Summa theologiae*, 48–61.

Van Nieuwenhove, Rik, and Joseph P. Wawrykow, eds. *The Theology of Thomas Aquinas*. Notre Dame, IN: University of Notre Dame Press, 2005.

Van Norden, Bryan W. *Introduction to Classical Chinese Philosophy*. Indianapolis, IN: Hackett Publishing, 2011.

———. "Mencius and Augustine on Evil: A Test Case for Comparative Philosophy." In *Two Roads to Wisdom? Chinese and Analytical Philosophical Traditions*, edited by Bo Mou, 313–36. Chicago and La Salle, IL: Open Court, 2001.

———. Ed. and trans. *Mengzi: With Selections from Traditional Commentaries*. Indianapolis, IN: Hackett, 2008.

———. *Virtue Ethics and Consequentialism in Early Chinese Philosophy*. New York: Cambridge University Press, 2007.

Verhoorn, Aat. "Friendship in Ancient China." *East Asian History* 27 (2004): 1–32.

Vijgen, Jörgen. "Job, Aquinas, and the Philosopher." In Levering, Roszak, and Vijgen, *Reading Job with St. Thomas Aquinas*, 42–67.

Wang, Huaiyu. "Piety and Individuality through a Convoluted Path of Rightness:

Exploring the Confucian Art of Moral Discretion via *Analects* 13 no. 18." *Asian Philosophy* 21, no. 4 (Nov 2011): 395–418.

Wang Huiyu. "Adjustments to the 'Accommodation Strategy' of the Early Jesuit Mission to China: The Case of Michele Ruggieri's *Tianzhu shilu* (1584) and its Revised Edition (ca. 1640)." *Journal of Religious History* 46, no. 1 (March 2022): 82–96.

Wang Ping, and Ian W. Johnston, trans. and annotators. *Daxue and Zhongyong: Bilingual Edition*. Hong Kong: Chinese University Press of Hong Kong, 2012.

Wang Xianqian 王先谦, compiler. *Xunzi Jijie* 荀子集解. Arranged by Shen Xiaohuan 沈嘯寰 and Wang Xingxian 王星贤. Beijing: Zhonghua shuju, 2014.

Wang Zheng 王徵. *Wei Tian ai ren* 畏天爱人. Published as Zheng Ande, *Mingmo Qingchu Yesuhui sixiang wenxian cihui* 明末清初耶稣会思想文献汇编. Vol. 34.

Wang, Xueying. "Mengzi, Xunzi, Augustine, and John Chrysostom on Childhood Moral Cultivation." In Slater, Cline, and Ivanhoe, *Confucianism and Catholicism*, 109–34.

Wang Zhixin 王治心. *Mozi zhexue* 墨子哲学. Nanjing: Jinling shenxue chubanshe, 1925.

Watson, Burton, ed. and trans. *Mozi: The Basic Writings*. New York: Columbia University Press, 2003.

Watts, Joel L. *Jesus as Divine Suicide: The Death of the Messiah in Galatians*. Eugene, OR: Pickwick, 2019.

Wawrykow, Joseph P. "Human Suffering and Merit." In Levering, Roszak, and Vijgen, *Reading Job with St. Thomas Aquinas*, 220–60.

———. "Wisdom in the Christology of Thomas Aquinas." In *Christ Among the Medieval Dominicans*, edited by Kent Emery, Jr. and Joseph P. Wawrykow, 175–96. Notre Dame, IN: University of Notre Dame Press, 1999.

Weinandy, Thomas G., OFM Cap. "The Supremacy of Christ: Aquinas' Commentary on Hebrews." In Weinandy, Keating, and Yocum, *Aquinas on Scripture*, 223–44.

Weinandy, Thomas G., OFM Cap., Daniel A. Keating, and John P. Yocum, eds. *Aquinas on Scripture: An Introduction to His Biblical Commentaries*. London: T&T Clark, 2005.

White, Kevin. "The Passions of the Soul (Ia IIae, qq. 22–48)." In *The Ethics of Aquinas*, edited by Stephen J. Pope, 103–15. Washington, DC: Georgetown University Press, 2002.

White, Thomas Joseph, OP. *The Incarnate Lord: A Thomistic Study in Christology*. Washington, DC: The Catholic University of America Press, 2015.

Wippel, John F. *Metaphysical Themes in Thomas Aquinas*. Washington, DC: The Catholic University of America Press, 1984.

———. *Metaphysical Themes in Thomas Aquinas II*. Washington, DC: The Catholic University of America Press, 2007.

Wong, Benjamin and Hui-Chieh Loy. "War and Ghosts in Mozi's Political Philosophy." *Philosophy East and West* 54, no. 3 (July 2004): 343–63.

Bibliography

Wong, David B. "Is There a Distinction between Reason and Emotion in Mencius?" *Philosophy East and West* 41, no. 1 (Jan 1991): 31–44.

Wong, Stephanie. "The Mind's Dynamism in Chinese Catholic Theology: A Comparative Study of Metaphysics and Knowledge in the Thought of Wang Yangming and Joseph Maréchal." *Journal of World Christianity* 8, no. 2 (December 2018): 109–33.

Wood, Jacob. *To Stir a Restless Heart: Thomas Aquinas and Henri de Lubac on Nature, Grace, and the Desire for God.* Washington, DC: The Catholic University of America Press, 2019.

Wright, N. T. *How God Became King: The Forgotten Story of the Gospels.* New York: HarperOne, 2012.

Wu John C. H. *Beyond East and West.* Notre Dame, IN: University of Notre Dame Press, 2018.

———. *Chinese Humanism and Christian Spirituality.* Jamaica, NY: St. John's University Press, 1965.

———. *From Confucianism to Catholicism.* Huntington, IN: Our Sunday Visitor Press, 1949.

Wu Leichuan 吳雷川. *Mo Di yu Yesu* 墨翟与耶稣. Shanghai: The Association Press of China, 1940.

Xinyue quanshu 新約全書 [New Testament in Chinese]. Translated by Studium Biblicum OFM (*Xianggang sigao shengjing xuehui* 香港思高聖經學會). San Francisco: The Archdiocese of San Francisco, 2017.

Yang Lihui and Deming An with Jessica Anderson Turner. *Handbook of Chinese Mythology.* New York: Oxford University Press, 2005.

Yao, Xinzhong. *An Introduction to Confucianism.* New York: Cambridge University Press, 2000.

Yearley, Lee H. *Mencius and Aquinas; Theories of Virtue and Conceptions of Courage.* Albany, NY: State University of New York Press, 1990.

Yeo, K. K. "Messianic Predestination in Romans 8 and Classical Confucianism." In *Navigating Romans through Cultures: Challenging Readings by Charting a New Course,* 259–89. Edinburgh: T&T Clark, 2004.

———. *Musing with Confucius and Paul: Toward a Chinese Christian Theology.* Cambridge, UK: James Clarke & Co., 2008.

———. *What does Jerusalem Have to do with Beijing? Biblical Interpretation from a Chinese Perspective.* Harrisburg, PA: Trinity Press International, 1998.

Yocum, John P. "Aquinas' Literal Exposition on Job." In Weinandy, Keating, and Yocum, *Aquinas on Scripture,* 21–42.

Yung Hwa. *Mangoes or Bananas? The Quest for an Authentic Asian Christian Theology.* Oxford: Regnum, 1997.

Zen, Joseph Cardinal. *For the Love of My People, I Will Not Remain Silent.* San Francisco, CA: Ignatius, 2019.

Zhao Binshi 趙賓實. *Ru dao sixiang yu Tianzhujiao* 儒道思想與天主教. Taipei: Guangqi Chubanshe, 1964.

Zhao Dunhua. "The Goodness of Human Nature and Original Sin: A Point of

Convergence in Chinese and Western Cultures." In Ruokanen and Huang, *Christianity and Chinese Culture*, 3–11.

Zhang Chunshen 張春申, SJ. "Jiaohui 'benweihua' de weijie 教會 (本位化) 的癥結." *Fujen daxue shenxue lunji* 33 (1977): 347–62.

———. "Zhongguo jiaohui de benweihua shenxue 中國教會的本位化神學." *Fujen daxue shenxue lunji* 42 (1979): 405–56.

———. "Zongjiao jiaotan de shenxue jichu 宗教交談的神學基礎." *Fujen daxue shenxue lunji* 45 (1980): 328–38.

Zhang Yangwen, ed. *Sinicizing Christianity*. Leiden: Brill, 2017.

Zhang Lifu 張立夫. *Jidujiao lunli yu Mozi zhi jianai lunli bijiao yanjiu* 基督教倫理與墨子之兼愛倫理比較研究. Taipei: Changqing wenhua chubanshe, 1980.

Zheng Jiewen 郑杰文. *Zhongguo Moxue tongshi* 中國墨學通史. Beijing: Renmin chubanshe, 2006.

Zheng Ande 郑安德, ed. *Mingmo Qingchu Yesuhui sixiang wenxian hui bian* 明末清初耶稣会思想文献汇编. Beijing: Beijing daxue zongjiao yanjiu, 2000.

Zhuo Xinping, ed. *Christianity*. Leiden: Brill, 2013.

Ziporyn, Brook, ed. and trans. *Zhuangzi: The Essential Writings with Selections from Traditional Commentaries*. Indianapolis, IN: Hackett Publishing, 2009.

Zizioulas, John D. *Being as Communion: Studies in Personhood and the Church*. Crestwood, NY: St. Vladimir's Seminary Press, 1985.

Zuijdwegt, Geerjtan. "'*Utrum Caritas Sit Aliquid Creatum in Anima*': Aquinas on the Lombard's Identification of Charity with the Holy Spirit." *Recherches de théologie et philosophie médiévales* 79, no. 1 (2012): 39–74.

Index

Aleni, Giulio, 1, 47n27
Allan, Sarah, 139, 140n38, 142n42
agape, 174
Ames, Roger T., 49; and David L. Hall, 17, 44n19
Amos (prophet), 235
Anselm of Canterbury, 28, 230n58, 231n63
ancestors, 30, 213, 217, 251, 280
ancestral sacrifice, 241, 251–52
ancestral veneration, 30n51, 241n81
anthropology, 83, 84n134, 103, 131, 147, 150n66, 151, 161, 171–72, 211
ascension narrative of King Shun, 52, 58, 61–62
ascension of Christ, 244, 280
Aristotle, XIn1, 3, 5, 68n93, 87, 108, 134–35, 149, 150n65, 177, 189, 190
Augustine, 3, 9n13, 14n19, 56n55, 87n137, 115, 119, 129, 130n5, 149, 165, 187, 192n53, 193, 199, 222, 228, 231, 248

Ban Gu, 160
Baptism, 130, 232
baptism, of Christ, 222–23
beatitude, 127, 190, 193, 196, 199–200, 271, 280
Behuniak, James, 42n12, 48n29, 83
benefaction, 193–95, 203–4
benefit (*li* 利), 92, 98–101, 107–8, 113, 118, 173n1, 176, 182–88, 202–6
benevolence (*ren* 仁), 7, 9, 113, 138, 140, 159–60

benevolence, 113, 190, 193–94, 203–4
Benxing 本性, 143
Beyer, Gerald J., 191
bie 別 (partiality), *See* partiality (*bie* 別)
Bonino, Serge-Thomas, 108n41, 136n22, 220
Book of Odes, 40n9, 46, 86
Brockey, Liam Matthew, 39n5
Bulgakov, Sergius, 32
burial, 250–52, 258, 270–72, 275, 279

cai 才 (resources), *See* resources (*cai* 才)
Chalcedon, 135
Charbonnier, Jean-Pierre, 38n2, 39n7
chaos (*luan* 亂), 98, 181, 208, 214, 216, 219, 238
charity (*caritas*), 10, 109, 169n114, 170, 174–79, 189–208
Chen, Ning, 55, 60n73
Chinese philosophy, XIn1, 1–37; background of, 289–96; as naturalistic, 5n7, 18n27, 41–45, 48n29, 48n30, 67, 69, 89, 91, 152
Chinese Rites Controversy, 30n51, 39, 241n81
Christ the king, 23, 212, 225
Christ's priesthood, 212–13, 220–46
Clark, Anthony E., 14n19
Clooney, Francis X., 7
communicatio idiomatum, 229
concupiscible powers, 162–64
Confucianism (definition of), 291–93
Conn, Christopher, 136

320   Index

Cosmogony, 20, 46–47

Cosmology, 20, 23, 32, 40n10, 48n30, 69, 72n106, 149–53, 160, 274

creation (doctrine of), 10, 32, 46–48, 67–71, 76n113, 86, 91, 93, 121–22, 125, 149, 232n67, 236, 244, 295

cross (of Jesus Christ), 228, 230–31, 239, 279–80

da fumu 大父母 ("great father-mother"), 31–33

dao 道, 9, 20–24, 61, 84n133, 145–46, 151, 214n7, 219, 255, 275–76

Daoism (or Daoists), 9, 20, 34, 49, 145, 294

Daodejing, 5n7, 9, 20–21

Defoort, Carine, 94n13, 95n14, 176, 180–81, 183, 293n12, 294

Deneen, Patrick, 24–25

Dupré, Louis, 43n15, 88

Elders, Leo J., 5n5, 76n115, 104n36, 108

emanation, 68–69, 149

emotions (qing 情), 138, 144, 146–48, 156, 159–61, 164–65, 171, 256–58

Eno, Robert, 43, 45n21, 49, 51n38, 52n43, 53n47, 55, 83

Ephesus, council of, 222, 224, 229

eschatology, 14, 85, 124, 127, 135–136, 169, 223n38, 232, 244n91, 262, 281

eternal law, 70–71, 86, 119, 156

Eucharist, 221, 226, 252

The Fall, doctrine of, 75, 130n4, 164–65, 167–68

Fang, Mark Zhirong, 33

Feng Youlan, 39n4, 49n34, 91, 176n10, 289n1

filial piety (xiao 孝), x, 30–31, 34, 151n67, 184, 188, 205–6, 251, 254, 261, 267, 269, 275–76

Flood, Anthony T., 119n64, 197

Fraser, Chris, 91, 125, 173n11, 176, 181n21, 187n37, 293n9, 295

Gaozi, 48, 138, 140–141, 154, 158

Gernet, Jacques, 17, 36n66, 47n27, 149n61

Goldin, Paul, 46n22, 129n1, 144n45, 147, 148n58, 165, 293n10

gospel (or Gospel of Christ), 3–4, 29–30, 33, 127, 261, 263, 270, 274, 279, 286

grace, 76n113, 109, 119, 130, 131n9, 169–71, 177–78, 190–91, 194, 196, 199–200, 204, 206–7, 225–27, 230–35, 240–41, 246, 249, 280, 283

Graham, A. C. (Angus), 94, 129n1, 133, 289n1, 294n13

Han Feizi, 9

Han-era Confucianism, 47, 48n29, 49n34, 160

Hao, Changchi, 91–92

happiness, 56, 80, 82, 85, 104, 113–14, 119, 123n7, 126, 154, 169, 197, 199, 202, 208, 270, 273–74, 280, 283

Hebrews (epistle), 213, 221, 223n40, 227, 229, 233–45

He Shiming, 35n64

heart-mind (xin 心), 50–52, 55n53, 60, 64–65, 79–80, 86, 103, 125–26, 138–40, 145, 147–48, 153, 155–56, 158–61, 165, 169–71, 208, 213, 235, 237, 245–46, 253, 256, 258

hell, doctrine of, 119, 135

Hengel, Martin, 261–62

Hittinger, Russell, 71, 154n74

Holy Spirit, 4, 109, 170, 178, 196, 204, 206, 210

hope (theological virtue), 162, 170, 234, 280

Huang, Paulos, 14, 35

human nature, 10, 36, 46, 50–51, 53, 64, 70–72, 75, 83, 129–31, 139, 149–54, 165–71, 191, 217, 220n27, 234, 246, 256; as Western theological concept, 134–37; of Christ, 211, 225, 226n47, 229–31, 233–34, 236, 238, 240

human moral nature (renxing 人性; or human xing), 8, 34, 41n11, 46, 60, 64, 137–48 214–16; as distinct from Western concepts, 131–35

Hypostatic Union, 224–25, 232, 249

imago Dei, 130, 136, 150, 153

Incarnation, 108, 135, 210, 223, 225, 228–31, 233–34, 239–40, 244, 276, 278, 282

irascible appetite, 162–64

Index

321

Israel, 3, 119, 212, 224, 235, 248, 281
Ivanhoe, Philip J., 41n111, 83n131, 138n24, 151n67, 157, 161n92, 289n1

Jenkins, Philip, 22n38
Jensen, Steven, 156–57
Jewish culture, 210, 220, 226, 241, 243n84, 248–49, 261–62, 278, 281
jian ai 兼愛, 11, 99, 114, 173–89, 201–9, 286; definition of 179–80
John Chrysostom, 268n48
John, Gospel of, 240, 248, 270
John Paul II, 15, 28
junzi 君子, 65–66, 84
Justin Martyr, 3, 19

Kerr, Gaven, 68, 77n120
Kierkegaard, Søren, 174, 194
Kim, Heup Young, 20–26
Kim, Myeon-seok, 139
kingdom of God, 261–63, 267, 279–80
Knapp, Keith N., 30n50, 251
Knasas, John, 73n107, 74n109, 75
Kwok, Pui-lan, 211n2, 282

Lee, Jung Young, XIIn2, 21, 25n44
Levering, Matthew, 72n124, 166n205, 220n28, 223n38, 224, 227n49, 229n56, 230n57, 239n79, 244n91, 249n6
Levitical priesthood, 223, 225, 231, 236, 239n78, 240, 243
Lewis, Mark Edward, 140n38, 141n40, 215n12, 217
li 利, *See* benefit (*li* 利)
li 禮, *See* ritual propriety (*li* 禮)
Lombard, Peter, 109, 196
Lombardo, Nicholas, 159n89, 161n93, 163n99
Luke, gospel of, 135, 222–23, 269,
Luo, Guang, 27n47, 49n34, 91n5
Luther, Martin, 187n38, 191

Ma Xiangbo, 178–179
MacIntyre, Alasdair, 2, 5n6, 150n65
Malloy, Christopher J., 190–91, 192n52
Matthew, gospel of, 222, 233, 235, 248–50, 260–71, 273, 276–78, 280
Melchizedek, 236, 243
Mengzi (or *Mengzi*): on burying parents,

258; critique of Mohism, 173, 184, 189, 204–5, 258; on fate, 55–57; on four "sprouts", 50–51, 64, 70–71, 83, 86, 138–40, 154–60; and "fundamental goodness" of *renxing*, 132–33; his understanding of *renxing*, 33–136; on King Shun, 52–53, 58–59, 61–62; on *qi*, 47–48; and natural law, 153–59; on *qing* (emotions), 159–61; on *renxing* as good, 137–43; on *renxing* and *Tian*, 150–51; on *Tian* as theistic concept, 40–45; on *Tian* as providential source in society: 54–63; on *Tian* as source of existence and order: 46–54; on *Tian* as source of goodness, 63–66
Mo Di (or Mozi as proper name); 93, 95–96, 181, 293–95; theories of his background, 294–95
Mohism (definition of), 293–96
moral anthropology, 70, 104, 137, 153–55, 160
moral self-cultivation (*xiushen* 修身), 82–84, 134, 144–45, 157–58, 164, 217n16, 252
morality of happiness, 154
mourning, 30, 241, 251–52, 254–56, 258–60, 268, 274, 276–78, 283
Mozi: on *jian ai*, 90, 114, 173–76, 178–89, 201, 203–9; in terms of Western moral theories, 90–94; on *li* 利 (benefit), 92, 98–101, 107–8, 173n1, 176, 182–88, 202–6, 208; on *luan* 亂 (chaos), 98–99, 181, 208; on mutual benefit (*xiang li* 相利), 92, 98–99, 182–86, 203–6; on punishment, 101–2, 115–19; on *Tian*'s love, 90–92, 99–103, 113–15, 118–19, 122, 124–27, 178, 201, 207–9; On *Tian* as moral exemplar, 96–98, 102–3, 106–7, 207–9; theories on composition of text, 295–96; structure of text, 94–95, 179–81, 295–96; on *yi* 義 as standard, 96–99

natura (distinguished from *renxing* 人性), 132–33
naturalistic interpretations of Chinese philosophy, 5n7, 125, 152
natural law, 39, 52–53, 63, 70–72, 79n121, 81, 83, 86, 100, 154–59, 168, 170, 178, 240, 273

322 Index

Neo-Platonism, 149
Neville, Robert Cummings, 25n44
New Covenant, 170, 231, 235, 239
New Law, 178, 206, 231, 246
Nuyen, A. T., 62n80
Nygren, Anders, 174

Old Testament, 79n122, 119, 223–25, 229, 231, 235, 243
ontology, 106–7, 136n22, 152
original justice, 130, 167–68
original sin, 36, 130–31, 166–68
Outka, Gene, 174

Pan Gu myth, 48
parent(s), 30–31, 77, 116, 173, 176, 186, 188–89, 206, 241, 243, 250–51, 253–54, 257, 259, 266, 268–70, 272–80
partiality (*bie* 別), 114, 186–87, 205
particular affection or particular attachment, 176, 184, 187–88, 203–4, 207
Passion of Christ, 228–30, 232–33, 240, 244–45
passions, 156, 161–64
Pasnau, Robert, 134
Phan, Peter, XIIn2, 15–19, 25
Plato, XIn1, 3, 28, 68n93, 76, 104n35
Platonism, 19, 290n3
Plotinus, XIn1, 108
Porter, Jean, 174, 195–96
privation of the good, 115, 166
Protestantism, 12, 14, 35, 89, 130n4, 167n109, 174–75, 225n45
Pseudo-Dionysius, 5n7, 120, 149
Puett, Michael, 42n12, 44n20, 152n68

qi 氣, 47–48, 171, 211
qiankun 乾坤, 32
qing 情 (emotions), *See* emotions (*qing* 情)
Qing dynasty, 1, 14, 30, 36, 149, 294

Rabbi, 247–48, 260, 281
Ratzinger, Joseph, 4n4
ren 仁 (benevolence), *See* benevolence (*ren* 仁)
rendao 人道 (way of humanity), 21, 290
renxing 人性, 3, 8, 10, 41, 128–34, 136–38,

140–45, 148–54, 159–60, 164–66, 168–71, 214, 286, 293
resources (*cai* 才), 47, 50, 52, 64, 139
resurrection of the dead, 135–36
revelation, 2, 4, 13, 35, 39–40, 45, 69, 72, 90, 113, 125, 179, 206, 212, 238, 269, 272, 283
Ricci, Matteo, 1, 29–31, 47n27, 132–33
righteousness (*yi* 義), 7, 9, 96, 98, 102–3, 106–7, 111, 138, 146, 160, 255
ritual or ritual propriety (*li* 禮), 144–48, 160–61, 165, 170, 173, 178, 213–20, 226, 228, 232–47, 251–52, 254–55, 257–60, 277, 281, 283, 292
Robins, Dan, 176, 182n23, 184, 207
Ruggieri, Michele, 1, 30n49

sage (*shengren* 聖人), 11, 51, 84, 147–48, 152, 161, 169, 171, 211–13, 215–20, 225, 232–37, 240–47, 250, 263, 272, 274, 276–78, 280–83, 291–92
sage kings (*shengwang* 聖王), 49, 52, 55, 58, 146, 148, 216–17, 219
sacraments, 170, 224, 226, 228, 241
saints, 199, 270, 280
satisfaction, 225, 230, 239
self-benefit, 183–84, 187–88, 202, 205
Simon, Yves, 80–81
sin, 6, 36, 116–19, 130, 135, 166–69, 208, 222, 225, 227–34, 236, 238–40, 244–45, 265
Shangdi 上帝, 39, 40n9, 57, 99–100
Shen, Vincent, 5n6, 27n47, 133n13
shengren 聖人 (sage), *See* sage (*shengren* 聖人)
shengwang 聖王 (sage kings), *See* sage kings (*shengwang* 聖王)
Sherwin, Michael, 192n53, 194–95, 248n4
Shijing 詩經, *See* Book of Odes
Shun (King), 52–53, 58–59, 62, 78, 88, 185–86
Shun, Kwong-loi, 41n11, 42n14, 43, 138n24, 139n25, 205
Slingerland, Edward, 17n26
soul-body relation, 123n71, 135–36, 150, 156, 245
spirits (equivalent of *guishen* 鬼神), 43n17, 62, 76, 78, 81, 88, 91n5, 99–100, 251
"sprouts" (*duan* 端), 50–51, 64, 70–71, 83, 86, 138–40, 154–60, 164

Index

323

Stalnaker, Aaron, 129n2, 130n3, 133n14, 144n45, 147n55, 165

Standaert, Nicholas, 14n19, 31n53, 32, 39n6, 40n9, 94, 96n16, 98n24, 291n5

Starr, Chloë, 27n48

Tabernacle, 240

Taiji (Great ultimate), 48n30, 84

Tan, Jonathan Y., 211–12, 282

Taylor, Rodney L., 93

teacher, 11, 22, 58, 217, 224n42, 246–50, 260–61, 263–64, 271–72, 274, 276, 278, 281–83

theodicy, 74

Tian 天, 1, 7, 10, 38–73, 77–88, 90–107, 111–16, 119–27, 139–40, 143, 150–52, 155, 173, 178, 202, 207–9, 213, 237, 275, 286, 290; as theistic term, 38–45; as *tiandi* 天地 (heaven and earth), 217–18

Tian's mandate (*Tianming* 天命), 38, 44, 49, 53, 59, 62, 65, 78–79, 81, 88, 97

Tian's intention/will (*Tianyi* 天意), 90–107, 111–16, 119–27, 173

Tiandao 天道 (or *dao* of *Tian*), 51, 64–65, 290

Tianzhu 天主 (as term for God), 38–40

Thomas Aquinas: on beatitude, 190, 193, 196, 199–200, 271, 280; on benefaction and benevolence, 193–95, 203–4; on charity, 108, 170, 174–79, 189–208; on Christ the teacher, 248–50, 260–61, 263–64, 282–83; on creation, 67–69, 76, 121–22, 125, 149–50; on divine goodness, 74–76, 82, 103–4, 106, 110–12, 115, 117, 120–23, 149–50; on divine governance, 67, 70–81, 86, 111; on divine love, 90–92, 106–9, 112–13, 119–25, 178–79, 196; on divine providence, 73–74, 77–78; on divine punishment, 115–19; on divine reason, 70–71, 150; on divine will, 82, 90–93, 102–25; on divine wisdom, 111–12, 150, 153, 192; and *divisio textus*, 263; and emanation theory, 68, 149; on emotions, 71–72, 156–57, 159n89, 160–65; on eternal law, 70–71, 86, 156; on friendship with God, 84, 177–79, 189, 190–92, 195, 197–202; on God as cause of goodness, 82, 104,

106, 110–12, 121–23, 125, 149–50; on God as final end, 113, 118; on God as first efficient cause, 67–69; on grace, 119, 131n9, 169–70, 177–78, 190–91, 194, 196, 199–200, 204, 206–7, 225–27, 230–34, 249, 280, 283; on the Holy Spirit, 109, 170, 178, 196, 204, 206; on the Incarnation, 108, 135, 223, 225, 228–31, 234, 244, 282; on justice, 103, 111–12, 116–18, 199, 204; on love of neighbor, 174, 176, 179, 191–93, 196, 198–203, 208; on love of self, 191–92, 197–98, 201–3, 205, 207–8; as model for theological engagement with Chinese philosophy, 3, 5–11, 28–29, 35, 285; on natural law, 70–72, 81, 83, 86, 154–59, 168, 178, 273; on natural love, 199–201, 205–8; and obligation to bury parents, 272–73, 277–78, 282–83; on original sin, 130–31, 166–68; on participation, 71, 73, 82n129, 104n35, 131n9, 150, 153, 197, 199; on priesthood of Christ, 212–13, 220–34, 238; on sacrifice of Christ, 226–31, 234n69, 238, 244; on satisfaction, 225, 230; on sin, 116–19, 130–31, 165–69, 208, 222–34, 244, 265, 271–73

Three-Self Movement, 12

Three Year Mourning period, 31n55, 241, 252–54, 256–60, 272

Torrell, Jean-Pierre, 220, 221n20

Van Norden, Bryan W., 41n11, 63, 91n6, 92–93, 129, 132–33, 138n27, 156–57, 158n86, 289n1, 290n2

vice, 9n13, 165–67

virtue(s), 6, 9–10, 21, 30, 41n11, 50–53, 55, 58, 61, 62, 64–66, 80, 84–87, 92–93, 102, 104, 111, 118, 126, 134, 137–38, 140, 142–45, 153–55, 157–71, 177–78, 184, 190, 195–96, 200, 205, 208, 213, 220n27, 234–35, 240, 245, 250, 260, 266–67, 273, 277, 279–80, 282–83, 285, 290n3

Von Balthasar, Hans Urs, 5, 243

Wang Yang-ming, 157

Wang Zheng, 18

Warring States period, 54, 128, 215, 251, 290, 293

Wawrykow, Joseph, 221

Wippel, John F., 67n91, 77n120, 104n36, 109n42
Wong, David B., 138, 139n31
Wu, John C. H., 1, 33
Wu, Leichuan, 89n2, 175, 294

xiao 孝 (filial piety), *See* filial piety (*xiao* 孝)
Xiaojing 孝經 ("Classic of Filial Piety"), 30, 254, 275
xiaoren 小人 ("small people"), 278–79
xin 心 (heart-mind), *See* heart-mind (*xin* 心)
xiushen 修身 (moral self-cultivation). *See* moral self-cultivation (*xiushen* 修身)
Xunzi: on artifice, 144, 147–48, 165, 169, 216–17, 238; on the cosmos, 149–53, 218–19; on mourning, 241, 256–59, 278; on *renxing*, 136–37, 143–48, 161, 214; on ritual, 144–48, 160–61, 165, 170, 213–20, 226, 232–33, 235, 238, 241–42, 246, 254–55, 257–59; on sage-kings, 146–48, 170–71, 213–19

Yang, Jing, 143,
Yang, Tingyun, 1, 31–32, 175
Yao (King), 53, 59, 88
Yearley, Lee, 5n6, 40n10, 155, 157
Yeo, K. K., 14
yinyang 陰陽, 20–21, 23, 32, 171
Yu (king), 59, 141n40, 185–86, 203

ziran 自然 (spontaneity or "natural"), 9, 97
Zhang, Aloysius Chunshen, 13, 33
Zhang Lifu, 89n1, 90n3, 175
Zhao, Binshi, 3, 8, 34, 149
Zhao, Dunhua, 35–36
Zhao, Qi, 51, 61, 64–65
Zhongyong, 49n34, 84, 160n90, 292
Zhou Dunyi, 48n30
Zhou dynasty, 38, 43–44, 46, 49, 54–55, 57–58, 79, 87, 185, 215–16, 219, 290, 292, 294n16, 295
Zhu Xi, 26, 132, 292
Zhuangzi (or *Zhuangzi*), 20, 42n12, 48n29, 145, 290

ALSO IN THE
THOMISTIC RESSOURCEMENT SERIES

Series Editors: Matthew Levering
Thomas Joseph White, OP

Theology as an Ecclesial Discipline
'Ressourcement' and Dialogue
J. Augustine Di Noia, OP
Edited by James LeGrys

Principles of Catholic Theology
Book 1: On the Nature of Theology
Book 2: On the Rational Credibility of Christianity
Book 3: On God, Trinity, Creation, and Christ
Thomas Joseph White, OP

Peace in the Thought of Thomas Aquinas
Philosophy, Theology, and Ethics
John Meinert

Trinitarian Ecclesiology
Charles Journet, the Divine Missions,
and the Mystery of the Church
John F. O'Neill

Catholic Dogmatic Theology, A Synthesis
Book 1, On the Trinitarian Mystery of God
Book 2, On the Incarnation and Redemption
Book 3, On the Church and the Sacraments
Jean-Hervé Nicolas, OP
Translated by Matthew K. Minerd

Liturgical Theology in Thomas Aquinas
Sacrifice and Salvation History
Franck Quoëx
Translated by Zachary J. Thomas

The Passion of Love in the
Summa Theologiae of Thomas Aquinas
Daniel Joseph Gordon

Reading the Song of Songs with St. Thomas Aquinas
Serge-Thomas Bonino, OP
Translated by Andrew Levering with Matthew Levering

Divine Speech in Human Words
Thomistic Engagements with Scripture
Emmanuel Durand
Edited by Matthew K. Minerd

Revelations of Humanity
Anthropological Dimensions of Theological Controversies
Richard Schenk, OP

The Trinity
On the Nature and Mystery of the One God
Thomas Joseph White, OP

Catholic Dogmatic Theology, A Synthesis
Book 1, On the Trinitarian Mystery of God
Jean-Hervé Nicolas, OP
Translated by Matthew K. Minerd

A Thomistic Christocentrism
*Recovering the Carmelites of Salamanca
on the Logic of the Incarnation*
Dylan Schrader